History and the Social Sciences

NEW APPROACHES TO THE TEACHING OF SOCIAL STUDIES

A Blaisdell Book in Education

CONSULTING EDITOR

John I. Goodlad, University of California at Los Angeles

MARK M. KRUG · *University of Chicago*

HISTORY
and the
SOCIAL SCIENCES

New Approaches to the
Teaching of Social Studies

BLAISDELL PUBLISHING COMPANY
A DIVISION OF GINN AND COMPANY
WALTHAM, MASSACHUSETTS · TORONTO · LONDON

FOREWORD

Anyone who knows Mark Krug well would expect him to write this book some day. And few persons could write such a book.

Professor Krug weaves into his manuscript several major threads of his own unique experience and preparation. As a student of history, with a doctorate in that field, he reveals his commitment to substance and method. As a teacher of teachers, he demonstrates the fact that history must not be brought into the classroom as immutable fact. It must be humanized for instructional purposes. As a sometime teacher of secondary-school students, he shows a sensitive awareness of adolescents' learning. His book, then, deals with the what and how of teaching the social sciences in high schools, with history predominating.

The themes in Professor Krug's book are too many for elaboration here. But four are so pervasive that a few words regarding them are in order. First, his approach to history is essentially humanistic. He carves out a place for history in the social science domain but, if pressed, probably would locate history in a university division of the humanities. Second, he plunges forthrightly into the current debate over how the social sciences should be organized for instructional purposes. Not rejecting current emphases on "structure," he nonetheless argues that this is not enough and, as a consequence, enriches the dialogue. Third, he joins content and pedagogy in the teaching of history, geography, and civics. Fourth, and perhaps most important, he transcends all of these themes through imbuing a mankind perspective, not just explicitly in the concluding chapter but implicitly throughout.

Professor Krug's previous books were about passionate men who helped to make history. It is a pleasure now to add his newest volume to the growing list of Blaisdell books in education.

John I. Goodlad

vii

PREFACE

Let me say with all candor that this book rests on a premise and a hope that there are vast numbers of social studies professors and social studies teachers who have serious doubts about the "new" social studies. I have assumed that many of my colleagues on the university and high school level have serious doubts, as I have, about centering the social studies curriculum on the idea of structure and on the teaching of concepts and generalizations without a solid foundation of content. I have also assumed that there is a need to make a case (hopefully an intelligent and convincing one) for the teaching of history—not history consisting of "facts and dates" —but great, inspiring, and instructive narrative history on the order of Prescott, Parkman, Gibbon, Macaulay, Trevelyan, and Morison.

If my assumptions are wrong, this book is destined to be neither bought nor read. It may be that the advocacy of a more effective teaching of history, geography, and civics is indeed old-fashioned and even perhaps reactionary. It may be "in" when one talks only about "structure," "concepts," and "generalizations." Those who have introduced these innovating and fresh ideas and approaches have made, and are making, an important contribution to the field of social studies. But the time has come to stop and thoughtfully examine the various proposals for the new social studies. Such an examination may well result in a decision to preserve what was worthwhile in the "old" social studies and in the simultaneous introduction of the new proposals with necessary scholarly caution.

Another educated guess which formed an essential element in the writing of this book, was the assumption of the existence of a large "silent vote" among social studies teachers in all parts of the country. These teachers seem to be overwhelmed by the many new curricula, projects, and approaches and are waiting out the storm by doing exactly what they have been doing for many years. Of course, if this situation exists, it is not a healthy development. Many aspects of the new ideas, curricula, and materials, ought to be evaluated, digested, and used in the classrooms. It is hoped that an examination of the new trends, even if in places not entirely dispassionate, may help the in-service and prospective social studies teachers to make intelligent decisions about the content and methods used in their classes.

The first part of this book, devoted to a discussion of the relationship between history and the social sciences and to an analysis of the new curricular approaches, is intended to provoke a thoughtful dialogue on the future of the social studies. The second part, which is mainly methodological, explores new approaches to the teaching of United States history, world history, geography, and civics.

The author is deeply indebted to his colleagues at the University of Chicago, Professors Roald Campbell, Francis S. Chase, Arnold Anderson, Eugene Gilliom, William D. Pattison, and to Research Associates in the Master of Arts in Teaching Program, Peter Gillies III, and John Poster, for their critical and helpful reading of the chapters of the book. Special thanks are due my secretary, Mrs. Violet Kraft, for her tireless efforts in typing and re-typing the manuscript. Most of all, my gratitude must be expressed to my students in the senior classes of the University of Chicago Laboratory High School, where I taught for a number of years, and to the students in the MAT Program who have given me the inspiration to write with deep conviction about the joy of teaching history, geography, and the social sciences.

CONTENTS

PART ONE / Rationale for a New Social Studies Curriculum

1. What History Is and What It Is Not   3

2. The Uses of History   20

3. History and the Social Sciences—How They Differ   37

4. Social Sciences and History: The Narrowing Gap—Prospects for
    Fruitful Collaboration   53

5. On the Use of Social Science Concepts in the Social Studies   73

6. Modes of Inquiry and Methods of Teaching in History and the
    Social Sciences   92

7. The Structure of the Social Studies—New Curricular Approaches   114

8. Case Study: Historians and the Moral Issues in the Civil War   139

9. Case Study: For a "Fair Deal" in the Teaching of Reconstruction   156

PART TWO / New Approaches to Social Studies

10. New Approaches to the Teaching of United States History   175

11. New Approaches to the Teaching of Civics (Part I)   198

12. New Approaches to the Teaching of Civics (Part II)   222

13. On the Teaching of Geography   248

14. For a Mankind Perspective in the Teaching of World History   261

    Bibliography   277

    Index   287

Part One

RATIONALE FOR A

NEW SOCIAL STUDIES

CURRICULUM

1

What History Is and What It Is Not

What is history? This seemingly simple question is not easy to answer. It might be a relatively easy task to define mathematics, geography, or anthropology, but in the case of history, the problem is complicated. Many have tried their hand in formulating pithy definitions of history:

Benedetto Croce: "All history is contemporary history."
J. B. Bury: "History is a science; no less, and no more."
Jacob Burckhardt: "History is contemplation based upon sources."
Henry Adams: "History is incoherent and immoral."
G. J. Renier: "History is the story of the experiences of men living in civilized societies."
Samuel Eliot Morison: "History is the Story of Man."
R. G. Collingwood: "All history is a history of thought."
Arnold Toynbee: "History is a search for light on the nature and destiny of man."
Sir John Seeley: "History is past politics."
Leopold von Ranke: "History is concerned with things as they really happened."
Paul Valéry: "History is the most dangerous product ever concocted by the chemistry of the intellect. Its properties are well known. It causes dreams, inebriates the nations, saddles them with false memories, exaggerates their reflexes, keeps their old sores running, torments them when they are at rest and induces in them megalomania and the mania of persecution. It makes them bitter, arrogant, unbearable, and full of vanity."

Valéry's indictment of history has been echoed in simpler words by Napoleon who said that history was "a fable agreed upon." Voltaire defined history as "tricks we play on the dead," and Henry Ford once exclaimed that "history is bunk." A distinguished English historian was reputed to say that history was just "one damn thing after another."

Disparaging definitions of history reflect disappointment with the products of historical research and writing. There is, however, considerable agreement among contemporary historians on what history is. History is concerned with the totality of human experience, past and present. It is not, as Sir John Seeley said, "past politics." It is past politics, past economics, past science, past society, past religion, past civilization—in short, past everything. History is no longer, as Voltaire charged, only the story of kings and wars. Historians, he complained, say nothing about the spirit of the time or the history of ideas. History written today records not only the story of kings, rulers, wars, and conquests, but also how men grew wheat and corn, how they sold their wares, built their homes, worshipped their gods, and how they lived and how they died. It is because of its concern with the totality of human experience that history, unlike many of the social sciences, has loosely defined boundaries.

History includes every conceivable trace of all past acts and ideas of men. It may describe the story of a great nation from its birth to its decline, or it may delve into the thoughts, feelings, and the modes of life of a humble villager in Russia during the reign of Catherine the Great. "The subject matter of history," wrote Sir Lewis Namier, "is human affairs, men in action, things which have happened and how they happened; concrete events fixed in time and space, and their grounding in the thoughts and feelings of men—not things universal and generalized."[1]

History attempts to provide society with an artificial collective memory. The tools used in this gigantic task of reconstructing the memory of mankind range from the stone artifacts of prehistoric man to this morning's newspaper. The sources of history have grown not only in quantity, but also in their complexity. The remarkable progress in archeology has greatly increased the treasure of physical remains such as the implements, sculpture, and inscribed stones. There has been a corresponding increase in available written materials ranging from papyri, cuneiform writing, manuscripts, chronicles, and the more recent accumulations of personal papers of important public figures.

The word "history" comes from a Greek word meaning to inquire. That is exactly the job of the historian, to inquire, to illuminate the past as best he can on the basis of available evidence. The earliest use of the word "history" is found in the Greek historian, Herodotus. In order to collect materials for his famous history, he traveled widely in the world known to

---

[1] Sir Lewis Namier, "History," quoted in Fritz Stern, ed., *The Varieties of History* (Cleveland: World Publishing Co., 1963), p. 372.

fifth-century Greeks and "inquired" about places and events, eventually writing a book known as *The History of Herodotus.* After that time, the Greek word for inquiry, *historie* or *historia,* began to mean a narrative dealing with the reconstruction of the past. The term passed into Latin as *historia* and then to all the modern European languages. Herodotus was basically a story-teller and a superb one, and his history is a combination of fact and fable. It contains shrewd and accurate observations and tales which are beyond reasonable limits of credibility.

A historian starts his inquiry basically with three questions: "What happened? How did it happen? Why did it happen?" The historian begins by collecting as much relevant data as he possibly can. He then organizes his evidence, tests it, and then proceeds, more often than not, painfully and laboriously to reconstruct a fragment of the past. R. G. Collingwood suggested that there are four characteristics of history:

(a) that it is scientific, or begins by knowing something and tells what it knows.
(b) that it is humanistic, or asks questions about things done by men at determinate times in the past.
(c) that it is rational, or bases the answers which it gives on grounds, namely, appeal to evidence.
(d) that it is self-revelatory, or exists in order to tell man what man is by telling him what man has done.[2]

The last characteristic cited by Collingwood is indeed essential for the understanding of the nature of history and its unique position among the scholarly disciplines. For a variety of reasons, some of which are easier to isolate than others, man *wants* to know what men who have preceded him have done or thought. Probably, because of his consciousness of the finite nature of human life, man is eager and even anxious to find a bridge to earlier generations which have faced this same disconcerting realization. Historical links to the past may well soften the fear or uncertainty about the meaning of existence by placing it in the perspective of past ages of human strivings, failures, and accomplishments. History seems to be an expression of, and an answer to, the deeply felt need of human beings everywhere to know of their collective past. Studies of amnesia victims reveal how unsettling and terrifying is the realization of the loss of memory of one's personal past, of the lack of roots, and how compelling is the urge to recover the lost past. No individual is ready to wipe out the memory of his past life, however unhappy or sordid it may have been.

---

2 R. G. Collingwood, *The Idea of History,* T. M. Knox, ed. (London: Oxford Univ. Press, 1946), p. 18.

Similarly, no society or nation would tolerate the loss of their collective memory and its replacement by a tabula rasa.

Consequently, the task of the historian is eased because of a strong pre-occupation with the history of human beings throughout the past. There is evidence that men in positions of leadership have paid great attention to the record and judgment of history. Kings, emperors, generals, chancellors, and popes have exhibited great curiosity about what history will say about them. They often spared no effort to "help" future historians in their verdict on their lives and accomplishments. Even humble folk have worried, and still do, about leaving a "good name." In fact, the existence of historical records including paintings, artifacts, sculpture, or inscribed clay tablets is one of the most important characteristics of progress and civilization. Interest in leaving a historical document, in whatever form, has always been a sure sign of civilization. In most ancient times early peoples, long before they possessed the art of writing, attempted to leave a record of their existence by painting animals and battle and hunting scenes on the walls of their cave dwellings. Others left strange and still unexplained stone structures like those at Stonehenge in England. Egyptian Pharaohs, the kings of Moab, Edom, Assyria and Persia, and other rulers of the ancient world made sure that posterity would know of their deeds and even of their misdeeds. They built massive pyramids and carved the tale of their accomplishments on huge monuments.

An inscription on the tomb of the Egyptian general Uni tells of punitive expeditions of the Egyptian army against unruly Bedouin tribes which were attacking Canaan. The campaigns were undertaken on orders of the Egyptian Pharaoh Phiops about 2300 B.C. Uni's report reads in part:

> His Majesty made war on the desert peoples and His Majesty gathered an army . . . I was entrusted with the whole campaign . . . The King's army returned in good order after laying waste the country of the desert peoples, after destroying their fortresses . . . after cutting down their fig trees and vines . . . And carrying off a large number into captivity.[3]

A clay cuneiform tablet relates the military triumph of the Assyrian King Tiglath Pilesser III. The chronicle describes the capture of Damascus:

> His noblemen I impaled alive and displayed this exhibition to his land. All his gardens and fruit orchards I destroyed. I besieged and captured the native city of Rezin of Damascus. Eight hundred people with their belongings, I led away. Towns in sixteen districts of Damascus I laid waste like mounds after the Flood.[4]

---

[3] Quoted in Werner Keller, *The Bible as History* (New York: Wm. Morrow & Co., 1956), p. 58.
[4] *Ibid.*, p. 248.

The famous Moabite Stone of the ninth century gives testimony to the determination of Mesha, the King of Moab to leave a clear record of his greatest accomplishment for history. The inscription reads:

> I Mesha, the son of Kenosh, King of Moab. My father was king over Moab thirty years and I became king after my father. And I made this high-place for Kenosh, for he saved me from my downfall and made me triumph over my enemies.
>
> Omri, King of Israel, was the oppressor of Moab for many long days because Kenosh was angered against his country. His son succeeded him, and he also said, "I will oppress Moab." It was in my day that he said it. And I triumphed over him and his house. And Israel perished forever.[5]

Being a work of theology, the Old Testament is concerned with historical events only to illuminate its main theme of the relationship of a people with their God. The Bible, however, makes repeated reference to the existence of more strictly historical works known as the Chronicles of the Kings of Judah and similar chronicles of the kings of Israel. A typical reference reads, "And the rest of the acts of Sholum, and his conspiracy which he made, behold, they are written in the book of the chronicles of the kings of Israel" (II Kings xv. 15). Unfortunately, these important chronicles were lost. In medieval and more modern times rulers and nobles showed the same concern with the verdict of history. Many of them employed monks and scribes to write their personal chronicles. The veracity of these chronicles varies as much as the types of caligraphy in which they are written.

History was for the Chinese not only a chronicle of the past, but a means of teaching good government and of inculcating ethical values. The past was a guide for the future and was consulted with great regularity, especially by the emperors. History in ancient and medieval China encompassed far more than political and military chronology; it included social mores, economics, philosophy, and moral precepts. The authors of old Chinese histories did not hesitate to praise or condemn the powerful, and the fear of the "verdict of history" dwelt not only in the palaces of the rulers, but also in the hearts of every government official.

Historical writing was an honorable and official occupation. Beginning with the powerful Han dynasty, which retained power for more than four centuries (202 B.C.–220 A.D.), it was the custom for the first ruler in each new dynasty to order the writing of a history of his predecessors. The author of a recent history of China describes the way in which the court historians went about their task:

---

[5] Edward Eyre, ed., *European Civilization* (New York: Oxford Univ. Press, 1934–1939), p. 271.

Since so much importance was attached to this work, the historian (or historians) who volunteered or had been assigned to its writing approached the task with a sense of mission almost sacred.   Groping through mountainous materials that had not been consumed by time, he sifted and winnowed until they were reduced to a manageable position.   He selected and discarded in accordance with his own judgment and conscience.   He should write factually and objectively; any slant or distortion would be a reflection on his personality and scholarship.[6]

The Chinese historian's lot was not without its perils.   On occasion, if the Emperor found his work unsatisfactory, the historian would be promptly beheaded.   Fortunately for historians such an execution was rare because of the abiding respect for scholars held by the Chinese.   Outstanding among these histories was the monumental work of Ssu-ma Kuang, significantly entitled *History as a Mirror*.   This work chronicled the events of 1,362 years (403 B.C.–959 A.D.) and was completed by Kuang in 1084 after seventeen years of labor.

Medieval and modern times produced much more sophisticated historical evidence in the form of letters, diaries, and newspapers.

Around 1365, the Italian poet Petrarch wrote to Boccaccio about the joy of learning.   The letter reads in part:

Neither love of virtue nor the thought of approaching death must distract us from the study of literature which, if pursued with good intentions, stimulates love of virtue and either diminishes or destroys the fear of death . . .   For literature is no hindrance to one who takes it in the proper spirit; to him it is not an obstacle but a comfort and an aid in the difficulties of the earthly voyage.   And as it happens with many foods that the same prove troublesome to a weak and queasy stomach, which to one healthy and craving offer grateful and timely nourishment, so it is with studies.   Those which might prove harmful to the weak minds seem beneficial to a keen and well disposed intellect.   This is particularly so, if, in both cases, the propensity be used in moderation.[7]

A historian, and for that matter, a high school student, can get an insight into the mind of Oliver Cromwell and may find at least a partial answer to the puzzling question of whether Cromwell was a deeply religious man or a hypocrite, in a careful reading of a letter from Cromwell to Colonel Hammond written in July 1648.   The use of primary historical documents such as letters is essential to effective teaching of a serious historical prob-

---

[6] Dun J. Li, *The Ageless Chinese—A History* (New York: Charles Scribner's Sons, 1965), pp. 227–228.
[7] Quoted in *Europe in Review*, George L. Morse, Rondo E. Cameron, Henry Bertram Hill, and Michael B. Petrovich, eds. (Chicago: Univ. of Chicago Press, 1957), p. 74.

lem. The letter, in which Cromwell tries to justify the attack of his Army of the "Saints" on Parliament, reads in part:

> You say: "God has appointed authorities among nations to which active or passive obedience is to be yielded. This resides in England in the Parliament. Therefore active or passive resistance," etc.
>
> Authorities and powers are the ordinances of God. This or that species is of human institution, and limited, some with larger, others with stricter bonds, each one according to its constitution. But I do not therefore think the Authorities may do *anything*, and yet such obedience is due. All agree that there are cases in which it is lawful to resist. If so, your ground fails, and so likewise the inference. Indeed, dear Robin, not to multiply words, the query is, whether this be such a case. This ingenuously is the true question . . .
>
> First, whether Salus Populi [the good of the people] be a sound position? Secondly, whether in the way in hand, really and before the Lord, before whom conscience has to stand, this be provided for; or if the whole fruit of the war is not like to be frustrated and all most like to turn to what it was, and worse? . . . Thirdly, whether the Army be not a lawful Power, called by God to oppose and fight against the King upon some stated grounds . . . And the Lord teach us.
>
> My dear Friend, let us look into providence; surely they mean somewhat. They band so together; have been so constant, so clear, so unclouded. Malice, swollen malice against God's people, now called "Saints," to root out their name; and yet, they "these poor Saints," getting arms, and therein blessed with defense and more! . . . Who acts, if he resolve not through God to be willing to part with all? Our hearts are very deceitful, on the right and on the left.
>
> What think you of Providence disposing the hearts of so many of God's people this way, especially in this poor Army, wherein the great God has vouchsafed to appear! . . . We trust, the same Lord who hath formed our minds in our actings is with us in this also . . . only desiring to fear our great God, and we do nothing against His will. Truly, this is our condition.
>
> And to conclude. We in this Northern Army were in a waiting posture; desiring to see what the Lord would lead us to . . . Dear Robin, beware of men; look up to the Lord. Let him be free to speak and command in thy heart. Take heed of the things I fear thou has reasoned thyself into; and thou shall be able through Him, without consulting flesh and blood, to do valiantly for him and His people . . .[8]

What a rich harvest for a fruitful class discussion can be gathered from this letter both on a high school and college level!

Newspapers are another important, although tricky and often suspect,

---

[8] *Ibid.*, pp. 74–75.

source for historical investigations. Their greatest value lies in the color and direct impressionistic testimony they provide. A great newspaperman and editor of the Cincinnati *Commercial*, Murat Halstead, left us this direct account of the nomination of Abraham Lincoln by the Republican Convention in Chicago in May, 1860.

> While this ballot (the third) was taken amid excitement that tested the nerves, the fatal defection from Seward in New England still further appeared—four votes going over from Seward to Lincoln in Massachusetts. The latter received four additional votes from Pennsylvania and fifteen additional votes from Ohio. It was whispered about—"Lincoln's the coming man—will be nominated on this ballot." When the roll of the States and Territories had been called, I had ceased to give attention to any votes but those for Lincoln and had his vote added up as it was given. The number of votes necessary to a choice were two hundred and thirty-three, and I saw under my pencil as the Lincoln column was completed, the figures 231½—one vote and a half to give him the nomination. In a moment the fact was whispered about. A hundred pencils had told the same story. The news went over the house wonderfully, and there was a pause. There are always men anxious to distinguish themselves on such occasions. There is nothing that politicians like better than a crisis. I looked up to see who would be the man who would give the decisive vote . . . In about ten ticks of a watch, Cartter of Ohio was up. I had imagined Ohio would be slippery enough for the crisis. And sure enough! Every eye was on Cartter, and everybody who understood the matter at all, knew what he was about to do. He is a large man with rather striking features, a shock of bristling black hair, large and shining eyes, and is terribly marked with the small pox. He has also an impediment in his speech, which amounts to a stutter; and his selection as chairman of the Ohio delegation was, considering its condition, altogether appropriate. He had been quite noisy during the sessions of the Convention, but had never commanded when mounting his chair, such attention as now. He said, "I rise (eh) Mr. Chairman (eh), to announce the change of four votes of Ohio from Mr. Chase to Mr. Lincoln." The deed was done. There was a moment's silence. The nerves of the thousands, which through the Law of suspense had been subjected to terrible tension, relaxed, and as deep breaths of relief were taken, there was a noise in the Wigwam like the rush of a great wind, in the van of a storm —and in another breath, the storm was there. There were thousands cheering with the energy of insanity . . .[9]

It is of interest to note that recent United States Presidents have, like the Pharaohs of old, made provisions during their term of office for the erection of separate libraries which would house their official papers, proclamations, letters, and even occasional doodlings, thus providing a con-

---

[9] Quoted in *The American Reader*, Paul M. Angle, ed. (Chicago: Rand McNally & Co., 1958), pp. 304–305.

venient source of information for future historians. We have the Franklin Roosevelt Library in Hyde Park, New York, the Truman Library in Independence, Missouri, the Eisenhower Library in Abilene, Kansas, the Kennedy Library at Cambridge, Massachusetts, and we will soon have the Johnson Library in Houston, Texas. These libraries are not only repositories of historical records, but are also centers of research, where historians work on various aspects of the various Presidential administrations.

Even our everyday language reflects the unique pre-occupation of many people at all times with history. Writers, debaters, government leaders on all levels, politicians running for office, and even people in everyday life use such expressions as "the lesson of history," "the verdict of history," "history teaches us," "history will show," "history proves," "history is on our side." It would be unthinkable and even seem ridiculous to hear a candidate for political office exclaim: "Sociology teaches us . . .", or "The lesson of anthropology is . . ."

We may well probe somewhat deeper into the reasons behind this universal and deep concern with history. We have already suggested that historical continuity gives human beings some assurance of immortality. History makes it possible for puzzled, bewildered men to contemplate their relationship with the past and bear the uncertain future with greater ease. The study of the historical record, with its repeated, if not orderly, patterns of successes and failures, progress and regression, periods of brilliance followed by chaos and decline, contributes to a sense of the unity and common destiny of all mankind.

Lord Acton wrote that while history is a record of the past, it is also, strangely enough, "a record told of ourselves, the record of life which is our own, of efforts not yet abandoned to repose, of problems that still entangle the feet and vex hearts."[10] The great piano virtuoso, Vladimir Horowitz, who in 1965 came out of a long, self-imposed retirement, expressed a similar idea in these words: "To people I am a legend, but I am still alive. In my way, my future is my past and my past is my present."[11] There is some consolation for mortal human beings in the realization that they are a link in the long chain of human generations. The English historian, George M. Trevelyan expressed this idea: "At bottom, the appeal of history is imaginative. Our imagination craves to behold our ancestors as they really were, going about their daily business and their daily pleasure . . . It is the detailed study of history that makes us feel that the past was as real as the present."[12]

There is indeed great fascination in getting a glimpse into the life of

---

[10] Lord Acton, *A Lecture on the Study of History* (London: The Macmillan Co., 1905), p. 19.

[11] New York *Times*, March 17, 1965, p. 22.

[12] Quoted in A. L. Rowse, *The Use of History* (New York: The Macmillan Co., 1948), p. 26.

generations long gone. History is the story of the lives and experiences of men living in civilized societies and as such it is about life and has the appeal of life, as revealed by imaginative reconstruction. The fascination with a good history book is akin to the excitement engendered by a good detective story. Indeed, the historian and the detective have much in common. The historian can reconstruct the event and the detective the crime only in their trained imaginations. Both painstakingly gather data and clues, evaluate the testimony of witnesses, and then formulate their conclusions. Neither the historian nor the detective can ever be sure that the event they finally describe *really* took place in the way in which they have reconstructed it. They can only hope that it did. Often new clues or new testimony appear which make it clear that the original judgment of the crime-hunter or the historian was wrong. While basically valid, this analogy can be carried only so far and no further. New evidence merely causes the historian to rewrite his book or compels successive generations of historians to provide new insights and new interpretations. Miscarriages of justice which result from faulty detective work may, of course, be much more drastic for the victim.

While reading good narrative history is an enjoyable experience, it seems that historians find the writing of history as laborious and often as painful as it may be rewarding and inspiring. In his autobiography Edward Gibbon described his feelings upon the completion of his monumental work, *The Decline and Fall of the Roman Empire.*

> It was on the day, or rather the night of 27th June 1787, between the hours of eleven and twelve that I wrote the last lines of the last page in a summer-house in my garden. After laying down my pen I took several turns in a berceau or covered walk of Acacias, which commands a prospect of the country, the lake, and the mountains. The air was temperate, the sky was serene, the silver orb of the moon was reflected from the waters, and all Nature was silent. I will not dissemble the first emotions of joy on the recovery of freedom and perhaps the establishment of my fame. But my pride was soon humbled, and a sober melancholy was spread over my mind by the idea that I had taken my everlasting leave of an old and agreeable companion, and that whatsoever might be the future fate of my history, the life of the historian must be short and precarious.[13]

Hundreds of similar testimonials, bearing on the pain and joy of writing history can be cited.

The reasons for this rather special relationship between the historian and his work are important because they have a bearing on the unique nature of history. History is a humane study—it is vitally interested in human emotions and in the virtues and follies of individual human beings. A

---

[13] Edward Gibbon, *Miscellaneous Works of Edward Gibbon, with Memoirs of His Life and Writings Composed by Himself* (London, 1796), p. 72.

historian who writes about the complex personality of Napoleon may soon become swept by human sympathy for this charismatic Corsican who even during the days of his pitiful exile on the island of St. Helena remained a leader of men. Even the madness and the depth of personal unhappiness of Ivan the Terrible can evoke pity and understanding in a sensitive historian. The historian cannot fail to be impressed by the realization that the history of the world has been affected, for good or for bad, by the length of Cleopatra's nose, by the eloquence of Churchill's oratory, and by the frustrated childhood of Lee Oswald. No such human sympathy is needed or expected in the study of mathematics, geology, or physics. The study of history results in the emotional involvement of the writer because it deals with man who is good or evil, or both, who has the capacity to distinguish between right and wrong, who can rise to great heights, create beautiful works of art, and perform good acts, but who also can be an agent of destruction and the cause of great evil. G. M. Trevelyan saw a close affinity between history and poetry.

> The appeal of history to us all is in the last analysis poetic. But the poetry of history does not consist of imagination roaming at large, but of imagination pursuing the fact and fastening upon it. That which compels the historian to scorn delights and live laborious days is the order of his own curiosity to know what really happened long ago in that land of mystery we call the past. To peer into that magic mirror and see fresh figures. There every day is a burning desire that consumes and satisfies him all his life and carries him each morning, eager as a lover to the library and the muniment because it is poetic. The dead were and are not. Their place knows them no more and is ours today. *Yet they were once real as we, and we shall tomorrow be shadows like them.*[14]

The imaginative reconstruction of the past which is scrupulous and scientific in method, but artistic in its conclusions, is the business of the historian. And it is a very stimulating and rewarding business indeed.

POLITICAL HISTORY

While history in general is concerned with the total, past human experience, few historians attempt to cover all of that experience. Consequently, there is political history, social history, economic history, military history, etc. While most historians reject the view that history is "past politics," a great deal of history now written and read is political history. Most textbooks, if not all of them, are basically political histories. Political history

---

[14] *The Varieties of History*, Fritz Stern, ed. (Cleveland: World Publishing Co., 1963), p. 122.

is concerned with the record of public events, the story of public institutions, of rulers and governments, wars, conquests, and the making of peace. In a broader sense, political history includes constitutional, administrative and diplomatic histories, and the great literature of historical biographies. The reason for the predominance of political history is simple. The reading public is interested in politics, in men who make politics, and in the consequences of political successes or failures. National rivalries, ideological conflicts, and the decisions affecting peace and war are of direct concern to most people, and they are the ingredients of political history. The most scholarly exposition of the economic causes of World War I cannot compare in readership appeal with the dissection of the personality of Lenin, the description of the Battle of Waterloo, or the analysis of the election to the presidency of John F. Kennedy. Some of the standard great histories, including the works of Thucydides, Macaulay, Bancroft, and Rhodes, are mainly political in emphasis.

The readers, who in the last analysis determine the longevity of any historical work, seem to be consistently fascinated with the story of the great men who shaped the history of mankind. There are never enough biographies of Alexander, Genghis Khan, Julius Caesar, Augustus, Constantine, Cromwell, Jefferson, Lincoln, Napoleon, Bolívar, Lenin, and Churchill to exhaust public interest. The public seems to be little concerned with the question of whether the respective ages produced their respective heroes or whether these great men created their particular eras. They merely want to get a glimpse into the workings of a great mind and to thrill at or abhor their deeds.

There can be little argument about the predominance of nationalism as a force in the shaping of the history of mankind. When confronted with the challenge of universal religions or international ideologies, nationalism has invariably proved to be the winner. Political history is basically national history; it is a history of conflicting nationalisms and this, too, is one of the reasons for its widespread appeal. How nations acquired their identity, how they gained or lost power, how they met internal and external challenges is the core of political history.

ECONOMIC HISTORY

Economic history has experienced remarkable growth in recent years. The great strides made in the discipline of economics have influenced many historians to do important research on how the societies in the past have earned their livelihoods. Economic historians deal with "economic factors" and "economic motives" in history and concern themselves with problems of land ownership and tenure, means and methods of production, commerce, currency, and the conditions of labor and management. Perhaps one of the greatest works in economic history was Adam Smith's *Wealth of Nations* (1776). He charted the road for future research in history from the point of view of economic development by analyzing how man has made use of his resources for his personal and societal needs. An economic historian, being a social scientist, is primarily interested in discovering uniform laws of development, rather than emphasizing disparate economic conditions.

Economic history received a great boost and entered into a prolonged period of controversy following the publication in 1926 of R. H. Tawney's *Religion and the Rise of Capitalism*. Tawney's main thesis that Protestantism was the ethic supporting, and mainspring responsible for the rise of European capitalism was defended and disputed by many scholars. The study of history centering on the economic choices made by man may be an important contribution to universal history. After all, economic functions have always been essential in the life of any society in the history of mankind. Consequently, economic history is the story of how man utilized his environment to obtain subsistence, and what he thought in the process of doing this. This process of utilization of resources of the environment was more often than not a social function which required some organization. The economist seeks to discover the unifying elements in this process. "The economic historian," wrote Professor W. H. B. Court, "dealing with the economizing principle of human nature, is on the face of things in touch with one of the most constant and rational and intelligible forces in history."[15] A general historian commenting on this unequivocal statement of a leading economic historian can only feel envious. In his work, the forces moving in history are seldom, if ever, "constant, rational and intelligible."

In discussing economic history one must note briefly the attempts to write general history from an economic point of view. Karl Marx, in his economic interpretation of history, maintained that the history of the world was shaped essentially by economic forces—by the constant struggle between the small property-owning class and the exploited, unpropertied masses. Political, social, and religious institutions, while important, were dependent upon, and determined by, the stage of the economic development of a particular society. A society's political and social superstructure was dependent upon the conditions of production and used in the constant struggle by those in control of the means of production. In Marx's works the range of choices in history is indeed limited by the inevitability of the eventual collapse of capitalism and the rise of communism.

The American historian, Charles Beard, while rejecting the Marxist phi-

---

15 W. H. B. Court, "Economic History," in *Approaches to History*, H. P. R. Fineberg, ed. (Toronto: Univ. of Toronto Press, 1962), p. 41.

losophy of historical determinism, causation, and the inevitability of social revolutions, asserted in his volumes *Economic Interpretation of the Constitution, Economic Origins of Jeffersonian Democracy,* and *Economic Basis of Politics* that political thought and action are dictated by the economic interests of individual groups and parties. While most historians today reject the specific findings of Beard about the making of the American Revolution and the causes of the Civil War, Charles Beard and his wife Mary, also an historian, made a lasting contribution to American historical writing by pointing to the importance of economic factors and economic motives in history.

SOCIAL HISTORY

George M. Trevelyan, the author of *English Social History,* defined social history as "the history of a people with the politics left out."[16] He went on to say that such a history is concerned with the daily life of the inhabitants of a land. It describes and analyzes the daily life of the people and their culture. Social history is the historical counterpart of sociology, and, as such, its scope is the life of man in society.

Significantly, Trevelyan wrote his social history of England after the completion of a number of masterful works in political history, including a trilogy on Garibaldi and a multivolume *History of England.* His interest in social history, Trevelyan explained (in the introduction to the *English Social History*), came from a growing realization of the importance of social change. Politics, he concluded, is both the outcome and the cause of social change.

Human society is complex, and social historians maintain that it cannot be viewed from all its many aspects at once. What is necessary is a focus. The focus for a social historian is society and social change. The social point of view is broad, indeed, and includes, in the words of W. W. Rostow, "the way people live, the culture and religion which they generate and regard as acceptable, their scientific pursuits, and above all, the general political concepts which serve to nationalize their relationship to the community."[17]

While social history is basically the history of various societies, it is not the history of all aspects of those societies. It is limited to the relationship of man to his society and the history of changes in that relationship. The dynamic nature of human societies, always subject to strain and stress and often to revolutionary upheaval, is also within the scope of social history.

---

[16] G. M. Trevelyan, *English Social History* (London: Longmans, Green, 1942), p. vii.
[17] W. W. Rostow, *British Economy in the Nineteenth Century* (Oxford: Clarendon Press, 1948), p. 134.

A social historian is interested in agriculture, industry, political parties, governments, and foreign policy, but only as they affect social activities and social institutions. Here again, social historians, by focusing attention on social change, social structure, and social fluidity, which moves upward or downward, have made an important contribution to the general history.

Subdivisions of these three main approaches to history writing, which include diplomatic history, military history, and moral history, describe aspects of past historical experiences and events from clearly defined perspectives. The naval history of the Second World War, written by Samuel Eliot Morison, is an example of excellent writing in the area of military history.

By now it should be obvious that history as the complete and fully accurate reconstruction of the past, of all the civilized past of mankind, does not exist. What we do have is what historians say about the past. The accumulated wealth of historical knowledge is the attempts of thousands of historians to recreate *segments* of past human experience, usually on the basis of incomplete evidence. Since no eyewitness can be called upon to testify if all participants in an era are dead, each historian faces the task of reconstructing the past with his own special cultural, national, ethnic, economic background and his own values and prejudices. Thus, what we have and what we read is what historians write *about* a particular period or event in history. That is why we have so many different interpretations of the American Revolution, the Civil War, the French Revolution and so many quite different biographies of great men like Cromwell, Napoleon, Peter the Great, and Lenin. The authors of these volumes often differ in their interpretation of the events and the people they describe. It would be foolhardy even to attempt to select one *true* history of the French Revolution or one really authentic biography of Oliver Cromwell.

It is very important that teachers and students alike, on the high school and college level, realize that a *history textbook is not history,* but an extended statement on American or world history by the author. The same is true of all history books, even those written by great historians. Even their views and interpretations have been subject to criticism and rejection. Not all historians, for instance, have agreed with Gibbon's central thesis on the fall of Rome, namely that Christianity was mainly responsible for the disintegration of Roman society, or with Parkman's hostility to French Catholics and to French colonization efforts in North America. One only has to read accounts of the American Revolution written by American and English historians, the story of Reformation written by a Catholic and a Protestant historian, or the history of British occupation of India written by English and Indian historians to realize that while history is a story about the past, or an investigation of the past, *it is not the past itself.* The past, the whole past, the absolutely true past, can never be reconstructed.

Consequently, it must be constantly borne in mind, especially by teachers of history, that the historian's task is not to deal with the past as it *really* was, but with the available traces and records of the past. The materials that the historian works with are the remains and relics of history. Those remains—tablets, documents, letters, monuments—are not history itself. They are materials, usually neither complete nor systematic, from which by the use of his *creative imagination* the historian reconstructs the past. Since creative imagination and acquired skills differ widely among even professionally trained people, two historians using the same materials can and often do come up with very different reconstructions of the past. If one adds the undeniable fact that all historians are human beings, with individual foibles, values and prejudices, it is no wonder that histories, which are the written attempts to reconstruct the past, differ so much.

The Soviet historian who accepts the Marxist-Leninist philosophy of history reconstructs the story of the French Revolution in a drastically different way than the English or an American historian who rejects the idea that all human history is essentially the history of class struggles and that the course of history is determined by the conflict over the possession of the means of production. Both groups of historians are true to their convictions and both use basically the same techniques in appraising available sources, but their differences about the essence of the story of human experience on earth make a fundamental difference in the conclusions arrived at in their works. For a discerning teacher of history, both approaches are valuable for joint teacher-student inquiry into the past.

These inherent problems do not make history writing either meaningless or less attractive. Disagreements about data evaluation are not peculiar to historians. Social scientists differ not only about the phenomena of the past, but seldom agree even about events and developments in contemporary society in spite of the opportunity for visual observation, direct analysis of the data, and examination and re-examination of witnesses. Sociologists trying to analyze a race riot do not often agree either on the diagnosis or on the remedies proposed, and distinguished economists seldom if ever agree on the best ways to prevent inflation or eliminate unemployment. The fact that historians differ in their reconstruction of events and in the interpretation of the past makes history alive, challenging, and dynamic. Carl Becker was correct when he maintained that each generation writes its own history. Consequently, the writing and the teaching of history can be an ever fascinating, challenging, and even inspiring occupation.

The realization that history is not the *past*, but the ever-changing, ever challenged attempts of historians to imaginatively reconstruct segments of the past, may be of great help to the teachers of history. The comparative study of differing interpretations of historians can be a fascinating motivation for the study of history. Students should be encouraged to conduct their small-scale investigations and pit their conclusions, as often as possible, against established historical interpretations. Jerome S. Bruner is convincing when he argues (in *The Process of Education*) that children on elementary and secondary levels are capable of engaging in such meaningful inquiries. In such a process the teachers are not the "givers" and the students "recipients." Both participate in the never-ending goal of education—namely the search for truth, however tentative it may be.

Historians reconstruct only a small part or some fragments of the past which are of particular interest to them. It is disturbing that few of our students and even many history and social studies teachers do not realize this simple fact. Such a realization may well lead to less reliance on textbooks, and it might lead to more exciting teaching of history by making both the teachers and students aware of the human qualities and limitations involved in the writing of history. The attempt to understand how a particular historian went about his work, how he has interpreted his data, can be a useful and absorbing learning experience for the students. Selected experiments with students acting like amateur historians and applying the historical method of inquiry to a particular event may be a rewarding and effective teaching strategy in the social studies.

2

The Uses of History

What is the use of the study of history? Why should generations of school children be compelled year after year to study history? What practical use can a knowledge of history have? These are legitimate questions which deserve serious consideration.

The answer can be found more easily if one frees himself of the widespread assumption that the past is the only component of history. Nothing could be more false and more misleading. Since the historian must reenact any past event in his own mind, history is an end product of two components; the past, as it can be reconstructed on the basis of discoverable evidence, and the historian's mind, his ideas, and his skill in reconstructing the past. Consequently, as the great Italian philosopher, Croce, said, "All history is contemporary history."[1] The past, he maintained, has no real meaning for us except as it is given that meaning by us. We deal with those aspects of the past in which we have an interest and which has some relevance to our interests, dreams, and hopes. Collingwood said, "The history of thought and, therefore, all history is the reenactment of past thought in the historian's own mind."[2] One does not have to accept Collingwood's extreme equation of history with the history of thought to agree that the historian's mind, thoughts, imaginative skill, personal values, and biases are part of the history that he is writing. All history has a direct

[1] Benedetto Croce, *Theory and History of Historiography* (London: G. G. Harrap, 1921), pp. 12–14.
[2] R. G. Collingwood, *The Idea of History*, T. M. Knox, ed. (London: Oxford Univ. Press, 1946), p. 232.

relationship and a direct influence on the present. The historian selects those fragments of the past in which he is interested, and he then proceeds to deal with the fragment of the past, not as it really was, but *as he sees it*, on the basis of historical evidence available. Consequently, the process of reconstruction is closely interwoven with and related to the present. Good history is neither stale nor is it irrelevant to the present—it vibrates with life because it is the product of men who receive their impulses, motivations, and inspirations from contemporary society. Valuable works of history have had and continue to have significant influence on the generation for which they were written. This was true of the histories of the Peloponnesian and Persian Wars of Thucydides and Herodotus, Voltaire's *The Age of Louis XIV*, Ranke's *Weltgeschichte*, Gibbon's *The Decline and Fall of the Roman Empire*, and H. G. Wells's celebrated *Outline of History*. It would be difficult to overestimate the influence on our own generation of Trevelyan's *English Social History*, Toynbee's *The Study of History*, McNeill's *The Rise of the West*, and Allan Nevins' *Emergence of Lincoln and the War for the Union*.

If history is to mean something and not be merely a dry chronicle and empty echo of the past, it must, as Croce put it, "vibrate in the soul of the historian," and consequently, be related to contemporary life and conditions.[3] A historian is interested in the past because he is interested in life. Only his interest in the present moves him to study the past. The true historian's interest in the past and his indefatigable labors to search for the traces of the past, answers a deeply felt need to assure the continuity of human life and discover its meaning, even if the goal is never fully realized. In the process of discovering the past, the historian discovers himself; those who read his works experience, in a smaller or larger measure, the discovery of their own relationship with the past and in the process, learn to know themselves. "History is," Collingwood wrote, "for human self-knowledge. It is generally thought to be of importance to man that he should know himself, where knowing himself means knowing not merely his personal peculiarities, the things that distinguish him from other men, but his nature as man. . . . Knowing yourself means knowing what you can do; and since nobody knows what he can do until he tries, the only clue to what man can do is what man has done. The value of history, then, is that it teaches us what man has done and thus what man is."[4]

History allows man to place himself in better relationship to himself and to preceding generations and gives him at least a clue to the meaning and

---

[3] Benedetto Croce, *Theory and History of Historiography* (London: G. G. Harrap, 1921), pp. 11–12.
[4] R. G. Collingwood, *The Idea of History*, T. M. Knox, ed. (London: Oxford Univ. Press, 1946), p. 10.

the mystery of life. This inquiry into the past seems to many to be an indispensable first step before a meaningful inquiry into the present can take place. John Dewey, who stressed the importance of educating children for their responsibilities in contemporary society said: "What is already known . . . is of immense importance; inquiry could not proceed a step without it."[5] It is history that makes it possible for us to see what is typical, new, unusual, in our time. This assessment, in turn, may be of great help in coping with contemporary problems and challenges.

All this is not to claim that knowledge of historical events will give the reader a perfect understanding of causal relationships or a scientific insight into conflict resolutions. Human societies are too complex, the variables of human life are too numerous to make direct applications of past solutions to present problems possible or even desirable. What is possible is to gain a sense of perspective and an understanding of the range of available alternatives. Thus, the effective study of history, the intelligent reflection on the past may be an important educative experience. The rationalizations offered by the political and intellectual leaders of the South in the twenty years before the Civil War on the "sacred institution" of slavery, their affirmation of the supremacy of the white race, and the glowing descriptions of the "civilizing" effects of human bondage do not give us the answer to the contemporary racial problems, but they may help us to understand better the difficulties in the road toward the full implementation of civil rights in a multi-racial society.

The study of history has been required of school children from ancient times. Most of the states in our Union require by law the study of United States history. The reason lies in the widespread belief that the study of history, especially of national history—the study of a nation's heroes and their deeds, of common dangers experienced, of victories and defeats—is useful as a creative and inspiring force in the molding of the minds of the younger generation. The study of the nation's past is considered by many, and with good reason, one of the best means of re-enforcing national unity and of instilling love of country and patriotic devotion. There is little doubt that the dramatic, heroic story of the American Revolution, of the genius of the Founding Fathers who in 1789 wrote a durable Constitution, which with few amendments is still viable in the 20th Century, of the story of Thomas Paine and of the patriotism of Patrick Henry, makes generations of young Americans proud of their heritage. The study of their past and of their rich heritage by the Jews, the Irish, and the Poles,

---

[5] John Dewey, "Experience and Nature," *The Paul Carus Lectures* (La Salle, Ill.: Open Court, 1929), p. 154.

and many others has enabled these peoples to survive centuries of dispersion or foreign occupation.

History also has been a powerful force in the creation of nations. What binds groups of people together in a community of nationhood is primarily a common past, a feeling of communality of interests in the present, and common aspirations for the future. The narration of history, the memory of past glories or grievances and the dream of unfulfilled future aspirations all forming a part of a nation's history, have contributed mightily to the rise of nationalism. The story of national heroes and their deeds is imbedded deeply in the national consciousness and has always evoked, and still does, profound emotions. The Hebrews remembered the exploits of King David, the Greeks, the glory of King Leonidas and the three hundred Spartans at Thermopylae, and the Romans, the bravery of Caesar. The Germans will always pay tribute to the political genius of Bismarck, the Poles to the bravery of Pulaski and Kosczusko, the English, to the greatness of Nelson at Trafalgar, and Americans to the moral stature of Abraham Lincoln.

While history has been a creative and inspiring force, at times it has also been a destructive one, especially when manipulated by unscrupulous demagogues. Excessive nationalism, nurtured by distorted and exaggerated teaching of national history, has often led to bloodshed and destruction. Potential foci of infection in the world have often provided a temptation to the inflammatory use of historical claims to justify the use of force. The Austrians are poised against the Italians over the Tyrol, the Pakistanis and Indians over Kashmir, the Chinese and the Russians over Sinkiang, the Greeks and the Turks over Cyprus, and the Poles and the Germans over Gdansk. While aware of the potentially beneficial effects of intelligent, dramatic, lively teaching of United States history, teachers must beware of nationalist indoctrination. The teaching of history must be a means of inquiry which allows students to become aware of worthy and not so worthy deeds, of the basic strengths and the occasional blunders, of the great accomplishments and the unfinished tasks in their nation's past. National history taught in this fashion will result not in cynical disillusionment, but in deep and abiding love of country and a personal commitment to its legitimate interests.

Perhaps the most persistently advocated use of history is the claim that the knowledge of the past helps in the understanding of the present. Marc Bloch, a great French historian, has said that in order to understand the present, one must step out of it. If one knows how men dealt with problems and crises in history, he may be more able to cope successfully with contemporary crises. To a limited extent this seems to be a valid assumption.

A. L. Rowse makes the equivocal statement that the prime use of history is that it "enables you to understand, better than any other discipline, the public events, affairs and trends of your time."[6] This strong claim is valid only if one keeps in mind its limitations. History is replete with examples of men in positions of power and influence who have assumed that their knowledge of history gave them a key to the understanding of the destiny of their peoples or of the world, but whose policies have ended in disastrous failures or whose prophecies proved to be false. The recent examples of Karl Marx, of Pierre Laval, Hitler, and Mussolini suffice to illustrate this point. It seems that their example has not been sufficient for a contemporary student of history, the Chinese leader Mao Tse-tung, who recently stated, "History has proved and will go on proving that the people's war is the most effective weapon against U.S. imperialism and its lackeys."[7]

There can be no doubt, however, that the knowledge of history, if used judiciously, may provide tools for a better understanding of contemporary problems and conflicts. It also provides the perspective needed for a dispassionate analysis of social and political conflicts. But the knowledge of history does not guarantee a correct diagnosis or fool-proof cure for contemporary ills. At best history is a fickle master.

Teachers who try to use the inquiry into the past for a better understanding of the present must remember that a comparison of present conditions with similar conditions in the past is not enough. Similarities between the past and the present are important—but so are the differences. Without the understanding of these differences there can be no history because the concept of change is a basic and valuable historical principle.

The English have shown great respect for history as an excellent school for statesmen. Many of their leaders and prime ministers, including Winston Churchill, were excellent historians. During the era of their imperial greatness, the British maintained that the best training for the governors and district commissioners in their far-flung possessions should include not courses in administration, but courses in history. Lord Acton believed that history was the most powerful ingredient in the formation of character and the training of talent.[8]

Thomas Jefferson shared Acton's views about the influence of history on young minds. When he wrote the famous Education Bill for his state of Virginia, he provided that children in the elementary school be required to read much history. "History," he wrote, "by apprising them of the past, will enable them to judge of the future; it will avail them of the experiences of other times and other nations; it will qualify them as judges of the

---

[6] A. L. Rowse, *The Use of History* (New York: The Macmillan Co., 1948), p. 18.

[7] New York *Times*, September 4, 1965, p. 2.

[8] Lord Acton, *A Lecture on the Study of History* (London: The Macmillan Co., 1905), p. 20.

actions and designs of men; it will enable them to know ambition under every guise it may assume; and knowing it, to defeat its views."[9] This statement may have very well represented Jefferson's appraisal of what history had taught him.

Some instances can be cited in which a thorough knowledge of history is indeed indispensable for an understanding of a current event or political development. Only a person knowledgeable about the territorial disputes over inner and outer Mongolia and Sinkiang and the nationalist rivalries between Imperial China and Czarist Russia can fully understand the growing rift between China and the Soviet Union. A student of Chinese and Russian history understands that the dispute over the correct interpretation of Marxism-Leninism is merely a cloak to cover the long-standing nationalist rivalry. Only one who knows the complicated, bloody, and dismaying history of Reconstruction in the South can understand, but not excuse, diehard resistance to Negro civil and voting rights in Mississippi and Alabama. There are also some cases of historical events the memory of which does not fade, but which were traumatic experiences for an entire nation influencing its national policy and behavior for many decades. For Spaniards, the Spanish Civil War was undoubtedly such an experience, as was the war with Russia in 1945 for Finland. American foreign policy seems to have been permanently influenced by the rejection of the Treaty of Versailles in 1919, and our economic policies are never free of the spectre of the economic disaster which threatened the nation during the Great Depression of 1929–1932. The memory of that depression has resulted in a bipartisan policy making it the duty of the Federal Government to take all measures necessary to prevent the advent of an economic recession.

But the lesson of history in determining later policies is more often neither so direct, nor so obvious, as the examples just cited would suggest. It is wiser to speak of lessons of history instead of a lesson of history, of uses of history rather than the use of history. History as the story of man's struggle to conquer the forces of nature and of his faltering attempts to attain the goal of a better and happier existence does make men more sophisticated and better equipped to deal with problems of their own life. The knowledge of how men acted in the past, how they have striven to order the life of their respective societies, and how they have striven to overcome diversity, may not always suggest ingenious solutions to present crises, but it undoubtedly makes the task easier by providing a background and a body of past experience. History is indeed an inexhaustible source of examples and modes of life and "styles of life," and as such, and to that extent, it is a school of wisdom.

---

[9] Quoted in Allan Nevins, *The Gateway to History* (Garden City, N.Y.: Doubleday & Co., 1962), p. 17.

In spite of the widespread use of such terms as "history teaches us" and "the lesson of history," history has always had difficulty in providing a source of accurate predictions. Unlike some social scientists, historians are reluctant to claim that their investigations and their conclusions can be used to predict future events and future developments. They are enormously impressed and humbled by the complexity of human nature, the varieties of human conditions, the variables that operate in any social organism, and the importance of accident in human life. G. M. Trevelyan concluded: "There is no utilitarian value in the knowledge of the past, and there is no way of scientifically deducing causal laws about the action of human beings in the mass. In short, the value of history is not scientific. Its true value is educational. It can educate the minds of men by causing them to reflect on the past."[10]

Historians have traditionally been reluctant not only to make predictions about the future, but even to formulate broad generalizations on the basis of their studies. They usually make "small" generalizations which are quite limited in scope. Historians have expressed many objections to large generalizations. First, that broad generalizations, like laws, are detached from the context of particular research findings and must be applicable in all similar situations. Most historians are unwilling, in view of the always incomplete character of their data, to make sweeping claims for the conclusions reached in their investigations. Second, very broad generalizations are often untenable because of the limited sources of information and the complexity and variability of the subjects of important historical studies. Third, historians must use their creative imagination and thus a good dose of fiction in their reconstructions of the past, and consequently, any attempt to formulate scientifically and generally applicable generalizations is bound to fail. Fourth, few broad historical generalizations can be proven empirically.

As just indicated there are a number of hazards in making historical generalizations. Nevertheless, a symposium of prominent historians conducted in 1960–62 under the auspices of the Committee on Historical Analysis of the Social Science Research Council, reached a surprising agreement that historians need and do use some generalizations in their work. They all agreed that the scarcity or the abundance of sources and the inability of a historian to deal with his material with absolute detachment make the formulation of immutable generalizations inadvisable. However, most historians participating in the symposium argued that while the attainment of scientifically accurate generalizations is impossible, historians do, indeed

---

[10] George M. Trevelyan, *Clio, a Muse and Other Essays* (London: Longmans, Green, 1914), p. 62.

must, formulate "lower" and even "higher generalizations," tentative as they may be. Even vulnerable generalizations seem to be indispensable in the work of the modern historian. Professor William O. Aydelotte wrote: ". . . All historians generalize in that the statements they make cannot be distinguished from generalizations by any defensible criterion and that the claim made by some historians that they merely recite the evidence and permit the facts to speak for themselves is unallowable. Written history, like any other coherent or intelligible presentation, is not a simple record, but something far more complex. Hence, the question whether historians should generalize or not is meaningless; as several essays in this volume insist, they must generalize if they are to say anything worth saying."[11] Professor David Potter maintained in the symposium that a historian, even if he tries to avoid making theoretical statements, is actually engaged in making low generalizations. According to Potter, commitment to some sort of generalization is inescapable in the writing of history. Summarizing the symposium, its editor, Professor Louis Gottschalk, concluded that historians willy-nilly use generalizations at different levels and of different kinds.[12]

Furthermore, in a limited way, the historian does engage in predictions of the future and he does present lessons of history by the mere fact that he analyzes and offers conclusions from his description of a past event or a past crisis. A reader and student of history who perceptively follows the historian's presentation and analysis of data and then formulates his conclusions can gradually develop his own critical faculties. The English historian, E. H. Carr, made a very apt comment on historical generalization and its role in making predictions:

> The historian . . . is bound to generalize; and in so doing, he provides general guides for future action, which, though not specific predictions, are both valid and useful. But he cannot predict specific events, because the specific is unique and because the element of accident enters into it. This distinction which worries philosophers, is perfectly clear to ordinary man. If two or three children in school develop measles, you will conclude that the epidemic will spread, and this prediction, if you care to call it such, is based on a generalization from past experience, and is a valid and useful guide to action. But you cannot make the specific prediction that Charles or Mary will catch measles.[13]

---

[11] William O. Aydelotte, "Notes on the Problems of Historical Generalization," in *Generalization in the Writing of History*, Louis Gottschalk, ed. (Chicago: Univ. of Chicago Press, 1963), p. 151.
[12] *Ibid.*, p. 108.
[13] Edward Hallett Carr, *What Is History?* (New York: Alfred A. Knopf, 1962), pp. 87–88.

In spite of the reluctance of most historians to attempt to formulate general historical laws, or to look for the same type of unifying principles that sociologists and anthropologists seek in their disciplines, some historians have made important attempts in that direction. Other historians reject the idea that history has a discernible pattern of general laws. H. A. L. Fisher wrote in the preface to his *History of Europe:*

> One intellectual excitement has, however, been denied me. Men wiser and more learned than I have discovered in history a plot, a rhythm, a premeditated pattern. These harmonies are concealed from me. I can only see one emergency following upon another as a wave follows upon wave; only one great fact with respect to which, since it is unique, there can be no generalizations; only one safe rule for the historian: that he should recognize in the development of human destinies, the play of the contingent and the unforseen.[14]

A few historians have tried to encompass the whole sweep of history and to derive a philosophy of history and a general historical law from their study. These attempts have usually met with severe criticism from professional historians, but they brought the authors much attention, fame, profit, and distinction. Apparently, while the task is difficult, if not impossible, the attempt to find sense, patterns, or laws in history responds to some deeply felt human need.

Immanuel Kant's *Idea of a Universal History* (1784) is an eloquent disquisition on the destiny of mankind and on the faith of the author in the idea of progress in history. To Kant, history was a constant progress towards rationality. Realistically, Kant pointed out that men are often governed by antisocial impulses and instincts, but he believed that the basic nature of man, which is ruled by reason, would eventually prevail. Thus, of course, he spoke as a faithful son of Enlightenment. "All tendencies of any creature," wrote this German philosopher, "to which it is predisposed by nature are destined in the end to develop themselves perfectly and agreeably to their final purpose." Consequently, man's essentially rational nature will assert itself in the end, and then we shall see the emergence of a "universal civil society founded on political justice."[15] Since man desires concord (although nature prefers discord), man will learn, often through the painful experience of wars and lawlessness, to establish an international rule of law and order. Mankind will eventually be forced to establish a supranational organization operating under international law. In that new society, all men will have complete freedom to use their reason in all private and public affairs. As Collingwood has observed, Kant's assertion that progress is a plan of nature belongs more to mythology than to phi-

---

[14] H.A.L. Fisher, *A History of Europe* (Boston: Houghton Mifflin Co., 1935), p. 111.
[15] Immanuel Kant, *Philosophical Works* (London: Oxford Univ. Press, 1932), p. 17.

losophy.[16]   A story was told at the University of Koenigsberg, where Kant taught philosophy, that when a student once pointed out that Kant had used some historical facts to support a particular philosophical theory, which upon examination proved to have been inaccurate, Kant allegedly replied, "Desto schlimmer für die tatsachen."—"so much the worse for the facts."

Hegel's *Philosophy of History* (1800) had a profound influence on the philosophy of history.   It created a whole school of historians who followed Hegel's theory in maintaining that all history is the history of thought and that every epoch was inspired and dominated by one idea.   These ideas, Hegel said, represented by such heroic figures as Caesar and Napoleon, dominate and shape whole periods of history.   Such heroes are "die weltseele," or the soul of the world in their times.   However, the great ideas are not static; they are subject to constant change because each great idea brings with it a counter-idea which is the negation of its truth.   These two contradictory ideas battle with each other until they give birth to a new idea.   The new idea marks the beginning of a new cycle of thesis, antithesis, and synthesis.   Hegel postulated that this dialectic method is the key to understanding history.

To Hegel history was the progress of reason through the all-powerful Providence of God.   Man's spirit, a reflection of the Divine inspiration, finds its fulfillment in history.   Consequently, history represents the reality of God.   The universal idea of history is best represented, according to Hegel, in a national state.   He wrote: "Thus the state is the definite object of world history proper . . . For law is the objectivity of Spirit, it is will in true form . . . Only that will that obeys the law is free, for it obeys itself and being in itself is free."[17]   Hegel glorified the national state and argued that real freedom can be attained only through complete and unquestioning obedience to the state.   The nation-state, according to Hegel, is the ideal vehicle for the development of mankind because it represents "the march of God through the world."   Herbert J. Muller, in an address to the American Historical Association in December 1962, stated:

> Whatever one thinks of his (Hegel's) dialectic, he accentuated the fundamental reality of *change*.   He gave philosophical dignity to change which in almost all the metaphysical systems had been treated as superficial, a much less kind of reality than permanence or immutable being . . . to be averted or arrested so far as possible in the interest of stability and order —the social ideal of almost all thinkers from Plato and Aristotle down to the Enlightenment.

---

[16] R. G. Collingwood, *The Idea of History*, T. M. Knox, ed. (London: Oxford Univ. Press, 1946), p. 104.

[17] Georg W. F. Hegel, *Lectures on the Philosophy of History* (London: K. Paul, Trench, Trübner and Co., 1896), p. 142.

Whatever historians may think of Hegel's key to history—thesis, antithesis and synthesis—teachers of history may find his concept of dynamic ideas and historical change a very useful methodological tool.

It is one of the ironic facts of history that Hegel's philosophy, with its deeply idealistic, religious, and nationalistic themes, found its most ingenious student in Karl Marx. No wonder Marx said that he "stood Hegel on his head," in developing his theory of historical, dialectical materialism. Marx created a comprehensive, unified theory of history using Hegel's concept of change and the concepts of conflict and disequilibrium in human society. All human history appeared to Marx in the context of allocation of scarce resources and of scarce power. The fate of men is determined by their relative relation to the productive power of society. The struggle over the possession and control of these productive powers in the society caused intrinsic contradictions in all societies in history and resulted in perpetual social conflicts. The economic struggle between the property-owning class and the exploited masses of have-nots is the determining factor in the history of human society. Morality, religion, metaphysics, while important, according to Marx and his collaborator Engels, do not have an autonomous existence. They are a "superstructure," directly related to the class struggle between control of the scarce economic resources and the many who struggle for that control. *The Communist Manifesto*, published by Marx and Engels in 1867, included their concise, capsule, general law governing all history. It said in part:

> The history of all hitherto existing society is the history of class struggles. Freeman and slave, patrician and plebeian, lord and serf, guild-master and journeyman, in a word, oppressor and oppressed, stood in constant opposition to one another, locked in an uninterrupted, now hidden, now open fight, a fight that each time ended, either in a revolutionary reconstitution of society at large, or in the common ruin of the contending classes.[18]

Having embraced a scientific approach to history, Marx embarked on making scientific predictions for the future course of historical development. So far, most of his predictions have proved to be false. Marx was correct when he said that a "specter of communism is haunting Europe" and in predicting that this new movement would spread all over the world. But Marx predicted that communist revolutions would come first in highly industrialized countries like Germany, England, and the United States where the capitalist, industrial system would collapse and where workers would rebel and seize power. He could not have been more wrong. A century of

---

[18] Quoted in George L. Morse *et al.*, eds., *Europe in Review* (Chicago: Univ. of Chicago Press, 1957), p. 306.

history since Marx made his predictions has proven the vitality and viability of the free enterprise capitalist system. This system has proven itself capable of coping with occasional economic depressions and recessions. England, the United States, and more recently the Federal Republic of Germany have provided their populations, including many millions of workers, with a standard of living incomparably higher than that attained in any communist country. Far from rebelling against their governments or planning a violent seizure of power, the powerful labor unions in America, the Labour Party in England, and the Socialist Party in West Germany are outspoken and determined foes of communism. Both leaders and the rank and file of workers in the United States, for instance, take pride in the tremendous gains made by the labor movement under the free American system. They cite the freedom to belong to unions, the right to strike, which is denied to workers in communist countries, and the right to bargain collectively with employers. Add to this, high wages, shorter working hours, unemployment compensation, Social Security and Medicare and you have an imposing list of social welfare developments in recent decades. No wonder that American proletarians are convinced that a victory of communism would mean losing all that they have gained. The victory of communism could only mean a tragic loss of the freedom to organize their life in a free society and to choose their rulers.

In spite of Marx's conviction that revolutions would not come in economically underdeveloped countries, the first successful communist revolution came in Russia, a backward country with a small number of industrial workers. In 1917 the Russian communists, the Bolsheviks, seized the government and established a "dictatorship of the proletariat." The Bolsheviks represented a minority, not only of Russia's population, but also a minority of the Russian laboring classes.

Not only was Marx wrong in his prediction of where revolutions would occur, but he was even more wrong in predicting the course of events and developments following a successful communist overthrow. He believed that the period of the dictatorship of the proletariat would be brief, to be followed by a broadly based socialist-communist government, and the eventual "withering away of the state" leaving a classless society. The communists seized power in Russia in 1917, and now forty-eight years after the Bolshevik revolution the Soviet Union is still a one-party dictatorship of the Communist party, which constitutes a small minority of the population. Only the 11,000,000 members of the Communist Party, have some say in a government which rules over a population of approximately 220,000,000 people in a country whose territory spreads over one-sixth of the globe.

Another general theory of history was formulated by the German philosopher, Oswald Spengler in *The Decline of the West* which gained great popularity and acceptance when it was first published in Germany in 1918.[19] History, according to Spengler, consists of self-contained units of culture whose life is analogous to that of the plants. Each culture lives and dies like plants and each has a life cycle consisting of a period of blossoming during which new forms of political organizations, arts, and music are developed. This stage is followed by the period of growth, followed by decadence, and, finally, the sinking of a civilization into barbarism. Spengler described four cyclical phases of world history and ended with his conviction that Western civilization was doomed to be supplanted by Asiatic domination. The ready acceptance of Spengler's gloomily prophetic work can be readily understood. It fitted perfectly the mood of Europe at the end of the bloody and often senseless holocaust of World War I. While Spengler's volumes show great knowledge of history and keen insights, his naturalistic and Darwinistic analogy between the lives of cultures and plants, and his denial of the importance of critical thought finds little acceptance today.

Arnold Toynbee, perhaps the most popular and distinguished contemporary historian, obviously was influenced by Oswald Spengler. Like Spengler, Toynbee sees the life of each culture as a self-contained cycle of origin, growth, and decay. However, unlike Spengler, Toynbee does not deny that different cultures have some sort of interrelationship and thus there is a continuity in history.

It is difficult to decide whether Arnold Toynbee, the "Great Generalizer" and cyclical historian, is an optimist or a pessimist about the progress of mankind or about the future of Western civilization. Believing that man is free to shape his destiny, Toynbee maintains that any civilization can have an unlimited future of progress and prosperity as long as its leaders and members respond to new challenges. Western civilization, a recent, tender growth, is now precariously attempting to deal with the new challenges facing it. Whether it will eventually succeed, says Toynbee, remains to be seen. The outcome will depend in a large measure upon the strength and vitality of the Christian tradition. According to Toynbee, religions and creative minorities make civilizations while schisms and the dead weight of majorities unmake them. Today we face a supreme contest between the *Western Way of Life,* which is essentially Christian and an *Eastern Way of Life* which is not. He decries the efforts to weaken the strength and influence of Christian thought:

When Descartes and Voltaire and Rousseau and Marx and Machiavelli and Hobbs and Lenin and Mussolini and Hitler have all done their best or worst,

---

[19] Oswald Spengler, *The Decline of the West,* 2 vols. (New York: Alfred A. Knopf, 1945), pp. 14–15.

in their diverse spheres, to dechristianize the various departments of our Western life, we may still suspect that their scouring and fumigating have been only partially effective. The Christian virus or elixir is in our Western blood if, indeed, it is not just another name for that indispensable fluid.[20]

Toynbee expressed his fervent hope that the doom of Western civilization may be averted if "we ask for it again in a contrite spirit and with a broken heart." This spirit of contrition will require "enrolling ourselves as citizens of the City of God, of which Christ crucified is King."[21]

Toynbee is the outstanding exponent of the theory that it is possible and instructive to formulate general conceptions about history and to seek an orderly developmental pattern in the history of mankind. In his six-volume work, *A Study of History*, Toynbee examined twenty-one civilizations which existed in the course of over six thousand years. To Toynbee, civilizations, not states or separate religions are the real units of history. He considers the history of nations or states as parochial and fragmented. Toynbee enumerates and characterizes various civilizations, then describes their life cycle of origin, growth, and disintegration. He concludes that civilizations come into being as a result of challenges and flourish by the contribution of a "creative minority." The collapse of a civilization comes when the "creative minority" becomes a "ruling minority" and when the weight of the majority and of schisms prevents successful and effective responses to new challenges. The course of history, according to Toynbee, consists of a series of challenges and responses. When a society breaks down and fails to respond to the challenges and demands of new times, it gradually collapses. After an examination of many civilizations, as he defined them, Toynbee concludes that all have decayed and perished with the exception of the Western, Latin-Christian civilization.

Toynbee's monumental work is world history on a large scale because it presents a study of the total experience of all the major civilizations and attempts to define one basic general law which governs human experience. Toynbee puts Western civilization in perspective when he portrays it as a relatively recent development beset by grave dangers to its very survival.

Unlike Hegel, Toynbee considers nation-states and nationalism both as obsolete and as dangerous to the survival of mankind. Nationalism breeds despotism and militarism. These, in turn, breed war, which in an age of atomic and hydrogen weapons threatens the very survival of the human species.

Many historians have challenged Toynbee's views, especially his insist-

---

[20] Arnold J. Toynbee, *A Study of History*, 6 vols. (London: Oxford Univ. Press, 1934–1939), Vol. V, p. 190.
[21] *Ibid.*, Vol. VI, pp. 279, 320.

ence that his generalizations are based on empirical evidence. Many historians maintain that Toynbee's conclusions are one man's opinions which are, in view of the variety and the contradictory nature of the evidence, impossible to prove scientifically. Arnold Toynbee's most effective and persistent critic, the Dutch historian Pieter Geyl, challenged Toynbee's use of "facts" to prove his theses:

> When you fish in a cauldron you cannot select, and to select is exactly what Toynbee is doing all the time; he selects the instances which will support his theses, or he presents them in a way which suits him, and he does so with an assurance that hardly leaves room for the suspicion not only that one might quote innumerable others with which his theses would not bear company but especially that those cases he does mention can be explained or described in a different way so as to disagree no less completely with his theses.[22]

Geyl admits that Toynbee soars above the earth while other historians wearily plod along the ground. He admires his erudition and the sweep of his imagination. His main objection is to Toynbee's assertion that his magnificent building rests on a foundation of strictly empirical investigation and the incontrovertible weight of factual evidence. Geyl maintains also that Toynbee uses religion as a panacea for the troubles of the contemporary world. He concludes:

> We need not accept his (Toynbee's) view that the whole of modern history from the sixteenth century on has been nothing but a downward course, following the path of rout and rally. We need not let ourselves be shaken in our confidence that the future lies open before us, that in the midst of misery and confusion, such as have so frequently occurred in history, we can still dispose of forces no less valuable than those by which earlier generations have managed to struggle through their troubles.[23]

Other critics objected to Toynbee's basically European assumption that history represents an ascending ladder of "progress." They correctly pointed out that the idea of progress was alien to the ancients and still is alien to many Oriental nations. Still others have charged that Toynbee has equated the role or position of religion with the condition and prospects of a particular civilization. *A Study of History*, one historian wrote, was "an anachronism, a book essentially backward looking, that seeks to rationalize the failures of religion into the terms of an indomitable and unquenchable faith."[24]

As in the earlier case of Spengler's *Decline of the West*, the buying public paid no heed to the criticism of the professional historians. Toynbee's vol-

---

[22] Pieter Geyl, *Debates with Historians* (Cleveland: World Publishing Co., 1958), p. 116.
[23] *Ibid.*, p. 164.
[24] Quoted by Arnold J. Toynbee in *Reconsiderations* (London: Oxford Univ. Press, 1959), p. 607.

umes enjoyed wide success with the general public. As we have said, it seems that macrohistory responds to a deeply felt inner need in the mass of the people to find a sense and a meaning in the story of human experience on earth. It seems that the intelligent reading public liked Toynbee's central theme of history, challenge and response. They shared his conviction that the interest in the study of history of mankind lies in the story of the indomitable spirit of man. They probably also agreed with Toynbee that the primary motivating force in man is spiritual.

An intelligent and well-informed teacher can make excellent use of Toynbee's basic "model" of a life of a civilization for effective teaching. He may well, and with profit, have his students participate in the great controversy over Toynbee's conception of history.

Finally, it should not be difficult to make a case for the study of history on the basis of the intrinsic pleasure that can be derived from such a study. It can be a fascinating and pleasurable aesthetic experience to be able to peer behind the curtain of time, to try to reconstruct the scene of Pericles delivering the funeral oration for his fallen Athenians or the drama of the barefoot Emperor Henry IV prostrating himself in less than sincere penance before Pope Gregory VII in the snow covered courtyard of the Canossa Castle. There might not be any immediate *practical* use in our youths learning about the heroic defense of Thermopylae by three hundred young Greeks, or about the stoic suffering of the underfed and ill-clothed Revolutionary soldiers in Valley Forge who were kept in the trenches only by the example, valor, and tenacity of General George Washington, but it is, if taught well, a glorious and self-edifying experience. The young generation of Americans, appalled by and often despairing of the sanity of their elders who confront them with cold and hot wars, may well benefit from an intellectual immersion in deeds of courage and faith in past history.

There can be great aesthetic pleasure derived and wisdom learned from reading aloud to the students passages from great historical works. Take, for instance, this dramatic portrait by Macaulay of Thomas Wentworth, the Earl of Stratford:

> But Wentworth—whoever names him without thinking of those harshly dark features, ennobled by their expression into more than the majesty of an antique Jupiter; of that brow, that eye, that cheek, that lip wherein, as in a chronicle, are written the events of many stormy and disastrous years, high enterprise accomplished, frightful dangers braved, power unsparingly exercised, suffering unshrinkingly borne; of that fixed look, so full of severity, of mournful anxiety, of deep thought, of dauntless resolution, which seems at once to forbode and to defy a terrible fate, as it lowers on us from the canvas of Van Dyck?[25]

---

[25] Quoted in C. V. Wedgewood, *Truth and Opinion: Historical Essays* (New York: The Macmillan Co., 1960), pp. 64–65.

This is not only a lesson in history, but an effective instruction in art appreciation.

Of what importance to a history teacher is an understanding of the possible uses of history? An intelligent teacher is aware that all history is in a sense contemporary history because every historian writes about the past from his own particular point of view and values, and can and should use the differing interpretations of historians of past events to suggest to students alternate analyses of contemporary problems. Differing historical judgments based on the same available evidence and "facts" allows a perceptive teacher to make his students aware of the importance of critical thinking and independent inquiry into the available data. A student who has been given the opportunity to read widely divergent newspaper accounts of the events which led to the Spanish-American War in 1898 would find it easier to critically analyze the following typical story in a popular news magazine:

> Observers in———say that the government of General———is much more popular than the previous government of General———. As one well-informed official said, "We now have a government which really governs."

Alert because of his experience with historical inquiries, the student would immediately tend to ask some searching questions. Who were the "observers?" "How many observers?" "How popular was the previous government?" Finally, he would chuckle at the device of ending the story by a meaningless, even if factual, quotation of somebody's opinion.

History mindedness and a historical perspective can prove invaluable for high school students when they attempt to cope with contemporary problems. Not that past experiences would provide them with easy answers to present issues and crises, but a reasonable knowledge of history—not specific and isolated, but organized and coherent knowledge—can greatly assist in gaining a better insight into a contemporary controversial issue. For example, some knowledge about the history and past decisions of the Supreme Court can help the students to understand the zigzag path of recent Court decisions on the publication of obscene materials; some basic knowledge about the history of China is essential for an understanding of the present foreign policy of mainland China.

3

History and the Social Sciences—

How They Differ

The debate on whether history is an art or a science, or both, has been long and protracted. In the last two decades of the nineteenth century and at the beginning of this century, the rapid growth of the natural and the social sciences encouraged many historians, especially in Germany, to demand that history be considered a science, subject to rigorous standards and methods of inquiry and capable of the formulation of empirically verifiable generalizations. Scientific historians demanded that the hypotheses and subsequent findings of historical investigations be tested by empirical evidence. Some adherents of the New History urged that scientific history attempt to develop general patterns and laws to explain the past and to help in predicting future developments. The pressure to have history generally accepted as a science resulted basically from a belief that science possessed final, ultimate, verifiable knowledge and that scientific history would be of great and immediate value to statesmen and leaders of society. Henry Adams, a vigorous exponent of scientific history, in a paper entitled "The Tendency of History" (1894), expressed his conviction that the political, religious, and business leaders would be able to ask the historian the question, "Is my conduct justified by and in history?" and receive a single, true answer.

Adams, the author of the *History of the United States During the Administration of Jefferson and Madison*, stated that the aim of his history was to grasp the "silent pulsation" and discover the natural laws which governed the history of the United States between 1800 and 1817. The first six chapters of this work, an economic, social, and political profile of America in 1800, are a worthy example of the new type of history writing. They have been recently published separately and are eminently suitable for classroom use.[1]

On the other side of the Atlantic, the English historian J. B. Bury (1861–1927), Regius Professor of Modern History at Cambridge and author of the *History of Greece*, declared in his Inaugural Lecture that, "History is a science, no less and no more." Bury continued:

> History is not a branch of literature. The facts of history, like the facts of geology or astronomy, can supply material for literary art; for manifest reasons they lend themselves to artistic representation far more readily than those of the natural sciences; but to clothe the story of human society in a literary dress is no more the part of a historian than it is the part of an astronomer to present in artistic shape the story of the stars.[2]

Bury claimed that scientific history can strip the "bandages of error" from the eyes of men, shape public opinion, and advance the cause of intellectual and political liberty.[3]

The influence on American historical writing of German historians, with their emphasis on "facts" and their adherence to Ranke's dictum that the historian's task was to describe things as "they really were," was strong in the writings of historians such as Richard Hildreth, John Draper, John W. Burgess, and, of course, Henry Adams. But the reaction against the Teutonistic historians, when it came, was sharp and furious.

Frederick Jackson Turner, in his presidential address to the American Historical Association in 1910, derided the search for absolute truths in history. Such a search, he declared, ignores both the fact that history is strewn with the wrecks of such truths and the relativity and transcience of historical interpretations. Instead of relying on the methods of the natural sciences, Turner believed that historians could be greatly aided in their work by insights and concepts adapted from the social sciences.[4]

Turner's student, Carl Becker, was even more skeptical than his teacher about the nature of facts and the scientific objectivity on the part of historians. He declared that "every man was his own historian" and maintained that facts, whatever they once really were, are only mental images

---

[1] Henry Adams, *The United States in 1800* (Ithaca, N.Y.: Cornell Univ. Press, 1957).

[2] J. B. Bury, "History as a Science" in Fritz Stern, ed., *The Varieties of History* (Cleveland: World Publishing Co., 1963), p. 214.

[3] *Ibid.*, p. 223.

[4] Frederick Jackson Turner, *The Frontier in American History* (New York: Holt, Rinehart & Winston, 1920), pp. 331–333.

in the mind of the historian. Becker wrote to Turner in 1910: "To me nothing can be duller than historical facts, and nothing more interesting than the service they can be made to render in the effort to solve the ever-lasting riddle of human existence."[5]

Charles Beard also dissented from the claims of scientific history. While adopting the economic interpretation of history, he rejected as false and mechanistic Marxist historical determinism. He endorsed the right of historians to make moral judgments in his famous address to the American Historical Association, which he entitled "Written History as an Act of Faith." He disagreed with scientific historians who espoused moral relativism on the ground that the job of the historian was to present the facts and leave value judgments to their readers. Progress, Beard argued, was neither automatic nor evolutionary. He urged historians to work for progress as an act of faith.[6] While Beard attracted a large following of younger historians who were happy to embrace social activism in the days of the Great Depression and the New Deal, his influence was somewhat diminished by the virtual demolition of the main thesis of his famous volume on the Constitutional Convention, *An Economic Interpretation of the Constitution.* The basic question asked by Beard was:

> If you were able to ascertain that substantially all of the merchants, money lenders, security holders, manufacturers, shippers, capitalists, and financiers, and their professional associates are to be found on one side in support of the Constitution and that substantially all or a major part of the opposition came from the non-slaveholding farmers and the debtors—would it not be pretty conclusively demonstrated that our fundamental law was not the product of an abstraction known as "the whole people," but of a group of economic interests which must have expected beneficial results from its adoption?[7]

Beard answered his question affirmatively, and based on his investigation of Treasury records became convinced that he had successfully debunked the idealistic interpretation of the motives of the Founding Fathers in the writing of the United States Constitution.

Beard's "axiomatic proposition" was refuted in the works of Robert E. Brown, Edmund Morgan, Merrill Jensen, and others. Brown, after a line by line analysis of Beard's work, concluded that "if historians accept the Beard thesis . . . their acceptance is founded on an 'act of faith,' not on an

---

[5] Quoted in Burleigh Taylor Wilkins, *Carl Becker* (Cambridge: The MIT Press, 1961), p. 32.

[6] Charles A. Beard, "Written History as an Act of Faith," *American Historical Review*, XXXIX (1934), pp. 219–229.

[7] Charles A. Beard, *An Economic Interpretation of the Constitution of the United States* (New York: The Macmillan Co., 1935), pp. 16–17.

analysis of historical method, or that they are indulging in a 'noble dream,' not history."[8]

While Beard's particular interpretation of the origin of the Constitution or of the causes of the Civil War, may no longer be generally accepted, his emphasis on economic concepts, insights, and factors has had a more durable influence. Historians became increasingly interested in seeking closer ties with their colleagues in economics and the other social sciences. These efforts were greatly accelerated by the establishment of the Social Sciences Research Council.

In 1942, Roy F. Nichols, an eminent historian, presented a report to the Council which stressed the inadequacies of present historical research and suggested a large program of fellowships to sponsor interpretative studies which would utilize insights from the social sciences in historical studies.[9] Following the recommendations of the Nichols' report, the Council appointed a committee, headed by Merle Curti and including Charles Beard and Louis Gottschalk, to prepare a manual on the relation between history and the social sciences and "to help clarify thought about history and to aid historians in teaching and writing about it."[10] Beard made a major contribution to the report of the committee by writing a dictionary of historical terms and a statement of fundamental propositions. The Curti-Beard report stated that the aim of the historian was not only to reconstruct selected fragments of the past, but also "to provide credible explanations of the development of contemporary events, thoughts, manners, and institutions."[11] One of the basic propositions asserted that historiography was essential to the social sciences because its findings were drawn from records or experiences of the past and the recorded work of the social scientists can survive only if it becomes a part of history.

There were indications that the leaders of the S.S.R.C. were disappointed that the Curti-Beard report did not address itself directly to the interrelationship between history and the social sciences. A year later, another committee on historiography was appointed by the Social Science Research Council. The appointment of the new committee was spurred by the publication in 1948 of an article by Roy Nichols who two years earlier urged the S.S.R.C. to forge closer ties between history and the social sciences. Nichols' article, "Post-war Reorientation of Historical Thinking," showed that Nichols had some second thoughts on the subject. He called for a declaration of intel-

---

[8] Robert E. Brown, *Charles Beard and the Constitution* (Princeton, N.J.: Princeton Univ. Press, 1956), p. 93.

[9] John Higham, Leonard Krieger, Felix Gilbert, eds., *History* (Englewood Cliffs, N.J.: Prentice-Hall, 1965), p. 129.

[10] *Theory and Practice in Historical Study: A Report of the Committee on Historiography,* Social Science Research Council (New York, 1946).

[11] *Ibid.,* p. 134.

lectual independence by historians and the rejection of the belief in the backwardness of history in comparison to the rapid advances in the social sciences. History, Nichols declared, was neither a social science nor an art or literature. As a discipline, it is unique. History, unlike the social sciences, cannot and should not tolerate "the slavery of present-mindedness," which characterized the social sciences.[12]

The new Committee on Historiography of the S.S.R.C. was headed by Thomas C. Cochran. Its report stressed the importance to the historian of the methods of inquiry and the techniques of proof used by the social scientists. The report asserted without equivocation that history is a social science and not a branch of the humanities. The historian's work must reflect the new scientific spirit and the practice "of making investigation more penetrating, analysis more precise, and demonstration more vigorous."[13] The committee denied the claim of the unique nature of historical events and declared that while each event is unique, it is also similar to other events. Consequently, formulation of generalizations and scientific laws in history is entirely feasible. The Cochran report was challenged by many distinguished historians, including Oscar Handlin and Robert R. Palmer, who maintained that the historian imaginatively reconstructs complex situations from the past and only occasionally lists the universals present. Thus, he is more of an administrator than a scientist. Handlin and Palmer argued that while a historian should use concepts from the social sciences in his work, he should not consider himself to be a social scientist.[14]

The third S.S.R.C. committee on historiography, headed by Louis Gottschalk, was appointed in 1956 and published its findings in 1963. This report was considerably more cautious in discussing the relationship of history and the social sciences. It did not repeat the assertion that history was a social science, and it did not urge the universal adoption of social science methodology by historians. The report, consisting of separate contributions by committee members, limited itself to a thorough, often brilliant discussion of the place of generalization in history. It cautiously concluded that historians do make "lower" and "higher" generalizations while clearly preferring the former. Gottschalk concluded:

> In sum, the historians who have written articles for this volume all agree that the historian willy-nilly uses generalizations at different levels and of different kinds. They all agree that some good purpose is served when he

---

[12] Roy F. Nichols, "Postwar Reorientation of Historical Thinking," *American Historical Review*, LIV (1948), pp. 78–79.

[13] *The Social Sciences in Historical Study: A Report of the Committee on Historiography*. Social Science Research Council, Bulletin 64 (New York, 1954).

[14] John Higham, "The Renewal of History," in John Higham *et al.*, eds., *History* (Englewood Cliffs, N.J.: Prentice-Hall, 1965), p. 139.

does so, if only to present a thesis for debate. They do not all agree that the generalizations he uses need be merely borrowed ones. He might, in the opinion of some of the authors, be independently able to construct modest ones. A few maintain even that, whether borrowed or independently derived, historical generalizations can in some persuasive manner be tested.[15]

The cautious nature of the conclusions of the Gottschalk report, which stressed the formulation of generalizations merely as a basis for discussion and which virtually advocated that historians limit themselves to "modest" generalizations, was nevertheless a far cry from the Cochran report. The Gottschalk committee represented a clear backing away from the previous classification of history as a social science. It also represented a greatly lessened confidence in the effectiveness of social science methods and research techniques to validate major historical generalizations.

While some historians still regard the testing of general laws by the empirical scientific method as the sole legitimate mode of historical investigation, most historians believe that a purely social science approach can only be partially applied to historical studies. Most historians today would probably agree with H. Stuart Hughes who wrote recently:

> Hence, the historian's supreme technical virtuosity lies in fusing the new method of social and psychological analysis with his traditional story telling function. If he can keep the "how" and the "why" moving steadily alongside each other . . . then he is a writer who understands his business well.[16]

History belongs to the social sciences, but it also belongs to the humanities. In an important sense, history is not a science, but an art. However, as we have seen, historical scholarship does have important ties with the social science disciplines, especially with their methods and research insights. To assert that history is both a science and an art or a branch of literature is one thing, but it is another to clearly delineate to what extent history is a science and to what extent it is an art. We may well be advised to admit that the boundaries are blurred, and therefore it may be impossible to make an accurate distinction. However, a general analysis of the relationship between history and the social sciences is possible and necessary.

The objectives of history and the social sciences are basically the same, and this identity of aims is one important common factor. The English historian, E. H. Carr, stated these aims:

> Scientists, social scientists, and historians are all engaged in different branches of the same study: the study of man and his environment, of the

---

[15] *Generalization in the Writing of History,* Louis Gottschalk, ed. (Chicago: Univ. of Chicago Press, 1963), p. 208.

[16] H. Stuart Hughes, *History as Art and as Science* (New York: Harper & Row, 1964), p. 77.

effects of man on his environment and of his environment on man. The object of the study is the same: to increase man's understanding of, and mastery over, his environment.[17]

A historian is a social scientist to the extent that he uses the scientific method. Historical investigations can usually be divided into three stages. In the first one, the research stage, the historian methodically collects his data, analyzes it systematically, and tests it for authenticity and credibility. In the second stage, the stage of analysis and interpretation, the historian looks for an inner logic in his accumulated evidence and subjects his evidence and data to thorough testing and scrutiny by comparing the evidence from a wide variety of source materials. By the use of inductive logic, the historian then arrives at his hypotheses and generalizations. After further tests and additional review of his evidence, the historian is now ready for the third and final stage of his work, which is the presentation. He now sets out to relate his findings in a coherent, meaningful narrative.

It would be tempting to say that during the first and the second stages the historian's work is scientific, while the third stage is artistic in nature. While this is generally true, the scientific and the artistic elements are present in all three stages, even if we do not know their exact ratio and even if the quality and the quantity of the scientific and artistic elements differ among individual historians. However, there is little question that the historian is basically a scientist during the investigative and analytical phases of his work and an artist (or should be an artist) when he puts his findings into writing. If an historical work is to survive and become a classic to be read by successive generations of school children and adults, it must be a work of substantial literary quality. The works of Thucydides, Plutarch, Macaulay, Gibbon, Trevelyan, Parkman, and Prescott continue to be widely read because they are masterpieces of literature as well as great histories. The reconstruction of historical events demands, in addition to a thorough knowledge and scrutiny of evidence, a flight of creative imagination which alone can fuse the raw material of history into a work of art. Our society has accorded a special place to works of history. Each year a Pulitzer prize is awarded for an outstanding volume in history, and such outstanding periodicals as *Harper's*, *Saturday Review* and the *New York Times Book Review* regularly review histories. These respected journals seldom review scholarly works in sociology and economics, and no Pulitzer Prize is awarded to works in the social sciences. These facts are undoubtedly related to the high literary quality of outstanding works of history. While an important work in sociology or in economics may survive even if it is poorly written and even if it is crammed with charts and statistics, a volume of history written in the best scientific tradition, but lacking

---

[17] E. H. Carr, *What Is History?* (New York: Alfred A. Knopf, 1962), p. 111.

the facility of style and the richness of language is not likely to be read or to endure.

No other factor contributed more to the gradual demise of the German school of New History than its dullness and pedantry. The dry, boring model German Ph.D. dissertation in history, so avidly imitated on American campuses at the turn of the century, was a far cry from history personified by Clio, the muse of history. The reading public did not take kindly to historical works which abounded in weighty, voluminous footnotes, but which had the effect of powerful sleeping pills. "People will read history," Trevelyan wrote, "if it fascinates them. It is therefore the duty of historians . . . not to conceal its fascination under the heap of learning which ought to overlie but not overwhelm history."[18] After the American Historical Association rejected his proposal for the publication of a popular history magazine, Allan Nevins, who came to his history chair at Columbia University from journalism, publicly attacked pedantic and boring historians. He charged that the pedant dominated the history departments in many universities. He declared:

> . . . though the touch of this school benumbs and paralyzes all interest in history, it is supported by university chairs, special foundations and funds, research fellowships, and learned bodies. It is against this entrenched pedantry that the war of true history will have to be most determined and implacable.[19]

The distinguished contributions of Allan Nevins to American history emphasizes another unique feature of history, namely the role of the amateur in history writing. History has been singularly hospitable to gentlemen of leisure, philosophers, journalists, and writers. In fact, the authors of some of the greatest historical works held no academic degrees in history. The list of non-academic historians in England includes the names of Macaulay, Gibbon, Carlyle, John Buchan, and Winston Churchill. In the last decades of the nineteenth century, five major works in American history were published. The authors, Moses Coit Tyler, Theodore Roosevelt (who became President of the American Historical Association in 1912), John Bach McMaster, Henry Adams, and James Ford Rhodes, were all amateur historians. One may argue that professional training would have made these amateurs even better historians, but this must remain a moot question. What is clear is that these gentlemen—historians since they accepted the necessity of applying rigid standards of historical method —considered themselves men of letters as well as historical scientists. All of them, including Roosevelt, who acknowledged Francis Parkman as his

---

[18] George M. Trevelyan, *History and the Reader* (London: National Book League, 1945), p. 24.
[19] Allan Nevins, "What's the Matter with History?", *Saturday Review of Literature,* XIX (February 4, 1939), p. 16.

master, took pains to produce works of high literary quality. They further enhanced the readability of their works by rejecting the dictum of New History which demanded from historians the presentation of facts and nothing but the facts. Such moral relativism was obnoxious to McMaster, Roosevelt, and Rhodes. They had their views and judgments of men and events and did not hesitate to express them. Some scientific historians may have frowned on this subjective writing, but the historical profession as a whole and the intelligent reading public have assured these men a distinguished place in American historiography.

In summary, historical inquiry is based on the scientific approach and method, but the final conclusions are intuitive and highly individual; in a word, they belong to the world of art. When history is written in the grand tradition of a literary narrative, it becomes important not only as a scientific record of a segment of the past, but also as an artistic and aesthetic experience. Thus, history is also a branch of literature and belongs not only to the social sciences, but also to the humanities. Thucydides' *The History of the Peloponnesian War,* Gibbon's *The Decline and Fall of the Roman Empire,* and Macaulay's *History of England* are not only great history, but also masterpieces of literature. They are both artistic and scientific achievements.

The same is true of American historians like William Prescott, the author of *The Conquest of Mexico* and *The Conquest of Peru,* and Francis Parkman, the author of *The Jesuits of North America* and *Montcalm and Wolfe.* Consider, for instance, this brief excerpt from Parkman. It is written in the best tradition of great narrative history. It is scientific and accurate because Parkman was a hard-working historian who, in spite of poor health and failing eyesight, pored days and nights over first-hand documentary sources, but it is also an artistic accomplishment because it is great literature.

> The peace was broken, and the hounds of war were turned loose. The contagion spread through all the Mohawk nation, the war songs were sung, and the warriors took the path to Canada. The miserable colonists and their more miserable allies woke from their dream of peace to the reality of fear and horror. Again Montreal and Three Rivers were beset with murdering savages, skulking in thickets and prowling under cover of night, yet when it came to blows, displaying a courage almost equal to the ferocity that inspired it.[20]

Another example of history of high literary merit is this description of Emperor Constantine in *The Decline and Fall of the Roman Empire* by Edward Gibbon:

---

[20] Francis Parkman, *The Jesuits in North America* (Boston: Little, Brown and Co., 1963), p. 404.

The person, as well as the mind, of Constantine had been enriched by nature with her choicest endowments. His stature was lofty, his countenance majestic, his deportment graceful; his strength and activity were displayed in every manly exercise, and, from his earliest youth to a very advanced season of life, he preserved the vigour of his constitution by a strict adherence to the domestic virtues of chastity and temperance. He delighted in the social intercourse of familiar conversation, and though he might sometimes indulge his disposition to raillery with less reserve than was required by the severe dignity of his station, the courtesy and liberality of his manner gained the hearts of all who approached him . . . In the despatch of business his diligence was indefatigable; and the active powers of his mind were almost continually exercised in reading, writing, or meditating, in giving audience to ambassadors, and in examining the complaints of his subjects. In the field he infused his own intrepid spirit into the troops, whom he conducted with the talents of a consummate general; and to his abilities, rather than to his fortune, we may ascribe the signal victories which he obtained over the foreign and domestic foes of the republic. He loved glory as the reward, perhaps as the motive of his labours. The boundless ambition which, from the moment of his accepting the purple at York, appears as the ruling passion of his soul, may be justified by the dangers of his own situation, by the character of his rivals, by the consciousness of superior merit, and by the prospect that his success would enable him to restore peace and order to the distracted empire.[21]

Who but a historian supremely endowed with exceptional literary gifts and with deep insights into human nature could have written this profile of the complex personality of Constantine? A teacher who attempts to have his students understand the motives of Constantine, which were and still are a subject of controversy among historians, without introducing his class to this memorable passage from Gibbon is indeed missing an opportunity to teach history at its literary best.

Samuel Eliot Morison, a distinguished historian, who demonstrated his narrative skill in his biography of Columbus, *Admiral of the Ocean Sea,* feels that "historians must write in three dimensions, . . . drawing not only on records, but on their own experience and background knowledge to recreate the past. An historian should yield himself to his subject, become immersed in the place and period of his choice . . ."[22] Like all literary historians, Morison has frequently admonished his colleagues to shun moral relativism. He has only scorn for "evasive historians, our mufflers of great passionate issues . . ."[23]

---

[21] Edward Gibbon, *The Decline and Fall of the Roman Empire,* an abridgment by D. M. Low (New York: Harcourt, Brace & World, 1960), pp. 266–267.
[22] Samuel Eliot Morison, *Vistas of History* (New York: Alfred A. Knopf, 1964), p. 23.
[23] *Ibid.,* p. 142.

History differs from the social sciences in other important aspects. While social scientists concentrate their efforts on the formulation of general concepts and on the discovery of widely applicable patterns, generalizations, and laws, historians (while not ignoring "laws" and "higher" generalizations) are at least equally interested in the *singular,* the *concrete,* and the *unique.* For instance, classical sociology, as defined by Max Weber, is interested in the constant and repetitive element in human society, past and present, in what social facts have in common, and ignores the unique aspects of events and treats them as social types. History, on the other hand, focuses its attention much more on the *special* event, the *outstanding* personality, and the *unique* trend of developments in a *particular* situation. The *particular* motives and personality of John Wilkes Booth are as important to a historian, in fact more important, than the discovery of common personality characteristics of assassins of great leaders in history. The *peculiar* combination of the jingo-imperialist and the pacific elements in the personality of Theodore Roosevelt, who contributed mightily to the start of the Spanish-American War and then received the Nobel Peace Prize for mediation between Russia and Japan, are as interesting to the historian as finding a common pattern in economic depressions. The human drama involved in the dismissal of Chancellor Bismarck by Kaiser Wilhelm is apt to excite a historian more than the temptation to discover a pattern or a generalization concerning border disputes among nations.

In general, while history is interested mainly in the uniqueness of cultures and civilizations, the social sciences prefer to look for elements and processes common to all cultures and civilizations. In order to reach its aims as a generalizing science, "commitment to sociology as an analytical science requires," wrote two sociologists, "a willingness to give up the study of all those very interesting historical phenomena that are unique, because no empirically verifiable generalizations about them are possible."[24]

While recognizing the existence of these differences in approach one should be careful not to overemphasize their importance. Many years ago Allan Nevins asked:

> Why should historians not be interested also in elements common to different situations, different societies, and different periods? Can a historian of the Russian Revolution exclude those parts of it which run parallel with the French Revolution? Comparative history may be made an exceedingly stimulating and fruitful study, even if it does come close to sociology.[25]

---

[24] Peter M. Blau and Joan V. Moore, "Sociology," in *A Reader's Guide to the Social Sciences*, Bert F. Hoselitz, ed. (New York: Free Press of Glencoe, 1959), p. 169.

[25] Allan Nevins, *The Gateway to History* (Garden City, N.Y.: Doubleday & Co., 1962), p. 326.

Past and present historians have drawn generalizations from the events they described. Spengler and Toynbee developed general laws governing all history, Gibbon concluded that the advent of Christianity did much to bring about the fall of Rome, Parkman concluded that the French and their Catholic faith were unsuited to the colonization of the North American continent, and Rhodes generalized that slavery was the central cause of the Civil War. Many historians have put forth the generalization that nationalism is the single most powerful force in modern history, usually victorious when confronted with the counter-forces of religion, international cooperation, or political ideology. Others have generalized that the lesson of history is that no one nation will ever be strong enough to dominate the world.

Two distinguished sociologists, citing the epigram "Sociology is history with the hard work left out; history is sociology with the brains left out," concluded:

> Sociologists, all too often, have tended to generalize either on uncritically accepted evidence or on evidence diligently assembled, but restricted in time and place; while some historians have rested secure in their knowledge of unique configurations and sequences without benefit of comparison or of conscious conceptualization.[26]

The authors correctly suggest that the work of historians and sociologists may well be complementary because while it is desirable to attain an understanding of specific events, it is also important, and often possible, to discover to what extent an explanation of a particular event is applicable to comparable situations existing in other places and other times. Ignoring the differences among facts leads to over-simplified and unsupportable generalizations. Similarly, lack of attention to the similarities among events ignores the existence of an important historical reality. The teacher of social studies would be wise to pay attention both to the uniqueness of historical events and to seek, where they can be found, unifying patterns in a number of historical situations.

The historian, unlike most of his colleagues in the social sciences, doubts whether many important questions and problems in history can be understood by quantitative empirical analysis, which is the preferred method of inquiry of the social scientists. For this reason, many historians have not accepted Toynbee's laws of behavior of civilizations. They have maintained that he fitted his empirical data to his own definition of a civilization as a rather neat bundle of phenomena and that his whole general law of history rests on the false assumption that history is repetitive. Repetitive phenomena are common in natural sciences and in some social sciences and

---

[26] Werner J. Cahnman and Alvin Boskoff, eds., *Sociology and History—Theory and Research* (New York: Free Press of Glencoe, 1964), p. 1.

can be duplicated in experiments. In history, which deals with the behavior of complex human beings in complex societies operating under diverse conditions, repetitive phenomena are too rare to allow the formulation of immutable laws. In history, situations seldom, if ever, repeat themselves in a discernible pattern because the actors in each of the innumerable dramas of the past are never the same. What is even more important, the awareness of actors in the second run of these dramas of the successes and failures of their predecessors makes repetition impossible. Any President in the White House faced with signs of an impending economic depression would be very conscious of the ordeal and policies of Herbert Hoover on the eve of the Great Depression in 1929. This knowledge of history would greatly influence his own course of action. G. M. Trevelyan explained this difference between history and the sciences in a particularly felicitous way:

> The study of mankind does not resemble the study of the physical properties of atoms, or the life history of animals. If you find out about one atom, you have found out about all atoms, and what is true of the habits of one robin is roughly true of the habits of all robins. But the life history of one man, or even of many individual men, will not tell you the life history of other men . . . Men are too complicated, too spiritual, too various, for a scientific analysis.[27]

The historian is increasingly impressed with the powerful role in history played by fate and accident, factors which distinguish history from purely scientific discipline. Was it not an accident that brought about the emergence of Mohammed in the deserts of the Hedjaz? Was it not an accident that gave Oliver Cromwell a weak son, Richard, who promptly lost the fruits of his father's revolution? What would have been the fate of the world if Napoleon, in 1799, after stealing away from Alexandria in the dead of night, deserting an army and a mistress, had not succeeded in miraculously evading capture by the British navy, which then dominated the Mediterranean? How different the present face of the world might have been if King Alexander of Greece had not died from blood-poisoning due to the bite of a pet monkey in the palace gardens. Had he not died, the Greek armies would not have taken the field against the Turks and would have avoided their complete rout in 1922. It was this Turkish victory that brought Kemal Ataturk to power in Turkey. Winston Churchill commented, "A quarter of a million persons died of that monkey's bite." Barbara Tuchman, who examined the causes of the First World War in *The Guns of August*, was awed by the erratic nature of human beings who, placed by destiny in positions of great power, passively allowed themselves to be swept into an abyss by the tide of events.

---

[27] Quoted in A. L. Rowse, *The Use of History* (New York: The Macmillan Co., 1948), p. 66.

It is no wonder that a historian finds it difficult to reconcile his discipline to some of the following claims made for sociology:

> Sociology is one of the social sciences. Its long-run aim is to discover the basic structure of human society, to identify the main forces that hold groups together or weaken them, and to learn the conditions that transform social life. In this sociology, like any pure or basic science, is a disciplined, intellectual quest for fundamental knowledge of the nature of things.[28]

History, unlike some of the social sciences, is vitally interested in values, attitudes, moods, and motives. While some of the scientific historians of the German school preached moral relativism and advocated a "pure," objective history, most historians agree that history is not only a scientific enterprise, but also a moral one. The anthropologist who lives in an Indian or Mexican village or in a tribal village in Africa and observes during his field work the daily mores and customs of the villagers, can and usually does abstain from making value judgments. He is, as a rule, not concerned whether a particular custom is "good" or "bad," "right" or "wrong." This is not true of the historian. He is constantly involved in value judgments, in the assessment of blame or praise on the dramatis personae of his story. While he rigidly attempts to apply objective criteria to the examination of his data, the facts and evidence he selects, the way he arranges them, and the conclusions he draws from them constitute in themselves a process of value judgment. One does not have to accept E. H. Carr's view of historical determinism to acknowledge that the historian's cultural, social, economic, and political background, his own conscious or subconscious presuppositions about the subject of his study, and the general intellectual climate of his time greatly influence his work. "The facts of history," Carl Becker wrote, "do not exist for any historian until he creates them." All history writing is essentially subjective. Most American historians would agree with their distinguished colleague, Samuel Eliot Morison, who said in his Presidential Address to the American Historical Association in 1951: "Unless it be the dull pedantry of the average doctoral dissertation in history, there is no quality more repugnant than chilly impartiality."

While historians and social scientists in general take a different position on value judgments and examination of motives, this difference should not be exaggerated, especially in view of recent developments. Many economists have begun to admit that some of their basic disagreements about inflation, welfare state programs, and price controls have more to do with ideological questions, belonging clearly to the area of values and social

---

[28] Leonard Broom and Philip Selznick, *Sociology*, 2nd ed. (New York: Harper & Row, 1958), p. 3.

attitudes, than with the question of distribution of limited resources. Similarly, an increasing number of sociologists would dispute the statement contained in most sociology textbooks that sociologists do not ask whether a particular social action is good or bad, they merely try to explain it. Professor Michael Polanyi, scientist, philosopher, and now a member of the Institute of Advanced Studies at Princeton, New Jersey, deplored this attitude because, as he put it, to assume that one can explain an action of human beings without considering whether it was good or bad is tantamount to the assumption that moral motives played no part in that social action. "To extend this assumption to all social action," Polanyi wrote,

> is to deny the very existence of genuine moral motives in man. When I protest against such doctrines, I am assured that sociologists who teach this moral nihilism are themselves men of high moral principles. . . . This is thought to put the matter right. It is considered quite in order that we should teach absurd views that we do not believe because we think that they are scientific.[29]

Some anthropologists, it seems, have also begun to veer away from moral relativism. Professor H. L. Shapiro, chairman of the anthropology department at the American Museum of Natural History and Professor of Anthropology at Columbia University, made some significant comments on the subject of value judgments and subjective involvement of anthropologists in his review of the book by the anthropologist Kenneth E. Read, *The High Valley.* Read was writing about the life of the natives in the highlands of northeastern New Guinea. The reviewer noted that Read presented his characters not dispassionately and objectively, as is the custom in anthropological field studies, but subjectively and with deep interest in them. Commenting on this departure from tradition in anthropological writing, Professor Shapiro wrote:

> Almost all anthropologists who spent months, sometimes years, living with primitive peoples, studying their behavior, their institutions, and every detail of their cultures, write reports on their observations as if the actors themselves did not exist as individuals. The passions that move primitive man become lost in the generalization that describes the rules under which he lives. And the traits that give him a distinct personality which attracts or repels the observer are considered to have little value to the portrait of his society . . .
> I can recall, however, in the older literature, only a few instances in which the professional anthropologist has broken this formula and attempted to portray as living people the subjects he has so sedulously cultivated and studied in the field. It may be something of a portent that within the last

---

[29] Michael Polanyi, "On the Modern Mind," *Encounter* (May 1965), p. 18.

4

Social Sciences and History:

The Narrowing Gap—Prospects

for Fruitful Collaboration

A variety of factors have contributed to the growing rapprochement and improving prospects for fruitful collaboration between history and the social sciences. The most important of these is the gradual recognition by leading social scientists that their respective disciplines are not as purely scientific as originally claimed and the frequently expressed conviction by prominent historians that they need and value the use of social science concepts and modes of inquiry in their work. More and more historians have declared themselves ready to explore new ways of looking at man, the ultimate object of their study, in order to gain a better understanding of the nature of man and his behavior in the past.

HISTORY AND SOCIOLOGY

The impressive growth of the social sciences and their great diversity make it hazardous and unwise to generalize too much about new trends and new orientations. However, it might be useful to indicate a few trends in a major social science like sociology which if viewed, on the whole, may explain the growing affinity and the greatly improved prospects for fruitful collaboration between history and sociology. The same trend, of course, is true of history in relation to the other social sciences.

Some sociologists have expressed the view that the stress in traditional Weberian sociology on recurrent social patterns, or on the concepts of order, stability, and social equilibrium have been rather one-sided. Conflict and disequilibrium, these sociologists maintain, are as important in the story of human society as order and equilibrium. Lewis Coser and others have suggested that while Marx may have been completely wrong in stating that the fate of men is determined by their relation to the productive power of the society, he did make a contribution to modern sociology by his emphasis on the mutable nature of human society.

A substantial and vocal group of sociologists has urged in recent years a shift from microsociology to macrosociology. They call for a broad analysis of large societal issues, such as peace and war and race relations. "The focus of social analysis," wrote its chief protagonist, Professor Amitai Etzioni of Columbia University,

> and its raison d'etre, are the problems of the age, the application of sociology to the understanding of society, its major sub-collectives, and a society's place in more encompassing communities . . . Social analysis is concerned with applying [sociological] concepts to the evolution of a world community, the redistribution of social wealth, efforts to advance the growth of civil rights, the development of "have not" nations, etc.[1]

Obviously, such an ambitious program of social analysis and social action cannot be totally reconciled with the view of traditional sociology which postulated "freedom from value-judgment."[2] Seeking support for his view that the sociologist, because he knows more about society than other observers, should be committed to societal issues and ought to express his concern about them, Etzioni observes that Max Weber was careful to make a clear distinction between a *wert-frei*, or value free and a *wert-los*, or valueless approach. A sociologist who is *wert-frei* withholds his judgment and lets his facts and findings speak for themselves, while a *wert-los* sociologist does not have any values. Professor Etzioni obviously suggests that sociologists today have the duty to present their data objectively, but they should not hesitate to support social analysis aimed at the betterment of society through peace, racial equality, and world cooperation. He thinks that sociology has paid too much attention to low-level, concrete social problems and has neglected the larger societal issues. "We will not learn much about the anatomy of elephants," Etzioni concluded, "by studying that of fruit flies. Hence, we ought to continue to study small groups for their own

---

[1] Amitai Etzioni, "Social Analysis as a Sociological Vocation," *The American Journal of Sociology*, LXX (March 1965),
[2] See Introduction by Robert K. Merton to Harry M. Johnson, *Sociology: A Systematic Introduction* (New York: Harcourt, Brace & World, 1960), p. 2.

sake and for the light they cast on social behavior in general, but we ought to invest more of our resources in macroscopic sociology."[3]

Another sociologist, Professor Robert Bierstedt of New York University, while basically agreeing with Etzioni's premise that sociologists have often "contented themselves with trivialities and have not taken into their purviews the larger problems that surround them," took issue with Etzioni's assertion that sociologists are better equipped to analyze and deal with the larger problems confronting contemporary society than editors, journalists, and commentators. Bierstedt maintained that in social analysis such commentators like Walter Lippmann and James Reston have few peers among professional sociologists. "It would be even more embarrassing," he continued, ". . . if we were to discover that undergraduate training in history, philosophy, constitutional law, or even English literature provides a better background for social analysis than sociology does."[4]

The new trend in sociology as represented by Etzioni, Bierstedt, and the colleagues who share their views greatly improves the prospects for fruitful collaboration between history and sociology. Concern for larger societal problems like racial integration and peace and war will result in a confrontation with the truly complex nature of human society and will make the formulation of broad generalizations difficult, if not impossible. Macrosociology is bound to play havoc with the inclination for scientific predictions of future behavior and future developments on social and political crises. In the study of macrosociology, the role of the unique and the specific will loom rather large, a situation bound to draw the sociologist and the historian closer together.

Even more important in this rapprochement is the growing respect among the sociologist and historian for each other's discipline. The somewhat hostile or disdainful attitude of sociologists and political scientists toward historians often had the characteristics of the reaction of grown-up children against domineering parents. While pioneering sociologists used historical sources to illustrate and substantiate their theoretical concepts and generalizations, the founders of modern sociology, such as Max Weber and Emile Durkheim, advocated that sociology as an analytical science should try to explain contemporary social institutions in terms of their functions and not in terms of their historical development. Dwelling on the unique features of a particular social system was actually thought to be detrimental to a sound study of societal problems. Many past and present sociologists have selected and arranged historical data without

---

[3] Amitai Etzioni, "Social Analysis as a Sociological Vocation," *The American Journal of Sociology*, LXX (March 1965), p. 617.
[4] Robert Bierstedt, "Comment," *The American Journal of Sociology*, LXX (March 1965), p. 623.

regard to their chronological sequence, in order to present a coherent sociological analysis.

Few sociologists and historians would now agree with the earlier mentioned sarcastic remark of an English sociologist, Donald G. MacRae, who remarked that "Sociology is history with the hard work left out; history is sociology with the brains left out."[5] Two important volumes published in 1964, *Sociology and History* and *American History and the Social Sciences,* testify to the growing affinity between history and the social sciences.[6] What is even more important, they indicate many promising avenues for fruitful collaboration. The first book includes contributions by a number of sociologists who employ sociological concepts for the illumination and sounder analysis of historical events and periods and by sociologists who use historical data to illuminate and test the validity of sociological concepts, models, and theories. Among the former are such eminent sociologists as E. Digby Baltzel, Werner J. Cahnman, and Sigmund Diamond, while the latter are represented by Alvin Boskoff, Thomas F. O'Dea, and Ernest Manheim.

The editors of this volume state that the rapprochement of history and sociology has become possible and desirable because sociologists have grown wary of generalizations based on doubtful evidence which is often severely restricted in time and place, and because historians feel the need to broaden the scope of their investigations by comparing analogous situations and by the formulation of broader concepts and generalizations. The interest of the historian in the unique and the interest of the sociologists in the general can be bridged, the editors assert, because while "it is desirable and possible to attain some measure of understanding of specific events and related periods, it is also desirable and possible to discover the extent to which explanations applicable to one situation may be extended to comparable situations from other times and places."[7] This cautious and wise statement should be carefully noted by social studies teachers. It might suggest to them an approach to the teaching of historical events and of general concepts from the social sciences not in an unrelated and disjointed way, but by a sensible fusion of both, whenever such fusion is logical and possible. The new sociology, the editors state, must steer its course between the Scylla of rigid generalization and the Charybdis of sheer empiri-

---

[5] Donald G. MacRae, "Some Sociological Prospects," *Proceedings of the Third World Congress of Sociology,* Vol. 8 (London, 1956), p. 302.

[6] Werner J. Cahnman and Alvin Boskoff, eds., *Sociology and History—Theory and Research* (New York: Free Press of Glencoe, 1964). Edward N. Saveth, ed., *American History and the Social Sciences* (New York: Free Press of Glencoe, 1964).

[7] Werner J. Cahnman and Alvin Boskoff, "Sociology and History: Reunion and Rapprochement," in *Sociology and History—Theory and Research* (New York: Free Press of Glencoe, 1964), p. 3.

cism.[8] "We believe," Cahnman and Boskoff wrote, "that the ways in which history and sociology are similar and complementary are as significant as the avowed differences, and that the specialized scholar ought to pause occasionally and look about to see whether his strivings and findings are in line with the general concerns of mankind."[9]

Among the many contributions to the volume, Professor Alvin Boskoff's paper represents an important example of fruitful collaboration between history and sociology. Boskoff examines the concept of a transitional society by the use of two historical case studies, Greece in the fourth and fifth centuries B.C., and Rome in the third to the eighth centuries A.D. He finds that the Greek society in the period discussed, suffered from social indecision caused by an unresolved conflict between oligarchy and democracy, the fruitless rivalry between Sparta and Athens, and the confusion over conflicting ideas of practical realism and utopian escapism. According to Boskoff, Roman society in the third to the eighth centuries A.D. was also a transitional society, because it was beset by a number of unresolved social crises. These included the problem of imperial succession which became the toy of the legions and the growing disorganization of the Roman army which became demoralized by politization. In addition, agriculture became stagnated by the escape of peasants to the cities, and trade and industry were severely hampered by lack of a clear economic policy.

In his essay on "Religion and Nationality," Cahnman uses sociological insights to explain the peculiar position of non-Moslems, particularly Jews and Christians, in the Ottoman Empire. They were tolerated, allowed to profess their faith, but they were considered tenants who had to pay tribute for themselves and their land to the Moslem state. Cahnman also studied the lack of a clear boundary between religion and nationality in Islam and in Judaism. He found the answer in the social pattern of the Middle Eastern region where tribal law prevented social stratification and where the ancient custom of adoption and naturalization prevailed. Also, in Islam the concept of Moslem brotherhood encouraged the conversion of peoples of different nationalities and races.[10]

American History and the Social Sciences gives ample proof that many historians see great benefits in a close working relationship with social scientists. However, while they are ready to acknowledge the value of empirical social research, they remain unwilling to take seriously the far-reaching claims made by some social scientists for their respective disciplines.

---

[8] *Ibid.*, p. 11.
[9] *Ibid.*, p. 11.
[10] *Ibid.*, pp. 271–280.

In an excellent statement on "Sociology and the School Curriculum," Professor Robert Perucci, of Purdue University, wrote:

> If the resources of sociology are to be used to help our youth understand the world in which they live, the curriculum must reflect our current knowledge about (1) the nature and importance of individual and social values, (2) how values shape institutions, groups and organizations, (3) how men react with one another through the various positions and roles they assume in groups and organizations, and (4) how the interaction between the individual and society may result either in the preservation or the modification of the values and institutions of society. This article describes these fundamental ideas and relationships.[11]

Perucci maintained that the basic ideas of sociology can be used in the social studies curriculum at all levels, either in separate sociology courses or to enrich the students' understanding of history.

HISTORY AND POLITICAL SCIENCE

The historian is ready to acknowledge the contributions made by political science in the development of rigorous research designs and the application of precise methods of analysis to the study of political behavior. But few historians will accept this claim made for political science by Professor Peter H. Odegard, former president of the American Political Association:

> There is a new look in the study of politics; . . . No longer a hostage to history, and freed at last from its bondage to the lawyers as well as from the arid schematism of the political taxonomists, political science is in the process of becoming one of the central unifying forces for understanding why we behave like human beings.[12]

When television audiences throughout the nation are intently watching distinguished political scientists differ diametrically in the diagnosis and prognosis of Viet Nam, in the analysis of relations between India and Pakistan and between Russia and China, and when almost every month a political upheaval takes place in the world which puzzles political scientists as much as historians, it is rather difficult to take such exaggerated claims seriously. A more realistic political scientist, Professor Heinz Eulau, observed that ". . . Professor Odegard's picture is still more in the nature of a snapshot of a possible future than of a richly painted canvas."[13]

---

[11] Robert Perucci, "Sociology and the School Curriculum," *Social Science Education Consortium Newsletter,* Vol. 1, No. 2 (July 1965), p. 3.

[12] Bert F. Hoselitz, ed., *A Reader's Guide to the Social Sciences* (New York: Free Press of Glencoe, 1959), p. 126.

[13] *Ibid.,* p. 126.

Arthur Schlesinger, Jr., addressing a meeting of the American Sociological Association in Washington in 1962, discussed frankly the historian's dilemma in his relationship to the social sciences. Schlesinger gratefully acknowledged his debt as a historian to the sociologists who have, as he put it, "so vastly broadened my own intellectual horizons and refined my conception of the historical enterprise."[14] He stated that he is in fact prejudiced in favor of empirical social research which aims at devising inquiries and experiments making possible a better understanding both of human behavior and social processes. But Schlesinger cautioned that the historian and the social scientist part ways when the latter suggests that the empirical method of inquiry is the only path to the understanding of past and present social phenomena and that social wisdom can be gained only through analytical quantitative analysis. Polls are useful, but they are often misleading and unreliable, and the quantitative method of inquiry in history would ignore many important psychological and philosophical variables. "For an indefinite future," Schlesinger concluded, "I suspect humanism will continue to yield truths about both individual and social experience which quantitative social science research could never reach."[15] It is of course one thing to assert that the quantitative method of empirical research cannot illuminate all, or even major historical events, and it is another, not to acknowledge the usefulness of this method in the exploration of many problems in historical research.

Professor Edward N. Saveth, the editor of *American History and the Social Sciences*, suggested that the traditional historical method of verifying data would profit greatly from the use of insights that the social scientists have gained on the nature of man. Such concepts as class, role, mobility, and decision-making may be of great help to the historian in his work.

HISTORY AND ECONOMICS

Economic history has been a distinguished branch of history for a long time.

In spite of the growing influence of econometricians in the discipline of economics, there is evidence to suggest the existence of large areas of cooperation between history and economics. W. W. Rostow suggested that the study of the problem of economic growth may become a fruitful meeting ground between history and economics. The study of economic growth, Professor Rostow wrote, would force historians to theorize about whole societies, while economists would be compelled to attempt a thorough analysis of the political, social, and cultural forces that affect

---

[14] *American History and the Social Sciences* (New York: Free Press of Glencoe, 1964), p. 52.
[15] *Ibid.*, p. 536.

economic growth.[16] Another indication of the increasing possibilities for collaboration between history and economics is the readiness of leading economists to acknowledge the existence of widely publicized differences in their discipline over the best ways to attain continued economic growth, the relation of interest rates to inflation, or the best method of preventing economic recessions or depressions. Basically, economists are obviously in disagreement on the issue of how economic growth is to be maintained. One group argues that maximum growth depends largely upon the incentive system developed and maintained by the private sectors of the nation's economy. Such an encouragement of the incentive system calls for minimum government intervention and spending and allows the consuming public to keep most of its income. The other school of economists believes that continued economic growth necessitates a great deal of government intervention through the juggling of the interest rate, government subsidies, and large welfare programs aimed at increasing productivity.

Basic disagreement in the discipline of economics may well bring historians and economists closer to each other. It seems clear that general economics, with the possible exception of econometrics, cannot make very serious claims as to the reliability of its predictions. What economists and, for that matter, other social scientists can do is to indicate certain trends, given a specific set of conditions, which may materialize in the future. Whether the trend will actually materialize depends upon the emergence or the non-emergence of a number of unforeseen and unforeseeable variables. Even more important, the sharp conflict among several schools of economists points to the inescapable conclusion that the root of the disagreements lies not in purely economic issues, but belongs in the realm of values. As Professor Seymour Harris of Harvard University, put it:

> But the major disagreements on welfare programs revolve around noneconomic issues. To what extent, for example, should the well-to-do subsidize the relatively underprivileged? Some will hold that old people who are unemployed or without savings deserve their fate, either because they have not worked hard enough or because they have not been thrifty.[17]

Obviously, these are moral questions which have nothing to do with the findings of an analysis of economic questions by the use of the quantitative empirical method of inquiry. The Medicare program for elderly people and federal programs to fight poverty have an important effect on the economy of the country, but they must be discussed also in moral and hu-

---

[16] W. W. Rostow, "Economics," in *American History and the Social Sciences* (New York: Free Press of Glencoe, 1964), pp. 25–38.

[17] Seymour E. Harris, "Economics," in Erling Hunt, ed., *High School Social Studies Perspectives* (Boston: Houghton Mifflin Co., 1962), p. 7.

mane terms. Disagreements among economists, Harris continued, "arise both in strictly economic analyses and in the application of different value systems to economic problems."[18]   On the basis of this acknowledgment, historians who wish to study economic problems in the broad content of the political, social, and cultural structure and values, and the economists who are largely concerned with the problem of distribution of scarce resources can find a large area of fruitful cooperation.

Setting aside for a moment the question of whether economics should be taught as a separate subject in the secondary school or be integrated in the study of history, civics, and government in the general framework of the social studies, the purpose in the teaching of economics is to provide students with a general understanding of economic principles and policies. Such an understanding would give students a knowledge of the ways in which our society and other societies manage their productive human and natural resources.   The basic scarcity of resources necessitates an understanding of how fully and efficiently they are used and in what proportion these resources are distributed among the different segments of the population.   In both totalitarian and democratic countries the role of the government in the allocation and use of scarce resources is an important subject of exploration.   One economist, Ben W. Lewis, sensibly argues that economic understanding is essential to the survival of our society:

> I argue simply that the demonstrated capacity of our democratic political economy to perform, and hence its capacity to survive, will be substantially affected in the years ahead by the extent to which our people become equipped to face up to public economic issues with an understanding of "what it's all about" and "how to get on with the job."[19]

Professor Lewis, who is a member of the National Task Force on Economic Education, which drew up a set of guidelines for the teaching of economics on the high school level, is open-minded on whether these guidelines should be taught as straight economics or be integrated in the study of history and government. If economics is to be taught as part of other courses, he urges that economics be integrated with them explicitly and imaginatively by competent teachers.

Richard Hofstadter, perhaps the foremost writer of American intellectual history, has repeatedly acknowledged his debt to social science and especially sociological insights and concepts which in his view greatly enhance the "speculative richness of history." In his Pulitzer prize winning volume,

---

[18] *Ibid.*, p. 7.

[19] Ben W. Lewis, "Economics," in *The Social Studies and the Social Sciences*, sponsored by the American Council for Learned Societies and the National Council for the Social Studies (New York: Harcourt, Brace & World, 1962), p. 115.

The Age of Reform: From Bryan to F.D.R., Hofstadter applied certain aspects of the method of sociological research to the study of Populism and Progressivism. He found such sociological and psychological concepts as status anxiety, self-deceiving image, role playing, alienation, and social mobility very useful in tracing the sources of social conflict in late nineteenth-century America and in gaining a better understanding of the character of the leaders of the Populist rebellion, of the Progressive movement, and of prominent Muckrakers. The Populists, Hofstadter suggested, failing to understand the true cause of the agricultural depression, projected their animosities and grievances on "alien" forces—Wall Street, New Yorkers, English capitalists, and Jewish bankers. The split personality and the paranoid tendencies of many of the Populist leaders became clear when such leaders of the People's (Populist) Party as Thomas Watson and Ben Tillman became bitter Negro haters. As for the Progressive leaders, most of whom came from the clergy, the law, and the universities, Hofstadter asserted that their reform crusades were an expression of resentment against their loss of status to the newly rich industrialists and the new breed of politicians representing the growing political strength of ethnic blocs in the big cities. Using a sociological term, Hofstadter spoke of "the status revolution." Similarly, talking about the abrupt conversion of the Mugwumps from anti-Populists to Progressives, Hofstadter concluded that the Mugwumps did so "not because of economic deprivations but primarily because they were victims of an upheaval in status."[20]

Professor Hofstadter is convinced that the modern historian must maintain close contact with the social sciences primarily because the social sciences have made impressive achievements, developed useful techniques of inquiry, and accumulated a body of substantive findings, intellectual concerns, and professional perspectives which can enrich the work of the historian.

> Questions associated with social status, social mobility, differences and conflicts between generations, child-rearing in its relation to culture, the sociology of knowledge and of the professions are questions which he (the historian) might properly take upon himself, and which are interwoven with his traditional concerns. It seems inevitable, too, that some of the discoveries made by modern social research about current mass political behavior and political influence will revise some of the historian's assumptions about political behavior of the past.[21]

---

[20] Richard Hofstadter, *The Age of Reform: From Bryan to F.D.R.* (New York: Alfred A. Knopf, 1955), p. 93.

[21] Richard Hofstadter, "History and the Social Sciences," in Fritz Stern, ed., *The Varieties of History* (Cleveland: World Publishing Co., 1963), p. 364.

Hofstadter was careful to state that for him these new social science perspectives were useful only as an addition to the traditionally rich and varied methods of historical analysis.

HISTORY AND PSYCHOLOGY

Psychological insights in the area of motives and personality traits are of great value to historians.

William L. Langer and H. Stuart Hughes seem to be fascinated by the potential contribution of psychoanalysis to history and especially to the field of biography. They agree that historians have, on the whole, ignored what Erik Ericson has defined as "the fateful function of childhood in the fabric of society." Professor Hughes sees a great affinity between historians and psychoanalysts. "For the historian as for the psychoanalyst," he writes,

> an interpretation ranks as satisfactory not by passing some formal scientific tests, but by conveying our inner conviction. For both plural explanations are second nature . . . Indeed, for both of them the word "cause" is admissible only if defined with extreme flexibility . . . For both deal in complex configurations, searching for a thread of inner logic that will tie together an apparent chaos of random words and actions.[22]

Hughes suggested that at least some Ph.D. candidates in history go through the process of psychoanalysis to be prepared to use psychoanalytical insights in their historical investigations.

A number of historians have recently testified to the debt they owed to psychology and psychiatry for a better understanding of the subjects of their inquiries. David Donald acknowledged the great benefit he derived from frequent consultations with psychiatrists in the course of writing his biography of Charles Sumner. He was especially grateful for the psychological insights which provided a better understanding of Sumner's complex character and especially his puzzling reaction to the assault on him by Congressman Brooks.[23]

This writer also has a special reason to acknowledge the importance of psychological understandings. In working on the life of Lyman Trumbull, a question emerged which was impossible to answer by the usual mode of historical inquiry. In 1871, Trumbull did all in his power to obtain the nomination for the presidency of the newly organized Liberal Republican party. When, however, the nomination was quite conceivably in his grasp,

---

[22] H. Stuart Hughes, *History as Art and as Science* (New York: Harper & Row, 1964), p. 47.
[23] David Donald, *Charles Sumner and the Coming of the Civil War* (New York: Alfred A. Knopf, 1960), Preface, viii–xii.

he suddenly and without explanation, either at the time or subsequently, lost all interest and did practically nothing to assure his nomination at the party's convention in Cincinnati. On the contrary, this able and experienced politician behaved like a bumbling neophyte in politics.[24] A plausible explanation for this enigma can be found in the psychological concept of dual personality which allows for contradictory drives in the same human being. Psychology has taught us to accept the bizarre fact that one may idolize Willie Mays and hate all other Negroes. Trumbull wanted the nomination because he was ambitious and thought himself well fitted for the White House, but he loathed campaigning and shuddered at addressing large crowds. Thus, his seemingly inexplicable last-minute paralysis becomes quite understandable.

WEAKNESSES IN THE HISTORICAL METHOD

The rapprochement between history and the social sciences has become easier because historians are occasionally willing to admit that there are weaknesses in the traditional historical method of investigation of the past. Lee Benson, a historian on the faculty of the University of Pennsylvania, has convincingly argued that the use of a classification system, favored by the social sciences, would help to undermine the long-standing dominance of American historiography by economic determinism. "By providing a framework for ordering data in some systematic and logical fashion," Benson wrote, "it (a classification system) brings into focus relationships among empirical data that are not readily apparent."[25] In analyzing American voting behavior, Benson illustrated the advantages of the classification system. He grouped voting patterns under three main categories: (1) pursuit of political goals by individuals or groups; (2) individual or group fulfillment of political roles and; (3) negative or positive orientation in reference to individuals or groups. The advantage of Benson's approach should be clear to any high school social studies teacher who ever attempted to teach and to make sense from the erratic behavior of American voters.

The tendency of some historians to rely too much on what may be called "footnote evidence" is a cause for legitimate concern. Too often a footnote reference to a single private letter is used as supportive evidence for a generalization. Take, for instance, this example chosen from an otherwise superior work of historical research. The author Lawrence W. Levine,

---

[24] Mark M. Krug, *Lyman Trumbull—Conservative Radical* (New York: A. S. Barnes & Co., 1965), pp. 303–314.

[25] Lee Benson, "A Tentative Classification for American Voting Behavior," in *Sociology and History* (New York: Free Press of Glencoe, 1964), pp. 415–421.

writing about the later years of William Jennings Bryan, makes the broad statement that the oratorical talents of Bryan in the 1920's had not diminished to any great extent.   He wants his reader to believe that the silver-tongued orator from the Platte was as good a speaker in 1920 and 1925 as he was during his memorable campaign against McKinley in 1896.   This indeed is a far-reaching statement.   How does he go about proving it? He cites in a footnote a single excerpt from a letter to Bryan written in 1923 by a man who was in one of his audiences.   The man wrote:

> I shall never forget your speech at Ogden . . .   A Republican sat by my side and made slighting remarks about you and your ideas before you began to speak.   He was cold-blooded and cynical.   His slurs began to weaken after you had spoken five or ten minutes and inside of twenty minutes you had him cheering lustily and even stamping his feet.   I have never heard anything so masterful as that speech.[26]

This is a very interesting letter, but it assuredly does not prove the generalization about the unimpaired oratorical powers of William Jennings Bryan in the late 1920's.

Some of the younger historians who acknowledge the importance of the unique and the specific in history, and who reject the idea of predictions in history are nevertheless convinced that the emphasis on detail in historical writing almost consciously discourages even a limited applicability to the future.   Too often results of historical investigations are presented in such detail and with such dull monotony that even the foundation for a broader analysis is lacking.   Martin Duberman complained, "No bit of information is too small to be worth having when used creatively as part of a larger mosaic, but all too frequently detail is elaborated in vacuo, the dead specifics of past action tirelessly rehearsed for themselves alone, without reference to a broader framework which might rescue them from antiquarianism."[27]

Historians often and with justice complain that the special professional jargon developed by their colleagues in the social sciences makes some of the latter's work incomprehensible to the uninitiated.   With equal justice social scientists may object to the tedious footnotes and dreary detail of many of the historical monographs which appear in scholarly journals. Reading some of these contributions to historical research, a bored reader may sometimes also be inclined to ask: "so what?"

Few readers, however, would either be bored by or have any doubts

---

[26] Lawrence W. Levine, *Defender of the Faith: William Jennings Bryan, 1915–1925* (New York: Oxford Univ. Press, 1965), p. 186.

[27] Martin Duberman, "The Limitations of History," *The Antioch Review* (Summer 1965), p. 286.

about the great value of Crane Brinton's *The Anatomy of Revolution*. No better example of the skillful utilization of social science concepts and methodology in history can be found in the historical literature of recent years. Brinton set for himself a deceptively simple task. Being the good historian that he is, he was quite aware of the unique and the specific in the major revolutions in history, but he decided to establish "as the scientist might, certain first approximations of uniformities" in the course of four successful revolutions: the English Revolution of the 1640's, the American Revolution, the French Revolution, and the Bolshevik Revolution.[28] The author disclaimed any desire to write a sociology of revolution and cautioned against any attempt to extend his conclusions to all revolutions. He was not ready to predict on the basis of his study when and where the next revolution would break out.

Since we have no desire to review in detail this important book, we shall limit our discussion to the observation that Brinton found the social science approach which he used in his study a very useful one. Without graphs, charts, and statistical correlations, but relying on his superb knowledge of the evidence and using a common-sense comparative technique, Brinton tested a number of generalizations concerning the four revolutions which he studied. He found some of them wanting and others quite reliable.

One major generalization which Brinton postulated—a pattern of uniformity among the leaders of the four revolutions—was found to be unsupportable. The leaders of the Puritan, French, American, and Russian Revolutions proved to be a varied lot. Some were aristocrats, others middle-class professionals, and still others proletarians. "To sum up," Brinton concluded, "it should by now be clear that it takes almost as many kinds of men and women to make a revolution as to make a world."[29] However, a number of "lower" type generalizations were supported by evidence. All revolutions were led by a minority of dedicated leaders who were conscious and very proud of their small numbers. Cromwell was proud of the relatively small number of his Saints and Lenin was happy with his select group of Bolsheviks. The revolutionary leadership group in all four revolutions was not only small, but was also fanatically dedicated. Among the other generalizations which Brinton found valid on the basis of his analysis of the four revolutions are summarized below.

1. Revolutions are not started by starving, miserable people. The revolutions under study came at a time when the respective societies were economically on the upgrade.

---

[28] Crane Brinton, *The Anatomy of Revolution* (New York: Random House, 1957), p. 6.
[29] *Ibid.*, p. 126.

2. A mass desertion of the existing regime by intellectuals preceded all four revolutions.
3. The pre-revolutionary governments were inefficient and unwilling or unable to make necessary reforms.
4. Many in the ruling group had lost faith in their own ability to govern and had lost faith in their own traditions and values.

Brinton's study combined excellent narrative history with a systematic search for patterns of similarity by the use of social science tools. It indicated how much promise there is in a meaningful working relationship between the historian and his colleagues in the social sciences.

HISTORY AND ANTHROPOLOGY

Since anthropology claims an interest in man, his works, and his thoughts at all times and in all places, its affinity to history is obvious. The differences lie in the points of emphasis and methodology. Anthropology is devoted to the scientific understanding of man as a whole through the comparative study of man in particular groups. There are two main branches of anthropology, physical and cultural. Physical anthropology is concerned with the biological origins of man—the evolution of man from other forms of animal life. Cultural anthropology concentrates on man's behavior in society, both shared and learned. Three themes emerge from cultural anthropology: (1) the basis in nature of the unity of man, (2) the existence of human diversity within the total human pattern, and (3) the universality of the process of cultural change.

The essential method of investigation in anthropology is the field study, the collection of data about peoples and cultures at their geographical location and the organization of this data in a systematic way which will aid our understanding of many societies. As we have observed in the previous chapter, cultural anthropologists, intent on the preservation of objectivity in their studies and guarding against ethnocentric "judgments" of other cultures, have been rigidly careful not to inject subjective value statements in their work. Recently, a number of anthropologists have produced highly praised field studies which have not been value-free.

The close ties between history and anthropology stem primarily from the fact that much of the research in anthropology, and especially in physical anthropology and in archeology, which is a branch of cultural anthropology, is both as scientific and artistic as is history. The physical anthropologist and archeologist, just as an historian, rely on a combination of available data and creative imagination. Indeed, it would be difficult to term physical anthropology a "hard" science. It abounds in conjectures and the controversies in which its celebrated practitioners engage are sharp and vocal. Consider for instance these excerpts from a paper titled "Human Beginnings," written by one of America's leading physical anthropologists:

> . . . We know virtually nothing about the precise way in which this tool using and tool-making propensity of man became an established attribute of his.
> . . . When and how this primate adjustment to partially upright posture became converted into a fully erect one is still obscure.
> . . . We cannot, therefore, assert with confidence that man's ancestors took to ground living because of burgeoning intellectual equipment.[30]

It is clear that because of scarcity of data the physical anthropologist, like the historian, must often rely on his best educated guesses in making conclusions. Archeology, which is called prehistory in Europe, is also as scientific and as nonscientific as history. Chemical carbon analysis has been of great help in dating ancient documents, but even this process is not absolutely reliable. For instance, archeologists are still locked in a bitter dispute about the exact origin of the Dead Sea Scrolls.

Two important voices have been raised recently which promise a closer relationship between historians and anthropologists. The dean of British anthropologists, Professor Evans-Pritchard, has pointed out that anthropology, especially cultural and social anthropology, have come so close to history that a complete merger of the two disciplines is within the realm of probability. Both the anthropologist and the historian have become aware that

> any event has the characteristics of uniqueness and generality and that in an interpretation of it both have to be given consideration. If the specificity of a fact is lost, the generalization about it becomes so general as to be value-less. On the other hand, events lose much, even all of their meaning, if they are not seen "as having" some degree of regularity and constancy, as belonging to a certain type of event, all instances of which have many features in common.[31]

The famous American anthropologist, Margaret Mead, argued recently that there is a special bond between anthropologists and historians not shared with other scientists and social scientists. While scientists have a single-minded devotion to abstract concepts, generalizations, and patterns of similarity which they test by repetitive experimentation, the historian and the anthropologist work with a concrete material, whether this be an

---

30 Harry L. Shapiro, "Human Beginnings" in Harry L. Shapiro, ed., *Man, Culture and Society* (New York: Oxford Univ. Press, 1956), pp. 4, 5, 7.
31 Quoted in Thomas C. Mendenhall, "Social Studies, History and the Secondary School," *Social Education* (April 1963), p. 203.

ancient document or a tribal initiation ceremony. The loving preservation of the detail, Professor Mead suggested, is a unique and unifying feature shared by history and anthropology. She has stated that traditionally

> historians and anthropologists have been distinguished from one another by the materials which they have studied: the historian dealing with past periods and the anthropologist with primitive peoples. This distinction is fast becoming obsolete, as both are turning their attention to contemporary problems of the great civilizations of the world—including our own.[32]

This statement may be a bit overdrawn and would probably be challenged by many practicing members of both disciplines, but it does reflect the new trends in both history and anthropology.

HISTORY, THE SOCIAL SCIENCES, AND THE SOCIAL STUDIES TEACHER

How important is this discussion about the relationship between history and the social sciences for the social studies teacher? It is hoped that he will draw several conclusions from this review.

First, a growing rapport between history and the social sciences has become possible. Prospects for a meaningful collaboration have become brighter because historians have become less dogmatic about their refusal to make generalizations, and social scientists have generally become wary about exaggerating the value of empiricism in the formulation of broad generalizations. In an address to the American Psychological Association, Dr. Gordon W. Allport of Harvard University warned against the dangers of "galloping empiricism."[33] Empiricism, objective experimentation, and analysis he said, "dash forth like a headless horseman." Too often, Allport complained, social science researchers over-generalize in limited and specific studies. A most vigorous attack on the dogmatic scientism of his own colleagues in political science came from Hans J. Morgenthau of the University of Chicago. In his brilliant volume *Scientific Man Versus Power Politics* Morgenthau argues that while scientism has given man a technical mastery over nature, it has failed to answer the most basic questions of human existence. Social science generalizations are only indicative of certain possible trends which materialize only when certain developments and conditions occur. "What can be stated scientifically," Morgenthau writes, "in way of prediction on the basis of a 'social law' is merely that, given certain conditions, a certain social trend is more likely to materialize than are others. . . ." Professor Morgenthau points out that there is a

---

[32] Margaret Mead, "Anthropology," in *American History and the Social Sciences* (New York: Free Press of Glencoe, 1964), pp. 90–91.

[33] New York *Times*, Sept. 7, 1965, p. 28.

fundamental distinction between natural and social phenomena and problems. Problems in the natural sciences are either solvable at a particular time or they are not. Once solved they stay solved. This is not true of the social problems. Morgenthau concludes:

> Social problems such as marriage, education, equality, freedom, authority, peace, are of a different kind. They do not grow out of temporary limitations of knowledge or temporary insufficiencies of technical achievement—both of which can be overcome by the progressive development of theory and practice. They are the result of those conflicts in which selfishness and the lust for power, which are common to all men, involve all men.[34]

Second, historians in an increasing number have become convinced that the use of social science concepts like status, social mobility, consensus, cultural change, and alienation can be of great value in achieving better understanding of an historical event or a personality. This realization holds great promise for social studies teachers in teaching United States history, world history, or civics and government. The concept of status politics may well make the teaching of basic motives of political behavior more explicable and more interesting. The concept of balance of power, as applied, let us say, to Europe on the eve of World War I, will make that tangled period more understandable and exciting to students.

Third, the increasing complexity of our society and the constant dangers to its survival are turning the attention of historians and social scientists to contemporary problems. Richard Hofstadter may have been right when he said that "the next generation may see the development of a somewhat new historical genre, which will be a mixture of traditional history and the social sciences."[35] However, one would be wise to assume that there will still be many kinds of historians in the coming generations.

Fourth, historians and social scientists are increasingly abandoning the sterile, pseudo-scientific approach to values in their investigation. There is an awareness that morally neutral history and value-less social science have weakened the spirit of personal responsibility for the improvement of human society. The practitioners in the disciplines of history and the social sciences are beginning to appreciate the importance of the moral relevance of their scholarship to a society direly in need of intellectual and ethical guidance. This point has a great bearing on the work of the social studies teacher who is called upon to deal with ever larger numbers of controversial issues. The only way that he can deal safely and intelligently

---

[34] Hans J. Morgenthau, *Scientific Man Versus Power Politics* (Chicago: Univ. of Chicago Press, 1965), pp. 136, 215.
[35] Richard Hofstadter, "History and the Social Sciences," in Fritz Stern, ed., *The Varieties of History* (Cleveland: World Publishing Co., 1963), p. 363.

with these problems is not by refusing to take a stand, but by insisting on high standards in the inquiry into any complex problem. Once he is able to establish a reputation for scholarship and scrupulous adherence to free inquiry, his personal position on controversial issues, which he should not hesitate to reveal at the last stage of the investigation, will be respected.

What remains to be discussed is the need for caution lest the opportunities for the infusion of social science concepts and methodology in the high school social studies be oversimplified. It is essential to realize that the term social sciences is becoming more and more complex. Too many people who should know better, and far too many social studies teachers, use the term social sciences as if the boundaries between the social sciences themselves and those between the social sciences and the natural sciences were clear and definite. There also prevails a widespread illusion that scholars in the social sciences are agreed upon one set of concepts and generalizations which are ready and waiting to be used by teachers in their social studies classrooms. It is likewise repeatedly assumed by some who write about the new social studies curricula that each of the social sciences has *one* particular and generally accepted mode of inquiry which can and should somehow be put to use in social studies instruction. Finally, there is the dangerous, and almost ridiculous assumption, that it is the duty of the high school social studies teacher to "integrate" into his classroom instruction, *all* concepts, insights, findings and methods of inquiry of the social sciences. These are dangerous illusions which have already caused much grief in the field of social studies. What is indicated and desired is the *selective* use of relevant concepts, generalizations, and modes of inquiry in the social sciences.

Even our brief review has indicated that there is a great variety of concepts accompanied by wide divergencies in basic aims and methods of inquiry within each of the social science disciplines. There are traditional economists and econometricians. There are the positivist and behavioristic political scientists who put their faith in quantitative analysis, and there are their colleagues who rely on the traditional analysis of politics and politicians. There is the deepening cleavage between the macrosociologists and the microsociologists. The prospect is that the tremendous accumulation of research and the refinement of many methods of inquiry will even more accentuate the differences and cleavages in each of the social science disciplines. It makes little sense and is even irresponsible to suggest that a high school teacher should integrate, or "make whole" as Webster defines the word, the social sciences, when even the scholars in each field have not succeeded in agreeing on integrated principles in their own disciplines. In fact, most scholars would agree that such an attempt at integration was impossible of achievement and unnecessary.

Finally, the glib talk about the grandiose plan for the inclusion of all the social sciences in the social studies curriculum, either in an *integrated* form or as separate disciplines, ignores the fuzziness of the lines of demarcation between the natural and the social sciences. A few examples will suffice to illustrate this point. Many psychologists are convinced that their discipline belongs to the natural sciences. Many physical anthropologists, concerned primarily with the biology of man, look upon themselves as natural scientists, while cultural and social anthropologists just as firmly see themselves as social scientists. In economics, the econometricians see themselves as hard-nosed scientists, unlike their colleagues, the classical economists, whom they consider rather old-fashioned social scientists.

These cautionary injunctions should in no way weaken the determination of social studies teachers to intelligently choose from the social sciences those concepts, insights, and modes of inquiry which will help them give more effective instruction aimed at attaining a better understanding of the past and present societies and cultures. The framework for the *selective* utilization of insights from the social sciences must be determined in view of the needs of high school students and the recognized objectives of the social studies.

History, because of its total concern with human experience and its flexible boundaries, can and should serve as a common body of knowledge for the other social sciences in the social studies curriculum. Social science concepts and modes of inquiry, intelligently selected, would add a new and promising dimension to the teaching of history by making all history, as taught on the high school level, conform to Croce's famous statement that all history is contemporary history. A fruitful collaboration between history and the social sciences will bring about a greater student motivation, and greater depth and dynamics in high school social studies. History, because it is a social science, a humanity, and an art, is in a position to accept and put to use selected materials, research findings, concepts, and modes of inquiry from all of the social sciences.

5

On the Use of Social Science

Concepts in the Social Studies

We have argued that it would be unwise and unrealistic to ask the social studies teacher to integrate, which in Webster's definition means "to make whole, renew," all the concepts and methods of the social sciences in the social studies curriculum. It is indeed a large order to attempt the integration in the high school social studies of the accumulated knowledge, research insights, and methodology in the social sciences. What can and should be done, is to encourage social studies teachers to use and correlate social science concepts relevant to classroom inquiries in history, broadly conceived.

Sociologists have suggested that in order to understand the world in which we live, our youth needs knowledge of

(1) the nature and importance of individual and social values, (2) how values shape institutions, groups and organizations, (3) how men react with one another through the various positions and roles they assume in groups and organizations, and (4) how the interaction between the individual and society may result either in the preservation or the modification of the values and institutions of society.[1]

Political scientists have told social studies teachers that an understanding of our society demands that the students study political philosophy, com-

---

[1] Robert Perrucci, "Sociology and the School Curriculum," *Social Science Education Consortium Newsletter*, Vol. 1, No. 2 (July 1965), p. 1.

parative government, choice and decision-making in politics, public administration, the drive for political power, and the art of political analysis.[2]

Anthropologists have suggested that young people of elementary and
high school age ought to become thoroughly familiar with the concepts of
culture and cultural change, with cultural lag, and with the relationship of
human behavior to the group and to biological factors. They ought to
know about the biological origins of man and the variations in human
species, including the study of race. The comparative analysis of societies
by the study of primitive communities in many parts of the world is also
deemed very important by anthropologists.[3]

Social psychologists also consider the study of their discipline on a high
school level very important because social psychology deals basically with
the interrelationship between group experience and the personality and
the psychology of the individual. Our youth, social psychologists maintain,
must be taught an understanding of the functioning of the man as a social
being. A knowledge of the nature of perception is essential. Similarly, it is
important for the student to understand how learning takes place. Central
emphasis in social psychology is placed on the effect that group influences
have on individuals and on personality formation. Motivation and emotional reactions must be studied, preferably by the introduction of "concepts of scientific method because there are good experiments on problems
of human motivation close to student interests."[4]

Economists, who had a special National Task Force on Economics Education work on an economics curriculum in high schools, concluded that
the minimum essential economic understanding needed by all high school
students would include the following areas:

an overview of the way in which our economic system solves the big, basic
economic problems:

1. What shall be produced . . .

2. How much can be produced in total . . .

3. Who shall get the goods and services produced?[5]

---

[2] Evron M. Kirkpatrick and Jeane J. Kirkpatrick, "Political Science," in Erling Hunt, ed.,
High School Social Studies Perspectives (Boston: Houghton Mifflin Co., 1962), pp.
99–125.

[3] Meyer Nimhoff, "Anthropology, Sociology and Social Psychology," in Erling Hunt, ed.,
High School Social Studies Perspectives (Boston: Houghton Mifflin Co., 1962), pp.
29–52.

[4] W. J. McKeachie, "Psychology," in Gordon B. Turner, ed., *The Social Studies and
the Social Sciences* (New York: Harcourt, Brace & World, 1962), p. 184.

[5] Ben W. Lewis "Economics," in Gordon B. Turner, ed., *The Social Studies and the
Social Sciences* (New York: Harcourt, Brace & World, 1962), p. 123.

Other areas of study in economics would include: economic growth and stability, the distribution of income, comparative economic systems, and important economic concepts and institutions. Students would also be introduced to the phenomena of cost, price, labor, savings, banking, investment, the law of supply and demand, and the workings of the stock market.

There is no need to belabor the point that no administrative genius could fit all the programs of the various social science disciplines into the required social studies curriculum which varies from a year and a half to two years. Even if successful, such a program of social studies would leave no room for United States, world history, and civics which are required by law in most states. Another serious question is the competence of the high school social studies teachers to teach the social sciences as separate disciplines. Scholars in economics and the behavioral sciences who have devoted thought and time to the question of the teaching of their respective disciplines in high schools are in complete agreement in stating that the success of this instruction demands a high level of competence in the discipline by the teacher. It would be unthinkable and harmful for teachers to instruct a course in economics, psychology, or sociology without an adequate background in these fields. A report in *The American Economic Review* which appeared in June, 1965, stated that a thorough survey showed that typical high school social studies teachers scored only a little higher than their students who had taken a one-semester course in high school economics. The leaders of this survey, which was conducted by the National Opinion Research Center, Professors G. L. Bach and Phillip Saunders, both of the Carnegie Institute of Technology, concluded that since most high school teachers have taken a one-semester course of college economics, "the findings raise serious questions about the effectiveness of most basic economic courses given in college to prospective high school teachers of social studies."[6] Professor Bach warned that if high school courses in economics are to be successful, social studies teachers offering these courses need intensive work with competent, interested, and understanding university economists, followed up by in-service help. But he warned that merely taking more courses in colleges in weak departments of economics or "going through weakly taught summer institutes or in-service programs apparently does little good for high school teachers."[7]

These conclusions apply equally to sociology, political science, anthropology, and psychology. It is clear that if the teaching of social science disciplines as separate subjects of instruction is to be successful, teachers require thorough and special training in each discipline under the guidance

---

[6] New York *Times,* May 23, 1965, p. 111.
[7] *Ibid.,* p. 111.

and supervision of able and dedicated university scholars. Anyone familiar with the interests and the priorities of economists, political scientists, sociologists, anthropologists, and psychologists in our colleges and universities knows that this is not a very realistic expectation.

There are a number of important schools of thought among the theoreticians in the field of social studies. The *simplifiers* in the social studies maintain that separate social science disciplines can be, and should be, simplified for pedagogical purposes and taught as social studies. "The social studies are the social sciences," wrote Edgar Wesley, a pioneer thinker in the field, "simplified for pedagogical purposes."[8] The job of the social studies teacher it is assumed, is to survey the knowledge, research materials, insights, concepts, skills, and techniques of the social sciences and to select that which can be taught on a high school level. This approach provokes several questions. What competencies do average social studies teachers have in order to survey the immense storehouses of knowledge in economics, anthropology, social psychology, political science, and sociology? What criteria and on whose authority will the selection of the "simpler" social science materials be made? Will not social scientists consider such a "simplification" process by outsiders a distortion of their basic organizing ideas and a threat to the integrity of their disciplines? Where will the teachers find time to do the job and how can adequate time be found for the teaching of the separate, even "simplified" social science disciplines in the social studies curriculum? Furthermore, as Lawrence Metcalf has sagely observed, the progressive simplification and boiling down of the content from the social sciences into broad generalizations will result in the presentation of their general prepositions as facts, supposedly derived from one of the social sciences without an attempt to test and verify the generalization.[9]

The *synthesizers* in the social studies contend that sociology, anthropology, economics, political science, and history are taught as separate disciplines only as a matter of convenience, but since they deal with a single basic theme—man and his society—they can and ought to be taught jointly. The new approach emphasizes the logical order basic to knowledge and the importance of the study and the comprehension of the structure of each discipline as a basic aim in school instruction. The teaching of the structure of a discipline, consisting of broad and connecting organizing ideas and principles, should be the basis of instruction starting with the lower grades of the elementary schools. "Any subject," Bruner maintains,

---

[8] Edgar B. Wesley and Stanley P. Wronski, *Teaching Social Studies in High Schools* (Boston: D. C. Heath & Co., 1958), p. 3.

[9] Lawrence E. Metcalf, "Research on Teaching the Social Studies" in N. L. Gage, ed., *Handbook of Research on Teaching* (Chicago: Rand McNally & Co., 1963), p. 960.

"can be taught effectively in some intellectually honest form to any child at any stage of development."[10]   Bruner has elsewhere stated:

> The structure of knowledge—its connectedness and its derivations that make one idea follow another—is the proper emphasis in education.   For it is structure, the great conceptual inventions that bring order to the congeries of disconnected observations, that gives meaning to what we may learn and makes possible the opening up of new realms of experience.[11]

We will discuss the structure approach in a later chapter.   However, some questions must be raised here.   Would it not be logical and more feasible, before an attempt is made to synthesize and unify the social sciences, to wait until the scholars in the social sciences themselves make an effort to find this synthesis?   The fact is that no such attempt has ever been made by the separate disciplines.

There is reason to believe that many social scientists would consider such an attempt either impossible or undesirable.   Those who agree with Bruner's position on the pre-eminent importance of the teaching of the structure of the disciplines may find that while it is relatively easy to define the structure and the broad organizing, logically connective principles in mathematics and in the sciences, the same task may well prove to be difficult, if not impossible, in the social sciences, especially history.   We shall for the moment leave out further discussion of whether the teaching of the structure of the disciplines is indeed the most desirable approach in social studies.

In his famous "Charter for the Social Sciences," Charles Beard denounced the exaggerated rigidity of boundaries among the social sciences, but he also wisely noted:

> This does not mean, however, that *a* or *the* social sciences has been created, a synthesis transcending the disciplines themselves.   Nor in the present state of things such an achievement seems possible.   Each of the disciplines inevitably has a center of gravity or furnishes a point of view from which materials are surveyed and an organization of knowledge.[12]

If Beard was right in 1932, the gigantic growth in the social sciences since that time would make integration and synthesis even less feasible.

The late Professor Alan Griffin wrote that while Bruner's approach is promising, he was seriously doubting the readiness of the theoreticians and

---

[10] Jerome S. Bruner, *The Process of Education* (Cambridge: Harvard Univ. Press, 1960), p. 33.
[11] Jerome S. Bruner, *On Knowing* (Cambridge: Harvard Univ. Press, 1962), p. 120.
[12] American Historical Association, *Report of the Commission on the Social Studies*, (New York: Charles Scribner's Sons, 1932), pp. 20–21.

practitioners in the field of social studies to integrate the social sciences. He wrote:

> Of the disciplines upon whose content social studies is said to depend, only history is by its nature precluded from experimentation. But if the social sciences, considered individually, are somewhat uncertain of structure, how much more difficult is the situation of the social studies considered as a grouping! It is exaggerated praise to say that the structure of the social studies is as yet inchoate; candor would compel us to say instead that the social studies are at best amorphous and at worst almost empty of scientifically-organized specific content.[13]

It is more realistic and worthwhile to explore the possibilities of using basic concepts and insights from the social sciences in the teaching of broadly gauged history courses. Professor Norton Long, a political scientist, has described this approach: "In fact, the use of history as a common body of knowledge for the other social sciences has much to recommend it both from the point of view of economizing on time and bringing the abstractions of analysis to bear on a historic reality that is rich in vicarious experience."[14] Professor Ben Lewis maintains that basic economic understanding may be acquired by students as a valuable by-product from courses other than economics, provided that "the economics be identified, and integrated explicitly, imaginatively, and with great care into the total body of material."[15]

History as taught on the high school level, if it is to become the core of the social studies curriculum, must be ready to view the past and the present not only through the traditional modes of historical inquiry and interpretation, but to become hospitable to *selected* concepts and materials from the social sciences. It must use, intelligently and selectively, the methods and techniques of inquiry from the social sciences. It must not be political history or economic history or cultural history. It must be history broadly conceived; in short, it must be great history in the tradition of Trevelyan, Gibbon, and Parkman. But it must also be a history aware of the limitations of its own methods and modes of inquiry and willing to improve its perceptions by making use of the rich harvest of social science knowledge and methodologies. Historians and teachers of history have much to gain by using more complex materials and more sophisticated methods of analysis sampling and classification accumulated and refined by the social scientists.

---

[13] Alan Griffin, "Revising the Social Studies," *Social Education*, October 1963, p. 295.

[14] Norton E. Long, "Political Science," in Gordon B. Turner, ed., *The Social Studies and the Social Sciences* (New York: Harcourt, Brace & World, 1962), p. 100.

[15] Ben W. Lewis, "Economics," in Gordon B. Turner, ed., *The Social Studies and the Social Sciences* (New York: Harcourt, Brace & World, 1962), p. 23.

Historians have always been concerned with the "what" and the "why" in the story of the past. They have encountered the greatest difficulty in assessing the "whys" of man's behavior and group actions. In this area the insights from social psychology and sociology on the principles and modes of personal and social interaction can be of inestimable value. Social science concepts and especially the many and varied methods of social science inquiry make it possible for the historian to look at the past from different and potentially rewarding angles. Professor C. Arnold Anderson wrote in a perceptive analysis of the future of social studies:

> It is possible also to teach pupils something of how social insights use their analytical abstractions, distinguishing from the historian's way of going about his tasks. Thus, a historical account can be shortened and simplified by omissions and telescoping; yet the thread of the story remains intact and meaningful . . . Social scientists simplify the world they deal with précis in a different way. They do not prepare a précis; rather they use "lenses" of different colors with which to look at human actions. Each specialist scrutinizes only threads of certain color in the "seamless web," but what he sees is a meaningful configuration . . . An economist observes the processes by which groups allocate their scarce resources . . . The sociologist focuses on recurrent social relationships . . .[16]

Anderson maintains that only historians can and should make the best use of these social science "lenses" in high school social studies courses. "Only history, among the social disciplines," he concluded, "is fully sensitive to the uniqueness of the configurations of actions and circumstances, the 'accidents' of experience and contact, personal creativity, the intrusions of circumstances."[17]

It would be a mistake to think that the acknowledgment by historians of the importance of social scientific investigations and techniques is of recent vintage. Frederick Jackson Turner asserted:

> no satisfactory understanding of the evolution of this American people is possible without calling into cooperation many sciences and methods hitherto but little used by the American historian. Data from studies in literature and art, politics, economics, sociology, psychology, biology, and physiography, all must be used. The method of the statistician as well as that of the critic of evidence is absolutely essential.[18]

It makes no sense to argue, as is done so often, for the introduction of political science or of economics into the social studies curriculum, on the

---

[16] C. Arnold Anderson, "A New Frame for the Social Sciences," *The School Review*, Vol. 72, No. 4 (Winter 1964), p. 429.

[17] *Ibid.*, p. 421.

[18] Frederick Jackson Turner, *The Significance of Sections in American History* (New York: Holt, Rinehart & Winston, 1932), p. 20. Turner wrote this passage in 1904.

basis that the study of these disciplines will provide students with the intellectual tools to deal with the problems of contemporary society and with their own personal affairs. History, it is often said, deals with the past, with "dry facts and dates," and therefore is of little use in understanding and in the search for solutions of problems besetting contemporary society. Therefore, it is suggested with almost monotonous regularity that the study of economics will help the future citizen to be wise in his investments or that the study of political science will make him cast his votes with intelligence and sophistication. The advocates of this utilitarian functionalism of the social sciences have somehow failed to note that the social scientists have vigorously denied the validity of such claims. Like their colleagues in history, leading sociologists, economists, and political scientists reject the crude and oversimplified theory of a direct transfer from learning to application and behavior. A prominent sociologist, Professor Gresham M. Sykes of Dartmouth College, decried the utilitarian approach to the study of sociology.

> Many college and university teachers of sociology are not primarily interested in "educating citizens" and many believe that the high school can perform a disservice by placing too heavy an emphasis on the utilitarian aspects of the social studies. For the professional sociologist, his discipline is . . . a science of human behavior . . . the professional sociologist is happy if a student becomes a better citizen . . . But the professional sociologist is also convinced that if his discipline is treated mainly as a means to an end . . . , his discipline will eventually be weakened and the student will be short-changed.[19]

Professor Evron M. Kirkpatrick, Executive Director of the American Political Science Association, disposed of the applied aspects of the study of political science briefly but succinctly. Political science, he wrote

> is an intellectual discipline, a body of knowledge about the political behavior of human beings. Its relevance to good citizenship is approximately the same as the relevance of economics to being a prudent consumer. Fortunately, it is possible to be a good citizen and know nothing about the methods or substance of the study of politics, just as it is possible to buy intelligently without regard to economic theory.[20]

Similarly, a number of leading social scientists have protested the "adoption" of various social science materials, including findings of research studies, to fit the short-range goals of social studies curriculum planners.

---

[19] Gresham M. Sykes, "Sociology," in Gordon B. Turner, ed., *The Social Studies and the Social Sciences* (New York: Harcourt, Brace & World, 1962), p. 158.
[20] Evron M. Kirkpatrick and Jeane J. Kirkpatrick, "Political Science," in Erling Hunt, ed., *High School Social Studies Perspectives* (Boston: Houghton Mifflin Co., 1962), p. 103.

They have protested, often in vain, that such "adoptions" for high school use have often distorted or violated the inner scholarly integrity of the book, document, or report of a scientific investigation.

We have already alluded to another claim made by some writers on social studies curriculum who make the invidious comparison between historians who are either unable or unwilling to make predictions or even broad generalizations and the social scientists who stress uniformities in social behavior, formulate universal propositions, and make scientific predictions. It has already been said that most uniformities that are discovered, while important, mainly concern minor problems. Macrosociology—large issues such as peace and war, freedom and compulsion—are singularly resistant to generalizing or broad scientific laws. The macroproblems in sociology and political science have not proven themselves amenable to Weber's and Durkheim's approach which ignores historical development and perspective and which abstracts from the reality of history those simple facts which are useful in arriving at a generalization which in turn can be proposed as a scientific law.

As to predictions of future developments, many leading social scientists seem to be ready to parallel the saying that "history must not be confused with prophecy." When Professors Hans J. Morgenthau and Zbigniew Brzezinski, both distinguished political scientists, after a thorough analysis of the conflict in Viet Nam came to opposite predictions of the results of U.S. policy, or when Professors John Galbraith and Milton Friedman, both leading economists, counsel diametrically opposite policies for fighting inflation, one may be pardoned a healthy dose of scepticism about the scientific validity of the predictions of the social scientists. Like the predictions of the historians, they are educated guesses. "Social scientists, we may conclude," writes Barrington Moore, Jr., "condemn themselves to unnecessary frustrations by trying to erect an intellectual structure that will permit predictions in the manner of the natural sciences. Meanwhile, preoccupied with its efforts to become 'scientific,' social science overlooks more important and pressing tasks."[21]

The struggle within political science between "behaviorists" and "traditionalists" should prove to be instructive to the uninformed who continue to talk and write about the scientism of the social sciences in contradistinction to the guesswork and the unscientific nature of history. The "behaviorists" demand that political science rely almost exclusively on rigorous and systematic empiricism and that it use more statistics, graphs, charts, and mathematical models in political analysis. They look down on the

---

[21] Barrington Moore, Jr., *Political Power and Social Theory* (Cambridge: Harvard Univ. Press, 1958), p. 159.

"think" methods of the traditionalist political scientists. The "traditionalists," led by Leo Strauss, Harold Lasswell, and Hans Morgenthau, have vigorously denounced the scientific pretensions of their behaviorist colleagues. The political scientist (like his colleagues in history) must still rely basically on his knowledge of the political world and political behavior, on commonsense and intuition. Writing about this struggle within the family, two political scientists pointed to the weaknesses of the behaviorist position. Curiously, in citing these weaknesses they have actually echoed the doubts often expressed by historians about the scientific nature of the social sciences. They wrote:

> . . . Something of a battle *does* rage over the new political science. The chief attack on it has come from those within the discipline who doubt the ability of empirical method to discover enough about political men and institutions to develop theoretical propositions. They point to the almost infinite complexity of human behavior and to the special difficulty of knowing human attitudes and motivations. They argue the inability of scholars to subject political phenomena to controlled experiments in the way he might if his actors were rats or primates. They note, too, that humans know when they are being studied and may adjust their behavior as a result . . . Above all, they argue that the scholar cannot achieve the same objectivity and detachment when his concern is political behavior as he may when it is the behavior of fruit flies or an isotope of carbon.[22]

Echoing the charges leveled by the social analysis sociologists and macrosociologists against each other, the "traditionalists" accuse their behaviorist colleagues in political science of frittering away their time and resources on the study of the obvious and the trivial to the neglect of the important, pressing political questions.

The great value of the study of selected concepts from the social sciences and the occasional use of their methods of inquiry in high school social studies lies in the use of the different social science "lenses" (using the term of C. Arnold Anderson) when examining historical events or contemporary social problems. Each social science asks different questions which almost automatically call for a different approach to the problem under study. Social scientists and historians have almost an infinite agenda of problems which they could study with great profit by pooling their insights and techniques of inquiry. We need more study and better understanding of the origins and phases of development of rural and urban communities, of the nature of political organization, of the political personality, of the stages and processes of the growth and decay of political units, of the dynamic in-

---

[22] Francis J. Sarauf and Charles S. Hyneman, *Political Science an Informal Overview*, The Charles Merrill Social Science Seminar Series, Raymond H. Muessig and Vincent R. Rogers, editors (Columbus, Ohio, 1965), p. 17.

terrelationships between various economic centers and between the economic "haves" and "have nots," of the impact of technology and modernization on societies past and present, of the impact of social class, social mobility, and social movements, of the impact of mass communication on modern societies, and of the role of race and racial prejudice during the various stages of human development. Of course, this is an incomplete list. It is merely intended to indicate some topics that social studies teachers may wish to study with the use of "lenses" from the appropriate social sciences.

It is important and potentially helpful to remember that while each of the social sciences has developed its own particular terms and even its "jargon," most social science concepts are truly interdisciplinary. "Class," "status," and "elite," for instance, are concepts freely used by sociologists, anthropologists, political scientists, and economists. However, in each science the concept is used in a different way and context, and each has produced a useful body of research results explaining the meaning of these concepts for a better understanding of human behavior and society. There is little duplication in this research among the social sciences. "Elite" to a political scientist means primarily the elite which holds the political power and prestige in the society, while "elite" to a sociologist would be more important as the apex in the ladder of social mobility. Both definitions are valuable to a historian when he tries to explain to his students the operation of the "elite" in the Greek democracy or in Rome in the age of Caesar or Augustus. There is great value in the acceptance of the interdisciplinary nature of concepts. "Once the priority of the concept to the discipline is recognized," Professor Edward N. Saveth argued,

> much of the argument among educators as to the relationship between history and the (social science) disciplines and the proper way of integrating them in school curricula is beside the point. Current efforts to cope with curricula, especially in high schools, generally result in a tug of war between teachers of history and teachers of social sciences . . . as to how much of the subject matter of history and the disciplines is to be included. The premises of this argument are false once the concepts are understood as being, by their nature, interdisciplinary and having a theoretical development in more than one social science. Much more could be accomplished if the social science teachers recognized that they were teaching concepts rather than disciplines and that the concept is illustrated best by concrete historical problems.[23]

A number of American historians have already fruitfully applied social science concepts and modes of inquiry to the study of history. Many of them have acknowledged that the application of insights and techniques

---

[23] Edward N. Saveth, ed., *American History and the Social Sciences* (New York: Free Press of Glencoe, 1964), p. 16.

from sociology, economics, political science, and anthropology have been very helpful to them in the study of the past. They have borrowed from the social scientists more sophisticated sampling techniques and have used social science terminology by asking questions about social mobility, role playing, status, social mobility, categories, and model building. Anthropologists have taught historians to become more aware of the evolutionary hypothesis in history and of the pitfalls of ethnocentrism. Historians with knowledge about the evolutionary processes, about the variety of cultures, and about race have avoided making many false assumptions about these subjects. Anthropology, which includes archeology, has given historians a deeper understanding of the early development of man which is indispensable to an effective study of ancient history. Historical writing has benefited from anthropological cross-cultural comparative studies. These studies have shown that while geographically scattered human beings have developed different cultural patterns, different modes of behavior, and different ways of believing, there is a large, discernible common area of regularity and similarity within that diversity.

The anthropological concept of culture as the total way of life of a people can be of great value to the social studies teacher. This concept when used in an anthropological analysis of, for example, Greek culture would include a look at Greek customs, housing, food, religion, beliefs, values, and attitudes. A typically anthropological comparison of the Greek culture with the Roman culture would be of great value to high school students. History teachers may accept or even partially reject the anthropologist's contention that all cultures are learned and acquired rather than innate or intuitive, but they would do well to allow their students an insight into the ways in which cultures are transmitted from generation to generation in various societies. Insight gained from such inquiries would help our students to overcome or at least control their deeply ingrained Western cultural bias and enable them to study with profit non-Western civilizations. An anthropologist has observed:

> If you saw a man spitting at another you would infer that he was expressing contempt for the victim. Well, that would hold in France, but you would be all wrong if it happened in East Africa among the Jagga Negroes. There spitting is a kind of blessing in critical situations, and a medicine man will spit four times on a patient or a newborn babe."[24]

Another anthropologist stated the problem this way:

> Each society of men possesses its own distinctive culture, so that the members of one society behave differently in some significant respect from the

---

[24] Robert Lowie, *Are We Civilized?* (New York: The Macmillan Co., 1929), p. 3.

members of every other society. We observe for instance, that the Andaman Islander from the Indian Ocean weeps with ceremonial copiousness when he greets a friend or a relative after a long absence; a Frenchman kisses his comrade on both cheeks; while we content ourselves with seizing his right hand to agitate it with a pumping motion.[25]

An understanding of or at least a respectful attention paid to cultural diversity would prove to be an enlightening and instructive experience to our students in the study of Commodore Perry's expedition to Japan or an inquiry into British rule in India. Many similar instances could, of course, be cited.

The role of cultural change, of the process of innovation in society, of a new mode of behavior, or the elimination or modification of old traits or cultural mores can be of inestimable value to the social studies teacher. The cultural revolution wrought in Turkey in the 1920's by Kemal Ataturk can be better understood in all its manifold and lasting implications by the application of the concept of cultural change. The same is true of the study of the new independent countries in Africa. Our students have much to gain from a deeper understanding of the complexities that usually accompany cultural change. They should understand that cultural innovation, cultural borrowing among cultures, or cultural integration are never simple or absolute processes. This realization would help to understand the difficulties and uncertainties entailed in the work of the Alliance for Progress in Latin America. They would learn to look more intelligently at the problem of political and economic reforms, technological modernization, or population control in the underdeveloped countries. Professor George Peter Murdock wrote:

> Certain anthropologists have erroneously assumed that the elements of any culture are in a state of nearly perfect integration, or equilibrium, at all times. Actually, however, perfect equilibrium is never achieved or even approached. The adjustment of other elements of culture to an innovation, and of it to them, requires time—often years or even generations . . . At any given time, therefore, a culture exhibits numerous instances of uncompleted integrative processes. . . .[26]

The truth of this observation becomes quite clear when one attempts to analyze the caste system in India, the status of women in Turkey, or the role of the family in Japan.

Many historians have paid handsome tribute to their indebtedness to

---

[25] E. Adamson Hoebel, "The Nature of Culture," in Harry L. Shapiro, ed., *Man, Culture and Society* (New York: Oxford Univ. Press, 1956), p. 168.
[26] George Peter Murdock, "How Culture Changes," in Harry L. Shapiro, ed., *Man, Culture and Society* (New York: Oxford Univ. Press, 1956), p. 260. Also see Ralph Linton, *The Tree of Culture* (New York: Alfred A. Knopf, 1959).

sociology. Professor Richard Hofstadter has gratefully acknowledged his debt to sociological insights and concepts.

It would, of course, be folly for any social studies teacher to accept Hofstadter's theories only because he uses psychological and sociological terms like "status alienation," "power," and "class." There is nothing magic in these concepts by themselves and use of them does not assure the soundness of a new historical interpretation. The importance of Hofstadter's approach is its newness and freshness. It allows the history teacher to look at a complex historical situation and to try to understand complex human beings from a new angle and with new tools. In addition, since the new approach uses terms and images (like "status," "jealousy," "power") close to the personal experience of high school students, their motivation and interest in the study may be heightened.

William L. Langer and H. Stuart Hughes seem to be fascinated by the potential contribution of psychoanalysis to history and especially to the field of biography. They agree that historians have, on the whole, ignored, in the words of Erik Ericson, "the fateful function of childhood in the fabric of society." David Donald has acknowledged his debt to frequent consultations of psychoanalysts in the process of writing his biography of Charles Sumner.[27] Professor Hughes sees a great affinity between historians and psychoanalysts.[28] Hughes suggested, apparently quite seriously, that at least some Ph.D. candidates in history should go through the process of psychoanalysis in order to be prepared to use psychoanalytical insights in their historical investigations.

The political science "lens" in the social studies and especially in the study of American history, civics, and world history can provide a much needed deeper understanding of political philosophies, political institutions, and politics. Broader political understanding is, of course, no royal road to responsible and good citizenship, and it is time that all the prattle to that effect should stop. Good citizens, as Plato, Aristotle, Aquinas, and Rousseau have told us, are formed by multiple influences from their birth. Political science courses do not make good and responsible citizens—many of the world's tyrants and dictators including Hitler, Lenin, Stalin, and Mussolini had an excellent background in political science. In fact, important studies in political socialization, which includes the whole area of the formation of values and attitudes in the area of politics, have indicated that these values and attitudes are acquired and formed largely by imitation in early childhood.

---

[27] David Donald, *Charles Sumner and the Coming of the Civil War* (New York: Alfred A. Knopf, 1960).

[28] H. Stuart Hughes, *History as Art and as Science* (New York: Harper & Row, 1964), p. 47.

Knowledge of basic concepts and techniques of inquiry in political science can help in educating our youth to understand political issues and vote more intelligently (although we can not guarantee or much less measure this effect). Some political scientists would reject even this modest expectation. Writing about the traditional belief that instruction in politics, government, and the political process can produce "better" citizens, two political scientists said:

> Without asserting that education in the field of government, politics and public policy has no role to play in helping form better citizens, we feel required to state at the outset, in the interests of clarity, that we regard this tradition and the beliefs on which it is based as mistaken and misleading: first, because it is based on a distorted conception of how citizens are made; second, because it is based on a distorted conception of democracy; and third, because it is based on a misconception of political science.[29]

However, there is no dispute about the role that political science can play in adding important new dimensions to the study of history. A case study in depth about *decision-making* in political affairs can provide the student with a valuable tool in the understanding of President William McKinley's tortured decision to make war on Spain, Prime Minister Neville Chamberlain's decision to sign the Munich pact, or President John F. Kennedy's decision to order the Bay of Pigs invasion of Cuba. *Comparative government,* a major division of political science, can be of invaluable aid in the study of American political institutions. The study of Congress, its structure, role, and relation to the other branches of our government, can become more intelligible and interesting if studied in comparison with the British Parliament. The typically American principle of separation of powers comes out in sharp focus when the students realize that Cabinet members in England must be members of Parliament (or in rare cases members of the House of Lords), while American Cabinet members cannot be members of Congress and, in fact, may come to the Capitol in their official capacities only when summoned to testify or when invited to hear the President or a foreign dignitary address Congress.

An understanding of the concepts of the political *elite* is essential to a meaningful study of history. It is important for our students to know that in all societies—democratic, partly democratic, and totalitarian—there is distribution of available values in the area of deference, income, and safety, as Harold Lasswell puts it, "Those who get the most are elite; the rest are mass."[30] A social studies teacher who wants to impart to his students an

---

[29] Evron M. Kirkpatrick and Jeane J. Kirkpatrick, "Political Science," in Erling Hunt, ed., *High School Social Studies Perspectives* (Boston: Houghton Mifflin Co., 1962), p. 100.
[30] Harold Lasswell, *Politics, What, When, How?* (Cleveland: World Publishing Co., 1963), p. 13.

understanding of the social and political structure of the antebellum South, so essential to the understanding of the Civil War and Reconstruction, would be well advised to learn what political scientists have to say about the behavior of political elites. The increasingly uncompromising attitudes of the Southern planter aristocracy on the inviolate nature of slavery as the "sacred institution" and the relentless drive toward secession becomes much clearer to students if they see these trends in the light of Lasswell's observation that "the fate of an elite is profoundly affected by the ways it manipulates the environment; that is to say, by the use of violence, goods, symbols, practices."[31] How the Southern white elite used the press, the Ku Klux Klan, the Mothers' Little Helpers, and the slogans of Caucasian solidarity to cripple and eventually topple the Reconstruction governments is a fascinating study of how a threatened elite managed to retain its status and power.

People of Plenty by David Potter is an ambitious and extensive effort by a prominent historian to apply the concepts and methods of the behavioral sciences to the examination of an historical problem.[32] Professor Potter focuses his study on the definition, description, and analysis of our national character. He is convinced that historians have repeatedly failed to write convincingly about man, his nature, and his motives because they have been neither willing nor able to form generalizations about human behavior from the mass of data they have accumulated. On the other hand, social scientists, according to Potter, have often neglected the importance of historical perspective and the variety of outside forces that usually impinge on important historical events.

Historians, Potter charges, have used the concept of national character too loosely and imprecisely. They have never made a systematic attempt to provide a rationale for this basic concept or to validate its use by agreeing about what constitutes national character. Consequently, they have often confused national traits with race traits, made no distinction between traits of character, traits of behavior, and cultural traits, nor have they made due allowance for the fact that traits considered quite basic to the national character of a particular nation are subject to marked and rapid changes. In Potter's view, social scientists have done much better in writing about national character. "A more factual demonstration of the reality of national character," Potter writes, "and a more scientific approach to the concept are being worked out, and, though the grounds on which it is defended are controversial, they are far more tenable than any in the past. The expo-

---

[31] *Ibid.*, p. 27.
[32] David Potter, *People of Plenty* (Chicago: Univ. of Chicago Press, 1964).

nents of this new interpretation are primarily the behavioral scientists . . . ."[33] Anthropologists and sociologists who have written about national character, unlike the historians, have recognized that national character is not a separate phenomenon but a particular manifestation of group character and group behavior. Using this and other insights from social science investigations, Potter arrives at a new definition of national character which he considers much more scientific and therefore more tenable.

> National character is a changing and not a fixed quality, for the culture itself changes; it means also that national character varies from one individual to another, partly because no two personalities are enough alike to receive the impact of the culture in precisely the same way, but even more because culture assigns diverse roles to various classes of individuals in the society.[34]

Professor Potter undoubtedly does not expect all historians to accept his new definition of the concept of national character. Some of them may well argue that while it is true that national character is subject to change, the changes take place over a long period of time and thus one may be well justified in speaking of a national character of Germans, Russians, or Turks over the span of many generations. The second part of Potter's definition, which postulates that individual citizens of a nation may or may not possess the traits attributed to their national group, is rather obvious and should not be considered a particular insight obtained from behavioral sciences. More valid and valuable are the research findings on the traits of the American national character of three social scientists—Margaret Mead, the anthropologist, David Riesman, the sociologist, and Karen Horney, the psychoanalyst. Mead isolated mobility and success drive as main components of our national character, Riesman stressed our concern for the opinions of the peer group, and Horney stressed competition and the contradictions and dilemmas in our culture.

Using as his point of departure the assumption that the task of history in relation to the behavioral sciences is "to identify and explain the determinants of the culture, and especially of cultural change,"[35] Potter proceeds to identify the determinant in the formation of the American national character. He concludes that economic abundance can be isolated as this determinant—the decisive factor that has shaped and is still shaping the national character of the people of the United States. This "state of relative abundance, of material plenty," Potter writes, "has been a basic condi-

---

[33] *Ibid.*, p. 31.
[34] *Ibid.*, p. 42.
[35] *Ibid.*, p. 66.

tion of American life and . . . has a pervasive, if undefined, influence upon the American people."[36] It is the factor of economic abundance, the fact that Americans have been and are the "People of Plenty," that explains the traits ascribed to the American national character by Margaret Mead, who focused on mobility and success drive, by David Riesman, who pictured the American as the other-directed man, and by Karen Horney, who spoke of the neuroses of modern Americans caused by the relentless pursuit of material goods, by competitive aggressiveness, and by exaggerated expectations of unlimited freedom.

Potter's book is a brilliant and completely successful attempt to fuse the insights and the "lenses" of both the historian and the social scientist in the examination of a problem of common concern to history and the social sciences. *People of Plenty* has a great deal to suggest to social studies teachers. It makes clear the central function of history as an integrating discipline capable of making good use of concepts and modes of inquiry of the behavioral sciences. A historian and a social studies teacher may, by providing the historical perspective, by isolating the historical factor from the amassed historical data dealing with a complex problem having to do with human motivation, decision-making, and group actions and interactions, find it very useful to seek help from the behavioral sciences. They will pay more attention to social structures and their influence on individual character, to the changing sets of values in various societies, and to the individual's conception of himself. They will also find it useful to consider the role of groups in the society and of the manifold ways in which societies condition their individuals and shape their values, attitudes, and modes of living.

As Potter points out in his successful effort to bring history and the behavioral sciences into fruitful collaboration, the greatest promise of such a combined effort is in the study of man. A better and deeper understanding of how and why man and societal groups act and interact can be of great value in the teaching of history in the program of high school social studies. In addition to the new opportunities to throw a stronger light on many difficult historical dilemmas, the consideration of man's motives and his erratic actions may prove to be of great value, to adolescents, who are vitally concerned with understanding their own motives and drives. The study of the *dramatis personae* in history would be stimulating for them and perhaps even beneficial. Using the insights and knowledge provided by the behavioral sciences, they will find fascinating the intelligent discussion of such questions as:

---

[36] *Ibid.*, p. 67.

1. Why did the young Alexander of Macedon decide to conquer the world and why did he wish to achieve a fusion of cultures and religions?

2. What were the true (and complex) motivations of the Abolitionist leaders like William Lloyd Garrison, Wendell Phillipps, and Gerrit Smith? Were they neurotic quacks or sincere reformers and true enemies of slavery, or both?

3. What were the common and dissimilar elements in the charisma of George Washington, Abraham Lincoln, Peter the Great, Napoleon, and Lenin?

4. What were the motivations of the various groups that joined Theodore Roosevelt's Bull Moose Party in 1912? (Obviously, the study of this fascinating question would require the pooling of resources from history, sociology, economics and social psychology.)

Great benefits can accrue from such a fusion of the specialized perspectives of the social sciences when applied to the study of history. David Potter's *The People of Plenty* provides conclusive proof that this can be done with success.

6

Modes of Inquiry and Methods of Teaching in History and the Social Sciences

Methods of teaching consist of a simple or complex set of procedures used in the teaching process. Some agreed rule governs the choice of these set procedures. The variety of teaching methods is staggering, and while the search for *the one, the best* teaching method will undoubtedly continue and claims for the discovery of this one method will be made, it is safe to assume that competent teachers will always use a variety of teaching methods. Broudy and Palmer have observed that "there are many methods of teaching and, for all we really know, there may be just as many methods of learning."[1] To assume that one or another method of teaching is the most effective under all circumstances is to suggest that we know how students learn best. In truth, our knowledge about the learning process is sketchy and inconclusive. This is not stated in disparagement of the splendid contributions of educational psychology toward our better understanding of the teaching-learning process. Rather, it is a reflection of the difficulty inherent in the clear comprehension of how one complex, changeable hu-

---

[1] Harry S. Broudy and John R. Palmer, *Exemplars of Teaching Method* (Chicago: Univ. of Chicago Press, 1965), p. 9.

man being teaches twenty-five or thirty much younger, but equally complex and changeable humans.

One may also argue that since the ways in which human beings obtain knowledge, perception, and insight about themselves and their environment are so varied and complicated, the ways of imparting knowledge must also be equally varied and often not fully explicable. In current discussions about the social studies there have been repeated attempts to find a relatively easy way to explore the subject of the methods of research in the social sciences.

One of the more popular myths perpetuated by some who have written about the "new" social studies curriculum is based on the assumption that each of the social sciences has its own unique method of inquiry which can be taught to and used by high school students in social studies classes. There is a basic fallacy in this proposition because sociology, anthropology, economics, political science, and social psychology have *many* methods of inquiry and these techniques are often used interchangeably. Professor Benjamin Cox, a thoughtful writer on the social studies, who has long advocated strong concentration on the social sciences, reported an experiment which undoubtedly brought him a great deal of disappointment. He requested a bright group of his students, all social studies teachers, to study the methods of research of leading scholars in the social sciences, to search the relevant literature, and to describe the distinctive modes of inquiry used by each of the social sciences. It was Cox's assumption that "each of the social science disciplines made use of peculiar modes of inquiry distinguishable in some ways from each of the other disciplines."[2] In spite of a diligent search, the students failed to identify the peculiar differences that were assumed to exist between the methods of inquiry of political scientists, economists, and sociologists. Disappointed, Professor Cox expressed his hope that an effort would be made to arrive at "some reasonably definitive descriptions of research methodology in each of the social science disciplines." If he persists in this hope, he will be disappointed. By using a simple, but ingenious investigation, Professor Cox laid to rest a myth and an illusion, and he ought to be content with his achievement. Cox indicated a reason for the lack of success in his investigation. "Human behavior," he wrote, "apparently categorizes itself poorly, for the sociologist must assay unemployment, for example, as he studies the habits of families, just as the economist must assay the habits of families as he studies unemployment."[3] Cox may be entirely correct when he concludes that social studies teachers and their students "remain in their original dark-

---

[2] C. Benjamin Cox, "An Inquiry into Inquiries," *Social Education* (May 1965), pp. 300–302.
[3] *Ibid.*, p. 301.

ness," because they are unable to describe and to differentiate the methodologies of the social sciences and to conduct intelligent and effective research in the social science disciplines as a classroom learning experience.   In fact, there is no reason for them to attempt such an ambitious and far-reaching task.   Neither is it the task or the area of competence of social studies teachers, in Cox's words, "to make qualitative judgments about the facts, principles, and generalizations which are produced for them."   Social studies teachers will have made a good start if they acquaint their students with some of the basic concepts and insights from the accumulated store of social science research and if they occasionally assist their students in the use of one of the many social science modes of inquiry in the study of a particularly complex social or historical problem.

In commenting on Cox's inquiry, Malcolm Collier, the director of the American Anthropological Association's Anthropology Curriculum Study Project, wrote that there is no need to be surprised at the variety of modes of inquiry used by social scientists.   "Each of the social sciences," she wrote, "is a dynamic entity with its own life history of internal change and development.   The social scientists who are the creators of this constant growth and differentiation are themselves never in unanimous agreement about their respective disciplines."[4]   She concluded that the social sciences do not differ greatly in their respective methodologies, but in the questions they ask of their data.   Sociologists, political scientists, anthropologists, and economists have different ways of looking at man and his activities.   They are looking for different answers to different aspects of the human condition and human behavior.   To attain these answers, social scientists use a *variety* of methods and they borrow and interchange modes of inquiry. Consequently, it may be well to put to well-deserved rest the oft-publicized myth that it is possible or even advisable to teach high school students the *separate* modes of inquiry of economics and sociology in order that they may use these methods to attain a broad economic and sociological understanding.   The whole idea is a snare and a delusion.

In many school systems social studies teachers are, on the whole, well-trained and well-educated, but very few of them are competent to teach the expanding and ever changing content and methodologies of any one of the social sciences.   How many teachers are there, even those who have taken a number of courses in anthropology, who are capable of dealing on a high school level with the explosion of knowledge and research in physical, cultural, and political anthropology, not to speak of linguistics, ecology, and archeology, which are also considered branches of anthropology?   "It is naive to believe," wrote a leading economist, "for one moment that any effective response to the drive for economic literacy can be made by teach-

---

[4] Malcolm Collier, "A Question About Questions," *Social Education* (December 1965), p. 555.

ers who are ill at ease, out of date, or just plain wrong in their understanding of basic economic principles."[5]

Recognizing this difficulty, a distinguished group of writers on social studies, including Professors Earl Johnson, Shirley Engle, and Paul Hanna, concluded that social studies must become a discipline with its own content and methodology. They are convinced that "improvement in the quality of beliefs which people hold in the broad areas of life experience is possible, and that such improvement, far from being a result of rigorous intellectual activity in a discipline, is to be reached only through direct experience in examining one's beliefs systematically and holistically."[6] Thus, systematic and holistic examination of one's beliefs, values, and attitudes cannot be attained by a rigorous and effective study of separate disciplines or by the use of separate modes of inquiry from the social science disciplines. The objective of changing and improving the quality of people's beliefs, through the rigid examination of values and through teaching the process of decision-making, can best be achieved by the attempt to "unify and synthesize the social sciences," and by the use of a separate social studies methodology which has "an integrity of its own and operates under rules and procedures that distinguish it from the methodology used in any of the social sciences, requiring intellectual veracity of an exceedingly high order and perfectable only through practice."[7]

It is difficult, if not impossible, to discuss this position intelligently because as yet its advocates have not told us exactly what this new independent social studies mode of inquiry will be and how it will differ from the modes of inquiry in history and the social sciences. Scholars, of course, will differ on what is meant by "intellectual veracity of an exceedingly high order." What has been written so far about the study of values and training in critical thinking and decision-making differs little from the rigorous examination of values and beliefs in the dialogues of Socrates, in the problem-solving methodology espoused by John Dewey, and in Johann Friedrich Herbart's and Samuel Clinton Morrison's steps in inquiry. The integrationists and the synthesizers have also, so far, failed to deal with the question of whether values can be taught and attitudes changed in formal school courses. Numerous studies in value formation and politization point to the crystallization of values and attitudes in early childhood or in lower grades of the elementary school.

Broudy and Palmer pointed out that learning skills, information, and

---

[5] John R. Coleman, "When Secondary School Teacher and College Economist Meet," *The Bulletin of the National Association of Secondary-School Principals*, No. 304 (November 1965), p. 68.

[6] Shirley H. Engle, "Objectives of the Social Studies," in Byron G. Massialas and Frederick J. Smith, eds., *New Challenges in the Social Studies* (Belmont, Calif.: Wadsworth Publishing Co., 1965), p. 12.

[7] *Ibid.*, p. 12.

explanations present a different task for the school than the task of learning to be a certain kind of person. ". . . Becoming brave," they wrote, "or temperate or wise, in short, becoming virtuous, calls for the building of dispositions that are to lie in wait for an opportunity to be exercised throughout one's life. The conditions under which one becomes brave, temperate and wise are not confined to school."[8] Furthermore, the question of "improvement in the quality of beliefs" (using Engle's terms) and the teaching of values brings us to the complex question of who decides when a belief has been "improved" and who selects the "right" values to be taught. Professor Engle is too careful a scholar not to recognize the dilemma. He writes: "A question remains which plagues both those who wish to synthesize the social studies curriculum and those whose goal is the mastery of individual subjects: What beliefs are to be taught (beliefs concerning values are an especially difficult problem here) and on whose authority?"[9] Engle's answer is that the emphasis is not on the kind of values or beliefs that are to be taught or improved, but on the acquisition of a method of inquiry which the student would use in the examination of values, beliefs, and the problems that he will face in life. "To the 'decision-making' group," Engle concludes, "the primary end is perfection of the process of inquiry into questions of value, all of which paints a far different concept of knowledge and a different image of the end product—i.e., the citizen—than is evident in any other position."[10]

Thus, the ground is shifted a bit and we come back to the teaching of a perfected process of inquiry as the chief aim of the social studies. We remain puzzled by the question of why and how this social studies methodology would differ from the historical method of inquiry or from the variety of the modes of inquiry used in the social sciences. It should not be too difficult to prove that if Professor Engle and his colleagues postulate the mastery of critical inquiry—the attitude of suspended judgment or of intelligent doubt as the chief aim in the social studies, it may be possible to achieve this aim by training the students in the use of, for instance, the historical method of investigation, or the sociological method of controlled experimentation.

A critical, skeptical spirit is the very essence of historical writing. A historian must train his mind to be critical and selective. The process of historical investigation has two basic elements: the materials of the past and the critical mind and skills of the historian. Lord Acton asserted that

---

[8] Harry S. Broudy and John R. Palmer, *Exemplars of Teaching Method* (Chicago: Univ. of Chicago Press, 1965), p. 5.

[9] Shirley Engle, "Objectives of the Social Studies," in B. G. Massialas and F. J. Smith, eds., *New Challenges in the Social Studies* (Belmont, Calif.: Wadsworth Publishing Co., 1965), pp. 12, 13.

[10] *Ibid.*, p. 15.

the historical spirit of doubt—in other words, what writers of the social studies have called critical or reflective thinking—is more important than amassed facts. Allan Nevins said: "The beginning of wisdom in history is doubt."[11] We could add, *intelligent* doubt. Thucydides, one of the earliest users of the historical method, told us that when writing the history of the Peloponnesian War, he attempted to check his own bias, thoroughly researching his available data by subjecting it to critical examination and verification. He wrote:

> And with reference to the narrative of events, far from permitting myself to derive it from the first sources that came to hand, I did not even trust my own impressions, but it rests partly on what I saw myself, partly on what others saw for me, the accuracy of the report being always tried by the most severe and detailed tests possible. My conclusions have cost me some labor from the want of coincidence between accounts of the same occurrence by different eyewitnesses, arising sometimes from imperfect memory, sometimes from undue partiality for one side or the other. The absence of romance from my history will, I fear, detract somewhat from its interest; but if it be judged useful by those inquirers who desire an exact knowledge of the past as an aid to the interpretation of the future . . . I shall be content.[12]

Modern writers on the historical method have elaborated on these principles related by the ancient Greek historian, but they have added little. In essence, Thucydides defined the historical method for all future generations of historians.

Historians who followed Thucydides began by assembling historical evidence.

What clay is to the sculptors, so are the "relics" the "traces" or the "sources" left by the past to historians. From these materials, and with the help of his imagination and narrative skill, the historian laboriously attempts to recreate events from the past. This record of the past is always fragmentary, never complete. Since some historical records were left intentionally to create a particular impression on future generations, they are naturally saturated with bias. Many remnants of the past reflect the deeds or thoughts of past generations, but the present day historian approaches them from his particular point of view. The Taj Mahal in India and Westminster Abbey in England, for instance, both have great emotional appeal to history writers.

It must also be remembered that the record of the past is uneven. We have a great deal of information about the early life, accomplishments, and downfall of Sir Walter Raleigh, but what we really know about the life of

---

[11] Allan Nevins, *The Gateway to History* (Garden City, N.Y.: Doubleday & Co., 1962), p. 67.
[12] *Thucydides*, Benjamin Jowett, trans. (Oxford, 1900), Book 1, p. 12.

William Shakespeare can almost be written on a postcard. All that we know about Carthage and Hannibal's struggle with Rome comes to us from obviously biased and fragmentary Latin sources. For some reason, Carthaginians were not interested in leaving a record for future historians. Thus, any history of Carthage is full of conjectures and more or less educated guesses.

The traces of the past most useful to historians are written records. These records, often compiled with much effort, expense, and labor, favor unusual events and happenings and often ignore the life of the ordinary people who have always comprised the great majority of mankind. The variety of materials which are the working tools of historians is truly staggering. It includes physical remains like ruins (including the Pyramids, the Kensington Stone and the Viking's Ruins and Smithy in Epaves Bay in Newfoundland), cave paintings (like those in the Cavern of Font-de-Gaume in France or at Altamira in northern Spain), cooking utensils, potsherds, weapons, chiseled stones, coins, and sculptures. Of great importance, of course, are ancient documents, like papyri, inscriptions on stones, and cuneiform writing. Again, it must be emphasized that these materials are not history, but are the *traces* of history, the raw materials from which history may be written. This body of evidence—of data on which the historian has to rely—is quite different from the data and evidence used by scientists. Unlike the chemist, the geologist, the biologist, the historian cannot subject his data to scientific experimentation. He has no control over his materials—he cannot increase or decrease the amount of oxygen or acid in his experiment and he cannot repeat his experiments. Even more important, a historian, unlike a natural scientist, cannot, and perhaps should not, stand impersonally aloof in relation to his work. No English historian is completely objective when writing about the execution of Charles II by Cromwell's troops, nor can an American historian be completely dispassionate in writing about the Civil War and Reconstruction.

With the passage of time, man left more and more extensive collections of documents in the form of parchment manuscripts (like the recently discovered Dead Sea Scrolls), chronicles, memoirs, official documents, and collections of private letters and papers. These documents are usually stored in libraries, archives, and museums, where the historian spends much of his time. In the United States, two of the great repositories of public documents and private collections of papers are the National Archives and the Library of Congress, both in Washington, D.C. A number of leading universities also house important collections of papers and documents.

Historical sources can be divided into two basic kinds: *primary sources,* which consist of testimony of eyewitnesses to a particular event (for instance, a memoir, a reporter's directly observed account in a newspaper, or a contemporary letter), and *secondary sources,* which are testimonies of anyone who is not an eyewitness. Only a contemporary of an historical event can produce a primary source. This does not mean that primary sources as such are necessarily more reliable and trustworthy than secondary sources. Many diaries, which are primary sources, are filled with distortions or even lies, whether intentional or unintentional. The famous diary of Gideon Welles, Secretary of the Navy under Abraham Lincoln and Andrew Johnson, is a valuable and interesting historical source, but hardly reliable for the history of the relations of Lincoln with Congress or for the story of the conflict between President Johnson and the Republican majority in the House and the Senate. On the other hand, some secondary source which is removed from the event itself, may be quite reliable because of its detachment.

An erroneous assumption, often made by those who know little of the problems of writing history, suggests that the study of more or less contemporary events yields more reliable results than the study of happenings long past. Consequently, it is often proposed that the study in high school social studies of contemporary sociological, economic, or political problems like race riots, crime, inflationary trends, or voting patterns would be of far greater value, far more reliable, and far more "scientific" than the study of history. First, it is unfortunately true that sociological studies of race riots have come up with few, if any, reliable causes for the riots and suggestions for preventing future race riots have differed little, if at all, from those made by historians, teachers, and politicians. For many years economists have studied ways of preventing inflation and have never failed to offer the government contradictory advice. Political scientists study the voting patterns of many elections, but are often mistaken in some of their assumptions and predictions, especially in national elections. All this is not said to disparage or belittle these investigations, because they are important and have yielded new information on all the above-mentioned problems. However, these investigations are neither more important, more reliable, nor more "scientific" than historical research into the causes of World War I, the role and influence of the Populists, or the reasons why John Wilkes Booth murdered Abraham Lincoln.

Those who see a magic advantage in the study of contemporary problems and who belittle the place of the study of history because of its alleged unrelatedness to present societal issues, would do well to reflect on the attempt to write a reliable story of the unfortunate Bay of Pigs invasion of Cuba by the United States in 1962. It seems that since the invasion was a contemporary event and since many of the main figures involved were alive and apparently eager to tell their version of the event, that the reconstruction of the invasion of Cuba by the Cuban exiles, supported by U.S. forces, would be a relatively easy task. Just the opposite is true. Two major books containing detailed accounts of the invasion have appeared. One was written by Theodore Sorenson, special assistant to President John F. Kennedy, who approved the operation, and the other by Arthur Schlesinger, Jr., a professional historian and a close aide of Kennedy.[13] A third account, given in testimony to a Congressional committee, came from Richard M. Bissell, who directed the Central Intelligence Agency participation in the invasion.

Without going into details, the three men give differing accounts about President Kennedy's actions during the invasion. One account states that the operation was doomed from the start, and another is adamant in insisting that the cancellation of a massive air strike on Cuba would have assured success. Two of the writers would have us believe that President Kennedy was thoroughly misled by information received from the military and intelligence experts, while the third insists that the information was completely reliable. The three eyewitnesses quote the President in statements made to each of them which are contradictory. A distinguished military analyst, S. L. A. Marshall, commented on these conflicting reports:

> All are men of character, talent and integrity, true insiders who worked right next to the seats of the mighty, absorbed all secrets through osmosis, and therefore collectively should be able to give us the real lowdown. A pity, but the three accounts do not agree among themselves, and where they chance to coincide, their unanimity but raises questions which await answers.[14]

The fact is that a reasonably true account, or at least an approximately true account about the Bay of Pigs invasion, will have to be written by a future historian long after the lifetime of the main participants. Then a dispassionate appraisal of the disastrous adventure may be possible.

As first outlined by Thucydides a historical investigation has to proceed in sequence.

The historical method involves a number of steps which the historian follows:

1. The selection of the subject for investigation. The historian must ascertain who and what anyone else has written on the subject in order to avoid duplication of effort.

2. The collection of as many of the printed, written, and oral materials bearing on the subject as possible.

3. The verification of the sources as to their genuineness and veracity.

4. The extraction and organization of the data pertinent to the subject under investigation.

---

13 Theodore Sorenson, *Kennedy* (New York: Harper & Row, 1965) and Arthur M. Schlesinger, Jr., *A Thousand Days: John F. Kennedy in the White House* (Boston: Houghton Mifflin Co., 1965).

14 Chicago *Sun-Times*, August 8, 1965, p. 28.

5. The commitment of the findings into a meaningful and interesting historical narrative.

Step number three, the process of verification, is the most difficult and the most exacting. Applying external criticism, the author tests the authenticity of the document. He must ask himself whether the document is genuine or a forgery. Forgery of historical documents is not an uncommon occurrence. There are hundreds of forged letters of Franklin, Jefferson, Washington, and Lincoln in circulation, many of them the work of Robert Spring, the greatest autograph forger of all times. Occasionally, historians have discovered that diaries have been tampered with and additional entries made at later dates, either by the diarist himself or by a friend or relative eager to "correct" the historical record or to improve the image of the diary keeper.

Internal criticism of a document concerns the establishment of its credibility. Is the document trustworthy? Are the facts or the sequence of events it relates reliable? In answering these questions, the historian must attempt to establish the reliability of the author from other sources. He must establish the date when the document was written in order to understand the circumstances surrounding it and to find out why a particular diary entry was made. Internal criticism also involves ascertaining, if possible, whether the author of a particular document was able to be a reliable witness to an event. If he was hundreds of miles away from Washington at the time of a dispute in the White House his report would, of course, be suspect. Even more important is to ascertain whether the author was prevented from telling the truth by his own emotional bias. Colonel House, writing after his abrupt dismissal from the inner circle of Woodrow Wilson, would not be the most reliable source in appraising President Wilson's thoughts and actions.

The historical method, Professor Louis Gottschalk observed, may be applied to the subject matter of any discipline to ascertain facts and to obtain a useful historical perspective. But the method has, of course, a special significance for the historian.

> The historian applies the historical method of evidence that has survived from the past and from it accumulates whatever credible data he can. These data may be used by the philosopher, the political scientist, the sociologist, the literary critic or the physicist to construct a history of thought, of political institutions, of social customs, of literature, of physics.[15]

This point is well taken. Historians should make use of the methods of inquiry perfected by the social sciences, like sampling, classification, and interview in the study of history, but it is also important for the social sci-

---

[15] Louis Gottschalk, *Understanding History* (New York: Alfred A. Knopf, 1950), p. 30.

entists to take advantage of the historical method in their own investigations. The social scientists may not always welcome the collaboration of the historians, but such a cooperation may be very useful. As Gottschalk points out, the historian often "provides a check upon the validity of social science concepts for the past. Social scientists, impatient with the historian who rejects their most favored concepts because he knows exceptions, would do well to remember that the health of science depends upon its ability to withstand challenge to its law and to reject or revise those successfully challenged."[16] An increasing number of social scientists acknowledge the importance of historical perspective and the historical method of testing evidence.

The intellectual integrity of the historian is tested during the fifth step—the writing stage. He may have to modify or discard his favorite hypotheses and theories in the light of evidence laboriously accumulated. The historical narrative, which includes the recital of the discovered facts and their interpretation, in which some imaginative reconstruction is indispensable, is of course much more subjective than the previous step the historian followed in using the historical method. In writing his narrative, the historian selects for inclusion certain facts and events. This process of selection is, of course, influenced by his education, social and economic status, and political views. It is the realization of the limits of his objectivity and scientism that makes the historian realize that absolute knowledge and truth are unobtainable in history. No wonder he is skeptical about the ability of his colleagues in the social sciences to stake a better claim to foolproof findings than he can.

Like any other method of inquiry, the historical method has a number of serious weaknesses. Data are often scarce, although this fact does not always deter historians. Scanty records and the completely inadequate evidence have not prevented some historians from writing of the Carthaginians and Etruscans. It has often been said that there are few hard facts in history, like the fact that Andrew Johnson's conviction failed by one vote. Most facts are facts because, as Carl Becker said, the historian by selecting them from the mass of evidence has subjectively made them *his* facts. At best, the attempt by the historian to recreate emotions, complex personality drives, and passions can only be partly successful. No historian can give a final and completely satisfactory answer to the reasons for the personal hatred between Woodrow Wilson and Henry Cabot Lodge, or the obsession of Andrew Johnson with rich Southern planters, or the psychological inability of General George B. McClellan to mount a military offensive.

---

[16] *Ibid.*, p. 255.

Historians as a rule have neglected, and still neglect, the impact of science and technology on history. Scientist and novelist C. P. Snow, who complained about the culture-gap between scientists and humanists, remarked that the steam engine helped shape the modern world at least as much as Napoleon and Adam Smith, but only rarely do historians admit the fact. The statement is obviously an exaggeration, but historians have until recently paid little attention to art, science, and technology. William H. McNeill, in his *The Rise of the West,* was not guilty of this omission and thereby greatly enhanced the importance and the influence of his study. The infusion of selected concepts and modes of inquiry from the social and even from natural sciences into the teaching of history on a high school level, may make it possible for many history courses to go beyond political history.

Historians can, with some justice, be criticized for passing historical judgments without sufficient evidence. The practice of establishing motives or finding a causal relationship on the basis of one footnoted reference to a letter or to a single speech is all too prevalent. An example is the following statement, commenting on the practice of some Northern states of naming agents to serve as liaison between the governors and the soldiers serving from the states in the Union Army: "Democrats sometimes dubbed the agents "political commissars" and charged Republicans with trying to protect the soldiers' political conscience from Democratic contamination."[17] In support of this serious charge allegedly leveled by the national Democratic party, the writer cites one source in one footnote, "*Madison Patriot, November 17, 1862.*" Thus, the entire statement is based on one reference to one rather obscure Democratic newspaper. On the basis of this evidence, the author could only have said: "One Democratic paper dubbed the agents, etc. . . ." Arthur Schlesinger, Jr., wrote disarmingly about the limitations of historical judgments:

Nothing in my experience of working for Kennedy was more chastening than my attempt to penetrate into the process of decision. In retrospect, I shudder a little when I think how confidently I have analyzed decisions in the ages of Jackson and Roosevelt, traced influences, assigned motives, evaluated roles, allocated responsibilities and, in short, transformed a disheveled and murky evolution into a tidy and orderly transaction. The sad fact is, that in many cases, the basic evidence for the historian's reconstruction of the really hard cases does really not exist—and the evidence that does exist is often incomplete, misleading or erroneous.[18]

---

[17] Frank L. Klement, *The Copperheads in the Middle West* (Chicago: Univ. of Chicago Press, 1960), p. 213. This is otherwise an excellent book. The example cited was merely used to illustrate the point.

[18] New York *Times,* Magazine Section, November 21, 1965.

Professor Martin Duberman of Yale, in an article entitled "The Limitations of History," frankly and perceptively discussed the imperfections and weaknesses of the historical method. He maintains that historians have been unaware of the distinction between human behavior and human personality. They are very competent in describing the past behavior of their heroes, but make no attempt to penetrate the inner world, the private thoughts, visions, passions, and frustrations of the individuals, the world that really constitutes their personalities. The external actions of the individual may or may not mirror or even give a clue to that inner personality. Duberman asks, "How can we fully understand past actions without fully understanding what occasioned them?"[19]

We have, Duberman reminds us, many biographies of Washington but we know precious little about Washington's inner thoughts, passions, and emotions. This neglect of the entire area of feelings and emotions has led many historians to footnote pedantry to the neglect of descriptive, evocative history. Duberman wrote:

> I am concerned that our analytic history is so devoid of evocative description that where it nourishes at all, it nourishes only the intellect. We seem willing to put up with any amount of pedestrian detail so long as it is concrete, but we are impatient with it when included "merely" to capture mood and evoke feeling. We distrust detail that speaks to our emotions, but not when it stultifies them; we seem suspicious of historians who excite us, but not of those who bore us.[20]

These are strong words, but important ones. Moral relativism, the dislike of any moral or emotional commitment on the part of the historian, is a fact of life in the historical profession. Luckily, more voices of protest are being raised against those who would always look for sinister motives of political or economic gain for any action indicating human compassion or noble ideas. It is still not entirely fashionable to maintain that abolitionists like William Lloyd Garrison and Wendell Phillipps were sincere in their detestation of slavery and not irresponsible fanatics, or to suggest that Abraham Lincoln issued the Emancipation Proclamation not only as a military measure, but also because he hated slavery, or to hold that Thaddeus Stevens wanted the South reconstructed not only to assure the continued ascendancy of the Republican party, but because he considered it his sacred obligation to help protect the personal safety and the rights of the Negro freedmen. The "tyranny of the footnotes" somehow prevents many modern historians from expressing their personal commitment and their moral

---

[19] Martin Duberman, "The Limitations of History," *The Antioch Review* (Summer 1965), p. 295.
[20] *Ibid.*, p. 295.

judgment, which if given after a thorough verification of the factual data (as selected and interpreted by the individual historian), is the task which the historian should not avoid.   Samuel Eliot Morison's standing as a historian has not been affected by his strong habit of making value judgments on matters large and small; in fact, his popularity has been enhanced by it.

The methods of inquiry used in the social sciences have much in common with the historical method.   They are all essentially scientific inquiries based on the rule defined by Auguste Comte that demanded the subordination of imagination to observation.   In the *positive* or scientific stage of man's intellectual development, Comte maintained that phenomena are explained by observation, hypothesis, and experimentation.   The advantages enjoyed by the social scientists over the historians are that they can use direct, empirical observation and that they have the opportunity to conduct controlled experiments.   Social scientists may observe certain phenomena under different conditions which they can often control.   They may then use sampling, polling, weighing, measuring, and classifying methods to study the phenomena.   The final stage is the attempt to generalize, to find patterns of similarity or differentiation, the attempt to formulate laws and make predictions.   The advantages of the social scientist over the historian are real, but ought not to be exaggerated.   Man and especially man in society is not an easy subject of study.   Much of the human phenomena that the social scientist observes are fragmentary, volatile, and mutable, and generalizations and predictions drawn from them are often questionable. The difficulty is often compounded because the perceptions of the social scientist of observed phenomena are highly colored by his own educational and cultural background, his value systems and biases.   The pitfalls are obvious.   "No one can read the literature of the social science," wrote Peter Odegard, "without noting how often hypotheses, generalizations, and abstractions are used, not as propositions to be tested, but either as truths to be demonstrated or as instruments of proof."[21]   Hans J. Morgenthau went even further in his attack on the presupposition of universality and scientific predictability of the social sciences:

> In the social sciences, the social conditions determine not only the ulterior purpose, but also the object of inquiry, the investigator's relation to it, his assumptions, methods, and immediate aims.   In all societies certain social problems cannot be investigated at all, or only at the risk of jeopardizing life, liberty, property and the pursuit of happiness.   The basic philosophic assumptions by which a society lives, such as Marxism in Russia, racial inequality

---

[21] Peter Odegard, "The Social Sciences in the Twentieth Century," in *The Social Studies: Curriculum Proposals for the Future* (Chicago: Univ. of Chicago Press, 1963), p. 24.

in certain regions of the United States, the profit motive and free enterprise in capitalistic societies, are generally not subjected to critical analysis by the members of these societies.[22]

These limitations in the social science methods of inquiry in no way diminish their basic worth and usefulness. By the use of these techniques of inquiry, the social sciences have reaped in a relatively short period of time a very rich harvest of new insight, new concepts, understanding and have greatly increased our knowledge in the area of the study of man and of society.

Observation as a mode of inquiry in the social sciences must be somewhat different than in the natural sciences. While a physicist measuring solar energy in the stratosphere knows more or less the limits of his observation, the anthropologist, studying the individual and social habits of the aborigines in New Guinea may, and often does, make new discoveries which go far beyond his original expectation. There is no question of values or biases involved in the measurement of solar energy, but values do play an important role in the observation of habits and mores of primitive people. Anthropologists in their field work make a valiant attempt to be value-free, but these efforts are seldom successful. As we previously observed, many anthropologists now maintain that bias is less dangerous when fully revealed. Robert S. Lynd wrote that an active bias is helpful in focusing the attention of the investigator on important phenomena and helps him in the selection and organization of his data.[23]

Students in social studies classes could greatly benefit from experiments in objective, prolonged controlled observation of the operation of the city council, state legislature, and clubs of all varieties. Such observation would clarify their ideas, and allow them to test their original hypothesis. Even more important, students can learn something about the limitations of their sensory perceptions, the danger of snap judgment, the complexity of human nature, and the erratic pattern of human behavior. They will learn that observation, to be meaningful and even partially trustworthy, demands practice and a high degree of empathy. Writing about his observations of the inhabitants of the Trobriand Islands, the famed anthropologist Bronislaw Malinowski observed that after learning the native language, "quarrels, jokes, family scenes, events usually trivial, sometimes dramatic, but always significant, formed the atmosphere of my daily life, or of theirs."[24]

---

[22] Hans J. Morgenthau, *Scientific Man Versus Power Politics* (Chicago: Univ. of Chicago Press, 1965), p. 162.

[23] Robert S. Lynd, *Knowledge for What? The Place of Social Science in American Culture* (Princeton, N.J.: Princeton Univ. Press, 1939), p. 24.

[24] Bronislaw Malinowski, *Argonauts of the Western Pacific* (New York: E. P. Dutton & Co., 1922), p. 5.

Polling, sampling, and, in general, the *statistical method* have gained an ever greater acceptance and respectability in the social sciences. The major objective of statistical polling is to make sure that the selected sample is representative of a much larger group. The polling process has two major phases. First comes the determination of the size of the population sample to be used. When a polling firm is asked by a soap company to determine whether American housewives prefer pink or yellow packaging, the first determination must be the number of housewives to be interviewed. Then comes the question of the selection of geographic regions where the sampling will take place and the economic and social strata of the respondents. The second part of the polling process involves the formulation of the questionnaire, the determination of the interview technique, and analysis of the findings.

Some of the present opinion polls, which were drastically revised after the disastrous failure in 1948 to predict Harry Truman's surprise re-election to the presidency, use the *quota-controlled system.* This way of polling relies on the isolation of those variables that have shown in the past a high correlation with the type of behavior under study. In a study designed to predict an election result, the pollster in selecting his sample makes every effort to poll the prospective voters on the basis of his knowledge of how age, sex, ethnic origin, and economic status have influenced past voting performance. The interviewers are then assigned to question quotas of Protestants, men, women, Negroes, whites, etc. Another factor which influences the selection and the size of the quotas is the geographic region of the country and whether the interviews take place in urban or rural areas.

In order to eliminate sampling errors and errors due to the bias of the interviewers, *random sampling* is used. Samples to be interviewed are drawn at random by lots or other methods. The basic principle of random sampling is that the final determination of who is to be polled is left to chance. Since the method is based on tested laws in statistics, the margin of error can be determined and discounted. In order to restrict the randomness of the selection, the population is divided into areas or is stratified in accordance with a special characteristic like age, religion, or wealth and polled by random selection accordingly. This method requires that each member of the specially stratified group has an equal chance to be selected as a sample.

Social scientists have greatly improved the techniques of obtaining information either through *questionnaires* or through *personal interviews.* These interviews, it is now agreed, should be conducted on the informant's home grounds, either at home, factory, or office, and must be conducted in complete privacy. While some experts feel that the results of the interviews should not be recorded in the presence of the person who is interviewed, in order to save time and preserve accurate reporting, most polling agencies and most scholars prefer taking notes during the interview. In assessing the veracity of the information obtained in the interviews, the social scientist is, in fact, asking himself the same questions that a historian asks when examining a letter or a diary which he intends to use to reconstruct an event in history. He asks, or should ask, whether the interviewed person has the ability to tell the truth, is competent to tell the truth, has direct knowledge of the subject in question, and most important, the researcher should ask himself whether the respondent is willing to tell the truth. Assessing the interview technique, and especially the issue of reliability, R. C. Oldfield wrote:

> In practice there are two principles used to increase the likelihood of reliability. The first is to seek information about matters which have no obvious or direct connection with accepted moral or conventional standards, or with the manifest purpose of the interview. The second is to insist upon a detailed, coherent account of *concrete* events, and not to allow the candidate to gloss over gaps with statements of what he generally does in given circumstances.[25]

John Madje considers the interview more reliable in the case of factual questions with "a low emotional content." He cautions the interviewer not to neglect or distort the issues which seem important to the informant even if they seem quite unimportant to the interviewer.[26] The difficulty with the obvious preference and greater reliability for factual questions "free from emotive content," as suggested by Madje, is that questions pertaining to truly important societal questions, like racial discrimination, sex standards, and religious prejudices are by their very nature loaded with emotional content.

Experimental research is at the very heart of social science modes of inquiry. Writing about social experimentation, the late Kurt Lewin maintained that experimentation permits the social scientist to work and manipulate the tools of his study long before he understands all the variables involved.[27] Social experimentation allows the social scientist to approximate, and sometimes to copy, real life situations and to observe them under controlled conditions. John Dewey observed that "if we want something to which the name 'social science' may be given, there is only one way to go about it, namely by entering the path of social planning and control."[28]

---

25 R. C. Oldfield, *The Psychology of the Interview* (London: Methuen and Co., 1941), p. 26.
26 John Madje, *The Tools of Social Science* (Garden City, N.Y.: Doubleday & Co., 1965), p. 288.
27 See Kurt Lewin in Dorwin Cartright, ed., *Field Theory in Social Science* (New York: Harper & Row, 1951).
28 John Dewey, "Social Science and Social Control," *New Republic*, January 14, 1931, pp. 276, 277.

The social scientist embarking on a research project based on an experimental design must contemplate a number of successive steps:

1. The identification of the problem to be studied. He must determine whether the subject of his study is worthy of investigation, whether it has already been investigated quite conclusively, and what are the possible limitations of the study.

2. The collection of pertinent literature, data, and background information on the groups to be studied.

3. The formulation of hypotheses to be tested. The hypotheses determine, in a large measure, the direction of the study. They also serve as standards for the testing of the finding of the study.

4. The selection of groups for study by matching certain variables. The experimental sample or group or groups are then exposed to the additional influence introduced by the investigator. The group which is not subjected to the additional influence is the control group. The influence of the additional factor is then studied, and the investigator attempts to determine to what extent the change is related to the experimentally introduced variable.

5. The evaluation of the hypotheses and the placement of the findings in some broader conceptual framework by the formulation, whenever possible, of generalizations and predictions.

The modes of inquiry used in the social sciences have yielded most impressive new knowledge and insight into the nature of man and the complex interrelationship of social groups. As far as possible, social studies teachers must become acquainted with this great harvest. Even more important is the usefulness of social science modes of inquiry in the study of world history, United States history, and contemporary American politics and society. But it makes no sense to suggest that the methods of inquiry of the social sciences are superior to the traditional historical method because they are the sure path to truth. "The exact truth," Madje wrote, "is both a proper objective and an unattainable one."[29]

Leo Strauss and Hans Morgenthau and their followers in the traditionalist wing in political science, who rely on common sense and knowledge of politics, have at least as much claim to the accuracy of their analysis of world politics as their "scientific" behaviorist colleagues. A trained historian studying recent race riots and using the historical mode of inquiry may be as right or as wrong in assessing the causes of the riots as a sociolo-

---

[29] John Madje, *The Tools of Social Science* (Garden City, N.Y.: Doubleday & Co., 1965), p. 335.

gist using the latest in polling and interviewing techniques. In fact, both approaches to the study of any complex social or political problem are needed. Eclecticism and the use of diverse modes of inquiry may well be the best approach to the social studies.

A great deal has been written recently about the central importance of the inductive method in the teaching of the social studies. The teacher, the adherents of this point of view maintain, should not impart knowledge, but rather lead young people "into the joy of discovering for themselves what is important and what is provisionally true. . . ."[30] The inductive method stretches the student's mind and enables him to interpret facts accurately and to apply the techniques of verification of data to the interpretation of events and people made by other historians. Students must be taught to order the facts, to ask the right questions, to separate facts from opinions, bias from objectivity, separate statements of facts from those laden with value judgments and emotions, and finally, they must be taught to solve problems in an orderly, dispassionate manner.

Professor Edwin Fenton, a historian at the Carnegie Institute of Technology, maintains that the development by the students of skill in the use of the inductive mode of inquiry by the historian is the primary objective in the social studies. "Only when a student can apply," Fenton writes, "the method of the historian, will he become a free investigator able to make sound judgments both in his personal life and on public policy."[31] What is important, he states, is to give the students the tools and the skills of inquiry which can be used all his life. "In contrast to those facts and generalizations, learned by rote and soon forgotten, the mode of inquiry can provide a tool useful throughout life."[32] Students using the inductive method will arrive at broad principles and generalizations and experience the same thrill of discovery allegedly enjoyed by scholars. Professor Fenton has also stated:

> . . . we must teach methods of interpretation if we claim to teach history. Students must learn the rules by which historians collect evidence, and use it to interpret the past if they are to read and write history intelligently. They must be able to judge whether an author's conclusions are supported by the evidence he presents . . .[33]

---

[30] John R. Coleman, "When Secondary School Teacher and College Economist Meet," *The Bulletin of the National Association of Secondary-School Principals*, No. 304 (November 1965), p. 70.

[31] Edwin Fenton and Richard B. Ford, "Organizing Summer Institutes for Teachers: Some Reflections," mimeographed and distributed in January 1966 by the U.S. Office of Education, p. 3.

[32] *Ibid.*

[33] Edwin Fenton, *Teaching the New Social Studies: An Inductive Approach* (New York: Holt, Rinehart & Winston, 1966), p. 150.

These views deserve serious consideration and social studies teachers may find the use of the inductive method rewarding. However, a number of questions suggest themselves. Why should all students be obliged, if not compelled, to deal with history in the way professional scholars do? Is it reasonable to ignore the fact that historians have used, and still use, a great variety of "rules" for gathering evidence and that many historians, who have followed the same or similar rules in collecting evidence and who have used the same historical methods for the interpretation of the evidence, have often arrived at diametrically differing conclusions? Professor Fenton's injunction that "students must be able to judge whether an author's conclusions are supported by the evidence he presents" may prove to be full of pitfalls for teachers who may wish to follow it. They will soon discover that judging the conclusions of historical works is a difficult and complicated task and that teaching this skill presents even more problems. In spite of the optimistic assertions of Bruner and his followers that almost everything can be taught on any level, in some intellectually honest form, many of our high school students are not capable of making intelligent judgments on the soundness of works in history. In fact, "judgments," for instance, on whether A. J. P. Taylor's conclusions on the causes of World War II and on Hitler's foreign policy are right or wrong, should be suggested only with extreme caution and reticence. The ability to use the historical modes of inquiry and to interpret historical issues and events is an important objective in social studies, but the potential achievements in this area ought to be kept within the realm of the possible and the attainable.

Furthermore, the formal approach to the rules of evidence, to the verification of data, and to the logical process of drawing conclusions should not obscure the role that intuition and imagination play in the work of the historian and in the writing of history.

There is, nevertheless, something very attractive in Fenton's ideas and proposals. If it is possible to give every young student, through the use of the inductive mode of inquiry in history and the social sciences, the tools and skills which will enable him to distinguish between truth and falsehood, to keep a cool head, and use sound judgment in emotion-charged situations, and to "make sound judgments both in personal life and on public policy," why not do so? There is no doubt, as was suggested in earlier chapters, that it may be quite useful to allow students to be occasionally "Little League historians" or "Little League sociologists" and go about the inquiry of a particular subject and a particular problem in the way in which a trained historian or an experienced sociologist would tackle these investigations. A great deal, Professor Fenton maintains, could well be gained from these experiments. However, if the suggestion is that the inductive method become *the* mode of inquiry in the social studies and that the attainment of the skill as individual inquiry becomes *the* objective in the social studies raises a number of questions which need to be considered.

Many events and problems in history are not susceptible to inquiry by the inductive method which, in Professor Fenton's interpretation is capable of yielding the truth, of dividing fact from opinion, and of separating emotional involvement from balanced judgment. Few questions have been studied as intensively and as inductively as the causes of the Civil War. While an inductive study of the subject in the classroom may be a worthwhile experiment, no expectation can be entertained that the truth, the whole truth, and nothing but the truth would result from such a study. Historians have long agreed that in viewing the tangled and complex emotion-charged period between 1850 and 1861 it is virtually impossible to separate opinions from facts and to deal with substantive differences between the North and the South without bringing to the study prior bias or personal value judgments.

How can one guarantee, even to a reasonable degree, that by the use of the inductive method students can arrive at "sound" judgments on the tangled passions and the frenzied emotions that were engendered by the Dreyfus Affair? The difficulty is with the word "sound." Two historians, both of unimpeachable integrity and complete masters of the historical method, can, and often do, arrive at diametrically opposed appraisals of that tragic period in French history. Both are convinced that they have arrived at "sound" judgments. Furthermore, to suggest that it is possible to achieve a skill providing a key to the solution of all the tangled and complex problems in the personal and in the public domains, through the repeated use of the inductive method, is to fly in the face both of accumulated experience in historiography and the methodology of the social sciences.

There is another expectation built in the inductive method which is bound to bring a considerable amount of chagrin and disappointment to many classrooms. The junior investigators who deal independently with new data will often arrive at totally different conclusions than those arrived at by competent scholars. What then? Will the teachers not be compelled to "correct" the thrilling "discoveries" of their students?

Some investigation of certain events in history, if studied by the inductive method in social studies classes, would be a waste of time. Instead of embarking on a long and tedious inductive study of World War I, it would be easier and more valuable for the students to read Barbara Tuchman's *The Guns of August*.

The inductive method requires a great deal of time, rich library resources, and expert guidance. If even one of these factors is in short supply, much of its effectiveness is lost. There is much that can be learned by the use of a deductive short-cut. There is also ground for suspicion that continuous or even too repetitive use of the inductive method would become intolerably boring both to students and their teachers. Realistically, it must also be remembered that the national tests which determine admissions to colleges basically test accumulated knowledge and agility of mind and not skill of inquiry.

It is doubtful whether the basic claim of its advocates that the inductive method is the best way to teach problem-solving skills can be substantiated by even a modicum of substantive evidence. It is *one* of the ways to sharpen the perceptions of students and to teach them to think intelligently about the problems of the past and the present, and it should be used as often as possible.

We shall end this chapter by returning to the emphasis on the complexity and variety of both methods of inquiry by scholars and methods of teaching by social studies teachers. Scholars in history and the social sciences daily use many methods to arrive at new understanding and discoveries about their discipline. They do not hesitate to borrow from each other the techniques of investigation. Social studies teachers should be as flexible as their colleagues in the academic fields.

7

The Structure of the

Social Studies— New

Curricular Approaches

Many voices have recently been raised to suggest that the emphasis in the teaching of social studies should be on the structure of history and the social sciences. Advocates of this position take much of their inspiration and rationale from the work of Jerome Bruner. Bruner, a Harvard psychologist, maintains that each discipline can best be mastered by teaching the basic organizing principles which, according to his view, form the structure of every natural and social science. These generalizations and broad ideas help scholars, who have invented them, to organize their respective inventory of accumulated knowledge into meaningful and connected patterns. Students who study any discipline by looking at its structure are bound to find the interconnecting spiraling logic of these sets of broad organizing principles. Bruner and his co-worker, Jerrold Zacharias, an M.I.T. physicist, contend that the stress on structure proved to be a great boon for the new mathematics and new physics and that there is no reason to doubt that the same can be true for the social studies. Consequently, both scholars, who are leaders in Educational Services, Incorporated, an endowed corporation, are now working to prepare a new social studies curriculum.

The new curriculum is to be based on Bruner's contention that "the structure of knowledge—its connectedness and its derivations that make one idea follow another—is the proper emphasis in education. For it is structure, the great conceptual inventions that bring order to the congeries of disconnected observations, that give meaning to what we may learn and makes possible the opening up of new realms of experience."[1] The implication is that learning one set of broad concepts will logically lead to the learning of a more complex set of conceptual frameworks.

It may be significant to note that in explicating his theory of the structure of disciplines, Bruner uses, almost without exception, examples from mathematics or from the natural sciences. His interpretation of the role and power of the organizing concepts seems to be best understood and related to the function and objectives of the natural sciences. For instance, Bruner stated that, "Knowledge is a model we construct to give meaning and structure to regularities in experience. The organizing ideas of any body of knowledge are inventions for rendering experience economical and connected . . . The power of great organizing concepts is in large part that they permit us to understand and sometimes to predict or change the world in which we live."[2] This statement has an obvious relevance to mathematics, physics, and chemistry. The question is whether Bruner and other scholars associated with him in his work on the social studies curriculum will be able to isolate some great organizing ideas in history or the social sciences which will help the students "to understand and sometimes to predict or change the world." Once this is done it remains to be seen whether historians will be ready to accept the structure of history as finally defined by Bruner.

Bruner cannot escape the task of defining the structure of history and of other social sciences because, according to his own conception, curriculum revision calls for two initial steps: the definition of the structure of the discipline by the scholars themselves and the organization of the discovered structure into meaningful patterns of relationships for purposes of classroom instruction. This means that Bruner would have to ask historians to define the structure of their discipline.

In the second chapter of his book, *The Process of Education,* Bruner wrote that whether school children would need to know Frederick Jackson Turner's ideas on the role of the frontier in American history before they could understand the general trends in American history, will have to be decided with the help of scholars in American history.

As we have tried to point out in the preceding chapters, the few historians who have tried to find some order, rhythm, or structure in history have done so with limited success and usually without the endorsement of the historical profession. Whether this task can be done by Bruner with the

---

[1] Jerome S. Bruner, *On Knowing* (Cambridge: Harvard Univ. Press, 1962), p. 120.
[2] *Ibid.,* p. 120.

help of several historians who are working with him is very doubtful. The task of identifying even a small number of fundamental ideas in world history and of finding their spiraling relatedness, may prove to be formidable, if not forbidding. An example of a great idea in history, which has been cited by Bruner, "A nation must trade in order to live" is so broad and so full of fuzzy implications that its value for classroom instruction may prove to be as useless as the generalization "in war there is no substitute for victory" or "appeasement of aggressors does not pay."

If we are to teach the structure of history or sociology in high school classes, scholars in these disciplines will have to agree on some list of fundamental ideas, basic skills, and methods and then show how these great ideas and skills are related to one another and how they represent the structure of history and sociology. This has never been attempted by historians or sociologists, and I doubt whether many would want to try. Commenting on this question, Professor Fred M. Newman of Harvard wrote:

> Can a discipline have a structure independent of the scholars' ability to articulate it? An affirmative answer carries with it an implication that some sort of intellectual natural law transcends scholarly endeavor, unaffected by the studies of human beings, that pre-existing structures are waiting to be discovered. On the other hand, a negative reply suggests that the utility of structure as a concept depends mostly upon a prediction that scholars will in fact be able to articulate the structure of their field. If the existence of structure is mainly a function of the scholars' ability to construct it, then there is no logical basis for assuming that any given discipline has a structure.[3]

Suppose that some historians, even as respectable and distinguished as those who serve as advisors to Professor Bruner at the E.S.I. project, concluded that they have discovered the "pre-existing" structure of history. Would their "discovery" be accepted by their colleagues? Is it probable that an interlocking, logically connected, progressively complex system of fundamental ideas in history, or for that matter in sociology or political science, could ever be identified? The basic obstacle, which apparently does not exist or has been overcome in mathematics and in the natural sciences, is the lack of any logical ladder of progression in the study of sociology or history. It is not absolutely essential for a high school student to have had a course in the American Revolution in order to study the Civil War. Students do learn about the Napoleonic Wars without ever having heard of the invasions and conquests of Alexander the Great. It would be rather difficult to formulate a generalization from the Napoleonic Wars which would have a logical or necessary relationship to the wars of

---

[3] Fred M. Newman, "The Analysis of Public Controversy—New Focus on Social Studies," *The School Review*, Vol. 111 (Winter 1965), p. 413.

Alexander or the conquests of Ghengis Khan. The same would undoubtedly be true about the broader questions in sociology. It may be possible and profitable to study about the apartheid policy in South Africa without any relation, or logically discoverable relatedness, to the situation of Indians in Peru or the Negroes in the United States. In fact, it can be argued that any attempt for instructional purposes based on a search for structure to develop an organizing idea which would relate the study of these three areas would be full of loopholes and would be misleading.

Even granting for a moment the legitimacy of the contention that the teaching of the structure of the disciplines is the proper emphasis in education, there is a question which would naturally occur to those who have taught social studies on a high school level. Would not the teaching of the broad concepts and generalizing principles, even if taught by inventive teachers by the inductive "discovery" method recommended by Bruner, prove to be boring for students during the long stretch of the school year? Granting that some of the students will, after engaging in an inquiry, by imitating the ways of research of sociologists, political scientists and historians, experience the "thrill of discovery," is it not sensible to assume that many other students would find this intellectual exercise not very challenging?

While there is no question that in the search for structure, Bruner's approach is valuable and should have a place in the social studies curriculum and in the lively, dramatic study of history and the social sciences, to build the entire social studies curriculum on the structure theory is fraught with grave dangers. There are many aspects of history and the study of human personality and group interrelationship which cannot and should not be fitted into a structure or even related to something else, yet are eminently worthy of teaching to our children. The way a historian or an economist goes about his work is interesting and may occasionally be useful as a mode of inquiry in the social studies class, but equally interesting and important is a deductive approach by a scholarly teacher who constructs his lesson by presenting to his students for discussion and analysis conflicting conclusions reached by historians, for example, about the causes of the Civil War or about the effectiveness of the New Deal legislation. Newman poses a legitimate query to Bruner and his followers:

> Why should a general lay population be taught to perform intellectual operations of a nature preferred uniquely by the academic profession? That is, why should all children be taught to ask and answer the kinds of questions that interest historians, political scientists, economists, etc.?[4]

---

[4] *Ibid.,* p. 414.

It is also disturbing to note that Bruner and the Structuralists in the social studies seem to assume that history and the social sciences each have one structure, when in fact most of them may have several sets or patterns of great conceptual ideas. Scholars who may eventually be induced to undertake the task of writing complete social studies curricula based on the structure theory, will undoubtedly find that historians and social scientists freely borrow ideas, methods, concepts, including fundamental ideas from one another. Professor Arno Bellack of Teachers' College, Columbia University, pointed out in his critique of Bruner's theories that:

> the social scientists today are characterized by a plurality of methods and conceptual schemes . . . Instead of a unity of method or a single universe discourse, we are confronted with a vast confederation of separate areas of study. Modes of thinking and analysis differ from field to field and even from problem to problem within the same field. In time, a Bacon of the Sciences that bear on social and cultural behavior may emerge, that time is not yet.[5]

The E.S.I. under the leadership of Professor Bruner has made considerable progress in preparing a new social studies curriculum. A preliminary report on the social studies published in 1963 by the Council of Learned Societies and Educational Services, Incorporated, included a basic statement of policy in the preparation of a course of study in the social studies. It reads in part: "History, sociology, anthropology, economics, and political science may for convenience be separated as academic disciplines, but they all deal with a single thing: the behavior of man in society. Accordingly, we propose to teach them jointly, not separately."[6]   One wonders what the reaction from academic mathematicians and natural scientists would be to a parallel statement: "Mathematics, physics, chemistry and biology may for convenience be separated as academic disciplines, but they all deal with one thing: man's attempt to understand and to control his natural environment. Accordingly, we propose to teach them jointly, not separately." The outcries of anguish and protest would undoubtedly be overwhelming. And yet, the Structuralists in the social studies do not hesitate to advocate an amalgamation of history and the social sciences and do not seem to be concerned about the integrity of these disciplines and the reluctance, if not outright opposition, of most historians and of many social scientists to a reductionist synthetic unification.

---

[5] Arno Bellack, "Structure in the Social Sciences and Implications for the Social Studies Program," *The Social Studies: Curriculum Proposals for the Future* (Stanford University, 1963), p. 102.

[6] From a mimeographed report issued by E.S.I., dated February 15, 1963 and entitled "A Preliminary and Tentative Outline of a Program of Curriculum Development in the Social Studies and Humanities," by the American Council of Learned Societies and Educational Servers, Incorporated.

The E.S.I. group has identified twenty-four broad generalizations which are to be taught in sequential steps by using interdisciplinary insights and techniques. Here is an example of one of these generalizations: "All societies have developed in different degrees of elaboration special institutions for ensuring conformity to other institutions (law) or changing institutions. All ultimately use the threat of force to try to ensure that conformity to institutions shall be rewarding." It is impossible to quarrel with such a broad generalization, but whether it can serve as an organizing, fundamental idea representing the structure of any discipline or the joint structures of history and the social sciences is another matter. Most scholars would undoubtedly have grave doubts.

Apparently the followers of the structural approach in the social studies are not as cautious as the scholars in Cambridge. The new social studies curriculum published in 1965 by the Wisconsin State Department of Public Instruction, on which twenty-six Wisconsin educators worked for three years, set down six major concepts for each of the following disciplines: history, political science, economics, geography, and sociology. These concepts, the authors claim, are applicable to all mankind. One of the major concepts in history reads: "Human experience is continuous and interrelated. Continuity is a fact of life: there is nothing new under the sun, all men, events and institutions are the outcome of something that has gone before, man is a product of the past and restricted by it."[7]

Some of the other concepts from history which are to serve as "a means of organizing subject matter in a most meaningful pattern" are:

Every effort at reform began as the private opinion of an individual.
It is difficult to separate fact from fiction. Every writer (sic!) has his biases.
Those who cannot remember the past may be condemned to repeat it.
Facts may often be interpreted in more than one way.
Nations with great power may not always use it wisely.

A similar concept in political science states, "Governments are established by men. In some situations, people delegate authority; in others authority is imposed.

One could, I hope not too irreverently, comment: "elementary my dear Watson" since some of these generalizations are obvious and even trite. However, several of the cited generalizing concepts in history would find little support from professional historians. Certainly, these statements do not constitute the fundamental concepts in history constituting its structure. More important concerns are the questions of how interested high school

---

[7] *A Conceptual Framework for the Social Studies in Wisconsin Schools*, Social Studies Bulletin issued by Angus B. Rothwell, State Superintendent of Public Instruction, Madison, Wisconsin (December 1964).

youngsters are in such high sounding generalizations and whether it is wise to build an entire social studies curriculum around these generalizations. It would, of course, be unreasonable and unfair to connect Professor Bruner's views with these "generalizations." They are cited here merely as an example of the excessive and misguided zeal of some of the followers of the structure theory.

In an E.S.I. Report published in the summer of 1965, Bruner gives a rather detailed description of a new social studies course of study which would be used, experimentally in grades 4, 5 and 6 and be entitled simply "man." "The content of the course," Bruner writes, "is 'man,' his nature as a species, the forces that shaped or continue to shape his humanity. The new social studies curriculum will center on "five great humanizing forces": tool-making, language, social organization, child rearing, and man's ways of explaining his world.

The section on language would discuss how humans and animals manage to send and receive messages, how language is acquired by young humans and other primates, and the origins of human language and its role in shaping human characteristics. This section, says Bruner, may take a month or year of study. The second section of the course would deal with "tools." The objective is to provide the children with an understanding of the relation between tools and our way of life. "Our ultimate objective in teaching about tools, is, Bruner writes, . . . not so much to explicate tools and their significance as to explore how tools affected man's evolution and still affect his life.[9] The study of tools and their role in the evolution of man is, according to Bruner, aimed at fulfilling one of the basic aims of the social studies program: "to get across the idea that a technology requires a counterpart in social organization before it can be used effectively by a society."[10]

The crux of the last statement is what is meant by the word "effectively." This statement represents one of the important objectives of the social studies as defined by Bruner. It is indeed strange and controversial. If one understands the main trend of thought of atomic scientists as reflected in recent years in the articles of the *Bulletin of Atomic Scientists*, it is the considered opinion of our leading atomic scientists that we have failed to build a "counterpart in social organization" to deal with atomic technology. However, our society has used atomic energy "effectively" to subdue Japan, to run atomic submarines, ships, and power stations, and to create some kind of equilibrium in the world by the reality of a balance of atomic terror.

---

[8] Jerome S. Bruner, *Toward a Study of Instruction* (Cambridge: Harvard Univ. Press, 1966), p. 74.
[9] *Ibid.*, p. 82.
[10] *Ibid.*, p. 82.

The third section of Bruner's new social studies course deals with social organizations. It is aimed at explaining to children "that there is a structure in a society and that this structure is not fixed once for all." It would seem that even our average students should have little difficulty in grasping this principle which is quite obvious to them from their own gangs, clubs, and school organizations.

The fourth section is devoted to the theme of child rearing. This study deals with the phenomenon of sentiment in human life which develops during the long human childhood and the influence of the special manner of childhood on future personality development.

The fifth and final section of this course of study aims to develop a world view and deals with man's drive to explicate and represent his world. "Central to the unit is the idea that men everywhere are humans, however advanced or primitive their civilizations." This seems to be essentially an anthropological unit aimed at proving that all cultures have inherent values and that there are no "superior" and "inferior" cultures. The objective is to combat an ethnocentric approach to world cultures. In explaining why this unit should be taught early on the elementary school level, Bruner presents an idealistic view of world history based on the idea of the rule of reason and continued progress, which few historians accept today. "We want children," he states, "to recognize that man is constantly seeking to bring reason (sic!) into his world, that he does so with a variety of symbolic tools, and that he does so with a striking and fully rational humanity."[11] Our students would be ready to accept this view only if we impose upon them and somehow enforce a total newspaper and television blackout and also frequently tape their eyes and ears so that they could not listen to their parents, friends, and casual acquaintances. Otherwise, they may tend to believe that, unfortunately, man is often not successful in bringing "reason into his world."

As for the methodology to be used in this new social studies course, Bruner wants to use three techniques, which seem to be quite unique. The first technique consists of using contrast, the second is the use of especially prepared games that "incorporate the formal properties of the phenomena for which the game is an analogue," and the third is "the ancient approach of stimulating self-consciousness about assumptions—going beyond mere admonition to think."[12] Little can be said about this new methodology in the social studies because few details have been given as yet. "The most urgent need," as Bruner sees it, is to teach the students to use theoretical

---

[11] Jerome S. Bruner, "Man: A Course of Study," Educational Services, Incorporated, *Quarterly Report* (Summer 1965), p. 92.

[12] *Ibid.*, p. 92.

models which will be "rather sophisticated." Evaluation will have to await the publication of the models and reports of their application will have to be analyzed. Enough, however, has been published to indicate that once the curriculum, which will include materials, games, films, and models all prepared under the supervision of academic scholars, is submitted to the schools, there will be a strong tendency to follow the new course of study with some rigidity. This is the usual course of all curricular innovations. The Educational Services Organization (the E.S.I.) is proceeding cautiously in the preparation of new curricular materials for social studies. If the unit on the Elizabethan Period, which has been published and made available for examination is a sample of the materials to come, the E.S.I. will make an excellent contribution to a more effective teaching of history.

Bruner and his associates are constantly emphasizing the importance of the child "doing" mathematics or physics instead of learning about them. The student should "do" the things on the blackboards or in the laboratory that mathematicians and physicists are doing. That sounds reasonable and exciting. But how does this apply to history or to English literature? Christopher Jencks, in his review of Bruner's book, *Toward a Theory of Instruction,* made an acute observation. "The analogy," he wrote, "between physics and history is at bottom misleading. The men who really 'do' history are not, after all, historians. They are politicians, generals, diplomats, philosophers. It is these people whom the young need to understand, far more than they need to understand the historians who judge them."[13]

Another new rationale for the social studies has been proposed by Professors Donald W. Oliver and James P. Shaver. It would center around the study of public, domestic, and international disputes. The originators of the Harvard University Project stated their objectives in these terms:

> The most broadly stated objective is to train students to examine and analyze, through discussion and argument, the kinds of disputes that give birth to social conflict. By considering a variety of situations throughout history and across cultures, by viewing the situations in terms of various social science concepts and theories, and by examining and weighing various methods for reaching and justifying positions, students will hopefully gain certain powers of analysis that will aid them in discussing value dilemmas on which public controversy thrives.[14]

Professor Fred Newman, a collaborator in the project, has emphasized that competence in political action and the social sciences, literary skills,

---

[13] Christopher Jencks, review of Bruner's *Toward a Theory of Instruction, Book Week* (Feb. 20, 1966), p. 5.

[14] Quoted in Dorothy Fraser, "Status and Expectations of Current Research and Development Projects," *Social Education* (November 1965), p. 425.

or a greater appreciation of the American past "are not central to our citizenship education." "The central focus," he continued, "is an intelligent national dialogue as a medium for clarification, justification, and resolution of social disputes."[15]

The study of public controversies that involve some basic conflicts in values necessitates an intelligent, thoughtful analysis of the apparent and the underlying issues involved. The study, for instance, of the social and political dilemmas involved in the enforcement of the 1965 voting bill, would, according to the basic approach of the authors of the Harvard Project, involve the study of the conflict between states rights and local autonomy arguments, of commitments to the political rights of all citizens, and of the obligation of the Federal Government to secure these rights.

The teaching of public controversies, Oliver, Shaver, and Newman argue, is the most promising approach to the social studies because it represents the best way to gain an understanding of the pluralistic nature of the American society which, while basically committed to a liberal tradition as secured in the Declaration of Independence and in the Constitution, generates a steady stream of public controversies reflecting the conflicts of values and commitments in a large and varied society. The essence of public controversies pertains to the set of values which constitute the American Creed. "The (Social Studies) curriculum," Newman writes, "reveals a two-fold commitment of its own, first to the creed and, second to the use of rational discourse in implementing the creed . . . We candidly recognize our faith that the best way to approach the resolution of social controversy is through rational discussion.[16]

Models for analysis of public controversies include questions, concepts and modes of inquiry from history and the social sciences. Social science disciplines and concepts are not taught as such, but are used to achieve the aim of a thorough, intelligent analysis and discussion of a public controversy. The list of public controversies included in the sample three year curriculum of the Harvard Project includes, "The Mutiny Act," "John Brown," "The Great Depression and New Deal," "The Bolshevik Revolution," "Kenya-Colonialism and Independence," and the "Nuremberg Trials."

The Oliver-Shaver-Newman proposals for a new rationale and curriculum in the social studies have many attractive features. The Harvard Project does not propose to integrate or synthesize history and the social sciences, neither is it embarked on the task of "simplifying" the social science research and materials for use in the social studies classrooms. The proposed curriculum indicates that the topics studied would include some of

---

[15] Fred M. Newman, "The Analysis of Public Controversy—New Focus on the Social Studies," *The School Review*, Vol. 111 (Winter 1965), p. 423.
[16] *Ibid.*, p. 425.

the most important periods of stress and conflict in U.S. and world history. The concept of public controversy is broadly interpreted to include such topics as the "Standard of Living," and "Anglo-American Developments from Roman England to the American Civil War: the Growth of Constitutionalism." These broader themes would be studied through a series of cases involving public controversies and conflicts of values.

One section of the curriculum in the higher grades is devoted to the general problem of peace and order. It involves the following topics:

A. Colonialism and the balance of power.
B. World War I and Versailles.
C. Diplomatic History through World War II.
D. Nuremberg trials.
E. Cases on the problems of international order: Israel, Hungary, Berlin, Cuba, Vietnam, Panama, South America.

Professor Oliver has made it clear that he wants the new social studies curriculum to center around conflict-resolution. He wisely points to the failure of the schools to give due consideration to the question of whether the school has the right to include the molding of personal values among its objectives. He also deplores the lack of emphasis on the continuous conflict over ideas and values.

Oliver has listed three major objectives of his curriculum based on the study of public controversies: first, "students should be taught to recognize and define areas of human conflict . . ."; second, "With reference to specific political and social issues, students should be taught to define alternative methods of regulating human affairs that are possible from the point of view of major value positions in society . . ."; third, "With reference to specific social and political issues, students should be taught to make thoughtful predictions about the consequences of various alternative methods of regulating human affairs."[17] The general objective of social science education, according to Oliver, is to "introduce young people into the fire and controversy that rage within a free society over regulating human affairs . . .[18]

As Professor Oliver admits, a curriculum built around his approach and rationale would omit large periods and events in American history. The approach is as he states "a combination of ethics and social science, with ethical consideration paramount because of the conscious attempt to teach

---

[17] Donald W. Oliver, "The Selection of Content in the Social Sciences," in Edwin Fenton, *Teaching the New Social Studies: An Inductive Approach* (New York: Holt, Rinehart & Winston, 1966), pp. 107–109. For a full exposition of the public controversy approach see Donald W. Oliver and James S. Shaver, *Teaching Public Issues in the High School* (Boston: Houghton Mifflin Co., 1966).
[18] *Ibid.*, p. 107.

students the analytical tools by which they may continuously redefine legitimate areas of personal liberty."[19]   Oliver is not unduly concerned by the omission of much of the historical content because he feels that history as taught now in public schools is a fact-myth-legend combination of limited value.

In a sense, this is a case study approach to the teaching of history or, in the term used by Charles Keller, the "post-holing" technique.   The difference, and this is an important difference, is the criterion that the cases or problems must involve a public controversy.   The criterion has the advantage of providing a rationale for the selection of case studies, and since most, if not all, important events or problems in history have contained some element of controversy, the Harvard approach guarantees that most important historical problems will be studied.

However, there are some potential weaknesses which ought to be indicated.   The leaders of the Harvard Project, whose writings have been singularly free of ambiguities or special pleading, do assume that public controversies can be dissected and resolved on a rational basis even if some of the "solutions" are left open-ended.   Analysis of great public controversies should not exclude the emotional entanglements, the complex and largely hidden motivations of the leading personalities, and the often unexpected resolution of major controversies.   Such omission, as Professors Oliver and Shaver would undoubtedly agree, would ignore some of the basic variables operating in great historical and contemporary problems.   The personal hatred between Woodrow Wilson and Henry Cabot Lodge played an important role in the Versailles Treaty ratification controversy.   In spite of Arthur Link's definitive studies of Wilson, we still do not know the reasons for Wilson's unwillingness or inability to compromise and it is not clear to what extent Wilson's stroke affected the final Senate vote on the treaty.   The study of the great controversy surrounding the causes of the Civil War must take into account the emotional involvement of historians and their personal attitudes toward slavery, Negroes, and civil rights, and their own loyalties to either the North or South.   The analyses of the causes of the Civil War by Avery Craven and by Kenneth Stampp are rational and intelligent, but they also reflect the cultural background, personal biases, and emotional commitments of both distinguished historians.   The point is that the study of conflicts in history ought to give due consideration to the accidental and irrational factors, as well as to the rational components of human behavior. How can one estimate how the course of progressive legislation and the role of the Federal Government on matters of public welfare has been affected by the murder of President William H. McKinley in 1901 and the totally unexpected elevation of Theodore Roosevelt to the presidency?

---

[19] *Ibid.*, p. 109.

The study of public controversies has some exciting possibilities but to build an entire curriculum based only on the study of public controversies may ignore the importance of chronological development and historical perspective. For some reason, dates and chronology have been the favorite whipping boys of the anti-historians among writers in social studies. In attacking the futility of cramming into the student's mind a number of unrelated dates and facts, these writers are storming at open doors. No historian would defend the teaching of dates unless they are relevant and important to an understanding of a historical development or essential to the comprehension of true relationships. Examples can easily be cited when dates, signifying a chronological sequence of related events, are important and should be taught. Take, for instance, the following dates:

1820 (Missouri Compromise) 1828–1832 (South Carolina Controversy), 1846–48 (Wilmot Proviso-The Texas Annexation Controversy), 1850 (The Clay Compromise), 1854 (Kansas-Nebraska Act–Popular Sovereignty) February, 1861 (The Washington Peace Conference).

It should not be difficult to prove that the knowledge of these dates, each marked by a flare-up in the national controversy over slavery and a futile attempt to find an acceptable compromise on this crucial issue, is essential to an understanding of the causes of the Civil War and of the failure of attempts made to avert the war after Lincoln's inauguration. Without this sequential historical perspective, the Civil War looks like a failure of statesmanship and a rather inexplicable unwillingness of the two warring sections of the country to compromise. There is some reasonable doubt whether the public controversy approach to the social studies curriculum would do full justice to the need of providing some chronological coherence and broad perspective to historical narrative and to historical developments. Of course, nothing should prevent a teacher who uses the public controversy approach from supplying chronological perspective when necessary.

One also wonders whether a social studies course based entirely on the study of successive public conflicts and controversies, would not, in the aggregate, lead to a distorted, Darwinistic view of history. The story of the United States and the story of mankind are much more than a sequence of conflicts. Periods of general contentment, relative tranquillity, often marked by great intellectual and technological creativity deserve as much attention as the study of conflict-resolution. Men were not always at each other's throat and "fire and controversy" do not always rage in a free society. The weariness, the striving for normalcy and pleasure, to cite an example, which characterized the period of the 1920's in our country, can be as instructive as the contemplation of periods of stress and upheaval. In fact, the exclusive focus on great conflicts may well distort the student's perspective on history. Daniel Boorstin speaks thoughtfully about the "bias of survival." He points out that there are great disparities in the documentary historical evidence. As a rule, controversies leave a lot of debris, while times of peace and peaceful pursuits leave few traces. We thus have a lot of material on the conflict over prohibition laws, but very little on the drinking habits of past generations. Similarly, we have much documentary evidence on great religious controversies, but know relatively little of what people believed in or how they worshipped. Thus, the study of a succession of controversies may give the students a somewhat distorted view of the past.

Some serious reservations may also be expressed about Professor Oliver's conviction that the study of past conflicts, always with the benefit of hindsight, holds great promise that our students would be able "to make objective predictions about how to control major conflicts in the regulation of human affairs."[20] This seems to be a doubtful path of raising false hopes in this complex and unpredictable world. It may be better to rest the case for the study of public controversies on the expectation that such an enterprise, if conducted by thoughtful and competent teachers, would give the students skills and sophistication helpful to them in grappling with new problems and new conflicts.

All new curricular approaches to the social studies are basically determined by the postulated objectives. It is the objectives set by the curriculum makers that determine the content of the particular courses of study proposed. Thus, Jerome Bruner hopes to achieve five ideals:

1. To give our pupils respect for and confidence in the powers of their own mind.
2. To give them respect, moreover, for the powers of thought concerning the human condition, man's plight, and his social life.
3. To provide them with a set of workable models to make it simpler to analyze the nature of the social world in which they live and the condition in which man finds himself.
4. To impart a sense of respect for the capacities and plight of man as a species, for his origins, for his potential, and for his humanity.
5. To leave the student with a sense of the unfinished business of man's evolution.[21]

These objectives deserve some scrutiny. They are far-reaching, ambitious, and, frankly, not entirely clear. How does one "give" or "impart" respect or a "sense of respect," and how would a teacher go about measuring

---

[20] *Ibid.*, p. 109.
[21] Jerome S. Bruner, "Man: A Course of Study," E.S.I. *Quarterly Report* (Summer 1965), p. 93.

whether he has done so? In setting before the social studies teachers the task of stressing the power of man's rational mind—an interesting throwback to the worship of man's rational powers by the philosophers of the Age of Renaissance and Enlightenment—do we not belittle or eliminate the evidence that suggests severe limits to the use of the "powers of thought" in dealing with the human condition? Are teachers expected to know the state of the "human condition" today and "man's plight and his social life." Is this not a tall order? Is this not too much to expect from high school teachers? Would not a world-conclave of scholars have a very difficult time in assessing the human condition and the very complicated plight of modern man? Why should one of the objectives of the social studies (if such basic personality changes are indeed feasible) not also be the imparting of a sense of *dis*respect for man's consistent refusal to live up to his potential and for his *in*humanity? An effective and imaginative study of history would certainly be more likely to give the student a better balanced picture of man's virtues and follies.

The Bruner objectives, especially the last one which aims to leave the student with a sense of unfinished business of man's evolution, have a distinct anthropological flavor. Indeed, the whole proposed course of study is anthropological in essence. The E.S.I. approach was to be an interdisciplinary one, teaching jointly all the social sciences. In fact, there is little political science or sociology in it, and as for history and geography, they are virtually non-existent. It is curious that the accumulation of a body of knowledge, yes, the acquisition of meaningful and related information, is not mentioned among the objectives. This attitude, of course, is in line with the recent trend of denigrating the importance of the transmission of the accumulated knowledge. The stress is on skills, concepts, and, in Bruner's terms, on "workable models." All this is based on the unproven and perhaps unprovable assumption that it is not really important to know much about, let us say, the English Civil War, about the American Revolution, the French Revolution, or the Bolshevik Revolution. Bruner and his colleagues seem to say that what a future intelligent man needs to know is the basic concepts and generalizations pertaining to all revolutions, or a workable model of *a* revolution, and possess the skills of critical inquiry. When the need arose, he would merely apply the generalization, the models, and skills to the study of any revolution he chose to investigate. We have already pointed out that Crane Brinton's careful study, *The Anatomy of Revolution,* has failed to come up with many generalizing principles about revolutions and clearly indicated that the differences and the variables involved in the American and the French Revolutions or between the English Civil War and the Bolshevik Revolution are so great that each of these great events should be studied separately. Even if it were possible to construct, in Bruner's words, "workable models to make it simpler to analyze the nature of the social world" and apply them to the study of revolutions, our pupils would be deprived of the opportunity of meeting and living with (through dramatic and effective teaching) such fascinating people as Theodore Roosevelt, Cromwell, Lilburne, Marie Antoinette, Dante, Lenin, and Trotsky.

Questions pertaining to the learning of a body of knowledge (carefully selected and logically connected) are rather simple. Is it or is it not important for high school graduates and college freshmen to know about the Populist Rebellion, the War of 1812, about Daniel Webster and Boss Tweed, about the Clay Compromise, the Teapot Dome Scandal, and the history of Reconstruction? Is it or is it not important for high school graduates to know about Pericles and the conquests of Alexander, about Caesar, the Carthaginian Wars, about Constantine, Genghis Khan, the reforms of Akbar, and the wisdom of Confucius, about Voltaire, Napoleon, and Waterloo? The assumption postulated here is that this type of knowledge, taught in an analytical and interpretative manner, is essential and worthwhile for any moderately well-educated man. I would shudder to think that a college freshman would have to see a Broadway play to become acquainted for the first time with the women of Troy, the complicated nature of Marat, or the tragic downfall of Charles Dilke. Historical knowledge, of course, may be gained through the partial use of Fenton's inductive method, the public controversy approach of Oliver and Shaver, the traditional chronological approach, the case study approach, or preferably by a combination of all these approaches.

Some of the new curricula in the social studies, based on Bruner's ideas, have drastically cut the time devoted to United States history and are drawing fire from some right-wing groups. This is unfortunate and it must be resisted as an unwarranted interference with the orderly process of curriculum revision.

However, it is legitimate to raise a voice in defense of the teaching of American history as an important element in the education of young Americans. Chauvinism has no place in the school because it is destructive and because it usually leads to unbridled cynicism. But it is proper to argue that to give the student an understanding and an appreciation of the ideas that brought about the founding of this nation, the men who helped to guide its destiny, and to make them aware of the constant struggle for the improvement of the democratic process are the proper concerns of social studies teachers and the schools. It should be stressed that the United States must be shown full face, with all the blemishes showing, and that teachers are duty bound not to gloss over the weaknesses and imperfections of our government and society.

The end-result of such teaching of United States history, based on integrity, scholarship, and imagination, will be a sense of pride in the unique genius of the American government and American politics. Professor James Quillen of Stanford put it this way:

> Through history a student comes to know his nation's ideals and traditions, the nature of its government, and the responsibilities of its citizens. In one sense, history is the door through which an individual can enter the edifice of his nation's culture. Without knowledge of history, patriotism has no roots and loyalty no bonds tying it to the past.[22]

John Dewey was not prone to postulating value-laden objectives in the education of the young. But in his remarkable but seldom read and even more seldom quoted, lectures on history, Dewey stated:

> There is one point which without controversy is desirable: that the child should recapitulate the progress of the race, that he should go back of present conditions where everything seems to be given, almost without the exercise of intelligence . . . should get himself back in his imagination to the primitive condition of man . . . and then follow in his constructive imagination the typical steps by which man has seized upon the salient points in the situation . . . and which have given the practical momentum onward in civilization . . .

> It requires the child to recapitulate in himself the occasions which have made the race think, and makes him appreciate in terms of his own experience, the sort of thinking that had actually to be done, with the motives for it on one side, and the results that were reached by it on the other side.[23]

Professor Bruner has recently made crystal clear his position on the place of history in the social studies curriculum in elementary schools and high schools. We should be grateful to him for his candor, and if he and his supporters succeed in emasculating or eliminating the study of history from school curricula, no one will be able to say that this was done surreptitiously or without proper warning.

In an article in the *Saturday Review,* which the editors described as a preview of his latest book *Toward a Theory of Instruction,* Bruner states that his work on a new social studies curriculum has led him to the conclusion that "we are bound to move toward instruction in the sciences of behavior and away from the study of history."[24] The basic reason for the need to shift from history to the behavioral sciences is that history looks to the past, whereas the behavioral sciences prepare the young to grasp and adjust to changing human conditions. "Recorded history," says Bruner,

---

[22] James Quillen, "American History in the Upper Grades and Junior High School," 31st Yearbook, National Council for the Social Studies (Washington, 1961), p. 345.

[23] John Dewey, *Lectures in the Philosophy of Education: 1899,* Reginald D. Archambault, editor (New York: Random House, 1966), p. 258.

[24] Jerome S. Bruner, "Education or Social Invention," *Saturday Review* (February 19, 1966), p. 103.

"is only about five thousand years old. . . . Most of what we teach is within the last few centuries, for the records before are minimal, while records after are relatively rich."[25]   However, Bruner continues, modern methods of retrieving and storing information will make it possible to accumulate large masses of information, and, consequently, "a thousand years from now we will be swamped." Because of this specter, if I understand Bruner correctly, we ought to stop the study of history right now because as he tells us, at that future time there would be little sense "to dwell with such loving care over the details of Brumaire or the Long Parliament or the Louisiana Purchase."

It is quite obvious that Professor Bruner never really enjoyed the study of the dramatic record of the Long Parliament which had a decisive influence on British political institutions and British democracy or the account of the brilliant and dramatic exercise of presidential powers by Thomas Jefferson, whose decision made it possible, in a large measure, for the United States to be the great power it is today. Bruner is disdainful of the record of history which includes only the most recent five thousand years— he seems to be much more interested, as his anthropologically centered curriculum clearly indicates, in teaching about the five-hundred million year old history of the evolution of mammals and man. Without in any way belittling the importance of the study of the origin of human species, one can and perhaps should argue that the study and the understanding of those "mere" five thousand years are of crucial importance for our young generations if they are to live intelligent and useful lives and if they are to be expected to make an effort to prevent the destruction of the human race in an atomic holocaust.

Bruno Bettelheim argued that educators should ask what kind of persons we want our children to be so that they may build a new world, different from the one that we live in, "a world in which they can live in accordance with their full potentialities." Answering the question on how this objective may be achieved, Professor Bettelheim recently wrote:

> Most of all, our schools ought to teach the true nature of man, teach about his troubles with himself, his inner turmoils and about his difficulties in living with others. They should teach the prevalence and the power of both man's social and asocial tendencies, and how the one can domesticate the other, without destroying his independence or self-love.[26]

History is superbly equipped to contribute a great deal to the attainment of these goals in education. It is the business of history to deal with the trials, tribulations, and the inner turmoils of man and the good and the bad

---

[25] *Ibid.*, p. 103.
[26] Bruno Bettelheim, "Notes on the Future of Education," *The University of Chicago Magazine*, Vol. XI, No. 5 (February 1966), p. 14.

in them. Effective history teachers allow their students to glimpse into the tormented soul of Ivan the Terrible and the social and asocial instincts and predilections of the Levellers.

For young people to adapt to changing conditions, Bruner argues, they must study "the possible rather than the achieved. It is the behavioral sciences and their generality with respect to variations in the human condition that must be central to our presentation of man, not the particularities of his history."[27] Thus, Bruner made his choice. Without equivocation and without any attempt to blur the real issue, he wants the social studies curriculum in elementary and secondary schools to be centered on the concepts, generalizations, and skills of the behavioral sciences. He is willing and ready to abandon the teaching of history with its stress on the unique, the separate, and the particular. We have discussed the uses of history and the importance of history in the education of the young in another chapter and we shall not repeat them here. It may suffice here if we observe that if Bruner's ideas on the nature, content, and objectives of the social studies should prevail, elementary and high school students would get a one-sided picture of the world. Generalizations and generalizing concepts are helpful to scholars as ordering devices, but the world as it impinges on the minds of the young is exactly the historical world of the specific, the unique, and the separate. Students want to study about racial problems and traffic laws in the cities, to learn more about the personality of the man in the White House, and about the nature of the war in Vietnam because they are personally and specifically interested in these problems. Teachers of social studies ought to be warned that making the study of structure and skills—"skills in handling and imagining, and in symbolic operations"—the principal emphasis in education, as postulated by Bruner, will transform social studies classes into many hours of unrelieved boredom. The elimination of history from the social studies would be an educational and a national disaster.

The teaching of facts of information is, of course, not an aim in itself. The study of well-analyzed data through the use of the inductive or deductive method, public controversy approach, or any other method must lead, whenever possible, to the formulation of concepts and generalizations. Engle put it well when he wrote that "in teaching the social studies, we should emphasize decision-making as against mere remembering."[28] While "mere" remembering may be useless, it is essential to stress that *without* remembering a great deal of information and data pertaining to the problem under consideration, no intelligent decision-making is possible. Engle goes on to postulate that the primary aim in the social studies is education

---

[27] *Ibid.*, p. 104.

[28] Shirley Engle, "Decision-Making—The Heart of Social Studies Instruction," *Social Education* (November 1960), p. 304.

for citizenship, and its primary concern is "the quality of the beliefs and convictions which students come to hold on public questions."[29]   Here we are again, as in the case of Bruner's stated "ideals," in the realm of values and attitudes.   It is suggested that social studies courses "ought to" impart "respect" and change the quality of the students beliefs and convictions. Leaving, for the moment, the question of the "right," "sound," and "desired" convictions and beliefs, the problem is not so much whether in the social studies courses we "ought to" influence the values and behavior of our students, but whether or at least to what extent this *can* be done.   The rather meager research on value and attitude formation available through courses of instruction has yielded little encouragement to those who believe in the power of schools to change values and attitudes.   Studies on how children form their ideas about politics and social problems indicate that these values and attitudes are formed in elementary school.[30]   The work of Easton and Hess of the University of Chicago concerning political socialization of children revealed that children learn and form attitudes and make value-judgments about politics and government and human behavior before they even enter school.   They suggest that the formative age of values and attitudes is from 3–13, which means that by the time the student enters his first high school social studies class his attitudes, prejudices, and values are quite firmly established.[31]

In spite of the indicated bleak prospects for changing the student's values and attitudes or for teaching them "sound" citizenship or imparting to them the ability to make the "right" decisions, social studies teachers are duty-bound to do all they can to try to change the student's behavior to conform, at least in part, with the ideal of a thinking and concerned citizen in a democratic society.   An effective, imaginative study of history (of truly great history, not "dry facts and dates") may well change or modify the values, attitudes, or thought-habits of students by giving them a sophisticated historical perspective.   The inductive method, as explained by Professor Fenton, may well imbue young people with the habit of careful sifting and analyzing of information or propaganda and avoid snap judgments. The analysis of the public controversy approach to the social studies may give many students skill in conflict resolution.   While conceding these potentially beneficial influences in the area of values and attitude formation, there is no justification to make personality changes the aim or the heart of the social studies.[32]

---

[29] *Ibid.*

[30] See Celia Stendler, *Children of Brasstown* (Urbana, Ill.: Univ. of Illinois Press, 1946).

[31] David Easton and Robert Hess, "The Child's Political World," *Midwest Journal of Political Science*, Vol. 6, No. 3 (August 1963), pp. 222–249.

[32] For difficulties involved in personality change see Philip Worchel and Donn Byrne, eds., *Personality Change* (New York: John Wiley & Sons, 1964).

Lawrence Metcalf has thoughtfully set the limits of the involvement and the responsibility of social studies teachers in the realm of values.

> Perhaps a return to subject matter, a reinterpretation of problem-solving, and a new emphasis upon logic will help teachers to entertain the hypothesis that teaching people to be good is not their province.   Teaching an understanding of how values affect and even distort perception is within their province. Teaching that certain values are inconsistent with other values is within their province as logicians.   It is even their job to teach that some values are democratic and how democracy is different from other systems in its effect on human development.   But no-one, least of all our teachers, can tell the American people what their values are to be.[33]

Social studies teachers cannot and should not be value-free.   They ought to state their views and judgments on controversial and other issues, provided they make it clear that they respect differing opinions and that their judgments are based on careful inquiry.   A teacher who has gained a good reputation based on scholarship and dedication to objective inquiry will experience little difficulty in discussing any and all controversial issues fully and completely.

Let us make our position clear.   What is being proposed here as the proper approach to and the right content in the social studies?   It is suggested that history remain the core of the social studies curriculum but that history teachers be encouraged and instructed to select and use often insights, concepts, and modes of inquiry from the social sciences.   Thus, social studies would become history, geography, and the other social sciences.   Professor Byron Massialas some time ago made a rather felicitous formulation of the aims of the social studies.

> In sum, instruction in history and social studies should be directed toward increasing the store of dependable and reliable knowledge, enhancing the ability of students to utilize analytical tools in historical and social science investigation, offering the opportunity to engage in intuitive thinking, and encouraging the judicious analysis of moral issues confronting the world or the local community.[34]

A history teacher discussing the ante bellum plantation system would study the influence of the planter aristocracy in the political structure of the South and would examine the concept of the elite, as it related to the slave owners, from the points of view of historians, political scientists, economists, and sociologists.   Slave social mobility upwards and downwards

---

[33] Lawrence E. Metcalf, "Some Guidelines for Changing Social Studies Instruction," *Social Education*, No. 4 (April 1963), p. 201.

[34] Byron Massialas, "Teaching History as Inquiry," in Shirley H. Engle, ed., *New Perspectives in World History* (Washington, 1964), p. 634.

from the field hands to the favored servants in the "Big House" would be examined as a system of social control. The economically almost self-sustaining structure of the plantation would be analyzed to discover possible implications for the contrast between the economics of the North and the South and the effect of this contract on the prospects for military victory of the South.

A study of the Populist movement would require the perceptive history teacher to include in addition to the historical narrative of events an inquiry centered around the various types of questions that a sociologist, a political scientist, and an economist would be apt to ask himself about Populism. Obviously, such teaching cannot be based on the use of a textbook which is only the interpretation of a unit or units of history by their author or authors. A history textbook, when used, should be presented to students as *one* possible approach to history or one man's interpretation of historical events. It is our position that there are many kinds of historical knowledge which are, or can be, useful for a future citizen and that a reasonable amount of historical information is indeed essential for any cultured individual. We shudder to think that a time may come when a high school graduate may know much about the structure of sociology, be quite at home with the concept of cultural change, be capable of using the inductive method, but nothing of Bryan's "Cross of Gold Speech," be unable to speak intelligently about the Spanish Armada, or plead ignorance of Cicero, Hannibal, and the Carthaginian Wars. Teachers of social studies should pose to themselves this simple query: "Is it or is it not important for young people entering college to know the "fact" that the murder of Prince Ferdinand at Sarajevo was the *casus belli* of World War I, or that Thomas Jefferson and John Adams died on the same day, July 4, 1826? Or, that Woodrow Wilson was the author of the "Fourteen Points" or that Franklin Delano Roosevelt used the memorable words: "we have nothing to fear but fear itself . . ." Thousands of similar "facts" can, of course, be cited. Masters of secondary schools in England defined their reasons for the teaching of history in simple terms: "One of the best reasons for teaching history to young children is to satisfy their love for a story . . . the teacher should consciously attempt to fire the imagination of his pupils and even to exploit the romance of history."[35]

As for the methods of teaching history, the teacher should be free to use the eclectic approach. He may dramatically present the "story of history" by simply imparting information, he may spend blocs of time on a study *in depth* of a public controversy, using the ingenious techniques developed by Oliver, Shaver and Newman, or he may, as occasion requires it, use the

---

[35] A.W.S. Hutchings, ed., *The Teaching of History* (Cambridge, England: Oxford Univ. Press, 1950), pp. 2–3.

inductive method, recommended by Fenton, by which the student applies the modes of inquiry and thinking of the historian to the problem or event under investigation.   In the area of method as in the area of content, the intellectual and pedagogical autonomy of the history and the social science teacher must be preserved. He should be free to guard against the tendency of downgrading the importance of knowing and within limits of time and capacity, acquaint the students with carefully selected research and findings of historians and of social scientists. The teacher would also be well advised to help students understand the chronological relationships among significant historical events and the time factor and dimension in history. History teaching, greatly enriched by the infusion of concepts and the social science "lenses," may profitably consist of the chronologically oriented historical narrative, made dramatic by the presentation of great personalities and carefully selected in depth case studies. The crux of the problem is whether history will be taught well and imaginatively by teachers trained in history who have also become informed and knowledgeable in at least one of the social sciences. As we have said, many methods of teaching history should be open to teachers. The inductive method, which would allow students to deal with original historical sources and to reach their own conclusions or write their own history, has its advantages, but it also has its weaknesses. Walter Rundell, Jr. wrote:

> The apparent danger with inductive teaching as promoted by some of its advocates, is that it would seem to eschew the collective knowledge of the historical profession garnered over the years . . .   It strikes me as highly unrealistic to disregard the work of generations of historians by making every child his own historian. If inductive teaching is carried to its fullest extent, then we surely will never stand on the shoulders of giants. Like Sisyphus, we will forever be rolling our stones. I trust that those who are promoting inductive teaching do not intend to deny students the use of conventional scholarship altogether.[36]

Not only will exclusively inductive investigations cover little material, but the inductive method also ignores the great potential in teaching contrasting interpretations and conclusions of historians. Historiography can be of great use and value in the teaching of history. A brief presentation of the different conclusions of historians about the causes of World War I and a summary paragraph from Barbara Tuchman's *The Guns of August*, stressing the unknowns and the imponderables in historical research of that great conflict, may provide an excellent motivation for the study of World War I. The use of historiography would also serve to prove to the students

---

[36] Walter Rundell, Jr. "History Teaching: A Legitimate Concern," *Social Education*, Vol. 29 (December 1965), pp. 523–524.

that history as such does not exist. What we have is the scientific and imaginative reconstruction of fragments of the past based on the "relics" left by the past generations. These reconstructions of the past differ from one work of history to another. The use of the various historical interpretations and evaluations of events and leading personalities in history would discourage the use of textbooks as the principal means for history instruction.

Historians have finally realized that unless they begin to discharge their responsibility for the improvement of the quality of instruction of history in elementary and secondary schools and unless they point the way toward a fruitful collaboration between history and the social sciences, the subject matter of history faces greatly diminished status in the social studies curriculum in high schools throughout the country. A special committee of the Organization of American Historians (formerly the Mississippi Valley Historical Association) was appointed in 1964 to study the status of history in secondary schools and to bring in recommendations for improvement. In its report, the committee suggested that history "should have a substantial place in the school curriculum as an independent entity" and be taught by well-trained history teachers.[37] History, the report continued, should be strengthened by the frequent use of social science materials, concepts, and methods. The committee criticized textbook learning of history and saw some benefits in the use of the inductive methods and Bruner's discovery approach to the study of history. But it warned that:

> . . . like every good idea, especially in the field of education, discovery learning could easily become a fad, embraced uncritically and carried too far by teachers who understand fully neither the psychology of learning on which it is based, nor the subject matter area in which it is applied. An over-enthusiastic application of the discovery principle might obscure the crucial time dimension of history, the chronological relationships between historical events.[38]

The committee apparently was only slightly apprehensive over the implications of Bruner's new social studies and cautioned only against "an over-enthusiastic application of the discovery principle." This caution may be interpreted hopefully and optimistically, as statesmanlike restraint and not as resulting from a lack of understanding of the full implication of Bruner's proposals. The report of the O.A.H. committee should be welcomed as a sign of a growing awareness on the part of historians that unless the profession takes cognizance of the new developments in the area of social studies, history may disappear as a subject of instruction in American high schools.

---

[37] "History in the Schools," Report of the Study Committee, Organization of American Historians, Signed by Richard H. Brown, Robert D. Cross, Angus Johnston, Charles Sellers, Chairman, December, 1965. (Mimeographed)
[38] *Ibid.*

8

Case Study: Historians and the

Moral Issues in the Civil War

Objective, value-free history is indeed rare, if it exists at all. This is especially true of periods of stress and conflict. The historiography of the Civil War reflects not only the complex problems involved in that bloody struggle but also the role of personal values, ideology, and background in the writing of history.

Two quite separate but related questions have engaged the attention of historians of the Civil War. What was the essence of the crisis that brought about this bloody war? Could that conflict have been resolved without resort to arms? The answers to both questions are crucial to the understanding not only of the Civil War, but also of the critical period of Reconstruction which still casts its shadow on the contemporary history of our nation. In order to put these complicated problems in perspective, it is important to sketch briefly the ever-changing course of Civil War historiography.

Those who wrote about the Civil War from the perspective of personal participation and involvement did not seem to have much difficulty in defining the basic issue between the North and the South. Two leaders on both sides of the great controversy agreed that slavery was the central issue of the conflict. Henry Wilson, who served during the Civil War as Senator from Massachusetts and was chairman of the Senate Armed Services Committee, wrote a three-volume *History of the Rise and Fall of the Slave Power in America*. Wilson, a self-educated cobbler from Natick, Massachusetts, published his volumes between the years 1872–1877. "This slavery and this Slave Power," Wilson wrote, "in their economical, social, moral and ecclesiastical, and political relations to the people and to the government, demoralizing the one and distracting the councils of the other, made up the vital issues of that 'irrepressible conflict' which finally culminated in a civil war. . . ."[1]

Jefferson Davis, the President of the Confederacy, unrepentant and unforgiving, wrote his history of *The Rise and Fall of the Confederate Government* in a cottage on the Beavoir plantation on the Gulf of Mexico at Pass Christian. In the peaceful surroundings of the plantation, Davis wrote a history of the war which was published in two volumes in 1881. Looking back on the long and costly struggle, Davis expressed only one regret. He was deeply grieved that his beloved South lost the war. Davis made his position clear in the opening sentences of his book:

> The object of this work has been from historical data to show that the Southern States had rightfully the power to withdraw from a Union into which they had, as sovereign communities, voluntarily entered; that the denial of that right was a violation of the letter and spirit of the compact between the States; and that the war waged by the Federal Government against the seceding States was in disregard of the limitations of the Constitution, and destructive of the principles of the Declaration of Independence . . . For the deplorable fact of the war, for the cruel manner it was waged, for the physical and yet sadder moral results it produced, the reader of these pages, I hope, will admit that the South, in the forum of conscience, stands fully acquitted.[2]

The intransigent attitude of some Southern states in the present struggle, more than a hundred years after the Civil War, to assure equal rights to Negroes may be better understood if one recalls that in the Deep South Jefferson Davis' birthday is a legal holiday.

Abolitionist propaganda and the denial of the right of the slaveholder to bring, his slaves with him into all of the new territories constituted, in the view of Jefferson Davis, the major cause of the civil conflict. "By the activity of the propagandists of abolitionism, and the misuse of the sacred word Liberty," Davis wrote, "they recruited from the ardent worshippers of that goddess such numbers as gave them in many Northern states the balance of power between two great political forces that stood arrayed against each other." Unlike some historians and most textbook writers, Davis was under no illusion that Lincoln was lukewarm on the issue of

---

[1] Henry Wilson, *History of the Rise and Fall of the Slave Power in America*, I (Boston, 1872–1877), p. 2.
[2] Jefferson Davis, *The Rise and Fall of the Confederate Government* (New York: Crowell-Collier & Macmillan, 1961), pp. 19, 21.

slavery. He knew that the Republican candidate for the presidency (as he stated in Chicago in 1858 at the opening rally in his senatorial campaign) hated slavery as much as any abolitionist. The election of Lincoln was, Davis asserts, the "casus belli" of the Civil War. "Still forbearing, still hoping, still striving for peace and union we waited until a sectional President, nominated by a sectional convention, elected by a sectional vote—and that the vote of a minority of the people—was about to be inducted into office, under the warning of his own district announcement that the Union could not permanently endure 'half slave and half free' " . . .[3]

The former President of the Confederacy, writing more than two decades after the outbreak of the Civil War, was still moved to write feelingly in defense of slavery.

> Generally they (the Negroes) were born slaves of barbarian masters, untaught in all the useful arts and occupations, reared in heathen darkness, and sold by heathen masters, they were transferred to shores enlightened by the rays of Christianity. There, put to servitude, they were trained in the gentle arts of peace and order and civilization; they increased from a few unprofitable savages to millions of efficient Christian laborers. Their servile instincts rendered them contented with their lot, and their patient toil blessed the land of their abode with unmeasured riches.[4]

The perceptive English writer, Harriet Martineau, who visited the United States in 1835 and wrote about her experiences with slavery had anticipated Davis' apologia of slavery. "I am frequently told," she wrote, "of the endearing relation subsisting between master and slave . . . As long as the above remains ignorant, docile and contented, he is taken care of. But the moment he exhibits that attributes of a rational human being . . . the most deadly hatred springs up; not in the black, but in his oppressors. It is an old truth that we hate those whom we have injured."[5]

The writing of the history of the Civil War based on primary documents began about seventy years ago with the publication by Congress of 128 volumes of the *Official Records of the Union and Confederate Armies.* Using this source and others, Edward von Holst, Chairman of the Department of History of the University of Chicago, published his *Constitutional and Political History of the United States* in seven volumes. Von Holst vigorously condemned the theory that the states had the right to secede and maintained (as Lincoln did in 1858) that the Union was older than the states. He castigated the Southern "slavocracy" and stated that the immorality of slavery was the cause of the Civil War.

---

[3] *Ibid.,* p. 62.
[4] *Ibid.,* p. 329.
[5] Harriet Martineau, *Society in America,* abr. ed. (Garden City, N.Y.: Doubleday & Co., 1962), p. 235.

James Ford Rhodes (1848–1927) looms large in the Civil War historiography. A wealthy amateur historian, Rhodes retired at the age of 37 and devoted himself to writing the *History of the United States from the Compromise of 1850 to the Final Restoration of the Home Rule at the South in 1877.* This massive work, based on meticulous research in all available sources, was published in nine volumes. Like von Holst, Rhodes considered slavery the cause of the Civil War and lauded the abolitionists and, especially John Brown, for having applied "moral ideas and Christian principles to the institution of slavery." Rhodes asserted that the South invoked the doctrine of states' rights and the right to peaceful secession merely as a means of preserving slavery. He stated a simple truism which many historians and almost all textbook writers have chosen to ignore. He said: "The question may be isolated by the incontrovertible statement that if the negro had never been brought to America, our Civil War could not have occurred."[6] According to Rhodes, the villain in the years immediately preceding the armed conflict was the senior Senator from Illinois, Stephen A. Douglas, who in order to further his presidential ambitions precipitated the crisis by his Kansas-Nebraska Bill of 1854. Aware of the efforts of historians (which have continued until today) to find extenuating circumstances for Douglas' actions, Rhodes still believed that the Illinois senator merited a "strong condemnation from history."

Later historians of the so-called "revisionist" school made a sincere and strenuous effort to make Douglas the hero of the story of the sectional conflict. George Fort Milton did not hesitate to state his position in the very title of his laudatory biography, *Stephen A. Douglas—The Needless War.* The thesis of the book was that if the North had followed the policy of "popular sovereignty" as defined by Douglas, the Civil War could have been avoided.

To Charles Beard, the Civil War was basically not a political conflict, but a social and economic cataclysm or revolution. In that struggle between the industrial North and the agricultural, cotton planting South, "the capitalists, laborers, and farmers of the North and the West drove from power in the national government the planting aristocracy of the South." The actual fighting, in Beard's view, was in the light of history only of fleeting importance. The social revolution was the most important outcome of the Civil War.[7]

The many followers of Charles Beard have always taken great pains to deny any affinity between their master's interpretation of American history

---

[6] James Ford Rhodes, *Lectures on the American Civil War* (New York: The Macmillan Co., 1913), p. 5.

[7] Charles A. Beard and Mary R. Beard, *The Rise of American Civilization,* Vol. I (New York: The Macmillan Co., 1927), p. 21.

and the Marxist theory of economic historical determinism. In general, this denial is valid. However, there is little, if any, difference between the appraisal of the causes of the Civil War made by Charles Beard and that of Karl Marx and Friedrich Engels. Marx and Engels wrote in *The Civil War in the United States,* "The present struggle between the South and the North is . . . nothing but a struggle between two social systems, between the system of slavery and the system of free labor." The *Great Soviet Encyclopedia* describes the conflict as a struggle between the "bourgeois Republican Party" which represented the industrial interests supported by workers-farmers of the North and the slave-owning big landowners of the South.[8]

Many present-day historians and some high school textbook writers have accepted the interpretations of the Civil War of two of the most influential "revisionist" writers, James G. Randall and Avery Craven. Thorough research into the period convinced both historians that the Civil War came because of a "blundering generation," as Randall termed it, that allowed the extremists of the North and the extremists of the South to dominate political thinking in the country. The armed conflict represented the dismal failure of the moderate majority in both regions to compromise their differences. These differences, including the issue of slavery, were blown up out of proportion by such fanatics in the North as Garrison, Phillips, Sumner, and Stevens and in the South, Toombs, Rhett, Slidell, Ruffin, and Yancey. It was the breakdown of statesmanship and the "breakdown of the democratic process," in the words of Craven, that caused the Civil War.

Randall maintained that there was really no basic difference between Lincoln and Douglas on the issue of slavery in their celebrated Debates in 1858. The issue of the extension of slavery which brought about the founding of the Republican Party and the election of Lincoln, did not, according to Randall, "mean much politically beyond agitation."[9] The Southerners cared little about taking slaves into Kansas and the Republicans knew in their hearts that Kansas because of its geography was not suitable to the use of slave labor. Thus, both sides could have accepted the Kansas-Nebraska Act as a workable compromise were it not for "the element of emotional unreason and oversold leadership." "If one word or phrase were selected to account for the war," Randall concluded, "that word would not be slavery, or state-rights or diverse civilizations. It would have to be such a word as fanaticism (on both sides), or misunderstanding or politics."[10]

---

[8] *A Soviet View of the American Past,* Prepared by the State Historical Society of Wisconsin (Chicago: Univ. of Chicago Press, 1960), p. 24.
[9] James G. Randall, "The Blundering Generation" *Mississippi Valley Historical Review* October 1940), p. 14.
[10] *Ibid.,* p. 27.

Paraphrasing Seward's words, Avery Craven had maintained that the Civil War was a "repressible conflict" and charged that "the distortions and the hatreds of the years had flowered in open battle. The irrepressible conflict of the politician had been reduced to the struggle of armies."[11] In the introduction to his volume *The Coming of the Civil War*, Craven deplored the orthodox histories of the Civil War by von Holst and McMaster, who viewed the conflict from the Northern point of view. Craven asserted in the introduction to the first edition that he and his colleagues approached the study of this terrible controversy not as partisans of either the North or the South, but as scientists. As a scientific historian, he saw the war as a national tragedy brought about by the inability or unwillingness of the leaders of the South and the North, induced by years of strain, to discuss issues and to find honorable and workable compromises. Undoubtedly stung by some of his critics, Craven wrote in the introduction to the second edition that "he had no intention of saying categorically that the war was a 'needless war'"—a term he has never used at any time. And even more certainly, he had no desire to defend slavery.[12] While Craven has not said "categorically" that the Civil War was a needless war, the whole gist of his argument was that the armed conflict was the result of unyielding fanaticism on both sides and the armed clash could have and should have been averted by reason and statesmanship. The insinuation, undoubtedly a false one, that Craven was a defender of slavery was the direct result of his laboriously "scientific" and objective analysis both of the abolitionist attacks on slavery and the Southern defense of the "sacred institution." For some reason, Craven condemned both with equal vehemence, without seeing a basic difference between men who saw evil and degradation in the enslavement of human beings and those who looked upon the existence of slavery as the mainstay in the building of a higher Christian civilization. Summing up the chapter on "The Southern Defense of Slavery," Craven wrote: "The extremists of the South, like their fellows of the North, stood thus self-convinced of their own righteousness and of the depravity of their opponents. Argument had deepened prejudices. Unreason had engendered unreason. Emphasis on faults had obliterated all understanding of virtues in other ways of life."[13] Obviously, Craven bemoaned the failure of the Northerners to see at least some virtues in the Southern way of life based on slavery.

A few years ago, Edmund Wilson apparently became fascinated by the leading figures of the Civil War period and wrote some biographical

---

[11] Avery Craven, *The Coming of the Civil War*, 2nd ed. (Chicago: Univ. of Chicago Press, 1957), p. 440.

[12] *Ibid.*, p. x.

[13] *Ibid.*, p. 412.

essays about them. Had he been satisfied with these splendid portraits presented in his lively and vivid style, he would have made an important contribution to the Civil War literature. However, our most distinguished literary critic decided to give his readers an explanation of the "real" causes of the great conflict. Without hesitation, and without providing any evidence, Wilson concluded that the idea that the North was fighting the South to free the salves is a naïve myth. Slavery, he asserts, was embarrassing to many people in the South as well as in the North—and many people in the South and in the North approved of it. Having made this rather superficial statement, Wilson proceeds with this dictum: "The institution of slavery, which the Northern states had by this time got rid of, thus supplied the militant Union North with the rabble-rousing moral issue which is necessary in every modern war to make the conflict appear as a melodrama."[14] The "real" reason for the War was the imperialist drive for power of the North. Lincoln, according to Wilson, realizing that the South and the North were in reality two different countries, decided on the unification of the United States in the same way as Bismarck and Lenin each were determined to unify Germany and Russia. In the end of this power-drive of the North, Lincoln "kept the Union together by subordinating the South to the North" in the same way as Bismarck imposed the Prussian hegemony on Germany and as Lenin succeeded in "binding Russia . . . in a tight bureaucratic net."[15] Surprisingly, reviewers of Wilson's book, many of whom know or should know better, failed to rebuke him for his excursion into Civil War historiography.

High school history textbooks, used in millions of copies throughout the country by many hundreds of thousands of high school students, almost without exception have adopted the "revisionist," Randall-Milton-Craven line. They picture Lincoln as lukewarm on the issue of slavery and unthinkingly parrot Randall's line that "Lincoln shared some of the Southern attitudes toward the Negro," completely ignoring the evolution of Lincoln's view on the Negro question. Some textbooks either ignore or belittle the importance of the Lincoln-Douglas debates or fail to see their real importance.

The debates not only provided a national forum for Lincoln and gave evidence that the Illinois politician was a knowledgeable and able debater, but even more importantly the debates clarified the basic ideological position of the newly founded Republican party and underscored its cleavage with the Democratic party on the issue of slavery. Randall and Craven have suggested that there was no basic difference between the debaters.

---

[14] Edmund Wilson, *Patriotic Gore—Case-Studies in the Literature of the American Civil War* (New York: Oxford Univ. Press, 1962), p. xvi.

[15] *Ibid.*, xvii.

The evidence clearly points to an opposite conclusion. At the Jonesboro debate, Stephen A. Douglas revealed himself as a determined believer in the principle of white supremacy. "I hold that this government," he said, "was made on the white basis, by white men for the benefit of white men and none others. . . . The signers of the Declaration (of Independence) had no reference to the Negro when they declared all men to be created equal."[16]

In his answer Lincoln rejected this thesis without equivocation, asserting that the Declaration pertained to all people, including Negroes, who were also endowed with the unalienable rights to life, liberty, and the pursuit of happiness. At the opening of the debates, Lincoln declared in Chicago: "I have always hated slavery, I think as much as any abolitionist." The claim that there was no real difference of opinion in the debates was not shared by Lincoln. After Douglas, who showed himself totally indifferent to the moral implications of slavery, stated that he did not care whether the people of Kansas voted slavery "up or down," Lincoln told the audience in Alton, Illinois: "The real issue in this controversy, the one pressing upon every mind is the sentiment on the part of one class that looks upon the institution of slavery as a wrong and of another class that does not look upon slavery as a wrong."[17]

The revisionist school of Civil War historians and most of the textbook writers find support for their view of Lincoln as a conservative on the Negro question by quoting his statement made in the Charleston debate in which he said that he did not favor social and political equality of the white and the black races. This statement proves that in 1858 Lincoln did not favor social and political equality for Negroes. But in 1858 even Lloyd Garrison and Thaddeus Stevens opposed racial equality. At that time, the only issue before the country was the existence of slavery. Using the Charleston statement to describe Lincoln's attitude to the rights of Negroes is as valid as it would be for a future historian to describe Lyndon Johnson's position on the Negro question by quoting his views and voting record on civil rights when he was a Congressman from Texas.

Almost all textbooks, both on the high school and college level, quote Lincoln's letter to Horace Greeley, dated August 22, 1862, in which he said: "My paramount object is to save the Union. . . . If I could save the Union without freeing any slave, I would do it; and if I could save it by freeing all the slaves I would do it; and if I could save it by freeing some and leaving others alone, I would also do it." This letter is cited as proof of Lincoln's ambivalent attitude to Negro slavery. Textbook writers, however,

---

[16] Edwin Earle Sparks, ed., *The Lincoln-Douglas Debates of 1858* (Springfield, Ill.: Illinois State Library, 1908), p. 225.

[17] *Ibid.*, p. 482.

fail to point out that when Lincoln was writing the Greeley letter, the text of the Emancipation Proclamation had already been read to the Cabinet and the President merely waited for a propitious moment to issue it. The Proclamation, which was issued on September 22, 1862, was essentially ready for publication some time before the letter to Greeley was published. Strange as it is, no textbook takes note of a letter written by Abraham Lincoln to General James S. Wadsworth. This remarkable letter, written in January, 1864, provides an excellent insight into the evolution of Lincoln's views on the position of Negroes. It reads in full:

> You desire to know, in the event of our complete success in the field, the same being followed by a loyal and cheerful submission on the part of the South, if universal amnesty should not be accompanied with universal suffrage.
>
> Now since you know my private inclinations as to what terms should be granted to the South in the contingency mentioned, I will here add, that if our success should thus be realized, followed by such desired results, I cannot see, if universal amnesty is granted, how, under the circumstances, I can avoid exacting in return universal suffrage, or at least, suffrage on the basis of intelligence and military service.
>
> How to better the conditions of the colored race has long been a study which has attracted my serious and careful attention; hence I think I am clear and decided as to what course I shall pursue in the premises, regarding it a religious duty, as the nation's guardian of these people, who have so heroically vindicated their manhood on the battlefield, where, in assisting to save the life of the Republic, they have demonstrated in blood their right to ballot, which is but the humane protection of the flag they have so fearlessly defended.
>
> The restoration of the Rebel States to the Union *must rest upon the principle of civil and political equality of both races;* and it must be sealed by a general amnesty.[18]

Many history textbooks either omit any serious discussion of the causes of the Civil War, follow the revisionist line of the "blundering generation," and ascribe the armed conflict to the rise of unbridled fanaticism on both sides. There are few high school history textbooks and very few college textbooks which discuss slavery as a moral issue. They usually ignore the widespread conviction in the North, which went far beyond the circle of Abolitionists, that the existence of slavery was a blot on American democracy and that the extension of slavery threatened to obliterate the line between slavery and freedom. Kenneth Stampp who has done significant research on the causes of the Civil War, has gradually been moved to look upon the war as a moral crusade. He writes in his *And the War Came:*

---

[18] Quoted in Grady McWhiney, ed., *Reconstruction and the Freedmen* (Chicago: Univ. of Chicago Press, 1963) (my italics).

"The impending Yankee crusade involved, like all such enterprises, a strange blending of human emotions. Into the blend went the idealism of strong-minded men who would foster political democracy, destroy slavery, and redeem the South. Into it also went the conviction that the shedding of blood was justified for these great objectives."[19]

Arthur Schlesinger, Jr. rejected the attempts of the revisionists to minimize the deep moral issues involved in the sectional conflict. The South, he stated, devoted half a century to the creation of a social system whose cornerstone, in the words of Alexander Stephens, was human bondage. Ideas of human dignity and freedom became inimical and threatening to such a society. Schlesinger decried the moral relativism of the revisionist, scientific historians. "A society closed in the defense of evil institutions," Schlesinger wrote, "thus creates moral differences far too profound to be solved by compromise. Such a society forces upon every one, both those living at the time and those writing about it later, the necessity for a moral judgment; and the moral judgment in such cases becomes an indispensable factor in historical understanding."[20]

Schlesinger's article appeared sixteen years ago, but it had little influence on textbook writers or on the way Civil War is taught in most high schools and in many colleges. There is still a massive resistance to allowing our young generations to see the terrible blood-letting of 1861–1865 as, at least in part, a moral crusade to safeguard the principles of American democracy.

Samuel Eliot Morison, who has repeatedly told his colleagues that "objective" history which avoids value judgments is dull history, concluded that slavery was the central cause of the Civil War. "Nobody who has read the letters, state papers, newspapers, and other surviving literature of the generation before 1861," he wrote, "can honestly deny that the one main, fundamental reason for secession of the original states which formed the Southern Confederacy was to protect, expand, and perpetuate the slavery of the Negro race."[21] Morison's assertion was confirmed years ago by Ulrich Bonnell Phillips, the outstanding historian from the University of Georgia and Yale University, who proudly and approvingly told the audience at the Conference of the American Historical Association in 1928 that the central theme of Southern history was "a common resolve indomitably maintained—that the South shall be and remain a white man's country."[22] Phillips, the

[19] Kenneth M. Stampp, And the War Came (Baton Rouge, La.: Louisiana State Univ. Press, 1950), p. 261.

[20] Arthur M. Schlesinger, Jr., "The Causes of the American Civil War: A Note on Historical Sentimentalism," Partisan Review, Vol. 16 (1949), p. 27.

[21] Samuel Eliot Morison, The Oxford History of the American People (New York: Oxford Univ. Press, 1964), p. 608.

[22] U. B. Phillips, The Course of the South to Secession, ed. Merton Coulter (New York: Hill & Wang, 1939, 1964), p. 152.

author of the monumental work *American Negro Slavery,* viewed slavery sympathetically and asserted the innate racial inferiority of the Negroes. Phillips claimed that slavery probably would have disappeared soon after 1860 had the South not been the victim of abolitionist propaganda and had not the North been determined on a policy of economic exploitation of the South.

It might be well to remember that the road to Fort Sumter was long and turbulent and strewn with shattered compromises, which when adopted were hailed as lasting agreements only to end in dismal failures. In the course of sixty years, major attempts to find a compromise between the North and the South by statesmanship and by the best use of the democratic process were made in 1820, 1832, 1846, 1850, and 1854. It is significant that these desperate attempts to find a modus vivendi between the two sections did *not* deal with economic differences or with states' rights. They were solely attempts to settle the controversy over slavery.

The story of the 1820 Missouri Compromise began in 1819 with the introduction of an amendment to the bill admitting Missouri to statehood which would have prohibited the further introduction of slaves into Missouri. This amendment, introduced by Representative James Tallmage, Jr. of New York, began a controversy which raged for two years. The controversy, in which Northern and Southern leaders exchanged denunciations and threats, was limited exclusively to the issue of slavery. The resurrection of the controversy over slavery terrified Thomas Jefferson like "a fire-bell in the night." He openly predicted that the conflict over slavery would bring about an armed clash. The bitter struggle was finally settled when under the leadership of Henry Clay, Congress admitted Maine as a free state, refrained from prohibiting slavery in Missouri, and forever prohibited slavery north of the line 36° 30′. After a tumultuous two years, the country breathed a collective sigh of relief. Slavery seemed secure where it existed and the North was assured that human bondage would not engulf any more territory in the North.

The peace lasted only until the South Carolina Nullification crisis, which began in 1828 and lasted until 1832. In part, the crisis concerned a high tariff bill passed by Congress, but the root of the crisis was South Carolina's concern and outrage at the growth of abolitionist propaganda in the North. Calhoun's *The South Carolina Exposition and Protest,* with its new doctrine defending the right of the people of any state to nullify a federal law or to secede from the Union, was a clear warning to the North not to interfere with the "sacred institution."

Governor George McDuffie of South Carolina, who was instrumental in winning Calhoun over to the extreme states' rights position, denounced in his 1835 message to the Legislature "the most offensive and inflammatory character of the abolitionist propaganda aimed 'to seduce our slaves from their fidelity.'" He warned the people of his state not to underestimate the small abolitionist movement led by "these wicked monsters and deluded fanatics." He asked the Legislature to urge the Northern states to punish these fanatics who disturbed the peace of the country. On slavery, McDuffie wrote:

> For the institution of slavery we hold ourselves responsible only to God . . . . No human institution, in my opinion, is more manifestly consistent with the will of God, than domestic slavery. . . . That the African Negro is destined by Providence to occupy this condition of servile dependence, is not less manifest. It is marked on the face, stamped on the skin, and evinced by the intellectual inferiority and natural improvidence of this race . . . .[23]

The Governor demanded that the Northern states issue forthwith "a formal and solemn disclaimer" that they would never interfere with domestic slavery in South Carolina. Significantly, McDuffie's message, coming only three years after the great tariff controversy, did not mention any economic issue. It was devoted in its entirety to the preservation of slavery. Craven's assertion that slavery mattered little in the South is, in view of this message and hundreds of similar documents, rather inexplicable.

Southern leaders consistently viewed slavery as the central issue in their controversy with the North. Twenty-six years after McDuffie's message, Alexander H. Stephens, Vice-President of the Confederacy, said in a speech in Savannah, Georgia: "Our new government is founded upon exactly the opposite ideas; its foundations are laid, its cornerstone rests upon the great truth that the Negro is not equal to the white man; that slavery, subordination to the superior race, is his natural and moral condition."[24]

The claim put forward by Jefferson Davis and other apologists for the South that secession was at least partly justified by the fact that the coercion of the South was ordered by Lincoln, a sectional President, cannot be squared with the fact that almost thirty years before a President born in South Carolina, and one who came to office by a landslide victory, told the South that he was determined to use all necessary force to prevent secession. Andrew Jackson stated in his Proclamation of December 10, 1832 that "disunion by armed force is treason." He told South Carolina that "dreadful consequences would fall on the heads of the would be nullifiers and secessionists. The federal government cannot accede to the mad project of disunion, of which you would be the first victims. Its First Mag-

---

[23] John A. Scott, ed., *Living Documents in American History* (New York: Washington Square Press, 1964), pp. 328–331.

[24] Kenneth M. Stampp, ed., *The Causes of the Civil War* (Englewood Cliffs, N.J.: Prentice-Hall, 1959), p. 127.

istrate cannot, if he would, avoid the performance of his duty." Using almost the same words that later were spoken by Lincoln, Jackson added: "If it be the will of Heaven that the recurrence of its primeval curse on man for the shedding of a brother's blood should fall upon our land, that it be not called down by any offensive act on the part of the United States."[25]

The Mexican War in 1846 and the prospect of the annexation of new territories again broke the short-lived peace on the slavery front. Many, including Clay and Lincoln, who at that time was a Whig Representative in Congress, looked on the Mexican war as an unjustified war of conquest, waged to expand slavery. Several times the House of Representatives had adopted the Wilmot Proviso which would have prohibited slavery in the territory to be acquired from Mexico, but each time the Senate, where Southern strength was great, prevented the passage of the amendment.

After the House in 1849 voted to organize the territories of New Mexico and California on the basis of the Wilmot Proviso, the bitter controversy over slavery broke out again. Once again, the Southern spokesmen threatened secession and Mississippi proposed to hold an all-Southern convention in Nashville, Tennessee to consider action to be taken in case of the passage of the Wilmot Proviso. Many leading men in South Carolina urged immediate secession, and their proposal received strong support in many other Southern states. Senator Robert Toombs of Georgia openly spoke of secession on the floor of the Senate. In 1850 the country was on the threshold of a civil war.

In the spirit of a well-functioning democratic process and in the display of superb statesmanship, in complete contradiction of the views of Randall and Craven, Henry Clay of Kentucky, Daniel Webster of Massachusetts, and Stephen A. Douglas of Illinois worked out an elaborate compromise which, at the last moment, averted the violent clash. This new formula for a settlement between the North and the South, known as the Compromise of 1850, involved no other issue, economical or political, except problems connected with slavery. California was to be admitted as a free state, a strong Fugitive Slave Law was passed, the slave trade was abolished in the District of Columbia, Texas was given compensation for territory added to slave-free New Mexico, and the Southwest was to be organized without the Wilmot Proviso.

This was an honorable settlement, a compromise that should have buried the issue of slavery for at least a quarter of a century. It was gratefully endorsed by most people in the country, who were tired of over thirty years of controversy over slavery. The compromise was the work of moderate, sensible people who overcame the objections of the fire-eaters in the North

---

[25] John A. Scott, ed., *Living Documents in American History* (New York: Washington Square Press, 1964), pp. 447, 449.

and in the South. If one bears in mind the strictures of the revisionist historians about the evitability of the conflict, the Compromise of 1850 should have been the way to avoid a national tragedy. But this was not to be. Even before the vote on the sections of the Compromise was taken, the foremost spokesman of the South, John Calhoun, predicted that the concessions made by Webster, at the peril of his political career, were not enough. He predicted that unless the North took more stringent measures to silence all agitation against slavery, the end would be disunion.

Calhoun, who, one would assume, was not considered an extremist by Randall, made it clear that the South would fight if "the relation between the two races in the Southern section, which constitute a vital portion of her social organization" were threatened.[26]

The responsibility for saving the Union, Calhoun stated, rested on the North. The South could offer no more compromises. He told the Senate: "How can the Union be saved? To this I answer, there is but one way by which it can be: and that is, by adopting such measures as will satisfy the states belonging to the Southern section, that they can remain in the Union consistently with their honor and their safety."[27] It is important to note that the safeguards demanded by this most articulate spokesman of the South did not pertain to economic issues, or states' rights—they were concerned solely with the demand that the North silence the critics of slavery, a demand that clearly was unacceptable and unenforceable because it ran contrary to the free speech and free press guarantees in the Bill of Rights. What this "moderate" leader of the South demanded can be better understood if one recalls a section from the introduction by Harriet Beecher Stowe to one of the later editions of *Uncle Tom's Cabin*. Mrs. Stowe, who according to a half-joking and half-serious jest of President Lincoln "made this big war," wrote about the enforced silence on the question of slavery in the period before she published her book. "It was a general saying," she wrote, "among conservative and sagacious people that this subject was a dangerous one to investigate, and that nobody could begin to read and think upon it without becoming practically insane; moreover, that it was a subject of such delicacy that no discussion of it could be held in the free states without impinging upon the sensibilities of the slave states. . . ."[28] Such was the pervasive, evil influence of salvery which extended its long shadow all the way to New England.

Calhoun, speaking from his deathbed, predicted that all the high hopes which were expressed for the 1850 Compromise would soon come to naught.

---

[26] *Ibid.*, p. 485.
[27] *Ibid.*, p. 490.
[28] Quoted in Edmond Wilson, *Patriotic Gore—Case Studies in the Literature of the American Civil War* (New York: Oxford Univ. Press, 1962), p. 5.

Only four years later the controversy over slavery broke out with a fury which in short order doomed the Whig Party, split the Democratic Party, gave birth to the Republican Party, and brought about the election of Abraham Lincoln. The 1854 crisis, which began with the introduction by Stephen A. Douglas of the Kansas-Nebraska Bill, centered solely on the issue of the extension of slavery. With the advantage of hindsight, revisionist historians have argued and most textbooks still argue, that the question over whether slaves could be brought into Kansas was basically irrelevant because the geography of that state was not conducive to the use of slave labor. This is, at best, an "iffy" argument. All contemporary evidence proves that the people on both sides of the "Bloody Kansas" controversy either did not know or did not care about such a sophisticated argument. Those who were determined to keep Kansas free were deeply stirred by the repeal of the cherished Missouri Compromise, the first compromise on the issue of slavery adopted in 1820. Men like Lincoln, Seward, and Greeley, supported by the mass of the Northern people, were not prepared to see the line drawn between freedom and slavery now erased. On the other hand, the Southern leaders, like Davis and Stephens, thoroughly alarmed by the rising antislavery sentiment in the North were convinced that without the extension of slavery the "sacred institution" would be strangled by the growing antislavery sentiment and power. An emotional crisis, even one induced by imaginary fears, can be as real and grave as one induced by apprehensions well-grounded in reality. Thus, in 1854, in spite of sincere efforts for peace and excellent statesmanship, the prospects for a lasting settlement between the North and the South were growing more and more remote.

Little wonder that by the end of 1860 Abraham Lincoln had finally despaired of any chance of reaching an honorable compromise with the South. The reason was not as has been suggested, that he underestimated the strength of the secession sentiment in the South. By December, he was not blind to the actual secession of South Carolina, Mississippi, Alabama, and Florida. It is rather that Lincoln concluded that any compromise which would by an amendment to the Constitution safeguard forever the existence of slavery was too high a price to pay for a temporary peace. He remained convinced that the nation could not remain forever half slave and half free. When rumors of compromising efforts reached him in Springfield, the President-elect wrote to Senator Lyman Trumbull and to several of the other Illinois Congressmen almost identical letters urging them to oppose any of the suggested compromises, especially the "Crittenden Compromise," aiming at appeasing the wrath of the South. In a letter to Lyman Trumbull he wrote:

> Let there be no compromise on the question of extending slavery—if there be, all our labor is lost, and ere long, must be done again—the dangerous

ground—that into which some of our friends have a hankering to run—Pop. Soc.—have none of it. The tug has come and better now than any time hereafter.[29]

One more final effort to use the democratic process of debate and accommodation was made at the initiative of Virginia by convening of a peace conference. The Conference met on February 4, 1861 in Washington, attended by most of the Southern states still in the Union and most of the Northern states. This was a distinguished gathering, presided over by John Tyler of Virginia, the former President. The Conference offered a last-ditch plan to settle the differences between the South and the North which called for seven amendments to the Constitution all aimed at making it impossible for Congress ever to interfere with slavery. The majority of the delegates from the North voted for this harsh plan, but the South was so intent on secession that even Virginia which called the conference and the president of the convention, ex-President Tyler, voted against the final plan.

Lincoln expressed his firm opposition to the plan proposed by the Peace Conference because as he stated on many occasions, he looked to the time when slavery as an evil would be abolished. He also clearly saw, especially from the vote of Virginia, that the sentiment for the South as an independent country was overwhelming. An interesting and little known episode during the Civil War fully confirmed Lincoln's convictions. On May 25, 1863, on the orders of President Lincoln, the Ohio Copperhead, Clement L. Vallandigham, was illegally escorted through the Union lines and delivered to the officers of the Confederate Army. It was expected that the Confederacy would welcome the man who opposed the war, predicted the Union's defeat and who hated Lincoln and called for "Union as it was and the Constitution as it is." On the contrary, the Southern press denounced their Northern sympathizer as an enemy because he advocated reunion. The Richmond *Sentinel* stated: "So odious to us has the idea of reunion with the North become that we denounce the party of which Vallandigham is chief."[30] The Confederate government declared the leading Northern Copperhead an "enemy alien" and deported him to Canada.

Slavery and only slavery was the theme of the Peace Conference. Samuel Eliot Morison, in a pointed rebuke to those who would deny that the Civil War was a war on human bondage and on the denial of human rights, wrote:

---

[29] Quoted in Mark M. Krug, *Lyman Trumbull—Conservative Radical* (New York: A. S. Barnes & Co., 1965), p. 175.

[30] The account of Vallandigham's exile in the South is based on an excellent study by Frank L. Klement, "Clement L. Vallandigham's Exile in the Confederacy, May 25–June 17, 1863," *Journal of Southern History* (May 1965), pp. 149–163.

I wish that some of our evasive historians, our mufflers of great, passionate issues, who are trying to persuade the American public that Negro slavery had nothing to do with the Civil War, would read the debates in this (February, 1861 Peace Convention. There is no suggestion in any of the Southern delegates' speeches of any grievance against the North, or against (Lincoln's) Republican party, other than hostility to slavery. Tariff, internal improvements, all those trumped-up issues which were the grist of the Confederate propaganda then, and since, were never even mentioned. . . .[31]

The existence of slavery, which was detested as a moral and political evil by the great majority of the people in the North and defended as a "sacred institution" indispensable to the Southern way of life, was the single, most important cause of the Civil War. Lincoln was not lukewarm, but hated human bondage as much as any abolitionist. The war did not come because of lack of statesmanship and the breaking down of the democratic process; it came after five major attempts at compromise had ended in failure and because no practical solution to the slavery controversy was found. If the war was avoidable, no one then and nobody since has suggested by what arrangement it could have been avoided. The North, under Lincoln, became convinced that the extension of slavery and, yes, the very existence of slavery in the South was a blot on American democracy and a violation of the tenets on which this democracy was founded. The survival of American democracy, and nothing less than that, was at stake in the Civil War.

---

[31] Samuel Eliot Morison, *Vistas of History* (New York: Alfred A. Knopf, 1964), p. 142.

9

Case Study: For a "Fair Deal" in

the Teaching of Reconstruction

The period of Reconstruction was a crucial and complex time in the history of our nation. The history of those years, extending only from 1865 to 1877, left such scars and so many unresolved problems that historians have found it very difficult to write about Reconstruction in an objective and factual manner. Yet it is imperative that we attempt to have clear knowledge of the events and issues of those years which followed the Civil War because such an understanding is essential for the understanding of the issue of civil rights, political alignments in the South, and a host of other related contemporary political, social, and economic problems. The significance of the civil rights planks adopted at the national conventions of the Democratic and Republican parties, the policies pursued on the racial question by Republican and Democratic administrations, and the political behavior of the South today can become intelligible and meaningful only on the basis of a thorough knowledge and understanding of the developments and issues involved in the Reconstruction of the South in the period between the end of the Civil War and the inauguration of President Rutherford B. Hayes. Our attitude toward the newly independent countries in Africa may also be shaped in a measure by the clarity of our understanding of the forces that shaped the destiny of the South and the North during Reconstruction.

In spite of a prodigious amount of historical documents and research, the period of Reconstruction has as yet failed to produce a definitive study. The abundance of evidence has enabled historians to find enough supporting data for utterly conflicting accounts, theories, and conclusions. It has evidently been difficult for historians to assess objectively the post-Civil War mood, attitudes, and frustrations of the people of South and North. Even more difficult is the task of evaluating the motives behind the actions of the principal characters like Andrew Johnson, Charles Sumner, General Nathan Bedford Forrest, and Wade Hampton. Lack of reliable documentary evidence makes it hard to understand the temper, aspirations, and behavior patterns of the four million freed slaves. The problem of the historiography of the period is further compounded by the fact that no period, with perhaps the exception of the early years of the New Deal, presents such baffling and complex constitutional questions. Questions concerning the legal status of the ex-Confederate states and the question of whether the President or Congress had jurisdiction over the restoration of the Union have not yet been resolved.

The great danger implicit in the study of this difficult and complex period is the temptation to simplify and condense its history. Such simplifications, unfortunately, lead to distortions and intentional or unintentional bias. One can sympathize with the difficulties facing authors of high school and college textbooks when writing about Reconstruction. They must, of necessity, write in a condensed fashion and must present clear-cut appraisals, snappy evaluations, and definitive judgments. The result, as far as the period of Reconstruction is concerned, is a black-and-white picture which lacks judiciousness, balance, and depth. The story, like the typical television Western, has heroes and villains; villains commit their crimes for a time, but at last the heroes prevail. The villains are the "vindictive" and "selfish" Radical Republicans like Stevens and Sumner who, with the help of the "barbarous," "illiterate" Negroes and the "rapacious" and "unscrupulous" carpetbaggers and scalawags, imposed on the South "Devil" and "corrupt" governments. The hero is usually President Andrew Johnson whose attempt to follow the merciful and magnanimous policies toward the South enunciated by Abraham Lincoln was frustrated and sabotaged by the "unscrupulous," "ambitious," and "vengeful" Radicals. The South, beaten and oppressed and despairing of getting justice and compassion at the hands of Congress, had no choice but to turn to massive resistance against the military Reconstruction governments. Occasionally, the southern whites were compelled to use extra-legal means of keeping the Negroes and their Republican allies from the polls by employing the scare tactics of the Ku Klux Klan and the Knights of the White Camelia. Finally, the efforts of the Southerners, aided by friendly elements in the North, succeeded in throwing off the yoke of the Reconstruction governments which had been dominated by ex-slave Negroes. The Union was restored and freedom and tranquility returned to the South.

What is wrong with this tale? First, it paints a picture of Reconstruction in black and white colors when the predominant color should have been gray. The tale assumes that all Radicals, or as James Randall called them, "the Vindictives," were devils, while in fact they were a varied group of diverse individuals. Similarly, the hero Andrew Johnson emerges from a close examination not as a knight in shining armor, but as a dour, dedicated, but rather ineffective President. In short, neither the tortuous story of Reconstruction nor the variety of its heroes lend themselves to narration as a simple tale of heroes and villains. A balanced presentation requires thorough research, balance and judicious weighing of the evidence—of all the evidence available.

It is rather unfortunate that even professional historians who have done valuable research of the period have not been able to overcome their personal bias and have failed to give us the findings of their historical investigations *sine ira et studio*.[1] Consider, for instance, these statements about Reconstruction made by two historians of high standing and reputation. Claude G. Bowers wrote in the introduction to his book, *The Tragic Era:*

> That the Southern people literally were put to the torture is vaguely understood, but even historians have shrunk from the unhappy task of showing us the torture chambers. It is impossible to grasp the real significance of the revolutionary proceedings of the rugged conspirators working out the policies of Thaddeus Stevens. . . . Brutal men inspired by personal ambition or party motives assumed the pose of philanthropists and patriots and thus deceived . . . vast numbers of well-meaning people of the North.[2]

W. E. B. DuBois, the Negro historian, wrote in his book *Black Reconstruction:*

> The real frontal attack on Reconstruction, as interpreted by the leaders of national thought in 1870 and for some time thereafter, came from the universities and particularly from Columbia and Johns Hopkins. . . . One fact and one alone explains the attitude of most recent writers toward Reconstruction; they cannot conceive of Negroes as men; in their minds the word Negro connotes "inferiority" and "stupidity" lightened only by unreasoning gaiety and humor. . . . Not a single great leader of the nation during the Civil War and Reconstruction has escaped attack and libel. The magnificent figures of Charles Sumner and Thaddeus Stevens have been besmirched almost beyond recognition. We have been cajoling and flattering the South and slurring the North because the South is determined to rewrite history, but the North is not interested in history but in wealth. . . . Three-fourths of the testimony against the Negro in Re-

---

[1] See Bernard Weisberger, "The Dark and Bloody Ground of Reconstruction Historiography," *Journal of Southern History*, Vol. 25 (November 1959).
[2] Claude G. Bowers, *The Tragic Era* (Boston: Houghton Mifflin Co., 1929), Introduction.

construction is on unsupported evidence of men who hated and despised Negroes and regarded it as loyalty to blood, patriotism to country, and filial tribute to fathers to lie, steal or kill in order to discredit these black folk.[3]

Obviously there must be some middle ground of historical objectivity between these two extreme and obviously exaggerated appraisals of the Reconstruction history and historiography.

It is essential, first of all, to assess as clearly and as objectively as possible the state of affairs and the mood of the South and of the North at the end of the Civil War. There are some facts about which no doubt can be entertained. The long, bloody, and ruinous war left the South in a shattered condition. The proud Confederacy ceased to exist as a political organism, and the economy of the region was utterly dislocated by the abolition of slavery upon which the whole plantation system was based. The South was beaten and forced to accept an unconditional, although honorable, surrender at Appomattox. The emancipation of nearly four million Negroes created an acute social and psychological problem. It was undoubtedly difficult for Southerners who believed in the sanctity and righteousness of Negro slavery and the superiority of the white race to accept Negroes, their former slaves, as free men. This problem was often aggravated by the presence of Negro regiments which formed a part of the Union conquering and occupying army. The prophetic statement made by Daniel Webster in an exchange with John Calhoun in 1850 that the South was making a tragic mistake in basing its entire economy on cotton and on slave labor certainly came true. Like other beaten and conquered peoples in history, Southerners found it painful to accept the reality of defeat. They were also either unwilling or unable to contemplate the future of the Negro freedmen in their midst.

The demise of the central Confederate organs of government and of the local governing bodies which were closely tied to the plantation system left the South a virtual political vacuum. The considerable damage by shelling and fire of most of the southern cities provided a visual testimony to the postwar defeat and desolation.

So much for the facts about the economic, social, and political situation in the South immediately after the war. There is, however, no agreement either among contemporary witnesses or among historians as to the mood and the state of mind of the South after the Civil War. In fact, the evidence is rather startlingly contradictory. General Ulysses S. Grant, who was sent by President Johnson in November, 1865, on a brief fact-finding tour of the South, reported in part:

---

[3] W. E. B. DuBois, *Black Reconstruction in America* (New York: Russell & Russell, 1953), pp. 719, 725, 726.

I am satisfied that the mass of thinking men of the South accept the present situation of affairs in good faith. . . . I was pleased to learn from the leading men whom I met that they not only accepted the decision arrived at as final, but now that the smoke of battle has cleared away and time has been given for reflection, that this decision has been a fortunate one for the whole country . . .[4]

Another Union general, Carl Schurz, who was also sent by President Johnson to survey the South, came to opposite conclusions. He found that the South had not accepted the defeat, was still despising the Yankees, and had no regrets for fighting the Civil War. He wrote in his report of the "incorrigibles" of the South and of the lack of "hearty attachment to the great republic" by most of the ex-rebels.[5]

There is also no agreement on the situation of the mass of the freed Negroes in the South. Some historians have described them as an undisciplined rabble. James G. Randall wrote "the masses of slaves were ignorant, poor, lacking in the sagacity which their new status demanded and in many cases intoxicated by the opportunity to be 'a free bird—free as a fool.' "[6] On the other hand, James W. DeForest, an agent of the Freedmen's Bureau who spent fifteen months in South Carolina, was impressed with their cheerfulness, good humor, lack of any desire to take revenge for their long years of oppression. "The Negroes themselves were not disposed to violence. They are a peaceable, good tempered set, and except when drunk, are no more likely to pick a fight than so many Chinamen. . . . The most hopeful sign in the Negro is his anxiety to have his children educated."[7]

Relatively little has been written about the mood and the expectations of the North after the Civil War. Eric McKitrick, in his book *Andrew Johnson and Reconstruction*, makes a serious attempt to assess the state of mind of the North. He points out that it is the traditional attitude of the American people to "get back to normal" and to "forgive and forget" quickly after a victorious war. This attitude was dominant in the North after the war. There was a curious absence of great vindictiveness or of unbridled hatred of the "Rebs." Grant's terms to Lee were generous and those offered by Sherman to the Confederate general, Joseph E. Johnston, were so generous that President Johnson and General Grant felt compelled to repudiate them. There was no strong sentiment to inflict on the South a savage punishment, and there was little support for trying and hanging Confederate

---

[4] Quoted in Henry Steele Commager, ed., *Documents of American History* (New York: Appleton-Century-Crofts, 1949), p. 10.
[5] Quoted in J. G. Randall and David Donald, *The Civil War and Reconstruction* (Boston: D. C. Heath & Co., 1961), p. 564.
[6] *Ibid.*, pp. 725–726.
[7] J. W. DeForest, "The Man and Brother," *Atlantic Monthly*, Vol. 22 (1868), pp. 339–343.

leaders, with the possible exception of Jefferson Davis. When there was talk of putting Jefferson Davis on trial for treason, Thaddeus Stevens volunteered to be his attorney without fee.[8]

However, it would be a mistake to assume that the North had entirely forgotten that the Civil War was bloody and savage, that the Union had suffered casualties of 370,000 men dead and 250,000 wounded, that Northern prisoners were, on the whole, treated with inhumanity in Confederate jails, that the South hauled down the Stars and Stripes, and that as a separate state the Confederacy had spared no efforts at home and abroad to bring about the Union's total defeat.

In spite of the general attitude of "forgive and forget," the North did expect certain changes and guarantees from the South.

1. It expected some tangible assurances and guarantees that the South would remain loyal to the Union and that it would give up forever any idea of nullification and secession.

2. It expected the immediate ratification of the Thirteenth Amendment abolishing slavery.

3. It expected that the human and civil rights of the freed Negroes and of the white Unionists would be respected and protected. The North felt a particular obligation to the 180,000 Negroes who had served, and served well, in the Union army as soldiers and laborers.

4. It vaguely expected that some Negro freedmen, at least the veterans and the educated ones, would be given the right of franchise.

5. It expected that the leaders of the Confederacy would not be returned, so soon after the war, to positions of leadership in the state governments or be elected Congressmen and Senators.

6. It expected the South, even in a purely symbolic way, to repent for the crime of secession and for the waging of a bloody war on the Union. The prompt repeal of the articles of secession and the repudiation of the Confederate debt would have constituted such proof of repentance.

Professor John Blum put the problem in this way in a recent college textbook, *The National Experience:*

> Their (the Republicans') attitude reflected the dominant public opinion of the northern people who could not believe that the "rebel" enemies in

---

[8] See Eric McKitrick, *Andrew Johnson and Reconstruction* (Chicago: Univ. of Chicago Press, 1960).

battle for four years had reformed in nine months. The victors intended to impose stringent terms for Reconstruction, conditions that would set so high a price for disloyalty that it could never occur again.[9]

The story of Reconstruction in the histories of the period and in college and high school textbooks usually begins with the statement that upon the tragic death of Lincoln his successor, Andrew Johnson, attempted to follow the magnanimous policies toward the South which President Lincoln had promulgated before his death.

The authors, as a rule, suggest that Lincoln had a workable plan for the Reconstruction of the South, that Johnson merely attempted to continue the work of his predecessor, but that his efforts were sabotaged by the evil and destructive designs of a "willful" and "selfish" group of Radical Republicans. Had Johnson been allowed, according to most historians and textbook writers, to put into effect his plan for the restoration of the South to the Union, based on Lincoln's policy of "Malice toward none and . . . Charity for all," the calamities and the iniquities of Reconstruction would have been avoided. And it happened, the usual argument goes, that the vindicative, unreasonable Radical Republicans willfully frustrated Johnson's (and Lincoln's) noble plans.

Generations of young Americans have been taught this interpretation of post-Civil War affairs in high schools and colleges. The time has come to subject this story to a careful examination. What were Lincoln's views on the future governments in the Southern states and on the return of the Southern states to the Union? Did Lincoln have a workable plan for the restoration of the South to the Union? To describe Lincoln's position on the postwar South, writers invariably cite the last lines in Lincoln's Second Inaugural Address, which reads:

> With malice toward none, with charity for all, with firmness in the right as God gives us to see the right, let us strive on to finish the work we are in, to bind up the nation's wounds, to care for him who shall have borne the battle and for his widow and his orphan, to do all which may achieve and cherish a just and lasting peace among ourselves and with all nations.

This is the last paragraph of the Inaugural Address and, like the closing passages in many presidential addresses, it is conciliatory and optimistic. One wonders, however, whether a preceding paragraph in the same speech —which has usually been overlooked by historians and textbook writers— is not more representative of the true feelings of Lincoln on the Reconstruction of the South. It says:

---

[9] John M. Blum, Bruce Catton, Edmund S. Morgan, Arthur Schlesinger, Jr., Kenneth M. Stampp, and C. Vann Woodward, *The National Experience* (New York: Harcourt, Brace & World, 1963), p. 360.

Fondly do we hope, fervently do we pray, that this mighty scourge of war may speedily pass away. Yet, if God wills that it continue until all the wealth piled up by the bondsman's two hundred and fifty years of unrequited toil shall be sunk, and until every drop of blood drawn with the lash shall be paid by another drawn with the sword, as was said three thousand years ago, so still it must be said, "The Judgments of the Lord are true and righteous altogether."[10]

These words of bitter condemnation of the evils of slavery and the injustices committed by the slave owners in the South for which retribution was surely to come were not much different from many passages found in the speeches of the arch-Radicals, Thaddeus Stevens and Charles Sumner.

There is another important clue to the true feelings of Lincoln on the conditions to be imposed on the returning ex-Confederate states. It can be found in a letter written on September 11, 1863, by President Lincoln to Andrew Johnson, who was at that time the military governor of Union-occupied Tennessee. Lincoln urged Johnson to proceed with the organization of a state government:

You need not be reminded that it is the nick of time for reinaugurating a loyal State government. . . . I only offer a few suggestions. The reinauguration must not be such as to give control of the State and its representation in Congress to the enemies of the Union. . . . Let the reconstruction be the work of such men only as can be trusted by the Union. *Exclude all others,* and trust that your government so organized will be recognized here . . .[11]

Obviously Lincoln had no intention of letting the new state government of Tennessee fall into the hands of the Democrats or of allowing rebel leaders to be elected to state offices or to be sent to Washington as the state's Representatives and Senators. In spite of his usual magnanimity, Lincoln arbitrarily ordered Governor Johnson to exclude from the voting lists and from the list of candidates all men suspected of disloyalty to the Union. The military governors of Arkansas and Louisiana received similar instructions.

On December 8, 1863, Lincoln issued a special proclamation which contained his plan for the restoration to the Union of the ex-Confederate states. The plan provided, in essence, that if ten per cent of the total number of citizens in each state who voted in the 1860 presidential election were found qualified they could vote for the establishment of a state government. Such a government would be recognized as "the true Government of the

---

[10] Henry Steele Commager, ed., *Documents of American History* (New York: Appleton-Century-Crofts, 1949), pp. 442–443.
[11] *Ibid.,* p. 429 (italics mine).

State," and that the state would then be eligible to elect Representatives and Senators to Congress. The proclamation provided for a loyalty oath pledging the potential voters that they would "henceforth" support the Union. The franchise was denied to high officials of the Confederate Government and to high-ranking officers in the Confederate army.[12]

Lincoln clearly stated that the reconstruction of any Southern state, in order to be complete, would have to involve the full cooperation of Congress because the decision to seat the Congressmen of the restored state rested, as Lincoln put it, "exclusively with the respective Houses, and not to any extent with the Executive." Furthermore, Lincoln made it clear that he did not consider his plan final or exclusive. "While the mode presented," he wrote, "is the best the Executive can suggest with his present impressions, it must not be understood that no other possible mode would be acceptable."

Lincoln's plan for the restoration of the South did not fare well. During 1864, Tennessee, Louisiana, and Arkansas established new state governments on the basis of Lincoln's ten per cent plan. However, the governments which were established were not viable. They were completely unable to cope with the massive resistance of the white population which continued to follow the lead of the old plantation oligarchy. In directing the campaign of ostracism, vilification, and abuse against the restored Unionist governments, the ex-Confederate leaders used the Southern press with great effectiveness.

The growing intransigence of the restored South, which refused to consider Lincoln's repeated suggestions that some Negroes should be given the right of franchise,[13] the official or unofficial boycott of state elections, and the evident weakness and lack of a popular base of support for the newly established state governments caused the Republicans in Congress (not only the Radicals) to withdraw their initial support for Lincoln's plan. On June 27, the Senate, by a vote of 27 to 6 refused to seat Messrs. Fishback and Baxter, who had been elected senators from Arkansas. The resolution of rejection declared that the rebellion did not appear to be suppressed in Arkansas to entitle the state to representation in Congress. The Senate

---

[12] Henry J. Raymond, ed., *The Life and Public Services of Abraham Lincoln, Together with His State Papers* (New York: Derby and Miller Publishers, 1864), p. 458.

[13] Lincoln wrote to Governor Michael Hahn of Louisiana on March 13, 1864: "I congratulate you on having fixed your name in History as the First Free-State Governor of Louisiana. Now you are about to have a convention, which among other things, will probably define elective franchise. I barely suggest, for your private consideration, whether some of the colored people may not be let in, or, for instance, the very intelligent, and especially those who have fought gallantly in our ranks." Henry J. Raymond, ed., *The Life and Public Services of Abraham Lincoln* (New York: Derby and Miller Publishers, 1864), p. 489.

and House were similarly not inclined to seat the congressional delegations elected by Louisiana.

In view of this impasse, Republican Senators and Representatives decided that the time was ripe for Congress to assert its leadership over the entire question of Reconstruction. In July, 1864, Congress passed the Wade-Davis bill which imposed more stringent conditions for the return of the South to the Union. The bill required the election of state legislatures by a majority rather than by ten per cent of the qualified voters. It also required a loyalty oath affirming past and future allegiance to the Union. The state governments were required to prohibit slavery, repudiate the Confederate debt, and deny voting and office-holding to former Confederate officials.

It is erroneous to suggest as so many writers have done, that Lincoln was enraged by the Wade-Davis bill and denounced it by a sharp veto message. Lincoln's pocket veto prevented the bill from becoming law, but the President took an unprecedented step and on July 8, 1864 issued a special proclamation in which he explained to Congress and the nation his refusal to sign the law. He was unwilling and unprepared, he stated, to make the Wade-Davis bill the only plan for the reconstruction of the Southern states, although he considered it as a very proper plan for the loyal people of any state who chose to adopt it. Lincoln added that should any state choose to accept the Wade-Davis plan, he would be ready to give it his full aid and assistance.[14]

Lincoln's realization that his plan for bringing the South back into the Union was not working and would have to be revised was made quite clear by him in his last public address, which he delivered on April 11, 1865 from a White House balcony to a crowd of people who came to thank him for the victory of the Union. This speech was devoted in its entirety to the question of Reconstruction. The President admitted that the people of the North and the South were not united on the best plan for Reconstruction. He refused to enter into the discussion of the legal status of the ex-Confederate states because such a discussion seemed to him unnecessary and eventually harmful. Discussing his own ten per cent plan, Lincoln stated, "I distinctly stated that this was not the only plan which might possibly be acceptable, and I also distinctly protested that the Executive claimed no right to say when or whether members (from the South) should be admitted to seats in Congress for such States."[15] He acknowledged that the new government of Louisiana, which was elected under his plan by less than 12,000 voters, was weak and imperfect, but he pleaded for its official recognition by Congress in the hope that once in the Union, improvements would be

---

[14] *Ibid.*, p. 495.
[15] *Ibid.*, p. 685.

possible. Three days after delivering this address, Lincoln was assassinated in Ford's Theater. Thus, it is true, as William Hesseltine states in his thorough study of Lincoln's reconstruction attempts, that "John Wilkes Booth's bullet found Lincoln without a plan of reconstruction."[16]

Is there much validity in the statement which is often repeated in textbooks that Johnson proceeded during the summer and autumn of 1865 to carry out the generous and magnanimous plan of Lincoln for the reconstruction of the South? The implication of this statement is that Lincoln and Johnson held similar views on the issues involved in the restoration of the South to the Union. Let us look at the record.

Johnson devoted his attention to bringing the Southern states into the Union immediately after he took office in April, 1865. In May and June he issued a Proclamation of Amnesty and a Proclamation of Reconstruction. In some respects, Johnson's plan was similar to that of Lincoln, but there were also striking differences:

1. While Lincoln stressed that his program for the restoration of the South did not exclude other possible plans, Johnson made no allowance for alternative programs. William B. Hesseltine, comparing Lincoln's and Johnson's plans of restoration, wrote, ". . . Johnson's inflexible adherence to his own program was far removed from Lincoln's experimental, pragmatic approach to the problem.[17]

2. While Lincoln was careful to stress that the process of reconstruction was a joint responsibility of the President and of Congress, Johnson interpreted Section 4, Article 4 in the Constitution, "The United States shall guarantee to every State in this Union a republican form of government . . ." to mean that this responsibility devolved on the President of the United States, who was bound by solemn oath faithfully to execute the office of President of the United States and to insure that laws are faithfully executed.

3. While Lincoln stressed in his proclamation that the question of whether Representatives and Senators elected from the former Confederacy were admitted to Congress rested constitutionally exclusively with each House, Johnson made no mention of this matter. In fact, the President in his veto message of the Freedman's Bureau Bill of February 19, 1866 specifically forbade Congress the right to deny seats to Southern Congressmen. In a curiously reasoned interpretation of the Constitution he said, "I would not interfere with the unquestionable right of Congress to judge [each House for itself] of the elections, returns, and qualifications of its own members; but that authority cannot be construed as including the right to shut out

---

[16] William B. Hesseltine, *Lincoln's Plan of Reconstruction* (Tuscaloosa, Ala.: Confederate Publishing Co., 1960), p. 14.
[17] *Ibid.,* p. 140.

in time of peace any State from the representation to which it is entitled by the Constitution . . ." In other words, Johnson had decided on his own authority that Congress had no right to exclude Congressmen from any state of the former Confederacy.[18] Furthermore, Johnson denied the right of Congress to pass any legislation relating to the South as long as that region of the country was not represented in Congress. His view was that such procedure was a violation of the principle of "no taxation without representation." There is no evidence to suggest that these views of Johnson's were shared, or would even have been entertained by Abraham Lincoln.

4. While Lincoln kept Congress, including the leaders of the Radical Republicans, fully informed about his efforts to reconstruct the South, Johnson issued his proclamations while Congress was not in session. He failed to consult the Republican leaders in Congress, many of whom suspected that the President wanted the whole process of Reconstruction to be completed before the opening of Congress scheduled for early December, 1865.

5. While Abraham Lincoln was a Republican and one of the founders of the Republican party in Illinois, Andrew Johnson was a Southern Democrat who was born in North Carolina and rose to political prominence in his adopted state of Tennessee. Showing remarkable courage and integrity, Johnson broke with the entire Southern delegation in the Senate and remained in Congress as a staunch supporter of the Union and a bitter foe of secession. Johnson, however, did not oppose slavery, being himself a slave-owner, but he detested the planter aristocracy of the South and considered himself to be the champion of the Southern poor whites. In spite of the fact that Johnson was selected by the Republican Union party in 1864 as Lincoln's running mate as a devoted War Democrat, Johnson had no loyalty to the Republican party. Once in office, Johnson made a determined effort to organize a new party comprised of pro-Union Democrats and conservative Republicans.[19] There is no reason to doubt that Lincoln would have exerted every effort to assure the "ascendency of the Republican Party" in the South. Johnson had no similar interest.

6. Probably the most crucial contrast between Lincoln and Johnson, which clearly contradicts the widespread assumption that their views on Reconstruction were identical or even similar, concerns their respective attitudes toward Negroes.

Abraham Lincoln detested slavery from his youth and desired its prompt abolition. In the early 1830's, as a young lawyer Lincoln devoted a great

---

[18] Henry Steele Commager, ed., *Documents of American History* (New York: Appleton-Century-Crofts, 1949), p. 14.

[19] For an excellent study on this subject see La Wanda Cox and John H. Cox, *Politics, Principle and Prejudice 1865–1866* (New York: Free Press of Glencoe, 1963).

deal of his time to destroying the legal basis of the Negro indenture system which amounted to the existence of de facto slavery in Illinois. In 1839, Lincoln in the case of *Cromwell* vs. *Bailey* won a decision in the Illinois Supreme Court on behalf of an indentured slave, Nancy. In an historic decision the court ruled that in Illinois the presumption was that a Negro was free and not subject to sale. In 1836, Lincoln, a Representative in the Illinois House of Representatives, inserted a protest in the Journal of the House in which he castigated pro-slavery resolutions passed by the Illinois General Assembly. In 1846, when in the House of Representatives, Lincoln fought to abolish slavery in the District of Columbia, but later despaired of a change in the slavery situation. In a letter to George Robertsen of Kentucky, dated August 15, 1855, he wrote:

> The condition of the Negro slave in America, scarcely less terrible to the contemplation of a free mind, is now fixed and hopeless of change for the better, as that of the lost souls of the finally impenitent.[20]

There have been frequent attempts to downgrade Lincoln's forthright stand on the Negro question by pointing to Lincoln's statement made during the Debates in Charleston that he did not favor social and political equality of the white and the black races. Chronology is most important in assessing this statement. It would have been unthinkable for any politician to advocate political and social equality with Negroes in 1858. What is important is to follow the gradual evolution of Lincoln's attitude toward Negro rights, especially during the tortuous years of the Civil War. Evidence suggests that by the end of the war he was very close to advocating full political equality for Negroes.

Lincoln was much impressed with the courage and valor of the 150,000 Negro soldiers who served in the Union Army. For some reason this chapter of history, which should show the Negroes as making an important contribution to the saving of the Union, is almost uniformly ignored by many historians and history textbook writers. Colleges and high school students know all about the letter to Horace Greeley in which Lincoln, who by that time had already prepared the Emancipation Proclamation, stated that if he could save the Union without freeing any slaves he would do it, but they seldom are told of his letter to James G. Congling written three days later on August 26, 1863. In that letter the President wrote:

> You say that you will not fight for the Negroes. Some of them seem willing to fight for you; but no matter . . . Peace does not appear so dis-

---

[20] Paul M. Angle and Earl Schenck Miers, eds., *The Living Lincoln* (New Brunswick, N.J.: Rutgers Univ. Press, 1955), p. 189.

tant as it did. . . . And there will be some black men who remember that with silent tongue, and clenched teeth, and steady eye, and well-poised bayonet, they have helped mankind on to this great consummation, while I fear there will be some white ones unable to forget that with malignant heart and deceitful speech they have striven to hinder it.[21]

Lincoln as we have seen in Chapter eight considered himself a guardian of the Negro people and advocated in 1864, an amnesty for the South coupled with franchise for the Negroes or at least for the Negro war veterans and for those who had some education.

How did these evolving views of Lincoln on the Negro question compare with those held by Andrew Johnson? We have already said that Johnson was a Southerner who had never opposed slavery or the extension of slavery to the free territories. Johnson made it clear in his veto of the Civil Rights Bill that he opposed the granting of citizenship to the Negro freedmen. He advocated that "persons who are strangers to and unfamiliar with our institutions and our laws should pass through a certain probation, at the end of which, before attaining the coveted prize, they must give evidence of their fitness to receive and to exercise the rights of citizens as contemplated by the Constitution of the United States."[22]

In fact, Andrew Johnson, in complete opposition to the views and convictions of Abraham Lincoln, was a believer in the principle of white supremacy. In his third Annual Message to Congress, submitted on December 3, 1867, President Johnson stated that the white man has proven his capacity for self-government but, "if anything can be proved by known facts, if all reasoning upon evidence is not abandoned, it must be acknowledged that in the progress of nations Negroes have shown less capacity for government than any other race of people. No independent government of any form has ever been successful in their hands. On the contrary, whenever they have been left to their own devices they have shown a constant tendency to relapse into barbarism."[23]

The burden of this essay was to prove that one of the basic assumptions often repeated by many historians and some textbook writers about the affinity between Johnson's and Lincoln's Reconstruction ideas should be revised. Traditional assumptions about the unrelieved evil of the carpetbaggers and the scalawags, about the role of the "barbarous and illiterate Negroes," about the Negro domination of the South during Reconstruc-

---

[21] Henry J. Raymond, ed., *The Life and Public Services of Abraham Lincoln* (New York: Derby and Miller Publishers, 1864), p. 443.

[22] Henry Steele Commager, ed., *Documents of American History,* Vol. 8 (New York: Appleton-Century-Crofts, 1949), p. 16.

[23] James D. Richardson, *A Compilation of the Messages and Papers of the Presidents,* Vol. VI (Washington, D.C.: Bureau of National Literature and Art, 1908), p. 565.

tion,[24] and about the record of the Reconstruction governments ought to be subjected to careful scrutiny and re-examined in the light of recent historical research, most of which significantly was done by historians in the South or of Southern origin.

Most contemporary historians of Reconstruction are agreed that the assertions concerning the uniformly oppressive nature of the Radical Reconstruction governments must be qualified and modified. Virginia, Tennessee, Georgia, and Texas were never ruled by a Negro-Radical Republican coalition. Negroes had substantial political influence in only three out of eleven former Confederate States.[25]

A Mississippi newspaper editor who wrote an able history of Reconstruction decried the attempt to picture the record of Reconstruction government solely by recounting the tales of corruption and inefficiency—without listing their solid achievements. "Their record in public school expansion was," he wrote, "in general, and despite accompanying corruption, better than were the performances of the Redemptionist administrations which followed Reconstruction, and, for that matter, better than the public educational achievements of the prewar South where the novel idea of free, mass education had not caught on."[26]

Some historians not only ignore the positive achievements of the Reconstruction governments, but fail to put their record of corruption in the proper perspective. The misrule, the inefficiency, the graft and corruption of the "carpetbag-scalawag-Negro" governments comes in for wholesale and unconditional condemnation. Many textbooks still continue to quote a tendentious and unreliable report written by James S. Pike on conditions in South Carolina as representative of the entire South. Pike's account was thoroughly discredited by Robert F. Durden who proved by a painstaking examination of Pike's journals and notebooks that Pike was a racist and that his

---

[24] John M. Blum, Bruce Catton, Edmund S. Morgan, Arthur M. Schlesinger, Jr., Kenneth M. Stampp, and C. Vann Woodward state in *The National Experience,* pp. 365–366:

"In the South the period 'Black Reconstruction'. cut new wounds. Southerners tended to remember the era as one in which government fell to uneducated Negroes, to selfish Northern transients—'carpetbaggers'—and to treacherous minority of Southern whites—'scalawags.' It was a time, according to memory, of unmitigated corruption. But the recollection drew evidence selected to confirm it.

Negroes never dominated the governments of the Southern states . . . In most of the Southern states, a majority of the voters were white, and most of them were not 'scalawags.' "

[25] John Hope Franklin, *Reconstruction After the Civil War* (Chicago: Univ. of Chicago Press, 1961), pp. 194–217. Writing about the myths of Reconstruction, Professor Franklin said: "Thanks to the fictional accounts of Reconstruction by novelists and the near-fictional accounts by influential writers in other categories, the many misconceptions and distortions regarding the period are tenaciously persistent."

[26] Hodding Carter, *The Angry Scar* (Garden City, N.Y.: Doubleday & Co., 1958), p. 406.

account was aimed at discrediting the Grant administration.[27]   C. Vann Woodward suggested that corruption in the South in the period of Reconstruction must be considered in the general framework of the Grant era with its Black Friday, Credit Mobilier, and Whiskey Ring scandals.

> The South, alternately at the mercies of the carpetbaggers and the Ku Klux Klan, was the most conspicuous example of corruption. But that was merely because the press dramatized the Reconstruction struggle as a continuation of Civil War issues and partisan politics. State legislatures in North, East, and West, with no carpetbaggers or Negro members, could match and often outdo those below the Potomac in jobbery, pelf and thieving.[28]

Finally the bitter controversy raging around the issue of Negro civil rights should make it much easier to understand the truly central issue of Reconstruction. The central issue was not corruption, inefficient military governments, or even states' rights, but the attempt to give Negroes political equality. It is the racial issue which provided the most powerful impetus for the solidarity of the aristocrats, the wealthy, and the poor whites to unite in resistance against the granting to former slaves even limited political influence. Professor Otis A. Singletary, writing about the determined effort of white Southerners to destroy the Negro militia, stated:

> Even had the neophyte Negro lawmakers been uniformly honest and capable, they would have been resented almost as much. . . . The restoration of white domination—which had been threatened seriously in its political aspects but hardly at all in the economic or social spheres—took precedence over all else, over material needs, basic political beliefs within the white groups, and even honesty in government itself.[29]

What is needed, and needed urgently, is a thorough revision of the chapters dealing with Reconstruction in many high school history textbooks. To continue to teach the story of Reconstruction, a crucial period in our history, without such drastic revisions, does violence to historical truth and constitutes an insult to twenty million American Negroes.

---

[27] Robert F. Durden, "The Prostrate State Revisited: James S. Pike and South Carolina Reconstruction," *The Journal of Negro History,* Vol. 39 (April 1959), pp. 87–110.
[28] C. Vann Woodward, "The Low Ebb," *American Heritage,* Vol. 8 (April 1957), p. 53.
[29] Otis A. Singletary, *Negro Militia and Reconstruction* (Austin, Tex.: Univ. of Texas Press, 1957), p. 182.

Part Two

NEW APPROACHES TO

SOCIAL STUDIES

10

New Approaches to the Teaching

of United States History

In hundreds of schools throughout the country, committees are busily at work on new social studies curricula. The catchwords most frequently used by the reformers are: "structure," "skills," "concepts," "interdisciplinary approach," and "critical thinking."

A report of the High School Social Studies Curriculum Committee which worked on a new social studies curriculum for the Naperville, Illinois, Public Schools stated in part:

> The dangers of the present world political situation impart an urgency to our task of emphasizing the basic concepts and providing the learning experiences through which students can achieve an understanding of the American way of life, an appreciation of our own democratic values, and also a realistic appraisal of cultures, relationships, and problems of the other nations of the world. The committee believes that these concepts and values can be built only through adequate social studies programs beginning in elementary grades.

Here are some examples of these "basic concepts":

1. The intelligent uses of the forces of nature.

2. Recognition of the dignity and worth of the individual.

3. Use of intelligence to improve human living.

4. The intelligent acceptance by individuals and groups of responsibility for achieving democratic social action.

5. Achievement of adequate horizons of loyalty.

6. The intelligent utilization of scarce resources to attain the widest general well-being.[1]

Why these vague and pietistic statements are to be considered "basic concepts" in the social studies is not very clear. This is not an isolated example. We could have cited tens of others. In fact, similar statements of objectives and similar lists of "basic concepts" are to be found in the revised, new social studies which have been laboriously prepared by special committees in schools and school districts from Maine to California. Obviously, curriculum makers who with great sincerity and devotion wish to teach long lists of concepts and generalizations can only give lip service to the teaching of history as that study has been understood for generations.

To talk about the teaching of separate disciplines, like history or geography, about "facts and dates," or about the acquisition of knowledge is considered old-fashioned, if not reactionary. The new proposed curricula greatly diminish the importance and the time devoted to United States or world history. The interesting thing about these projected, far-reaching reforms of the social studies is that few administrators, teachers, parents, and, if the truth was to be told, students, shed any tears over the injury done to the ancient muse and discipline of history. Unfortunately, this apathy is not surprising.

Historians and history teachers are merely reaping the poor harvest of years of neglect and inattention to the teaching of history. While one can find in almost every community some superb high school history teachers, the subject matter of U.S. or world history is universally in a state of disrepute. In a number of studies, high school students have placed history at the bottom or near the bottom of their preferences. They, and their teachers, find history a "boring" subject. And boring it often is. Usually taught on the basis of cautiously written, inane textbooks, filled with a dull narrative of distilled historical judgments and conclusions, history as a subject of instruction is often pedestrian and unimaginative. The great men of history—Peter the Great, Wellington, Napoleon, Garibaldi, Churchill, Tamerlane, Bolívar, Confucius, Jefferson, and Lincoln—remain merely names, not great and dramatic personalities brought to life in the classroom to inspire admiration or revulsion. It is no wonder that few college freshmen can write two brief, intelligent biographical paragraphs on the men listed above. The blame for ineffective and dull teaching is traceable to the textbooks only in part. First, some of the recently revised textbooks are great improvements over previous editions, and second, an able, well-informed,

---

[1] *Report of the High School Social Studies Committee,* Naperville Public Schools, Naperville, Ill., 1964 (Mimeographed), pp. 1, 2.

imaginative teacher can teach an excellent history course with the use of any textbook.

History teachers, who themselves often are not very enthusiastic about the romance, adventure, and lessons of history, and who do not enjoy continuous reading in history, can hardly be expected to imbue their students with a love of or at least a respect for their discipline. Teachers who have stopped the study of history upon receipt of their diplomas, who fail to follow the trends, new findings, and new interpretations of historiography, are obviously not in a position to impart to their students the excitement and the thrill of historical investigations. While history is, of course, not "facts" and "dates," the history taught in many high schools is exactly that. No wonder that the reformers in the social studies, the "structuralists" and the "synthesizers" who are bent on pushing history out of a position of prominence in elementary and high school social studies, are meeting such little resistance. It has become acceptable and even fashionable at meetings of social studies teachers to speak sarcastically and with ill-concealed derision about the teaching of history. The only resistance which is occasionally encountered comes from outside pressure groups which see in the suggested curriculum revisions a "communist plot" aimed at substituting anthropological globalism for the teaching of United States history. This, of course, is nonsense. There is no plot—there is only a misguided effort to make hasty, drastic, and not well thought out changes based on a temporary (one hopes) infatuation with an interesting, attractive, but unproven theory of teaching and teaching objectives.

A recently published study of the teaching of history in Indiana, which received nationwide publicity, leaves much to be desired as a piece of scientific research, but it nevertheless provides an important insight into the present status of the teaching of history.[2] The study was conducted by three distinguished history professors from the University of Indiana and while limited to Indiana, the authors are undoubtedly correct in suggesting that their findings pertain to other states. Using rather unsophisticated and sometimes even unfair techniques, the researchers interviewed over thirteen hundred high school history teachers in Indiana—a large and representative sample. They also spoke to many students and visited many classrooms. The results of the study confirmed the worst fears of the professors. They discovered widespread apathy and even hostility toward American history as taught on the high school level.

In assessing the causes for the situation, the Indiana researchers concluded that the major part of the blame rests with the teachers. They found them inadequately trained, often having no more than fifteen to eighteen hours of undergraduate work in history. They contended that a

---

[2] Maurice G. Baxter, Robert H. Terrell, and John E. Wiltz, *The Teaching of American History in High Schools* (Bloomington, Ind.: Indiana Univ. Press, 1964).

large percentage of the teachers interviewed did "C" work at college, doing nothing to improve that record by taking some tough graduate courses. Basing their conclusions more on intuition and speculation than on hard data, the authors concluded that the failure of history teachers to read history and their ignorance of the works of important historians such as Nevins, Morison, and Catton can be explained by the fact that "teachers came from an unbookish background and teach in an unbookish environment."[3]

The young teacher learns very soon that the entire school atmosphere is "unbookish" and anti-intellectual and that "other teachers do not read books or dispatch students to the library."[4] This blanket indictment, supported only by circumstantial evidence, is undoubtedly an injustice to many Indiana history teachers and the authors were rightly taken to task for it. However, anyone who, like this author, visits high school classes cannot but be appalled at the lack of acquaintance of many teachers with even the most standard works of history.

The Indiana professors have, with justice, condemned history lessons, frequently observed by them, which consist of a superficial interrogation of students from a list of questions prepared by the teacher from a textbook chapter. They complained about "the amazing lack of *esprit de corps* among high school teachers of history. Seldom do they think of themselves as members of the historical tribe . . ."[5] Nor do they read the scholarly professional journals like the *Journal of American History* or the *American Historical Review*. The complaint is valid, but it is directed to the wrong address. Why should history teachers feel any solidarity with the fraternity of historians when many academic historians are completely indifferent to their problems and ignore their existence? Why should history teachers read the historical journals when even professional historians often find the lead articles pedantic and of interest to only a few specialists? Most historians usually limit themselves to the reading of the book reviews, especially those in which the reviewer employs the latest techniques of "scholarly reviewership" to "abolish" an author.

The remedies suggested by the authors of the Indiana survey are not new but they deserve respectful attention. They want teachers to take graduate courses in history and demand that separate history courses be preserved. However, they maintain these courses ought to be taught not as a "narrow political narrative," but broadened and deepened by the inclusion of the treatment of such topics as "immigration," "labor," "civil rights," and by the study of historical issues, problems, and controversies.

There is general agreement that American history courses must be en-

---

[3] *Ibid.,* p. 30.
[4] *Ibid.*
[5] *Ibid.,* p. 33.

riched and that once enriched and taught competently and imaginatively, the students will become curious and actively interested. Child psychologists, parents, and teachers know that it is unnatural for a child not to be interested in a well-told tale of the past or not to be thrilled by an occasional peek into the past. Children, even more than adults, are naturally fascinated and curious about events far distant from their own experience, be it the story of Daniel Boone or the latest explorations of the surface of the moon. But to exploit this interest, the past must be made alive and presented dramatically. We will cite a few examples on the following pages.

The 1828–1832 Nullification crisis is one of the most dramatic events in United States history, but is seldom taught in a meaningful manner to provide the students with a lasting and useful educative experience. The narration of the simple facts of the controversy relating to the "Tariff of Abominations," Calhoun's *South Carolina Exposition,* the Webster-Hayne debates, the passage in the South Carolina Legislature of the nullification resolution is important, but unless tied to some coherent, overall reconstruction of contemporary events, it will not long endure in the memory of students.

High school students would, however, have the Nullification crisis imprinted in their memories by the dramatic re-living of the Jefferson Day Dinner of May 12, 1832. This was indeed a remarkable event. The hall was filled to capacity by Congressmen, distinguished Washington officials, and their families. It was announced that President Andrew Jackson would attend the dinner and make a speech. The assembled dignitaries and the country at large were waiting to hear what the President, himself a Southerner, a native born Carolinian, and a former senator from Tennessee, would say about the action of South Carolina which not only "nullified" the new tariff law, but openly threatened secession.

When the President, tall, erect, his white hair a bit tousled, entered the hall with Martin Van Buren, his Secretary of State, the audience rose to bid respectful welcome to "Old Hickory." Jackson sat between Vice-President John Calhoun, the father of the doctrine of nullification, and Senator Robert Hayne of South Carolina, who two years earlier succeeded in holding his own in the famous Senate debates with Daniel Webster over states' rights.

The President engaged in a friendly conversation with his fellow South Carolinians, but ate very sparingly and only toyed with his glass of wine. At one point, Senator Hayne turned to Jackson and gallantly suggested that if the President needed more time for his speech, he would gladly relinquish his own part on the program. Jackson thanked the Senator for his kindness, but indicated that his own remarks would be quite brief.

As the program began, the speakers, most of whom were Southerners, while extolling the virtues of Thomas Jefferson, gave vigorous support to the nullification action of South Carolina and to the doctrine of states' rights. The eyes of the audience were glued on Jackson's face in an effort to detect his reaction to the speeches, but the old Indian fighter's face was impassive and no expression or gesture gave a clue to his thoughts. The tension in the hall reached almost unbearable proportions.

Finally, the chairman said, "Ladies and Gentlemen, the President of the United States." The assembled guests stood and gave Andrew Jackson a thunderous ovation. The President, holding his glass, said in a quiet, but firm voice: "Our Federal Union: It must be preserved." He then lifted his glass as a sign for the audience to rise again and to drink the toast standing. For a few seconds there was a deathly silence in the hall and then suddenly came a roar of cheers, shouts of approval, and applause. Only the Southerners remained seated and silent. Some observers stated that John Calhoun's hand trembled so much that he spilled much of his drink. With the ovation still in progress, the President left the dais and walked to the door, greeting old friends as he passed by.[6]

It is unfortunately true that few high school graduates would be able to write two or three paragraphs about the two presidential terms of Grover Cleveland. The accomplishments of Cleveland, who as most historians agree must be ranked among our greatest Presidents, are not easy to remember because the crises which he battled and overcame were domestic and largely financial. It is not easy for our students to remember Cleveland's courageous struggle against the raids on the United States treasury by the "private bills" which he vetoed in the hundreds, his desperate and successful efforts to overcome the economic panic of 1893, the rapid dwindling of the gold reserves, the threat to the currency, growing unemployment, and his wise stand against the imperialist intoxication.

Grover Cleveland can, however, become a meaningful and inspiring figure for our young people if we tie his accomplishments and policies to some "biographical hooks." Our students ought to "see" Grover Cleveland, the three-hundred pound bachelor from Buffalo, who fooled the wisest Washington newspapermen by marrying the eighteen-year old Miss Folsom, when they had expected that he would marry her charming mother. But most of all, they ought to be allowed to thrill at an act of courage displayed by President Cleveland which should have earned for him a chapter in John F. Kennedy's *Profiles of Courage.*

On June 30, 1893, in the midst of the economic depression, Cleveland was told by his doctors that the large tumor they detected in the roof of his mouth was cancerous and that an immediate operation was imperative. Given the state of medical knowledge and surgical techniques at the end of the nineteenth century, one can only imagine what a shocking experience this diagnosis must have been. However, Cleveland was aware that a

---

[6] This account is based on Paul I. Wellman, *The House Divides* (Garden City, N.Y.: Doubleday & Co., 1966), pp. 107–112.

public announcement of the nature of his illness would have disastrous effects on the economy of the country and he determined that the operation would take place in complete secrecy.

On June 30th the President left the White House by train for New York. Since in those days there was no Secret Service, and reporters as yet did not guard all the exits of the White House, Cleveland was able to slip away unobserved. In New York harbor he boarded the yacht *Oneida*. In the darkness of night, several surgeons and doctors, all sworn to secrecy (which they faithfully observed for many years), boarded the yacht.

The next day the President, dressed in pajamas, was strapped to a deck chair and given the newly discovered nitrous oxide gas for anesthesia. Then the surgeon, Dr. Joseph Bryan, using an electric knife, performed the two-hour operation, removing the large lethal tumor from the palate and plugging the big hole with a rubber ball. The next day after a restful sleep, the President took a short walk in his room. Although in terrible pain, he did not complain, but thanked the doctors for saving his life.

As early as July 12th the President was back at his desk in the White House working on his message to Congress, but his ordeal was not yet over. On August 17th Cleveland was again on the *Oneida* because the doctors discovered that not all of the cancerous tissue had been removed. Once again the President was given gas and the palate was thoroughly scraped. And again, not a whimper, nor a complaint emerged from the long suffering patient. A few days later Cleveland resumed his work on the message, writing 2,800 words by hand. This operation was fully successful, the President lived a long and useful life, and the country was not exposed to the danger of an economic collapse.

What student would not thrill to this story skillfully told and have the memory of a courageous President implanted in his mind? Many teachers may ask where they can easily obtain this material. This description of Cleveland's ordeal is based on an article by John Stuart Martin which appeared in October, 1957 in the *American Heritage*, which has recounted hundreds of similar dramatic events. *American Heritage* deserves to become the standard reference source for all teachers interested in making their history courses alive, dramatic, and effective.

Contemporary newspaper accounts can also be used most effectively. Newspapers are the source for the following account:

The Attempted Assassination of Theodore Roosevelt

Disappointed with the choice of William Howard Taft as the nominee for the presidency of the Republican party, Theodore Roosevelt bolted and organized his own Progressive party, also called the "Bull Moose party." The new party gathered at a convention on August 5, 1912. Like all third party conventions in our history this was an emotional, enthusiastic, singing gathering. The delegates and the people who filled the galleries frequently joined in choruses of "Onward, Christian Soldiers" and the "Battle Hymn of the Republic."

Theodore Roosevelt appeared before the convention on the second day and was given a frenzied ovation. In his "Confession of Faith" Roosevelt affirmed his devotion to progressive reforms, condemned the "invisible" government of big business, and ended with the war cry, "We stand at Armageddon, and we battle for the Lord!" He was nominated by acclamation for the presidency as the candidate of the Progressive party.

During his furious and inspired campaign, Roosevelt criss-crossed the country several times. On October 14th he attended a dinner in his honor at the Gilpatrick Hotel in Milwaukee. After the dinner Roosevelt went in an open car to the hall where he was slated to give a major address. The streets were packed with enthusiastic supporters who waited for the candidate of the new Progressive Party. In the crowd waiting for Roosevelt was John Schrank, who had come to America from Bavaria and owned a saloon in New York. Schrank was obsessed with the idea that it was his duty to prevent Roosevelt from becoming President for a third term, because he feared that Roosevelt would become an American dictator. Schrank, in his warped mind blamed Roosevelt for McKinley's murder in Buffalo, in 1901.

Outside the Milwaukee Hotel the assassin saw his chance to kill the potential "dictator" of the United States. As Roosevelt stood in his car waving to the cheering crowd, Schrank drew a gun from his vest pocket and fired. He was seized almost instantly by Roosevelt's secretary, Albert Martin. Witnesses later related that Theodore Roosevelt, wounded and bleeding, turned to his assailant and asked him softly, "Why did you do it?" Before Schrank was able to answer, several voices were heard in the crowd demanding that the assailant be lynched. As the would-be murderer was about to be seized, Roosevelt shouted, "Don't hurt him!" The police stepped in and took Schrank away.

The assassin's bullet had penetrated Roosevelt's chest, but its force was partly spent by its passage through a heavy manuscript of his speech and a spectacle case. Roosevelt's campaign aids and his hosts urged him to get medical aid, but he insisted on proceeding to the auditorium. A large bloodstain was visible on his chest as he stepped up to the speaker's platform. The audience of nine thousand people, aware of the assassination attempt, sat stunned as Teddy Roosevelt began his speech. During his speech, the pain and the loss of blood caused Roosevelt to sway. He was held up by the chairman who urged him to stop and get medical attention. Roosevelt, disregarding the request, turned to the audience and shouted, "Go away. I have a bullet in my body, but I have a message to deliver. . . . It will take more than a bullet to kill a Bull Moose." By summoning almost superhuman courage, Roosevelt finished his speech and was then rushed to a hospital.

Roosevelt's stamina and courage brought praise and admiration even from his opposition. The New York *Herald*, a strong supporter of William

Howard Taft, Roosevelt's bitterest rival, wrote, "We are against his politics, but we like his grit." After several days, Roosevelt resumed his campaign and spoke in almost every state of the Union. The American people liked and admired Teddy, but refused to vote for his third party. The majority elected Democrat Woodrow Wilson. The popular vote was 6,296,547 for Wilson, 4,126,020 for Roosevelt, and 3,486,720 for Taft.

What seems to be lacking most in our history courses is an awareness by the teachers of the fact that history has been made by people—living, breathing people. It follows that biography, the dramatic presentation of the complex nature of historical figures, with their strength, weaknesses, contradictions, great deeds, acts of cruelty, stupidity, and aberrations, must form an essential part in the teaching of history. In arguing his case for biography, the great teacher of history teachers, Henry Johnson, made these points:

1. Children have a natural and healthy interest in persons: they live and suffer with their heroes and thus enlarge their own experience in a manner scarcely thought of in dealing with social groups.
2. Individuals can be made to represent social groups, so that a study of the characteristics and experiences of individuals is in effect a study of the characteristics and experiences of social groups themselves.[7]

"Everybody is interested in personality," wrote A. L. Rowse,

everybody loves a story; he is a very dull dog who does not. That makes me very much in favor of the biographical approach, especially with children, in teaching history in schools. Everybody knows or should know, that the important thing is to arouse their interest . . . The life of a human being, particularly an exciting one, fascinates me; and the great figures of history have all had exciting lives. There is no end to the interest in the extraordinary personalities of people like Elizabeth, Cromwell, Nelson, William the Silent, Richelieu, Benjamin Franklin, the Roosevelts, Winston Churchill.[8]

Rowse does not insist that the biographical approach is the only or the best approach to the teaching of history, but biography can be of immeasurable value in providing motivation and excitement in the teaching of history. Social studies teachers seldom seem to realize that history is not in essence a scientific undertaking, but an ethical and moral one. History is the story of human beings as they have endeavored to shape their relatively short lives, how they grappled with their problems, successes, triumphs, disappointments, and defeats. Looked at from this point of view, history and the teaching of history can be a fascinating enterprise,

---

[7] Henry Johnson, *Teaching of History* (New York: The Macmillan Co., 1940), p. 132.
[8] A. L. Rowse, *The Use of History* (New York: The Macmillan Co., 1948), p. 36.

provided, of course, that it is taught as a human drama. There is no history without man and therefore there should be no history instruction without considerable stress on biography. Biography well taught and intelligently interwoven in the fabric of historical narrative and chronology can be, in the words of Page Smith, "an inexhaustible reservoir of 'life styles,' of models and examples, as a means of identification and completion."[9] Unfortunately, biography seems to be a most neglected art in our social studies courses.

Jonathan Edwards, Aaron Burr, Thomas Jefferson, Patrick Henry, John Brown, Ulysses S. Grant, Alexander Hamilton, Henry Cabot Lodge, Sr., Robert La Follette, William Jennings Bryan, and even Lincoln and F. D. R. do not come alive in the classroom. One of the difficulties is that they are usually *talked about* and are seldom allowed to speak for themselves. This situation brings us to the discussion of the use of sources, documents, and primary materials in the teaching of history. There seems to be general agreement that original historical data and documents can be used with great profit. The advocates of the inductive method in the teaching of history are firmly convinced that students should be encouraged to gather and evaluate historical raw materials and information in the same way as historians do. The supporters of this approach, led by Professor Edwin Fenton, believe that the achievement of effectiveness in the teaching of history in secondary schools is directly related to the degree in which students will use inductively the raw stuff from which history is written. Professor Richard Brown, who is directing the Amherst College project in history, recently wrote:

> To give him (the student) the new materials of knowledge—the evidence— rather than what some one on a different wave-length has said about it, is to invite him to grapple with truth on his own, to start where he is, to fit it into his own experience, to make it something useful and therefore worthwhile to him.[10]

There is much merit in Brown's contention. The intelligent, selective use by students of original sources can be a worthwhile and highly motivating learning experience. But it will only be so if used sparingly and with great care. Social studies teachers who expect the student to be able to fit his historical inquiry "into his own experience," and to "make it something useful and therefore worthwhile to him," will often be disappointed. The "thrill of discovery" is a blessed, but rare occurrence. Furthermore, the study of the results of the investigations conducted by such artist-historians

---

[9] Page Smith, *The Historian and History* (New York: Alfred A. Knopf, 1964), p. 246.
[10] Richard H. Brown, "History as Discovery: An Interim Report on the Amherst Project." Address given to the 25th Annual Convention of the National School Boards Association, April 15, 1965 (mimeographed), p. 5.

as William Prescott, Francis Parkman, or Samuel Eliot Morison should not be denied to students. Keeping these cautionary injunctions in mind, selected attempts to make the students act and work like "Little-League" historians should be greatly encouraged. These "post hole" experiences in historical inquiry and in the use of sources can be exciting and may help in the development of a "feel" for history and in training for critical thinking and analysis, provided that the sources are carefully selected and judiciously used. The historical source selected must be of interest—it must tell a story and it must be on the general level of comprehension of the students who will read it. The most important condition for success in the use of the document is in the preparatory stage. The examination of a "new document" or even of a "blind" document whose author and date are withheld from the student can be an interesting and instructive learning experience. The dating of documents is a good teaching device, and it may be fun for the teacher and the students.

However, the most important condition for the effective use of a historical document, a condition seldom even thought about, is the need for the presentation of the document in its proper setting. McKinley's message to Congress, half-heartedly recommending a declaration of war on Spain or Franklin Delano Roosevelt's First Inaugural Address giving heart to the nation in the throes of a depression will have the desired impact only if preceded by a brief, concise, and dramatic presentation of the circumstances surrounding these messages. Understanding the setting for a speech, letter, or excerpt from a diary is an essential element in the use of sources. Consider, for example, the introduction of Lincoln's Farewell Address to a class. The teacher would be well-advised to precede the reading of this remarkable address by a short, but dramatically delivered lecture.

Soon after his election in 1860, Abraham Lincoln realized quite clearly the tasks that lay before him. He received the largest number of votes of the four candidates, but together the three other candidates, Douglas, Breckinridge and Ball, received a million votes more than he did. Thus, only a minority of voters elected Lincoln, and almost no votes were cast for him in the entire South.

In those days Presidents elected in November did not take office until March. During the long and crucial months before his inauguration, the President-elect remained at his home in Springfield, Illinois, finishing the business of his law practice and receiving visitors from all over the country, including thousands of office-seekers who made his life quite miserable. Not wanting to infringe on the authority of President Buchanan, Lincoln was reluctant to offer solutions to the slavery crisis which was keeping the nation at a high pitch of tension. Helplessly he watched the Union being split asunder by the secession in December of Mississippi, Florida, Alabama, Georgia, and Louisiana, and of Texas in early February. Almost daily he received warnings that the "Copperheads" in Maryland and the District of Columbia would prevent his inauguration even if it meant his assassination.

Disregarding these warnings and forebodings, Abraham Lincoln decided to go to Washington by the longest possible route, taking twelve days, in order to see as many people as he could. After many weeks of self-enforced silence, he was eager to talk and listen to the people of the North who had elected him to the highest office in the land. Surrounded by a handful of friends, Lincoln arrived at the railroad station in Springfield to board his train. The day was cold, damp, the skies overcast, and a steady bone-chilling drizzle fell. Mr. Lincoln wore a black coat, a top hat, and had a shawl over his shoulders. Around the rear platform of the train stood a wet and rather gloomy crowd of friends and neighbors who had come to bid farewell to their illustrious native son. They, of course, expected to hear a few words of farewell from the man they knew and loved so well.

Mr. Lincoln mounted the platform and said:

My Friends: No-one, not in my situation, can appreciate my feeling of sadness at this parting. To this place, and the kindness of these people, I owe everything. Here I have lived a quarter of a century, and have passed from a young man to an old man. Here my children have been born, and one is buried. I now leave, not knowing when or whether ever I may return, with a task before me greater than that which rested upon Washington. Without the assistance of that Divine Being who ever attended him, I cannot succeed. With that assistance, I cannot fail. Trusting in Him who can go with me, and remain with you, and be everywhere for good, let us confidently hope that all will yet be well. To His care commending you, as I hope in your prayers you will commend me, I bid you an affectionate farewell."

The rain was falling harder and as the engine whistle blew, Lincoln rather wearily entered his car. The people stood for a while in the rain watching the train pull out of the station and then slowly dispersed.

How does a teacher "teach" this moving speech? First, as we said, he must place the speech in a setting and in a perspective and then after the proper mood of expectation is achieved, he could with benefit read the speech to the class reflecting the sadness and the drama of the circumstances in which it was given.

The discussion can center on a number of points.

1. Why is the Farewell Address one of Lincoln's finest speeches?

2. What words or sentences added or detracted from the Address, would "improve" it?

3. Would a President-elect today refer to himself as an "old man"? What does this tell us about Lincoln and about our times?

4. What are the reasons and the significance of Lincoln's prophetic statement that he might never return alive to Springfield?

5. In what way was Lincoln's task more difficult and more complex than that which faced Washington?

6. Was Lincoln, while not a church-goer, nevertheless a man of profound faith in God?

7. What passages in the speech mark it particularly as a literary masterpiece?

Often speeches, or excerpts from speeches, can and should be used to refute a widespread but erroneous interpretation of a historical event or outright historical myth.

For example, it is usually asserted by textbook writers and some historians that in April 1898, President William McKinley recommended that Congress declare war on Spain. A careful reading of McKinley's message to Congress, dated April 18, 1898, does not support this contention.

In his message, McKinley who courageously resisted the pressure of the war hawks, led by Theodore Roosevelt, gave Congress a calm and objective summary of the developments of events which followed the revolutionary efforts of Cubans to gain their independence.

The President recounted that the revolution caused serious losses for American business interests in Cuba. The American Government, wishing to avoid a foreign entanglement, attempted to mediate the conflict, but was not successful because the Spanish authorities rejected outside arbitration. In fairness to the Spanish Government, President McKinley reported to Congress that the new government of Spain had released from custody all American citizens "held under one charge or another connected with the insurrection . . ." On orders from Madrid, General Weyler, the Spanish commanding general in Cuba, was ordered to disband the concentration camps. The Spanish Government also allocated $6,000,000.00 for public works to provide employment for Cuban workers.

The United States, McKinley stated, cannot allow the war in Cuba to continue indefinitely. The President, therefore, considered it his duty to "seek to bring about an immediate termination of the war." For that purpose, McKinley related, he submitted to the Spanish Government a number of proposals leading to an early armistice in Cuba.

The President then reviewed the alternatives of the United States: declaring its neutrality or intervening in the conflict to bring about the cessation of hostilities. He argued that intervention would be justified on the basis of humanity, for the protection of American citizens and American trade interests in Cuba.   The President concluded this review of alternative actions by this request:

> In view of these considerations I ask Congress to authorize and empower the President to take measures to secure a full and final termination of hostilities between the Government of Spain and the people of Cuba, and secure in the island the establishment of a stable government . . .

The message should have logically ended with this request.   While not requesting specifically a declaration of war on Spain, the President did request authority to use American forces in Cuba.

But, strangely enough, McKinley reflecting his own personal reluctance for armed intervention, added the following postscript:

> Yesterday, and since the preparation of the foregoing message, official information was received by me that the latest decree of the Queen Regent of Spain directs General Blanco, in order to prepare and facilitate peace, to proclaim a suspension of hostilities, the duration and details of which have not yet been communicated to me.

> This fact, with every other pertinent consideration, will, I am sure, have your just and careful attention in the solemn deliberations upon which you are about to enter.   *If this measure attains a successful result, then our aspirations as a Christian, peace-loving people will be realized.*   If it fails, it will be only another justification for our contemplated action.

This last paragraph makes it clear that this was not, as it is commonly labeled, "McKinley's War Message."   On the contrary, the President clearly implied that Congress should wait until the success or the failure of the order of the Spanish Government to suspend hostilities in Cuba could be ascertained.   Only if that step would fail, American intervention could be justified.

Congress, long impatient with McKinley's preference for peace and negotiation, was in no mood to procrastinate.   It disregarded the last paragraph in the President's message and the use of American forces in Cuba was authorized.

The reading of the text of the message by the students would help them to better understand the events that led to the Spanish American War and the position of President McKinley on the question of war and peace.

An original historical document can give the students a first-hand insight, almost "a taste," of a particular event or personality in history.   In addition to talking *about* Jonathan Edwards and his special brand of theology and *about* his almost hypnotic influence on his listeners, the teacher might read to his class a few carefully chosen passages from Edwards' famous sermon, "Sinners in the Hands of God."   It is one thing to lecture about the fury of the New England revivalism and it is another to allow the students to hear the words of the great preacher:

> There is nothing that keeps wicked men at any moment out of hell, but the mere pleasure of God . . .
>
> There is no want of power in God to cast wicked men into hell at any moment. Men's hands cannot be strong when God rises up; the strongest have no power to resist him, nor can any deliver out of his hands. He is not only able to cast wicked men into hell, but he can most easily do it.
>
> They deserve to be cast into hell; so that divine justice never stands in the way, it makes no objection against God's using his power at any moment to destroy them. Yea, on the contrary, justice calls aloud for an infinite punishment of their sins . . .
>
> They are now the objects of that very same anger and wrath of God, that is expressed in the torments of hell. . . . Yea, God is a great deal more angry with great numbers that are now on earth; yea, doubtless, with many that are now in this congregation, that, it may be, at ease and quiet, than he is with many of those that are now in the flames of hell . . .
>
> The wrath of God burns against them; their damnation does not slumber; the pit is prepared; the fire is made ready; the furnace is now hot; ready to receive them; the flames do now rage and glow . . .

Yes, original sources, if used prudently, can often offer an excellent link between the past and the present and brightly illuminate the importance of history for a better understanding of present problems. This is especially true when an old document has a fascinating relevance to a current social or political issue and thus highlights the continuity of human experience. A scholarly and effective history teacher who is confronted with the need for a judicious inquiry into the problem of school segregation would do well to prepare a "blind" copy of some primary material for all his students, containing a few paragraphs dealing with this issue. The mimeographed material should not give the name of the author or the date of the document. Students should be asked to seek for clues as to the authorship and the date in the body of the source.

Consider, for example, this quoted paragraph:

> The separation of children in the schools, on account of race or color, is in the nature of *caste,* and, on this account, a violation of equality. The case shows expressly that the child was excluded from the school nearest to her dwelling—the number in the school at the time warranting her admission— on the sole ground of color . . .
>
> It is absurd to suppose that the committee, in their general charge and superintendence of schools, and in determining the number and qualifications of scholars, may engraft upon the schools a principle of inequality, not only unknown to the Constitution and laws, but in defiance of their letter and spirit. In the exercise of these powers they cannot put colored children to personal inconvenience greater than that of white children. Still further,

they cannot brand a whole race with the stigma of inferiority and degradation, constituting them a caste. They cannot in any way violate that fundamental right of all citizens, equality before the law.

It may prove to be somewhat of a shock to the students and perhaps to
some of the teachers to learn that this statement formed part of a brief
presented to the Massachusetts Supreme Court on December 4, 1849 by
Charles Sumner, later Senator from Massachusetts and a great champion of
Negro rights.

How many students would continue to believe another popular myth, still
perpetuated by some historians, according to which there really was no
great difference on the issue of slavery between Abraham Lincoln and
Stephen Douglas during their famous 1858 debates, if the teacher had the
wisdom to read them the following passage from Douglas's speech at Gales-
burg:

> I will tell you that this Chicago doctrine of Lincoln's—declaring that the
> Negro and the white man are made equal by the Declaration of Independ-
> ence and by Divine Providence—is a monstrous heresy. The signers of the
> Declaration of Independence never dreamed of the Negro when they were
> writing the document. They referred to white men, to men of European
> birth and European descent, when they declared the equality of all
> men . . .

The teaching of a great speech can be a valuable and inspiring educative
experience, a learning experience of great value in history, and also in
literature. Let us examine, in some detail, the opportunities for learning
experiences in a study of William Jennings Bryan's "Cross of Gold" speech.

First, of course, would come "the setting" for this great speech. The
Democratic convention opened in Chicago on July 7, 1896. It was a hot,
humid summer in Chicago, and over two thousand delegates and alternates
and an estimated crowd of eighteen thousand spectators were sweating and
uncomfortable in the steaming hall. This was an "open" convention, meaning that no strong contender for the nomination had emerged. The real
issue was the battle over the platform. While the silver men had an upper
hand, their opposition, which had the support of President Grover Cleveland, was strong and articulate. The silver men needed a spokesman who
would present their case to the convention, and, if possible, sweep the delegates off their feet. While the silver issue was the most frequently mentioned, other problems and grievances were even more important. Farmers
were in rebellion over low prices for their products, high mortgage interest
rates, and foreclosures, laborers felt like exploited cogs in the rapidly growing industry, and small businessmen, faced by growing monopolies, felt
threatened and insecure. Silver became the rallying cry of millions of dis-
contented Americans.

It was rather surprising that the leaders of the convention would turn to Bryan to be the spokesman of the silverites. William Jennings Bryan, a young Congressman from Nebraska, came to the convention without even knowing if he would be a delegate. After a prolonged dispute, he and his delegation were seated as the legitimate representatives of Nebraska Democracy.

But Bryan was not a political unknown. He had served two terms in Congress and had already distinguished himself in debates over the silver and tariff issues. He had already earned the nickname of the "Boy Orator of the Platte." However, at the opening of the convention, few, if any, believed that Bryan would emerge as the nominee for President. Not one delegation, not one delegate was pledged to vote for him. There was, however, one man who had no doubt on this question. That was William Jennings Bryan himself. In his hotel room, he spent many hours preparing his speech. He knew that his views represented the mood of the convention and he was ready to grasp the opportunity that history offered him. It may not be true that Bryan got the nomination only because of his "Cross of Gold" speech, but it is true that he would not have gotten it without it.

Bryan himself described the response of the delegates to his speech. "The audience," he wrote, "seemed to rise and sit down as one man. At the close of a sentence it would *rise* and shout, and when I began upon another sentence, the room was still as a church. . . . The audience acted like a trained choir—in fact, I thought of a choir as I noted how instantaneously and in unison they responded to each point made." When Bryan concluded his speech there ensued the wildest and most spontaneous demonstration that has ever been seen by any political convention.

What made the "Cross of Gold" speech so effective? In order to reproduce the effect of the speech, the teacher would do well after the presentation of the background and the setting, to read aloud, dramatically, and with proper emphasis the more important parts of the speech. Analysis of the speech might center around the following topics:

1. *Bryan attempts to capture the attention of the Convention by adopting the stance of humility and by presenting himself as a champion of a great public cause.*
   "Mr. Chairman and Gentlemen of the Convention:
   I would be presumptuous indeed, to present myself against the distinguished gentlemen to whom you have listened if this were a mere measuring of abilities; but this is not a contest between persons. The humblest citizen in all the land, when clad in the armor of a righteous cause, is stronger than all the hosts of error. I come to speak to you in defense of a cause as holy as the cause of liberty—the cause of humanity."

2. *Bryan presents the winning coalition for the forthcoming election.*
By an ingenious stretching of the definition of a businessman, Bryan
includes in his coalition, the laborers, the farmers, the small merchants,
the professionals in smaller towns and the miners. "We come to speak
to you for this broader class of businessmen."

3. *The heart of the coalition will be the farmers and the people in the*
Western part of the country.
"Ah my friends, we say not one word against those who live upon the
Atlantic coast, but the hardy pioneers who have braved all the dangers
of the wilderness, who have made the desert to blossom as the rose—
the pioneers away there (pointing to the West), who rear their children
near to Nature's heart, where they can mingle their voices with the
voices of the birds—out there where they have erected schoolhouses
for the education of their young, churches where they praise their
Creator, and cemeteries where rest the ashes of their dead—these
people, as we say, are as deserving of the consideration of our party
as any people in this country. It is for these that we speak."

4. *Appeal to national pride and to the always popular anti-British senti-*
ment. The United States does not need to consult England if it
decides to abandon the gold standard.
"My friends we declare that this nation is able to legislate for its own
people on every question, without waiting for the aid and consent
of any other nation on earth; and upon that issue we expect to carry
every State in the Union. . . . It is the issue of 1776 over again.
Our ancestors, when but millions in number, had the courage to declare their political independence of every other nation; shall we, their
descendants, when we have grown to seventy millions, declare that we
are less independent than our forefathers? No, my friends, that will
never be the verdict of our people."

5. *Bryan offers a fighting threat to the Eastern interests and to the opposi-*
tion party.
"We do not come as aggressors. Our war is not a war of conquest;
we are fighting in defense of our homes, our families, and posterity.
We have petitioned, and our petitions have been scorned; we have
entreated, and our entreaties have been disregarded; we have begged,
and they have mocked when our calamity came. We beg no longer;
we entreat no more; we petition no more. We defy them."

6. *Bryan electrifies the convention by a rousing finish.* (This part can be
read by the teacher or a contest may be held for the best dramatic
reading.)
"If they dare to come out in the open field and defend the gold stand-

ard as a good thing, we will fight them to the uttermost. Having behind us the producing masses of the nation and the world, supported by the commercial interests and the toilers everywhere, we will answer their demand for a gold standard by saying to them: You shall not press down upon the brow of labor this crown of thorns, you shall not crucify mankind upon a cross of gold."

The teacher may then ask the students to select the most single telling paragraph of the speech. Many suggestions will be offered, but agreement will surely be reached on this passage:

"You come to us and tell us that the great cities are in favor of the gold standard; we reply that the great cities rest upon our broad and fertile prairies. Burn down your cities and leave our farms, and your cities will spring up again as if by magic; but destroy our farms and grass will grow in the streets of every city in the country."

The analysis of this beautiful passage should include the critical question whether this paragraph, which the delegates cheered to an echo, did not in fact bring about Bryan's defeat. Bryan's unfortunate use of the words "our" farms and "your" cities was skillfully exploited by Mark Hanna, McKinley's manager. He branded Bryan as a sectional candidate of a few Western states and an enemy of the cities. An analogy suggests itself to the famous statement made by Barry Goldwater at the 1964 Republican Convention in San Francisco: "Moderation in the pursuit of justice is no virtue. Extremism in pursuit of liberty is no vice." These rousing words also brought the delegates to their feet, but they plagued Goldwater throughout the campaign.

History teaching can be greatly improved and enriched by the judicious use of historiography—The varying conclusions of historians on controversial issues and the reasons on which they base these conclusions—can greatly motivate the students to do their own critical thinking and make their own investigations into historical problems. The vigorous, and sometimes bitter, polemics among historians over such issues as the guilt or innocence of Aaron Burr, Madison's responsibility for the War of 1812, Wilson's role in the controversy over the Versailles Treaty, the character of Augustus and Cromwell and the firing of General MacArthur by President Harry Truman are, to cite only a few, examples of good readings that can lead to effective teaching experiences. When given access to the views of historians, preferably through direct contact with their works, students will learn how historians go about their work, will realize that history is what historians *say* about the past, and, most importantly, will be forced to do their own thinking and judging of past events.

The causes of the Civil War have long been the subject of spirited dispute among historians. What were the major causes of the almost continuous conflict between the South and the North during the years from 1815 to 1861? Was slavery as evil as the abolitionists have pictured it or was it as benevolent as described by the spokesman of the South? Could the bloody war have been avoided? These and other related questions are absorbing and perplexing, but the textbooks, for a variety of reasons, gloss over them or treat them superficially. When intelligently posed in the classroom and made subject to collective and individual inquiries, these questions could become interesting and instructive experiences for both the students and the teachers.

A teacher could well begin this inquiry deductively by putting on the blackboard the names of some important Civil War historians and by adding a summary statement of their particular views of the causes of the Civil War, which could look something like this:

James Ford Rhodes: Slavery the single cause.

Charles Beard: An economic conflict between an agrarian South and an industrially expanding North.

James G. Randall: *Central cause of the Civil War*—a blundering generation.

Avery Craven: Civil War was not inevitable; it came because of the extremist pressure and agitation of the Northern abolitionists and Southern fire-eaters.

Bernard De Voto: Civil War—a moral struggle for the very soul of American democracy.

Allan Nevins: Civil War came because South and North were rapidly becoming separate countries.

The discussion and investigation which would follow the presentation of these divergent views of historians could make for exciting teaching of Civil War history. It could not only lead to a better understanding of that important period, but would also provide an excellent opportunity for training students in critical and analytical thinking. Critical thinking should be particularly in evidence during class discussions. Unfortunately, many discussions conducted in social studies classrooms are of little value. Some teachers believe that the mere fact that they had a "good" discussion results in effective teaching. This, of course, is not often the case.

It is not unusual for Johnny, a high-school junior, to come home and at supper time have this conversation with his father:

Father: "What did you do in history today, Johnny?"
Johnny: "Oh, we had a discussion."
Father: "What did you learn from it?"
Johnny: "Nothing."

Why didn't Johnny learn anything from this discussion? Probably because the teacher paid no attention to setting up some essential conditions needed to make class discussions productive. First, the discussion ought to follow a logical sequence with a beginning, a middle, and an end. While flexible, the discussion must have a direction. Many classroom discussions are particularly lacking an end and a summary. Such a summary, in the form of a teacher's or student's brief summation, either oral or written down on the blackboard, and preferably formulated by a student, would provide a sense of accomplishment, the sense of the completion of a learning task. Secondly, a discussion must not be allowed to deteriorate into an exchange of mutual ignorances. There must be an occasional infusion of *new* information into the discussion, either by the teacher or the students. Thirdly, and probably most importantly, a discussion is good and effective when it is stimulated by intelligent questions. How to ask questions is a crucial problem in the social studies. There is no sense in talking about critical, reflective thinking when the teacher only asks questions which begin with "What," "Why," "When," and "Where"? These questions, as a rule, do not stimulate profound or subtle thinking. They are, of course, necessary, but should be supplemented with questions which begin with:

What do you think?
Put yourself in his (or her) position . . .
How would you compare . . . ?
How would you contrast . . . ?
How would you evaluate . . . ?
Try to characterize . . .
Which would you choose . . . ?
Suppose that and that happened—what would have been the result . . . ?
List the causes of . . .
List the effects of . . .
What alternatives were there in this situation?

New teachers and even experienced ones ought to prepare at least five such imaginative questions for each lesson and on occasion declare a short moratorium on the use of more simplistic questions.

The lecture has fallen into disrepute in the social studies. It is suggested that students do not listen to lectures and dislike teachers who "talk too much." Lecturing, it is said, merely increases the child's passivity and lack of involvement. Thus, it is an imposition from above and undemocratic. These are weighty arguments, and yet, under proper conditions, lectures can be effective and pleasurable educational experiences. What are these conditions:

1. The teacher must tell a good story. To do that he must be well prepared and he must "ham it up." A dramatic telling of Woodrow Wilson's speaking tour and his collapse from a stroke can have the students
   glued to their seats.

2. Lectures must be brief and infrequent.

3. There must be a specific purpose for giving the lecture. These purposes may include: motivation for an inquiry into a new historical
   period or problem; a summation at the conclusion of an extended historical investigation; or a lecture modifying prevalent misconceptions
   and misinterpretations of the problem under study, as revealed, for
   instance in a test or in class discussion.

Much has been written about the advantages of the problem-solving
approach in the teaching of United States and world history. There is no
question that this method of teaching does correlate best with the postulated objectives in the social studies and fits very well in the framework of a
school in a democratic society. Problem-solving is, as Dewey pointed out,
tantamount to education in the best sense of the word because it increases
the intellectual sophistication of the child and teaches him skills of inquiry.

Unfortunately, much of what appears as problem-solving in textbooks,
teacher guides, and curricula are no problems at all. Many books that
carry the word "problems" in their titles do not deliver what has been
promised. A problem, according to Webster, is "A question proposed for
solution, hence a perplexing question or situation." Thus a problem is a
problem if it is perplexing and if it requires research, illumination, and
resolution. Obviously, then, not all events in history which are worthy of
attention are problems, and, consequently, teachers must exercise great care
in the selection of problems which they wish to investigate and "solve" with
their students. Based on Dewey's approach, problem solving consists
basically of these five steps:

1. A feeling of perplexity (something akin to the state of mind of the
   King of Siam, who in the musical *The King and I* exclaims, "That's a
   puzzlement!").

2. The definition of the problem.

3. Suggesting and testing of hypotheses.

4. Development of the best possible solution or solutions by reasoning.

5. Testing and re-testing of conclusions.

However, even using Dewey's criteria, it makes no sense to base the
entire course of study on "problems." Much in history which cannot be de-

fined as problems is worthwhile teaching. Also, students should not be wearied by an endless succession of problems or given the impression that all crucial issues in history are amenable to problem-solving.

Thomas A. Bailey of Stanford has long advocated a multi-faceted approach to the teaching of history. He has suggested several ways of infusing life into the United States history course. Exploding popular historical myths, or in other words a responsible job of debunking a common but false interpretation, can be a motivating and stimulating experience. The student, Bailey suggested, may even be encouraged to keep a Myth Book.[11] The teacher can also contribute to a greater interest in his subject matter by

> acting as the Devil's advocate in presenting the neglected, forgotten, or unpopular side of the major lost causes. . . . Yet, we must also remember that the offbeat approach, like every good thing, can be overdone. Teenagers can become so angry that they will close their minds rather than open them.[12]

These words of caution by Professor Bailey seem fitting for the closing paragraph of this chapter. We have discussed a number of new and "oldnew" approaches to the more effective teaching of American history. Not one of them will work if used exclusively or to excess. But the judicious addition of a variety of new methods and new approaches may prove to be a boon in history classrooms in secondary schools.

---

[11] Thomas A. Bailey, "Revitalizing American History," *Social Education* (December 1960).
[12] *Ibid.*, p. 42.

11

New Approaches to the

Teaching of Civics (Part I)

It might be advisable at the opening of this chapter to make clear what is meant here by the word "civics." It is used in its broad sense to include the study of the Constitution, the structure of American government on Federal, state, and local levels, and citizenship education. This broad definition of civics has been accepted by Congress in a report of the Senate Committee on Labor and Public Welfare which interpreted the addition of institutes for teachers of civics under the 1964 Title III of the National Defense Education Act. The report stated:

> It is the intent of the committee that the Commissioner of Education in carrying out these provisions of the Bill shall construe broadly the terms used . . . for example, in the committee view . . . civics includes the function as well as the structure of American government at all levels, including the impact on government of current developments at home and abroad. . . . The committee further understands that support may be given to combinations of subject matter areas of this section of the bill in accordance with the current usage of the local school systems. Such interdisciplinary studies could well include the study of international affairs which have a direct influence in shaping American life and it is hoped would include an understanding of the *responsibilities* of citizens in a democracy. Knowledge of these responsibilities of citizenship, the committee believes, is essential if we are to strengthen the intellectual and moral fiber of our nation."[1]

---

[1] Quoted in an article by Robert E. Cleary, "Current Weaknesses in Civic Education and Opportunities for Improvement," *Social Education* (November 1965), p. 445. Professor Cleary's study contains an excellent discussion of the problem of teaching values in civic education.

This is an interesting and important statement on the nature of civics. A group of legislators has somehow done well in attempting to define the scope of citizenship education. Civics, they said, should not only be concerned with the structure of government, but with the process of government. American government, in the view of the congressional committee, cannot be studied in isolation from the international scene because foreign problems, pressures, dangers, and opportunities exert a great influence on domestic policies and on the functioning of the entire machinery of the Federal Government. Finally, the members of Congress said nothing about the direct teaching of values of patriotism and loyalty. They wisely limited themselves to the study of the "responsibilities of citizenship" which when understood and accepted would "strengthen the intellectual and moral fiber of the nation." Thus, love of country could be expected to be a natural outcome of effective citizenship education.

Let us take a look at another statement on the scope and aims of civics in a paragraph taken from the 1954 Yearbook of the American Association of School Administrators which dealt with the general aims of American education. It said:

> Knowledge by itself is not enough . . . knowledge coupled with faith and loyalty is still not enough . . . skill by itself or action by itself in conjunction with any of the others is not enough. Only when all four are blended so that each supports the other do we have the kind of person that civic education seeks to produce.[2]

Here professional educators postulate that the aims of civics are the obtaining of knowledge, the instilling of faith and loyalty, and the acquisition of skills. And if that were not enough, there is also the demand that all these ingredients be properly blended and balanced in the graduate who is to be "produced" by civic education. Obviously, the legislators approached the vexing and complicated problem of spelling out the objectives of education for citizenship in a democratic society in a more realistic manner than did the school administrators. The congressional committee exhibited in its statement an awareness of the grave doubts engendered by a number of studies as to the ability of the school to teach values and of the even greater difficulty faced when attempts are made to change political and social values and attitudes which seem to be well entrenched by an early age. The statement of the committee makes clear that the aim of the school is not to "produce" persons whose behavior patterns have been changed, but to educate (from Latin, to "draw out") people to the maximum of their

---

[2] *Educating for American Citizenship,* Thirty-Second Yearbook, American Association of School Administrators, National Education Association (Washington, D.C., 1954), p. 335.

individual potential and to blend that individual potential with some societal needs and responsibilities.

Political scientists who, by the nature of their discipline, are the most competent to discuss the objectives and contents of high school civics, are adamant in their opposition to the notion that there is a direct correlation between the study of government and good or wise citizenship. They state that while political science may help its disciples to become better citizens, this effect can neither be measured nor guaranteed. Political socialization or the formation of political values and attitudes, political scientists maintain, is a long process involving many components. Some of them, like home, church, and neighborhood, are much more powerful influences than social studies instruction. Furthermore, they point out that in view of the great expansion of our government and the complex domestic and foreign problems faced by it, it makes little sense to speak of *knowledge* of political life. Even experts in political science are only experts in their particular area of interest and are basically laymen in the area of public policy. The analysis of political institutions and behavior has little or no relationship to performance as citizens. How a man casts his ballot is determined by many factors, and erudition in some aspect of political science usually plays a minor role.[3]

There is a strange paradox in the far-reaching demands made for civic education and the reality that one encounters in civics classrooms. As a rule, civics education is limited to the study of the Constitution which culminates in a test on the Constitution, usually administered by the state, and to the study of the structure and functions of the United States government. Much can and should be done to bring more life, more drama, more interest, and more excitement to citizenship education. Obviously, there can be little of that drama and excitement as long as so many teachers make the civics textbook the cornerstone of their instruction.

Many civics and government textbooks are well written, describe the structure and functions of the executive, legislative, and judicial branches of the Federal Government, and deal with the state and local governmental units in a scholarly fashion. Yet, these textbooks suffer from a number of grave shortcomings. First, like all textbooks they constitute a body of *conclusions*, some correct, some partly correct, and a few representing the personal opinions and judgments of the author or authors. It is exactly *conclusions* and *judgments* that our students need *least*, especially on such complex issues as the seniority rule in Congress or the growing involvement of the Federal Government in education. By presenting "conclusions," one should not assume that the textbooks take a clear-cut position on some con-

---

[3] Evron M. Kirkpatrick and Jeane J. Kirkpatrick, "Political Science," in Erling Hunt, ed., *High School Social Studies Perspectives* (Boston: Houghton Mifflin Co., 1962).

troversial issues. On the contrary, the "conclusions" are more often than not inane and lifeless summaries of two opposing viewpoints on the complex issue at question. It is exactly such a succession of inane summaries that makes effective teaching of civics so difficult. By glossing over some of the most important problems facing our body politic, most textbooks make citizenship instruction dull and uninteresting.

After reading in the textbooks that "some say that the seniority rule is good because . . . ." and "some say that seniority rule is bad because . . . ," why should any bright youngster feel very stimulated to investigate this complicated and important dilemma for himself? This leads us to another difficulty. Many textbooks fail to present the United States of America as it is—a powerful democratic country which, using the criterion set down by Alexis de Tocqueville, has proved capable of providing the most good for the most people, but a democracy which is in constant need of a conscious and determined effort at improvement and perfection and which is challenged to deal successfully with a variety of new problems, new issues, and conflicts that result from the ever changing conditions of a modern society. Too many textbooks, in attempting to avoid giving offense to various interests, levels of authority, and legitimate and not so legitimate pressure groups, often omit any discussion of some controversial issues. What is worse, there is often lacking a clear commitment to the refinement and improvement of our democracy. After reading through a civics textbook which treats explosive questions like civil rights and prayers in the public schools gingerly and superficially, why should a high school student feel puzzled, disturbed, and stimulated to do some hard thinking on these complex issues?

Hunt and Metcalf listed six "closed areas" which they contended are largely excluded from discussion in social studies textbooks.[4] These are:

1. *Economics.* Students and teachers are often inhibited to discuss freely such subjects as the shortcomings in the "free enterprise system," the evil of mergers, the whole scandal of the "loan industry."

2. *Race and minority relations.* Some publishers, eager for the sale of the textbook in all states, insist that the discussion of the civil rights issue be done very "diplomatically" without giving offense to the entrenched sensibilities and fears.

3. *Social class.* Hunt and Metcalf contend that this area is "neatly ignored" as a result of the widespread belief that "there are no social classes in America."

---

[4] Maurice P. Hunt and Lawrence E. Metcalf, *Teaching High School Social Studies: Problems in Reflective Thinking and Social Understanding* (New York: Harper & Row, 1943), p. 230.

4. *Sex, courtship, and marriage.* Again, there are too many taboos in this area and truly significant issues are ignored or just lightly touched.

5. *Religion and morality.* Civics teachers are usually politely but firmly advised to stay away from religious issues.

6. *Nationalism and patriotism.* The evil excesses of nationalism are seldom discussed and the pitfalls of the "my country right or wrong" attitude are not subjected to searching analysis.

Professors Hunt and Metcalf assert that the study of these highly controversial areas should constitute a proper function of civic education. One could question this overemphasis on highly controversial issues which can be overdone and can lead to a distorted picture of our society. It would seem that the *occasional* study of controversial and relevant issues in the context of an honest and scholarly critical study of civics would be enough to stimulate and challenge our growing and restless adolescents and at the same time assure effective and well-motivated teaching. Students will hardly be challenged by such bland and underplayed "analyses" of the 1954 Supreme Court desegregation decision as found in one textbook:

> The problem of equal educational opportunity is especially real in some sections of the country where different schools are provided for children of different races. In such cases, the minority group often suffers because of its inferior schools.
>
> In 1954, the United States Supreme Court made a decision stating that separate schools for Negro children were unconstitutional. This decision caused much controversy, but there has been general agreement, however, that some system must be developed to provide equal educational opportunities for all children—regardless of race, nationality, religion or whether they live in cities or rural areas.[5]

The studied omission of the words "South," "Negro," the cautious words "often suffers," the lack of any expression of outrage at the violation of a basic civil right, and the lack of any reference to the stubborn resistance to the decision in the Deep South would be almost amusing if the situation were not so serious. It has to be noted that the authors do not suggest that the Supreme Court decision, as the law of the land, must be obeyed and that public schools ought to be desegregated. They merely state that "some system must be developed to provide equal educational opportunities

---

[5] The name of the textbook is withheld. The quotation is given in full and accurately, but the passage cited should not be allowed to obscure the fact that the textbook is admirable in many other respects. Furthermore, subsequent editions of the textbook have been considerably revised. For an extended discussion of the civics textbooks, see "'Safe' Textbooks and Citizenship Education," *The School Review* (Winter 1961).

for all children." Thus, the textbook inexplicably resurrects the "separate but equal" doctrine which the 1954 decision declared unconstitutional.

Another textbook wrote about the poll tax:

> Some states have one or more requirements for voting in addition to those already named. For example, several states require the payment of a poll tax. This means that a voter must pay a certain amount of money in order to vote. The amount is small, perhaps, one or two dollars. However, some states which require a poll tax also require that it be paid for a certain number of years before the election. If a voter has neglected to pay his tax, he may find that he owes ten dollars or more. If the voter is poor, he will probably (sic!) not be able to pay his poll taxes and therefore lose his vote.

This is indeed a gentle treatment of an iniquitous practice which has deprived large numbers of native-born American Negroes of their right to franchise and which has been repeatedly denounced by Presidents, leaders of Congress, and religious leaders, and was finally declared unconstitutional (in Federal elections) by a special amendment to the Constitution.

The existence of slums, the growing problem of narcotic addiction, race riots, and increasing crime on the streets of the big cities are treated in most civics textbooks with great circumspection. The student would have real difficulty in perceiving that these and similar issues are tough, perplexing, and dangerous in their implications. Some textbooks deal with the slum situation in most big cities, but they give the distinct impression that urban renewal is successfully coping with the problem.

The almost ridiculous lengths to which textbook writers, or should we more properly say textbook publishers, go to avoid offending anyone can be seen most glaringly in the chapters dealing with the United Nations. This issue is considered by publishing houses a real "hot potato." There is a determined effort not to provoke those who maintain that the U.N. is an arm of the communist conspiracy and an infringement on our national sovereignty. Take this example:

> In our country two extreme positions exist in addition to the middle-of-the-road group that supports the U.N. One group wants the United States to depend less on U.N. . . . They represent the isolationist position . . . . At the opposite extreme are those who feel that the U.N. is not enough. These people believe that only some form of world government can prevent mankind's destruction.

The statement is a classic example of the typical "some say" and "some say" balancing act so frequently found in civics textbooks. The authors of this particular passage have carefully failed to point out that the "middle-of-the road" group includes the United States government, a succession of Democratic and Republican Presidents who have given the United Nations strong support and endorsement, the Congress which has passed a succession of resolutions and money bills in support of the U.N., the major religious bodies, and, as shown in several public opinion polls, over eighty-five per cent of the American people who support the U.N. as an important instrument for the settlement of international disputes by peaceful means.

We have put the blame for this situation on textbook writers and on textbook publishing companies. However, fairness and candor require that we state that many social studies teachers are also apparently convinced that an honest and critical acknowledgment of some weak spots in our democracy would confuse and undermine their students' devotion and faith in our system of government. Some teachers feel that high school students should not be burdened with these crucial problems which bewilder and confuse the adult society. They have time to find out about the imperfections and difficulties after they leave high school and are more mature and better able to deal with controversial issues. They tend to believe that the important thing is for young people to learn how our government functions and recognize that it deserves the active concern, participation, and support of all our citizens.

This reasoning is based on several doubtful assumptions. First, it assumes, erroneously I believe, that the mind of a high-school student is a *tabula rasa*, a clearly wiped board, as far as information, attitudes, and values on civic issues are concerned. It assumes that our students are unaware of the racial issue, of restrictive covenants in housing, of the existence of slums, and of the complexities of conducting a successful foreign policy in a complex and explosive world. Anyone who has taught in a high school or talked to high school students knows how keenly aware many of them are and how much information and misinformation they have about the Harlem and Watts riots, about occupancy ordinances, about juvenile delinquency, about the occasional corruption scandals in their communities and in Washington, and about skid rows and slums. In fact, many of them can speak on these problems from personal experience. Civics textbooks may have "closed areas," but for our students, because of television, the involvement of their parents, and their peer groups, there is little that remains unknown and untouched. On the contrary, there is an imperative need to submit controversial issues to a searching, honest, and scholarly scrutiny in the classrooms. If our young people are to gain new understanding and insights, and gradually adopt intelligent and sophisticated attitudes as involved citizens, their bits and fragments of "knowledge," their beliefs, values, and prejudices must be challenged and subjected to the test of critical research and critical thinking. In this way effective and interesting learning can take place, and we may prepare our young generation for intelligent decision-making as citizens in a world that abounds in conflict and controversy. By this approach, we may succeed in preparing the young generation to compete effectively in the battle of ideas between democracy and totalitarianism.

The ostrich-like attitude adopted by many civics textbooks is not only a distortion of the real society in which the students live and in which they will have to make their way, but it is also one of the major causes of boredom that reigns supreme in many civics classrooms. "We can scarcely expect to motivate," wrote a leading political scientist,

> to any lasting and strong desire to effectively participate in the community politics with the milk-and-water moralism of the average civics text, nor is the bland emptiness of a junior chamber of commerce get-out-the-vote campaign such that it inspires a ritual of even ceremonial significance. Political competence can stem from a hard material purpose that schools itself to a realistic study of facts.[6]

It is relevant also to point out that the bland diet which is enforced in citizenship and government instruction contradicts what we know about the conditions needed for effective teaching. Researchers in the area of the teaching-learning process are agreed that learning takes place when what is in the student's mind is confronted, challenged, and puzzled by new information and new insights. Ralph Tyler writes: "As long as the learner does not recognize that his earlier modes of behavior are inappropriate, he will keep on doing what he has been doing and will not really learn anything new."[7] And Herbert Thelen maintains that

> Our schools have the responsibility of helping children live as self-realizing people, not in a vacuum or a hermitage, but in a complex society. . . . They are going to manage others; interpret the world around them; make discoveries; create social, political, and economic alternatives; ferret out facts; and persuade, promote, criticize, analyze, guide, console and teach.[8]

It would seem logical to assume, upon some reflection, that our young people will love the United States more, not less, when they arrive at the realization that in spite of its difficulties, conflicts, and weaknesses, a free democratic society provides the best opportunity for its citizens to enjoy the benefits of a "Good Life." They will love the United States more, not less, when they understand that generations past have built the nation soundly and well, but have left for their successors the task of improving and refining our way of life. They ought to realize that it is in the nature

---

[6] Norton E. Long, "Political Science," in Gordon B. Turner, ed., *The Social Studies and the Social Sciences* (New York: Harcourt, Brace & World, 1962), p. 97.

[7] Ralph Tyler, "Criteria for Curriculum Content and Method," in Francis S. Chase and Harold A. Anderson, eds., *The High School in a New Era* (Chicago: Univ. of Chicago Press, 1958), p. 178.

[8] Herbert A. Thelen, "The Triumph of 'Achievement' over Inquiry in Education," *Elementary School Journal* (January 1960), p. 194.

of a democracy to always seek improvement and perfection. Furthermore, realistic and challenging teaching of civics would prevent our students from becoming disillusioned cynics when they find out from their first college instructor or from some life experience that all is not sweetness and light in our politics and society. Whether we like it or not, our ideals and way of life will be challenged in coming years, directly or indirectly, peacefully or violently, by representatives of totalitarian regimes who will cite chapter and verse in an attempt to prove that communism or fascism are the "wave of the future." Our young people must be ready to accept the challenge. To do so they must be deeply imbued with, and committed to, the "American Creed," but they must also be aware of the shadows in our society and of the still unresolved conflicts and problems. They must be prepared to defend intelligently the advantages of our way of life and of our system of government and we, the older generation, must make sure that they can point with pride to progress that is being made.

Instruction in government and civics has been woefully inadequate in giving our high school students a clear comprehension of the unique genius of the American government and in fostering in them a commitment to the basic ideals on which this republic was founded and which still constitute the bedrock of its existence.

How does one make students understand the uniqueness of American democracy? One of the ways not to do it is to attempt to *indoctrinate* the students with love of country or to preach the gospel of the superiority of the American system over any other system of government. An appreciation of the uniqueness (not of the superiority) of our form of government should be the hoped for result of intelligent, honest, and vivid instruction in citizenship education. The particular and peculiarly attractive features of the Constitution and of American politics are not easily perceived or articulated. This problem has made the attainment of this objective in the teaching of civics so difficult. The difficulty, however, does not free us from an obligation to find new ways and new approaches.

Let us make three suggestions and then elaborate on them in order. First, we want to suggest a thorough study of four books, available in paperback editions and surprisingly, all written by foreigners. The authors of these books have understood and articulated the most important features of the American government and society. They were also superb writers, and therefore their books or at least excerpts from them are quite intelligible to the average high school student. They should be used in all civics classes as supplementary readings. The second suggestion concerns the study of the United States Constitution which if it is to be effective, must be completely revamped. Finally, it is suggested that politics, an area almost completely ignored in civics classrooms, be given a distinguished place in citizenship education.

The four books which deserve to be in the hands of all students may well become the standard references in civic instruction. They are: J. Hector St. John de Crèvecoeur's *Letters from an American Farmer,* Harriet Martineau's *Society in America* (edited and abridged by Seymour Martin Lipset), Alexis de Tocqueville's *Democracy in America,* and James T. Bryce's *The American Commonwealth.* Crèvecoeur's short but important volume, was first published in London in 1782. The author was a Frenchman who in 1764 became a naturalized American citizen. He was a farmer in Pine Hill in New York State, and his letters relate his experiences on his farm and reports on his travels in New England and in the South. Crèvecoeur was a lover of nature, a keen observer of life in the colonies, and a good writer, but what is of interest for us here, is his ability to comprehend the uniqueness of the early American experience. Letter number three, "What is an American?" is an absorbing and insightful attempt to set down the differences between the life of an American and an English or a French farmer. An Englishman when he first lands in America, Crèvecoeur writes, beholds a rich land with "fair cities, substantial villages, extensive fields, an immense country filled with decent houses, good roads, orchards, meadows, and bridges, where a hundred years ago all was wild, woody, and uncultivated." But even more important is the special spirit of the people in America.

> We are animated with the spirit of an industry which is unfettered and unrestrained, because each person works for himself. If he travels through our rural districts he views not the hostile castle, and the haughty mansion, contrasted with the clay-built hut and miserable cabin, where cattle and men help to keep each other warm, and dwell in meanness, smoke and indigence . . .

When Americans in the countryside went to church on Sunday there was an atmosphere of equality. "There is not among them an esquire, saving the unlettered magistrate . . . *We have no princes for whom we toil, starve, and bleed. We are the most perfect society now existing in the world.*"

The traveler from abroad, Crèvecoeur says, would wish to know the background of this idyllic situation and ask, "What then is the American, this new man?" He answers:

> He is an American, who, leaving behind him all his ancient prejudices and manners, receives new ones from the new mode of life he has embraced, the new government he obeys, and the new rank he holds. He becomes an American by being received in the broad lap of our great Alma Mater.

> Here individuals of all nations are melted into a new race of men, whose labors and posterity will one day cause great changes in the world.[9]

---

[9] J. Hector St. John de Crèvecoeur, *Letters from an American Farmer* (New York: E. P. Dutton & Co., 1957), p. 39 (italics mine).

An American, says the author,

> extinguishes all his European prejudices, he forgets that mechanism of sub-
> ordination, that servility of disposition that poverty had taught him . . .
> Ye poor Europeans, ye, who sweat, and work for the great—ye, who are
> obliged to give so many sheaves to the church, so many to your lords, so
> many to your government, and have hardly any left for yourselves—ye,
> who are held in less estimation than favorite hunters or useless lap-dogs, ye,
> who only breathe the air of nature, because it cannot be withheld from
> you . . . it is here the laws of naturalization invite everyone to partake
> of our great labors and felicity, to till unrented, untaxed lands![10]

How astounding it is for an immigrant Frenchman to have been able to
comprehend and articulate so well the spirit of the new country on the
American continent. To Crèvecoeur the American was a man in love with
his big and rich land, who prized his freedom and who despised servility.
With a keen eye he perceived the advantages of this new frontier society,
free of squires, counts and oppressive government exactions and regulations
and prophesied that this "new race of men" would build a great and powerful nation.

Harriet Martineau, an Englishwoman, writer, and social worker came to
the United States in 1834 and stayed for two years studying American society. Miss Martineau was a reformer and abolitionist, but she was also
a thorough and objective researcher of American politics, society, and government. She published the results of her study, *Society in America*, in
1837. She found Americans remarkably different from their European fore-
bears.

> I regard the American people as a great embryo poet; now moody, now
> wild, but bringing out results of absolute good sense, restless and wayward
> in action, but with deep peace in his heart, exulting that he has caught the
> true aspect of things past, and at the depth of futurity which lies before
> him, wherein to create something so magnificent as the world has scarcely
> begun to dream of. There is the strongest hope of a nation that is capable
> of being possessed with an idea, and this kind of possession has been the
> peculiarity of the Americans from their first day of national experience till
> now.[11]

How remarkable it was for Harriet Martineau, in 1835, to perceive the
essence of the American Dream and to stress a unique feature relating to
the origin of this country. She realized that the United States, unlike most
if not all countries, was born of an idea that all men were created equal,
that all men have the right to life, liberty, and the pursuit of happiness, and

---

[10] *Ibid.,* p. 56.
[11] Harriet Martineau, *Society in America,* abr. ed. (Garden City, N.Y.: Doubleday & Co.,
1962), p. 73.

that Americans, possessed by this idea, were determined and capable of building a new society the like of which the world had never seen.

Fascinated as she was by the vibrant and promising new society, Harriet Martineau fully comprehended the evils and the potential dangers to the integrity and well-being of America that were to result from the existence of slavery. She was not one to be fooled by the Southern apologia for slavery as a benevolent institution which civilized and Christianized the barbaric Africans.

> I was frequently told of the "endearing relation" subsisting between master and slaves. . . . As long as the slave remains ignorant, docile and contented, he is taken care of, humored, and spoken of with a contemptuous, compassionate kindness. But from the moment he exhibits the attributes of a rational being, from the moment his intellect seems likely to come into the most distinct competition with that of whites, the most deadly hatreds spring up; not in the black, but in his oppressors. It is an old truth that we hate those whom we have injured. Never was it more clear than in this case.[12]

The corrosive effect of the existence of slavery on the mind of the South has seldom ever been put more succinctly or perceptively. In spite of the black spot of slavery, Harriet Martineau had no doubt about the validity of the American Dream and of the destiny of America. She wrote in the concluding paragraph of her book:

> No peculiarity in them is more remarkable than their national contentment. If this were the result of apathy, it would be despicable, if it did not co-exist with an active principle of progress, it would be absurd. As it is, I can regard this national attribute with no other feeling than veneration. Entertaining as I do, little doubt of the general safety of the American Union, and none of the moral progress of its people, it is clear to me that this national contentment will live down all contempt and even all wonder; and come at length to be regarded with the same genial and universal emotion with which men recognize in an individual the equanimity of rational self-reverence.[13]

These words of a wise and noble Englishwoman who wrote about the United States of 130 years ago, if presented in the proper setting and dramatically, should prove to be a source of inspiration to any civics or government classroom.

However perceptive Crèvecoeur and Martineau were, no one understood the workings of the American Constitution, government, and society as deeply as the young French aristocrat, Count Alexis de Tocqueville. De Tocqueville, who was an assistant magistrate or junior judge, was sent in 1831 to America by the French government to study the prisons in this

---

[12] *Ibid.*, p. 33.
[13] *Ibid.*, p. 357.

country. He and his traveling companion, Gustave de Beaumont, soon became so entranced by the United States that they decided to study much more than the prisons—they were determined to learn all that they could about this remarkable land. Tocqueville and Beaumont arrived in the United States on May 11, 1831 and sailed for France on February 20, 1832. The New York *Evening Post* carried an item which took notice of their arrival: "Two young magistrates . . . have arrived in New York, sent here by order of the Minister of the Interior, to examine the various prisons in our country, and make a report on their return to France." It is remarkable how much de Tocqueville, who remained faithful to his aristocratic heritage and traditions, learned and appreciated about the United States, a democratic republic.

Upon his return to France, de Tocqueville published in 1835 a report on his travels entitled, *Democracy in America*. The prevailing theme of his book was that American democracy works and that it has been able, in spite of many shortcomings, to assure the greatest amount of happiness to the greatest number of its citizens. Professor George Wilson Pierson, the foremost American scholar on de Tocqueville, summarized de Tocqueville's observations on the uniqueness and the sources of strength of the American people in the following points:

1. Their origin. Fine starting point, intimate mixture of religion and spirit of liberty.

2. Their activity, commercial and industrial. Even their vices are now helpful to them.

3. Their geographical position. No neighbors.

4. The Material Happiness which they enjoy.

5. The religious spirit which reigns. A Republican and equalitarian religion.

6. The diffusion of *useful* education.

7. Very pure morals.

8. Their division into small states.

9. The lack of a large capital where everything is centered. (Like Paris and London.)

10. Communal and provisional activity, which enables everyone to find employment at home.[14]

---

[14] George Wilson Pierson, *Tocqueville and Beaumont in America* (New York: Oxford Univ. Press, 1938), p. 295.

De Tocqueville was greatly impressed with the egalitarian character of America. He considered the pervasive spirit of equality "an extraordinary phenomenon." "Men are there," he wrote, "seen on a greater equality in point of fortune and intellect, or, in other words, more equal in their strength, than in any other country in the world . . ."[15]

While on the whole de Tocqueville saw America as an exciting, strong, and viable democracy, he was not blind to the weaknesses and difficulties it faced. He warned against dangers lurking in the "tyranny of the majority," possible in a system in which 51 per cent may theoretically rule a 49 per cent minority. However, de Tocqueville's most insightful and prophetic chapters are those dealing with the fate and the future of Indians and of Negroes in America. Excerpts from these chapters, in a mimeographed form, can form the basis for excellent discussions of the Indian problem and of the slavery question. Teacher and students should note that this profound analysis of two complex issues was made by a young French visitor nearly thirty years before the Civil War.

De Tocqueville saw an important difference between the Indian and the Negro in the American society. While the Negro

> makes a thousand fruitless efforts to insinuate himself among men who repulse him; he conforms to the tastes of his oppressors, adopts their opinions, and hopes by imitating them to form a part of their community. . . . The Indian, on the contrary, has his imagination inflated with the pretended nobility of his origin, and lives and dies in the midst of these dreams of pride. Far from desiring to conform his habits to ours, he loves his savage life as the distinguishing mark of his race and repels every advance to civilization, less perhaps, from hatred of it, than from a dread of resembling the Europeans.[16]

It is hard to believe that a young visitor to this country, not a trained political scientist, without the benefit of polls, charts, and computers, after an inquiry which lasted only nine months was able to make such an acute analysis of the complex sets of relationships between white Americans, Indians, and Negroes.

"The Negro," de Tocqueville continues, "who earnestly desires to mingle his race with that of the European, cannot do so; while the Indian, who might succeed to a certain extent, disdains to make the attempt. *The servility of the one dooms him to slavery, the pride of the other to death.*"[17]

The French observer was unerringly and almost uncannily correct in his predictions of the future. These prophecies, the fruit of diligent observa-

---

[15] Alexis de Tocqueville, *Democracy in America*, Vol. I (New York: Random House, 1945), p. 55.
[16] *Ibid.*, pp. 346, 347.
[17] *Ibid.*, p. 354 (italics mine).

tion, research, and analysis, can prove to be a source of great interest to the students if properly presented. Consider the following brief selections:

> I believe that the Indian nations of North America are doomed to perish and that whenever the Europeans shall be established on the shores of the Pacific Ocean, that race of men will have ceased to exist. The Indians had only the alternative of death or civilization . . .[18]

De Tocqueville, who wrote his book in 1835, twenty-six years before the Civil War, did not see any hope of a lasting compromise between the South and the North on slavery. In that view he differed and still differs from many historians of the Civil War. He wrote:

> Whatever may be the efforts of the Americans of the South to maintain slavery, they will not always succeed. Slavery, now confined to a single tract of the civilized earth, attacked by Christianity as unjust and by political economy as prejudicial, and now contrasted with democratic liberty and the intelligence of our age, cannot survive. By the act of the master, or by the will of the slave, it will cease; and in either case great calamities may be expected to ensue.

Abraham Lincoln, speaking in 1858, stated a similar view on the incompatibility of slavery with America and the ideals on which it was founded in one sentence, "I believe this government cannot endure permanently half slave and half free."

As if this insight into the future were not enough to make us stand in awe and wonder, de Tocqueville added a dire prophecy of the racial difficulties that would develop after the abolition of slavery: *"If I were called upon to predict the future, I should say that the abolition of slavery in the South will, in the common course of things, increase the repugnance of the white population for the blacks."*[19] This is as accurate a prediction of the period of Reconstruction as one could have expected from a truly inspired Prophet of old.

James Bryce, the author of the thorough and penetrating analysis of American government, society, and politics which he entitled *The American Commonwealth,* was an Englishman who at the age of twenty-four had already gained renown as a historian. After his appointment as professor at Oxford, Bryce visited America frequently to study its institutions, mores, and problems. *The American Commonwealth* was published in 1888 and was received with great acclaim in the United States and in England. While not uncritical, the author is sympathetic and understanding. In 1907, Lord Bryce was appointed British Ambassador to the United States, a post which he filled with distinction for a number of years.

---

[18] *Ibid.,* p. 397.
[19] *Ibid.,* p. 390 (italics mine).

Students in civics classes could benefit greatly from a discussion of this list of basic strengths of American democracy as listed by Bryce:

1. The first is that of Stability . . . The Federal Constitution is, to their eyes, an almost sacred thing, an Ark of Covenant, whereon no rash man may lay rash hands. Everywhere in Europe one hears schemes of radical change freely discussed. . . . But in the United States the discussion of political problems busies itself with details and assumes that the main lines must remain as they are forever.

2. Feeling the law to be its own work, the people are disposed to obey the law. . . . The habit of living under a rigid constitution superior to ordinary statutes—indeed two rigid constitutions, since the State Constitution is a fundamental law within its own sphere no less than is the Federal—intensifies this legality of view. . . .

3. There is a broad simplicity about the political ideas of the people, and a courageous consistency in carrying them out in practice. When they have accepted a principle, they do not shrink from applying it "right through," however disagreeable in particular cases some of the results may be. . . . Take, for instance, the boundless freedom of the press. There are abuses obviously incident to such freedom . . . but Americans deliberately hold that in view of the benefits which such freedom on the whole promises, abuses must be borne with and left to the sentiment of the people and the private law of libel to deal with.

4. It is a great merit of American government that it relies very little on officials, and arms them with little power of arbitrary interference.

5. There are no struggles between privileged and unprivileged orders, not even that perpetual strife of rich and poor which is the oldest disease of civilized states. One must not pronounce broadly that there are no classes, for in parts of the country social distinctions have begun to grow up. But for political purposes, classes scarcely exist . . . Everything that government, as the Americans have hither to understand the term, can give them, the poor have already, political power, equal civil rights, a career open to all citizens alike, not to speak of that gratuitous higher as well as elementary education, which on their own economic principles the United States might have abstained from giving, but which for political reasons have led them to provide with an unstinting hand.

6. Wealthy and powerful such a country must have been under any form of government, but the speed with which she has advanced, and the employment of the sources of wealth to diffuse comfort among millions of families, may be placed to the credit of stimulative freedom.

7. The government of the Republic, limited and languid in ordinary times, is capable of developing immense vigour. It can pull itself together at moments of danger, can put forth unexpected efforts, can venture on stretches of authority transcending not only ordinary practice, but even ordinary law. This is the result of the unity of the nation. Now the American people are united in movements of national concern from two causes. One is that absence of class divisions and jealousies which have been already described. The people are homogeneous; a feeling which stirs alike rich and poor, farmers and traders, Eastern men and Western men—one may now add, Southern men too. . . . The other source of unity is the tendency in democracies for the sentiment of the majority to tell upon the sentiment of the minority.

8. Democracy has not only taught the Americans how to use liberty without abusing it, and how to secure equality; it has also taught them fraternity. . . . The natural impulse of every citizen in America is to respect every other citizen, and to feel that citizenship constitutes a certain ground of respect. The idea of each man's equal rights is so fully realized that the rich or powerful man feels it no indignity to take his turn among the crowd, and does not expect any deference from the poorest.[20]

Bryce's interpretation of the essence of American democracy can still be used as a basis for discussions and investigations in civic classrooms.

Those engaged in training prospective history and social studies teachers know of their hesitancy and even resistance to speak clearly about those objectives in civics education which relate directly to the student's intellectual and emotional stance in relation to the United States. They do not feel uncomfortable when encountering such vague terms as "good citizenship" or "responsible citizenship," but they draw back when told that "devotion to American democracy" and "appreciation of American ideals" are postulated as objectives in citizenship education. The hesitation, if not an outright objection, center on the fear of indoctrination and a grave doubt about the efficacy of "teaching" devotion and appreciation. In addition, many of our brighter prospective teachers react almost instinctively to the shrill and bombastic propaganda for "true" patriotism in schools conducted by some small but vocal extremist pressure groups.

Making due allowance for this difficulty, it must nevertheless be said that an understanding and then, hopefully, an appreciation of the American Creed and the American Dream are legitimate objectives in the teaching of civics. In fact, the attainment of these objectives is the most important

---

[20] James Bryce, *The American Commonwealth*, Vol. II (New York: G. P. Putnam's Sons, 1888), p. 211.

reason for teaching civics in schools. The study and discussion of the particular sets of ideas and values that made America and which form the core of our basic national character are a legitimate subject of study in social studies. "That each nation has its own character," wrote Henry Steele Commager, "is taken for granted, and it is neither chauvinistic nor provincial to observe that the United States is no exception."[21] What are the basic elements in this American national character?

A group of leading businessmen and intellectuals was commissioned some time ago by the Rockefeller Foundation to draw up a document on the future thrust of American education. That report, *The Pursuit of Excellence,* was widely distributed and contained the following brief statement on the essence of our free society:

> We believe that man—by virtue of his humanity—should live in the light of reason, exercise moral responsibility, and be free to develop to the full the talents that are in him.
>
> Our devotion to a free society can only be understood in terms of these values. It is the only form of society that put at the very top of its agenda the opportunity of the individual to develop his potentialities. It is the declared enemy of every condition that stunts the intellectual, moral, and spiritual growth of the individual. No society has ever fully succeeded in living up to the stern ideals that a free people set themselves. But only a free society can even address itself to that demanding test.[22]

The last sentence is a crucial one and it serves as an answer to the "realistic" critics who when confronted with a general statement that the United States stands for the opportunity of all individuals to the fullest pursuit of their liberty and happiness will point to continued discrimination against Negroes and to the existence of poverty in the midst of prosperous America. The crucial point is that these grievous shortcomings are by the general consensus considered to be contradictory to the American Creed, and are actively combatted by the powers of all the branches of the federal government. Furthermore, our society is addressing itself to the demanding task of redressing just grievances. It is that national determination to eliminate inequalities that proves the stability of the American national character. The great poet and teacher Archibald MacLeish wrote:

> We not only have a national purpose, we have a national purpose of such aspiration, such potentiality, such power of hope that we refer to it, or used to—as the American Dream. We were dedicated from our beginnings to the proposition that we existed to be free. This dedication was real in

---

[21] Henry Steele Commager, ed., *America in Perspective* (New York: New American Library, 1951), p. 111.
[22] *The Pursuit of Excellence: Education and the Future of America,* Rockefeller Brothers Fund (Garden City, N.Y.: Doubleday & Co., 1958), p. 1.

spite of the fact that it took a bloody war to eliminate slavery from within our own frontiers. It was real in spite of the fact that the full practice of freedom is still a delusion in numerous pockets of hypocrisy across the nation.[23]

The articles of the American Creed are a legitimate object of instruction of inquiry and instruction in civics classes. The components of this Creed are many and varied. There is a surprising agreement in this country on what they are. A few examples should suffice:

We believe in the worth of the individual to live his life as he chooses.

We believe in the rule of law, in a government in which the men in authority are subject to law under the Constitution.

We believe in freedom, in peace, and justice. Whatever the occasional mistakes and shortcomings of our foreign policy may be, no American Government could or would pursue a course of imperialist aggrandizement.

We believe in the right to free discussion, to the right of dissent, and to the right of petition for the redress of grievances.

We believe in spite of the growth of the power and responsibilities of the Federal Government, in limited government and in the government as the servant, not the ruler of the people.

We believe in a government whose members present themselves in regular intervals to the inspection of their records and accept the decision rendered by the electorate.

In an essay titled "Some Generalities That Still Glitter," which should be put to frequent use in civics classrooms, the great historian Carl Becker wrote on the essence of democratic faith:

To have faith in the dignity and worth of the individual man as an end in himself, to believe that it is better to be governed by persuasion than by coercion, to believe that fraternal good will is more worthy than selfish and contentious spirit, to believe that in the long run all values are inseparable from the love of truth and the disinterested search for it, to believe that knowledge and the power it confers should be used to promote the welfare and happiness of all men rather than to serve the interests of those individuals and classes whom fortune and intelligence endow with temporary advantage—these are the values which are affirmed by the traditional democratic ideology.[24]

Having said all this, the question still remains—how does one *teach* the American Creed? Professor Donald Oliver, in an article in the 30th Yearbook of the National Council for the Social Studies, deals with this question

---

[23] Archibald MacLeish: "We Have a Purpose . . . We All Know It," in *The National Purpose* (New York: Holt, Rinehart & Winston, 1960), p. 39.

[24] Carl Becker, "Some Generalities That Still Glitter," in Hillman M. Bishop and Samuel Hendel, eds., *Basic Issues of American Democracy* (New York: Appleton-Century-Crofts, 1948), p. 39.

incisively and imaginatively.[25] He suggests that in the elementary grades the sense of national identification be through the legends about Columbus, the Founding Fathers, the Revolution, the discovery of the West, and the Civil War. Children should get to understand the American Creed, says Oliver, emotionally and symbolically.

This emotional approach should be supplemented in a high school with what Oliver calls a jurisprudential approach. Basically, the jurisprudential approach is similar to the Oliver-Shaver public controversy curriculum in social studies. This curriculum would center primarily on broad areas of conflicts on questions relating to the rights of individuals and groups in a free society and the relationship of the individual citizen to his government. Professor Oliver does not equivocate about the objectives of citizenship education. He properly asks that the main objective be the fostering of a basic commitment to the democratic process and to our free society. "The most important reasons for teaching the great image," Oliver wrote,

> as a crucial initial step in citizenship is the need to provide a concrete basis for our dynamic faith in a truly liberal society. Otherwise, there is a real possibility that some men may never be trained to see the world beyond their own petty personal interests. We must commit our children so completely to a system of government which protects constructive non-conformity that day-by-day contact with the hazards and realities of the system will not tarnish the ideals for which the system stands.[26]

It is clear or it should be clear that teachers cannot bring about such a commitment to our system of government unless they themselves have such a commitment, unless they themselves experience a surge of emotion when they read the Declaration of Independence or the Gettysburg Address. Teachers who neither understand, nor stand in awe in the face of the utter devotion to freedom and to the government of law of George Washington, Thomas Jefferson, Abraham Lincoln, John Marshall, and Oliver Wendell Holmes cannot inspire their students with a sense of appreciation for the American Creed. Only such a primary commitment can lead to a fruitful and exciting, even if often disturbing and irritating, critical inquiry into the yet unsolved problems and conflicts which beset our society.

Oliver's judicious use of the public controversy approach to the teaching of civics holds great promise. Let us give one example of how it can be used in practice.

The states' rights controversy, the conflict between the rights of states and the rights and prerogatives of the Federal government, is of crucial importance in the study of civics. The complicated problem and public controversy which has yet to be resolved can be illuminated by an inquiry into

---

[25] Donald W. Oliver, "Educating Citizens for Responsible Individualism," in *Citizenship and a Free Society* (Washington: National Council for the Social Studies, 1960), p. 211.
[26] *Ibid.*, p. 214.

the conflict between the governor of Illinois, John P. Altgeld, and President Grover Cleveland during the Chicago Pullman Company strike in 1894.

When in the spring of 1894, the Pullman Company, suffering from a loss of business due to an economic depression, cut wages and laid off almost a third of the employees, the workers went on strike. They soon received the support of the American Railway Union, led by Eugene V. Debs. The A.R.U. ordered a boycott of all Pullman cars on all railroad lines in the West. Members of the American Railway Union began to cut off the Pullman cars, leaving them standing on the sidetracks. In a short period of time, some regular trains were also halted, and in spite of the strenuous efforts of the railroad owners to keep the lines operating, railroad traffic was only sporadic between Chicago and San Francisco. The halting of the trains brought about riots of strikers, the burning of engines, and considerable damage to railroad property. The railroad owners countered with use of force by hired strike-breakers and armed Pinkerton men. It became clear that law and order had to be restored, especially at the Chicago railroad yards. The railroad operators had no confidence in Governor Altgeld, whom they considered a dangerous radical because he had pardoned the anarchists convicted in the Haymarket Riot. They urged President Grover Cleveland to send in federal troops. (The President's dilemma was duplicated later when President Dwight D. Eisenhower in 1954 was faced with the necessity to intervene in force in Arkansas to enforce a federal court order to integrate a high school in Little Rock.) President Cleveland realized that the Constitution authorized the sending of federal troops to a state for the purpose of restoring order only "on application of the legislature, or of the executive." Neither the Illinois governor, nor the Illinois legislature asked for help and intervention. On the contrary, Governor Altgeld insisted that the state forces were fully capable of maintaining law and order.

Nevertheless, on July 4, 1894, Grover Cleveland sent in two thousand troops to restore order. The President announced that his step was justified because the strike interfered with the free transport and distribution of the United States mail and that it was his responsibility under the Constitution to assure the proper functioning of the Post Office. Once in Chicago, the troops not only assured the movement of the mail cars, but actually broke the strike.

Governor Altgeld vehemently protested the use of federal troops as an unconstitutional usurpation of power by the federal government. He branded Cleveland's action as a violation of states' rights and an unjustified imposition of military power over lawful civilian authority.

Students in civics classes, ought, after understanding the background and the issues involved in the strike, to have the benefit of reading and analyzing the correspondence which ensued between Altgeld and Cleveland.

On July 5, 1894, Governor Altgeld wrote the President in part:

I am advised that you have ordered Federal troops to go into service in the State of Illinois. Surely the facts have not been correctly presented to you in this case, or you would not have taken this step, for it is entirely unnecessary, and, it seems to me, unjustifiable. Waiving all questions of courtesy, I will say that the State of Illinois is not only able to take care of itself, but it stands ready to furnish the Federal government any assistance it may need elsewhere. . . .

At present some of our railroads are paralyzed, not by reason of obstruction, but because they cannot get men to operate their trains. For some reason they are anxious to keep this fact from the public, and for this purpose they are making an outcry about obstructions in order to divert attention. . . . Very little actual violence has been committed. . . . The newspaper accounts have in many cases been pure fabrications, and in others wild exaggerations . . .

I repeat that you have been imposed in this matter; but even if by forced construction it were held that the conditions have come within the letter of the statute, then I submit that local self-government is a fundamental principle of the Constitution. Each community shall govern itself so long as it can and is ready and able to enforce the law, and it is in harmony with this fundamental principle that the statute authorizing the President to send troops into States must be construed . . .

As Governor of the State of Illinois, I protest this and ask the immediate withdrawal of the Federal Troops from active duty in this State . . .

> I have the honor to be, yours respectfully,
> John P. Altgeld, Governor of Illinois

On the same day, the President replied:

Sir:

Federal troops were sent to Chicago in strict accordance with the Constitution and laws of the United States, upon the demand of the post-office department that obstruction of the mails should be removed, and upon the representations of the judicial officers of the United States that the process of the Federal courts could not be executed through the ordinary means, and upon competent proof that conspiracies existed against commerce between the States. To meet these conditions, which are clearly within the province of Federal authority, the presence of Federal troops in the city of Chicago was deemed not only proper, but necessary, and there has been no intention of thereby interfering with the plain duty of the local authorities to preserve the peace of the city.

> Sincerely yours,
> Grover Cleveland

Altgeld dispatched another letter to the White House, dated the next day, July 6th. It said in part:

Sir:

Your answer to my protest involves some startling conclusions and ignores and evades the question at issue—that is, that the principle of local self-government is just as fundamental in our institutions as is that of Federal supremacy.

First, you calmly assume that the executive has the legal right to order Federal troops into any community of the United States, in the first instance, whenever there is the slightest disturbance . . . Inasmuch the executive is the sole judge of the question as to whether any disturbance exists in any part of the country, this assumption means that the executive can send Federal Troops into any community in the United States at his pleasure, and keep them there as long as he chooses. If this is the law, then the principle of self-government did not exist in this country or else has been destroyed . . .

Second, it is also a fundamental principle in our government that except in times of war the military shall be subordinate to the civil authority. . . . The troops you have ordered to Chicago are not under the civil authorities . . .

Fourth, You say that troops were ordered into Illinois upon the demand of the post-office department and upon representations of the judicial office of the United States. . . . All of these officers are appointed by the executive. Most of them can be removed by him at will. They are not only obliged to do his bidding, but they are in fact a party of the executive. If several of them can apply for troops, one alone can, so that under the law, as you assume it to be, an executive, through any one of his appointees, can apply to himself to have the military sent into any city or number of cities, and base his application on such representations as he sees fit to make.

This assumption as to the power of the executive is certainly new, and I respectfully submit is not the law of the land, and not a government by the caprice of an individual, and further, instead of being autocratic, it is a government of limited power . . .

Inasmuch as the Federal troops can do nothing but what the State troops can do there, and believing that a State is amply able to take care of the situation and enforce the law, and believing that the ordering out of the Federal troops was unwarranted, I again ask your withdrawal.

Respectfully yours,
John P. Altgeld

The President's answer was brief and curt:

Sir:

While I am still persuaded that I have neither transcended my authority nor duty in the emergency that confronts us, it seems to me that in this hour of danger and public distress, discussion may well give way to active efforts on the part of all in authority to restore obedience to law and to protect life and property.

Grover Cleveland

This correspondence presents a public controversy in a revealing, instructive and dramatic manner. It is, using Oliver's term, a typical jurisprudential problem in citizenship education which is ideally suited to a classroom inquiry. Obviously, just talking about the controversy without the intelligent use of the letters would not be effective teaching. Altgeld's passionate appeals for the principle of self-government and local autonomy and Cleveland's cool and detached stand for law and order and his confidence in the overwhelming power of the Presidency can be conducive to a dispassionate and critical analysis of the issues involved. Students should be encouraged to think of alternative ways in which this conflict could have been resolved. This would be teaching civics of high order and of course, if done by an imaginative and learned teacher, who would fully participate in the inquiry, would be an exciting learning experience.

12

New Approaches to the

Teaching of Civics (Part II)

The teaching of the Constitution of the United States is, as we have said, obligatory in most of the states. Much new thinking and planning is needed to make this study worthwhile and effective. One assumes that the state legislatures which have passed laws requiring the teaching of the Constitution did so in the hope that knowledge about the Constitution would lead to an appreciation and veneration of the basic legal document on which our government rests. This hope is not often realized. In many schools the study of the Constitution becomes a rather boring exercise in memorizing the content of the various sections and articles. The questions, often listed on a mimeographed sheet of paper distributed by the teacher, contain no-nonsense factual questions pertaining to the "enumerated powers of Congress," the qualifications required of the candidates for the presidency, and so on. This instruction is then culminated in an examination, usually administered by the state which, on the whole, requires only recall information.

No wonder that many students find the study of the Constitution tedious and uninspiring. Several things are radically wrong with the present procedure. First, the Constitution is taught as a document or a historical source without an origin, a background and a setting. Second, the emphasis is on the language, the content of that great document, not on the presentation of *a living Constitution*, the constantly evolving *constitutional process*, and the actual application of the various articles and provisions. Thirdly, and probably most importantly, the Constitution is usually taught completely divorced from politics and from the political process. These three major shortcomings will be discussed, *seriatim*.

The Constitution has a unique place in American life, and that uniqueness must become clear to our students. Once explained and perceived it may prove to be a powerful motivation for the effective study of the Constitution. Americans can refer to *the* Constitution because it is the only constitution this country has ever had. While the United States is a relatively young country, nevertheless, among the major powers it has the oldest written constitution in the world still in effect. This lack of an enduring constitution is, of course, true of the totalitarian countries and the newly independent countries, but it is also true of several of the Western democratic states. Great Britain has never had a written constitution, and Germany, Italy, and France have had several constitutions in the last century.

Our Constitution, written at the end of the eighteenth century, when railroads were still unknown, is still a viable instrument of government in the second half of the twentieth century, an age of jet planes and atomic energy. The teaching of the Constitution in the classrooms throughout this land should be preceded by the discussion of this truly phenomenal fact. How did the Founding Fathers in 1787 succeed in drawing up a body of laws, a blueprint for a functioning government which with but a few changes is fully compatible with the radically changed conditions of our times? The answer to this question must lead the teacher and the students to an inquiry into the composition and the workings of the Constitutional Convention of which Thomas Jefferson, at the time the American Minister in Paris, wrote to John Adams in London, "It really is an assembly of demigods."

The "assembly of demigods" deserves several weeks of study in any civics class. The benefits of the insights gained should prove to be most important for the study and the understanding of the Constitution. Even more importantly, students will be able to "see" the founders of this country, not just as political leaders engaged in complicated disputations, but as men of great stature. The sense of awe for the members of the Constitutional Assembly and for their masterpiece is an essential prerequisite for an effective study of the Constitution. Obviously, this sense of awe should not preclude a searching and critical examination of the conflicting interests and pressures which brought about the many compromises in the final text of the great document.

It was indeed remarkably good fortune from which all future generations of Americans have benefited that when the Convention convened in the red brick State House in Philadelphia, on the second Monday of May, 1787, in the room among the fifty odd delegates were such "demigods" as George Washington, Benjamin Franklin, Alexander Hamilton, and James Madison. Thomas Jefferson and John Adams would have also been present were it not

for their foreign assignments in the service of the new country.   Among
the delegates of the twelve states were other very able and distinguished
men: the thirty-four year old Governor of Virginia, Edmund Randolph,
New Jersey's Governor, William Livingston, the financier of the Revolution
and the richest man in the Colonies, Robert Morris of Pennsylvania.   The
Pennsylvania delegation also included one of the ablest men at the Convention, Gouverneur Morris, brilliant in his mastery of the English language
and style.   It was this Morris who on one occasion during the Convention,
declared that he was not afraid of anyone—Hamilton, who heard the boast,
offered to bet Morris that he would not dare to slap General Washington's
shoulder in a gesture of familiarity.   Morris sought out an occasion and did
act on Hamilton's dare, but later reported that he was greatly embarrassed
when Washington reacted by a cold and reproachful look.   Other delegates
of note were John Dickinson of Delaware, a noted writer, Charles Pinck-
ney, of South Carolina, who at twenty-nine was the youngest member of
the Convention, Rufus King of Massachusetts, and, finally, the cunning and
shrewd Roger Sherman of Connecticut, who was Mayor of New Haven.[1]

Portraits of the leaders of the Convention should be drawn for the students in greater detail.   There was no question that General George Washington would be the president of the Convention.   There was no one who
equaled in prestige and fame the man who was "first in the hearts of his
countrymen."   His integrity and devotion to duty were exemplary and he
was a leader of men.   If anyone could have preserved the dignity of the
deliberations during the long and hot summer of 1787, it was General
Washington.   He and he alone was aloof enough to contribute to the composition of the differences of views which were known to exist among the
delegates concerning the basic structure of the federal union.   The people
in the former Colonies trusted him even more because he made no secret
of his longing to return permanently to his serene life as the squire of his
plantation at Mount Vernon.

Benjamin Franklin was eighty-one years old in May 1787, but one could
not detect any sign of this advanced age from his sprightly walk, his regular attendance at the sessions, and his profound wisdom.   "The wisest man
in the world," as Franklin was acknowledged to be, used his wit to smooth
the tempers of the delegates, which were sorely tried by interminable disputes and the hot and humid weather of a Philadelphia summer.   The first
veritable genius produced in the Colonies was known and respected all over

---

[1] This and other anecdotes about the Founding Fathers may be found in the classic
study of Max Farland, *The Framing of the Constitution of the United States* (New
Haven, Conn.: Yale Univ. Press, 1962), Paperback edition.   Another newer and excellent volume on the making of the Constitution is Clinton Rossiter's *1787: The Grand
Convention* (New York: The Macmillan Co., 1966).

the world as a writer, scientist, printer, newspaper editor, philosopher, civic improvement leader, and diplomat. Franklin used his great reputation to foster a spirit of compromise and accommodation in order to assure the successful outcome of the Convention.

No student in a class where the Constitution is taught should be deprived of the opportunity to read and discuss Franklin's speech given on September 17th, the last day of the Constitutional Convention. Franklin's sentiments expressed on that occasion have an enduring relevance. We give it here in part:

> Mr. President, I confess that there are several parts of this Constitution which I do not at present approve, but I am not sure I shall never approve them. For, having lived long, I have experienced many instances of being obliged, by better information or fuller consideration, to change opinions, even on important subjects, which I once thought right, but found to be otherwise. It is therefore that, the older I grow, the more apt I am to doubt my own judgment, and to pay more respect to the judgment of others. Most men, indeed, as well as most sects in religion, think themselves in possession of all truth, and that wherever others differ from them, it is so for error . . .
>
> In these sentiments, sir, I agree to this Constitution, with all its faults, if they are such; because I think a general government necessary for us, and there is no form of government, but what may be a blessing to the people if well administered for a course of years, and can only end in despotism, as other forms have done before it, when the people shall become so corrupted as to need despotic government, being incapable of any other. I doubt, too, whether any other convention we can obtain may be able to make a better constitution. For, when you assemble a number of men to have the advantage of their joint wisdom, you inevitably assemble with these men all their prejudices, their passions, their errors of opinion, their local interests, and their selfish views. From such an assembly can perfect production be expected? It therefore astonishes me, sir, to find this system approaching so near to perfection as it does. . . . Thus I consent, sir, to this Constitution, because I expect no better, and because I am not sure that it is not the best.

What better text can be found to lead the students to an appreciation of critical thinking and of the greatness of the makers of our Constitution. But, once again, it should be emphasized that even this superb speech will be taught effectively only if presented in its historical setting and content.

Alexander Hamilton of New York was at the time of the Grand Convention only thirty years old, but he was well known to his countrymen. His was a uniquely American success story. He was born on the island of Nevis in West Indies but historians have still not resolved the question of the legitimacy of his birth. At any rate, Hamilton, as a youth of eighteen, came to America and studied at King's College, now Columbia University. He soon threw himself eagerly into revolutionary activities which culminated in his service in Washington's army. Hamilton was a gallant and brave officer, and General Washington made him his private secretary and confidential aide. After the war, Hamilton married into the rich and aristocratic Schuyler family in New York and served in the Continental Congress.

At the Constitutional Convention, Hamilton represented the aristocratic point of view. The new government, he argued, must be put in the hands of the wealthy and the well-educated because the masses are ignorant, shiftless, and cannot be trusted. Arrogantly, he once told the Convention "Take mankind in general, they are vicious." His fellow delegates remembered his oft-quoted opinion that the people are "a great beast." Speaking to the Convention, Hamilton stated on one occasion:

> Take mankind as they are, and what are they governed by? Their passions . . . One great error is that we suppose mankind more honest than they are. Our prevailing passions are ambition and interest . . . All communities divide themselves into the few and the many. The first are rich and well-born, the other the mass of the people. The voice of the people it has been said is the voice of God; and, however generally this maxim has been quoted and believed, it is not true in fact. The people are turbulent and changing; they seldom judge and determine right. Give, therefore, to the first class a distinct, permanent share in the government. They will check the unsteadiness of the second, and, as they cannot receive any advantage by change, they therefore will ever maintain good government.

Hamilton advocated a President who would serve for life, have an absolute veto over all federal legislation, and have the power to appoint the state governors. The Senate, if Hamilton had his way, would have been elected only by the well-to-do and its members would have served for life. The New York delegate advocated a strong central government and considered the states obsolete.

Hamilton propounded his views with clarity, although on occasion his manner was haughty and overbearing. His point of view found little support in the Convention and most of his proposals were not incorporated in the Constitution. However, when his two colleagues from New York withdrew from the Convention, Hamilton remained, actually representing himself and not his state. The Journal of the Convention, after listing the delegates of the several states attending could only state: . . . "and Mr. Alexander Hamilton of New York." In spite of the fact that the final document of the Constitution was far too democratic to accord with Hamilton's views and rested far too much on the principle of the "checks and balances," Hamilton signed the Constitution in behalf of New York. He then waged a hard and finally successful struggle in the New York Legislature for the ratification of the Constitution. The vote for ratification was 30 for and 27 against.[2] Were Hamilton not ready to subjugate his own views to the decision of the majority in the Convention, New York state would have surely rejected the new Constitution.

Hamilton's views on aristocracy and on the dangers of a people's or a democratic government ought to be thoroughly discussed. Such a discussion, in addition to providing an exciting teaching and learning experience, should go a long way to undermine the common and totally false view of all the Founding Fathers as stalwart supporters of the rule of the people. Presenting the makers of the Constitution as great men, differing on the issues of suffrage, slavery, and the powers of the Federal Government, will not diminish their stature in the eyes of our young. On the contrary, it will enhance it because it will emphasize their genius for intelligent compromise and their overwhelming devotion to the welfare and well-being of the new country.

What we know about the Constitutional Convention we owe to James Madison. A contemporary onlooker who would have chanced upon the Virginia delegation entering the convention hall would not have been impressed by the slender, small man, who, as we are told, was always dressed in an immaculately clean and well-cut black coat. But appearances would have been deceiving, because Madison, a young man of thirty-six, was undoubtedly better steeped in the study of governments and constitutions than any of the delegates. For several years before the convening of the constitutional assembly he read deeply in Plato, Aristotle, Locke, and Rousseau and studied all available constitutions of many lands to prepare himself for the task ahead. In addition to his scholarship and his complete devotion to his responsibility as a Convention delegate, James Madison was a very influential debater. He was knowledgeable, logical, agreeable, and, therefore, persuasive.

It was indeed fortunate for future generations of Americans and for students of government everywhere that Madison, on his own initiative, but with the wholehearted support of Washington and of the delegates, kept a daily journal of the proceedings. Since the convention debates were conducted in complete secrecy (amazingly no information "leaks" have developed), Madison's notes, or Journal of the Convention, are the only source of information on the Grand Convention now available. In order to report the proceedings as accurately as possible, Madison sat facing the delegates

---

[2] Another useful resource book, available in paperback, on the teaching of the Constitution is Saul K. Padover's *The Living U.S. Constitution* (New York: New American Library, 1954).

with his back to Washington who presided. "In this favorable position," Madison later wrote, "for hearing all that passed, I noted in terms legible and in abbreviations and marks intelligible to myself what was read from the Chair or spoken by the members; and losing not a moment. . . . I was enabled to write out my daily notes during the session or within a few finishing days after its close."[3]   Madison's notes were published by order of Congress, a few years after his death.

The setting and the background of the Constitutional Convention should, of course, be expanded and tailored to the particular needs of the class. What is argued here is that the teaching of the Constitution ought to be done in that setting, and that the Founding Fathers must not remain, as they often do, only shadows in history.   Having laid the foundation for an intelligent and insightful inquiry a discussion of the deliberations of the Convention and the compromises achieved should follow.   One would hope that the dramatic story of the ratification of the Constitution would be given full justice in the classroom.   The students should not be allowed to nurture the illusion that once the Constitution was signed it became the law of the land.   In fact, the new basic instrument of our government after its approval at the Convention faced an uncertain future.   The arguments (read, in part from primary sources) against the ratification by Patrick Henry, Amos Singletary and for the ratification by James Madison and of Dr. Benjamin Rush should be made available to the students.   The middle-road position of Thomas Jefferson ought also be explored.   This could be done effectively by arranging a mock ratification convention in which students would present opposing views on ratification.

Historiography is as important in the teaching of civics as it is in the teaching of history.   This is especially true of the rich and controversial historiography of the Constitution.

Students would be excited, challenged, and stimulated to do their own thinking if confronted with the economic interpretation of the decisions taken in Philadelphia in 1787, argued so brilliantly, if not very convincingly, by Charles Beard.   Passages from Beard's *An Economic Interpretation of the Constitution* pertaining to the author's view that the framers of the Constitution voted as they did on the various articles to protect their investments and interests in stocks, bonds, ships, land, or slaves, should be mimeographed and made available to all students.   In advanced classes Beard's book could be read by all students and reported on and discussed. This discussion, however, should not come before the class had an opportunity to read, at least in part, the rebuttal and refutation of Beard's theory in Edmund Morgan's *The Birth of the Republic*, and Forrest McDonald's

---

[3] Quoted in Saul Padover, *The Living U.S. Constitution* (New York: New American Library, 1954), p. 16.

We the People: The Economic Origins of the Constitution.[4] Both of these authors, retracing the research steps of Charles Beard, concluded that the makers of the Constitution often voted against their own personal economic interests and that the economic interpretation of the making of the Constitution was untenable. Recent historical scholarship seems to be agreed that the Founding Fathers were, on the whole, an idealistic, almost heroic group of men, who during the long and hot summer of 1787 in Philadelphia rescued the newly independent country from disaster and wrote the finest constitution that the world has ever seen.[5] While the teaching of the American Revolution can be made more effective by the dramatic presentation of the Constitutional Convention, the teaching of civics would be enriched by the study of the functioning of our political systems.

If one were pressed to single out the one most important weakness in the study of civics in high schools, it would be the almost complete exclusion of *politics*. Somehow, and very mistakenly, it is assumed by almost all textbook writers and by many teachers that the study of politics does not belong in the study of government. In fact, it seems to us that the study of the Constitution, of government, and of citizenship is almost meaningless without the teaching of the political process. The Constitution, to take one example, enumerates the powers of the President and it prescribes the mode of his election, but it says *nothing* of the long process of nominating candidates for the Presidency, about the party conventions, and the election campaigns. It should not be difficult to argue that knowledge and understanding of how we go about selecting a President is essential and indispensable to the understanding of the role and the functions of the presidency.

The exclusion of politics from our civics classrooms is even more incomprehensible and inexcusable if one looks at it from a purely didactic, methodological point of view. Politics as the art of the possible and the struggle of men for power is interesting and dramatic in itself and thus the teacher would have little difficulty in motivating his students. Intelligent and effective infusion of political content would make the study of the Constitution and civics interesting and absorbing. Theodore White's books on the 1960 and 1964 presidential elections became bestsellers, while many scholarly books on government can hardly sell a few thousand copies. Why? What is the secret of White's success? It is in the masterful way in which the author presents the fascinating and absorbing game of poli-

---

4 Edmund A. Morgan, *The Birth of the Republic* (Chicago: Univ. of Chicago Press, 1956); Forrest McDonald, *We the People: The Economic Origins of the Constitution* (Chicago: Univ. of Chicago Press, 1963).

5 This is the basic theme in Clinton Rossiter's study of the Convention, *1787: The Grand Convention* (New York: The Macmillan Co., 1966).

tics. The Purdue University surveys of attitudes of high school students on political issues, reveal that politicians are held in general contempt by our young people. For some reason, most students equate the politician with the image of a short, corpulent political boss, smoking a big, fat cigar and trampling on the rights of the people. Theodore White, while not gilding the lily, emphasized a truism, which is somehow often overlooked, that without politicians our system of government could not function for a month. It is distressing to note that in almost no civics or government textbooks can a student find an explanation of some of the most frequently used terms pertaining uniquely to American politics. As the presidential elections approach every four years, young people frequently encounter such typically American terms as "Presidential timber," "dark-horse candidate," "favorite son," "smoke-filled room," "barnstorming campaign," "climbing on the bandwagon," and many others without ever having been taught their meaning or significance. It is almost unbelievable, but a search in a great many of the most widely used civics textbooks showed that these and many other household expressions of our political life are not even mentioned.

Theodore White's books should be in the hands of all students in civics and government classes. The uniquely American way of selecting a President, a way which truly bespeaks the genius of our political system is the main theme of White's books. "Nowhere," he notes, "are more people more freely engaged in active, responsible participation in the choice of national leadership than in the United States during the fall season of any American Presidential election."[6] This process, this trial of fire, this long endurance contest that lasts many months and leads the nominee from the early spring primary in still cold and snowy New Hampshire, through the convention ordeal and exhilarated triumph, through the most grueling campaign to the White House, is not found in the Constitution, but it should be included as an integral part of the teaching of our basic instrument of government. It would infuse life, interest, and *meaning* into the study of the legal structure of the Government.

The American people do not bestow the high and powerful office of the presidency lightly. They want to be convinced that the man who would lead them and be their spokesman, who would have in his hands the decisions of war and peace, is worthy of that honor and responsibility. A candidate must prove that he is a man of stamina, wisdom, and knowledge. Then he must convince his party leaders, by winning at least some of the presidential primaries, that he has popular support and that his nomination will be supported at the party convention. That means that he must make

---

[6] Theodore H. White, *The Making of the President, 1960* (New York: Atheneum Publishers, 1961), p. 31.

a good showing in the primaries held in New Hampshire, Wisconsin, Oregon, and a number of other states. In 1960, John F. Kennedy, who battled Hubert Humphrey for the Democratic presidential nomination, won the primary in Wisconsin, but since his victory came by a slight margin, he had to continue the struggle in West Virginia where his victory was so overwhelming that it assured him of a strong position at the forthcoming Democratic Convention.

A dry and not very accurate paragraph in a civics textbook on the conventions, usually written in the typical "some say the convention is good because . . . and some say the convention is bad because . . ." does not constitute teaching about one of the most important and indigenous phenomena in American politics. All students ought to be required to read the accounts of the 1960 and 1964 Republican and Democratic conventions in White's book. In addition, some of the more crucial and interesting conventions in American history, including the Democratic conventions of 1896 and 1912 and the Republican convention of 1940 ("We want Willkie!") should be reported and discussed.

It is now fashionable to sneer at national conventions as televised circuses. Some needed reforms in their antiquated procedures have been suggested, but the conventions remain a colorful and uniquely American institution. They will not be eliminated because they serve an essential role in American politics. "Conventions and caucuses—like primaries," White noted, "are uniquely American political institutions; had they not been invented 130 years ago, they would have to be invented now."[7] There is both truth and wisdom in this statement. While not overlooking the negative features of the convention, the circus atmosphere, the bombastic and exaggerated oratory, the behind-the-scene maneuverings and bargaining, the convention remains the best method for nominating candidates for the presidency of the United States. No better method has, as yet, been suggested by the severest critics of the convention system.

In addition to providing the means for selection of candidates for the presidency, the national party convention has other important advantages. First, it serves as a valuable testing ground for aspiring politicians. The convention conducts a great deal of its business under the glare of television lights, and when microphones are stuck practically under the noses of politicians, their intelligence, political acumen, and wisdom are put to a severe test.

Second, the convention subjects the candidates contesting for the presidency to a searching scrutiny. The political conventions, which had began in the age of Andrew Jackson in 1831, ended a long era during which

---

[7] *Ibid.*, p. 226.

American voters did not see or hear the man they put in the highest office of the land until he was actually in the White House. When in February of 1861, Abraham Lincoln began his long and roundabout trip from Spring-field, Illinois to Washington, D.C. to attend his inauguration, the American people had the first opportunity to see and hear the man they had elected President.

Third, the convention is an excellent means of educating American people of all ages in the workings of American politics. It also educates the voters about the issues in the campaign. Studies have shown that many voters analyze their political views and preferences most intensely during the conventions.

Fourth, the convention forces the party to place a great deal of emphasis on party harmony. Neither of the major parties can afford an open schism or the walk-out of an important group. Hence, continuous efforts are made at the conventions to satisfy, at least in part, the views, needs, and interests of all sections by compromise and accommodation. Convention leaders go to great length to avoid prolonged internecine disputes.

Fifth, in view of the fact that party organization in the United States is basically local and statewide and not national in character, the convention functions as a meeting ground for these diverse party units. The voting procedure forces the delegations from many states to caucus in order to exchange views, learn of each other's problems, and often to bargain and compromise.

Sixth, in spite of all their shortcomings, national party conventions have, on the whole, done very well in choosing candidates for the presidency of the United States. It is safe to predict that the party convention will remain an important institution in our political system for a long time to come.

If skillfully taught, with the use of primary sources, pictures, films, tapes, records, the drama and the color of the party conventions could make for valuable educational experiences. Students would not have to be prodded to that study if the mores and the peculiar customs and language of the convention were expounded with dramatic effect. These would include such terms as "the Permanent Chairman," "the Temporary Chairman," the "planks of the platform," "favorite son delegations," "the releasing of the delegates," and the booming voice of the delegate shouting: "Mr. Chairman, the delegation of the Peach State of Georgia casts a unanimous vote for the next President of the United States. . . ." A knowledgeable teacher would give his students the *flavor,* the unrestrained enthusiasm of the convention, and, yes, its occasional pathos by quoting, for instance, the following two paragraphs, from nominating speeches made in past conventions. The man who nominated Thomas E. Dewey to oppose F.D.R., at the 1944 Republican Convention, concluded with these words:

We are here to restore the Presidency of the United States to the American people. We are here to bring Washington, D.C. back to the United States. We are here to make the American people masters in their own household. For that job we have the means and the man. I give you the nominee of the Republican Party, the spokesman of the future, Thomas E. Dewey.

The delegate who nominated Franklin Delano Roosevelt at the Democratic Convention of the same year, said in the closing part of his speech:

I present to the Convention for the office of President of these United States, the name of one who is endowed with the intellectual boldness of Thomas Jefferson, the indomitable courage of Andrew Jackson, the faith and patience of Abraham Lincoln, the rugged integrity of Grover Cleveland, and the scholarly vision of Woodrow Wilson—Franklin Delano Roosevelt!

It is difficult to imagine boredom and disciplinary problems in classes where such teaching would take place.

The long grind of the election campaign, which begins for both the Republican and the Democratic nominees immediately after the convention and culminates in November, should be made vivid and dramatic to the students not only because it is interesting, but because it can teach some profound lessons about the American political process and government. In the jet age, candidates are now expected to visit almost all of the fifty states and give thousands of speeches. On the campaign trips the nominee is accompanied by large numbers of newspaper and television reporters who daily inform the nation about what the candidate said, whether he was losing his voice, and what the reaction of the street crowds and his audiences were. No man is scrutinized and analyzed more thoroughly and no man enjoys less privacy than a nominee for the presidency. Americans insist on knowing *all* that can be learned about their future chief executive. In a sense this is testimony to the vitality and the resilience of the American system. However exalted and guarded the occupant of the White House is, as a presidential candidate he must mingle on the most familiar terms with the people who elect him. He shakes hands with farmers in New England, with Negro laborers in Harlem, with well-groomed ladies in Grosse Point, with recent immigrants from Poland and with the orthodox Jews in Brooklyn. He must wave and respond with a smile (genuine on most occasions) to people yelling, "Give 'em hell, Harry," or "We like Ike," or simply, "Hello, Lyndon." There is nothing disrespectful in this familiarity. This is merely a way in which Americans tell their leaders where their real power lies. It is a humbling and exhilarating experience which is repeated every four years.

Students in civics classes ought to become acquainted with some interesting bits of American political mythology. That mythology dictates that candidates must take a picture with their wives and children to assure the voters that all is well with their private home life. In the midst of the campaign, a candidate who bone-weary boards a plane at dawn for another parade and another speech, when asked by the reporters how he feels, must always say that he "never felt better in his life." It is somehow believed that if he told the truth—that he is dead-tired and thoroughly bored with repeating himself—the consequences would be disastrous. Similarly, no matter how cold and rainy the weather is, custom prescribes that a candidate ride in an open car in a parade, coatless and hatless. The purpose, it seems, is to prove to the people that he is a vigorous and hardy man who would have no trouble in carrying the burdens of the presidency.

It is also time to open to free discussion and inquiry in high school classrooms some of the "closed areas" in the study of civics and government. We refer to the place of religious and ethnic factors in American politics. The usual stance taken by curriculum writers, textbooks, and many teachers, which either ignores or glosses over the place of ethnic origin and religion in elections, is indefensible on factual and pedagogic grounds. Religious and ethnic factors have a considerable influence on American elections and politics. Negroes, on the whole, vote for candidates who are pledged to the support of equal rights and opportunities for all citizens. Americans of Irish, Polish and Italian ethnic origins, usually vote Democratic, especially those who live in the big cities. The pattern of voting of Jews clearly indicates that they usually vote for candidates who favor welfare legislation, who are internationalists, and who are intellectuals like T. R. Roosevelt, Wilson, or Stevenson.

The United States has been a melting pot of many cultures and national groups, and in time a general American consensus on political, social, and cultural issues and mores has emerged. But, and we would add, fortunately, the melting pot has not obliterated all cultural differences and the sense of ethnic loyalty. This fact does not testify to America's weakness, but to its strength. This powerful country is stronger, not weaker, because the Irish, wearing the green, march proudly in St. Patrick's Day parades, the Italians celebrate Columbus Day and the Jews express their support for Israel. There is no need for the teacher of civics to feel apologetic when he or she points to the phenomenon of ethnically and religiously balanced tickets in federal, state, and even local elections. Both parties which nominate candidates for state offices in the larger states, including New York, California, Illinois, or Massachusetts make sure that if the candidate for Governor is an Anglo-Saxon Protestant, the candidate for Lieutenant Governor is an Italian Catholic, the Attorney General is a Jew, and the State Treasurer is an Irish Catholic. Some important posts especially in the North, are reserved for Negroes. Usually, this practice of balancing is deplored, if not entirely condemned, as unworthy of a united country where all men should be judged by their merit and not by their religion or ethnic origin. Even such an astute observer of the American political scene as Theodore H. White wrote:

> A national ticket for the Presidency is not chosen by this squalid method of racial and ethnic balancing. Yet once it is selected, its leaders must concern themselves with all the delicate inheritances of the subordinate tribal communities of America and address themselves to the imposing task of convincing each little group that somewhere in the candidate's mind and affections they will find a reflection of their own concerns and aspirations.[8]

One wonders why White is so opposed to the racial and ethnic balancing of election tickets, provided that the candidates selected are of the highest caliber. It may be reasonable to argue that the attempt to balance tickets, if done with due regard to the qualifications for respective offices, is good for our national political health. The minority ethnic and religious groups apparently need an occasional reassurance that they enjoy first-class citizenship. Election to high offices of their compatriots has proven to be most effective in providing a feeling of belonging and of being important. It was good for the Catholics in 1960 to know that a Catholic can be elected President of the United States, and Americans of Polish and Italian origin found it reassuring and a boon to their pride as Americans when President Kennedy appointed John Gronouski and Anthony Celebrezze to be Postmaster General and Secretary of Health, Education, and Welfare, respectively. The appointment of a Negro, Robert Weaver, as the first Secretary of Urban Affairs, was warmly greeted by Negroes, and Jews found great comfort in the appointment of Arthur Goldberg as U.S. Ambassador to the United Nations. It can be argued that attention to the "inheritances" of the ethnic groups is one of the more attractive traits of our democracy. White's objections notwithstanding, there is something reassuring in regard to the vitality and viability of the democratic process to see candidates for the presidency, for the Senate, or for state governorships attentive and responsive to the concerns and the aspirations of the various voter blocs in the country. What better testimony can there be to the American principle of unity in diversity and to the paramount sovereignty of the voters? Due attention to ethnic and religious influences in American politics can provide exciting teaching material. Students would undoubtedly enjoy inquiries into the 1928 presidential campaign of Alfred E. Smith and John Kennedy's election in 1960. Election results in some selected states could be analyzed and discussed with great profit.

Consideration of ethnic, social, and religious differences seems essential for the study of the two-party system. The differences between the Democratic and Republican parties can best be understood by a close study of

---

[8] *Ibid.*, p. 266.

groups of population which support them in elections.   Professor Neal McDonald in his study of political parties observed:

> For every one hundred votes cast for the national ticket of each major political party in the United States, the Democratic one hundred votes will include more young persons, more Catholics, more urban residents, more union labor members, more Southerners, more low-income persons, more Negroes, more Jews and recent immigrants in general, more lower class and more poorly educated persons, than would every one hundred Republican votes.   The one hundred Republican votes would contain more older persons, Protestants, rural and small town residents, professional and managerial persons, Northerners, wealthy whites, English, Scotch, German and Scandinavians, upper class and well-educated.[9]

This succinct summary of the role of ethnic and religious differences in elections can be used in civics classrooms for intelligent discussion and searching and enlightening inquiries into the relationship between, age, education, economic status, ethnic, and religious background and voting preferences.   Such studies would infuse life, drama, and interest into the study of government, especially if the teacher is skillful enough to tactfully bring into play the personal impressions and experiences of the students as members of one of the potential blocs of voters.   The taboo on racial, ethnic, and religious issues in American politics ought to be discarded. Politicians, and in that group we include bosses of big-city political machines, the chairmen of the Republican and Democratic National Committees, most Presidents and Congressmen, have always been aware of the "Polish vote" in Chicago, Buffalo, and Detroit, of the "Scandinavian vote" in Minnesota and Wisconsin, of the "Irish vote" in Boston, of the "Jewish vote" in New York, and of the "Negro vote" in the Harlem section in New York City and in the Watts district in Los Angeles.   These "votes" are complicated concepts and ought not be oversimplified, but they are, as our political leaders know, realities and vital factors in our democratic body politic.   We are duty bound to make this reality comprehensible to our students.   Properly presented, the infusion of politics into civics instruction may well help in lifting the fog of apathy and boredom in the classrooms.

It makes no sense to teach about Article III in the Constitution dealing with the Supreme Court and the jurisdiction of the federal courts without including a great deal of *additional* material about the judicial process, about the historical role of the Supreme Court, about the great Chief Justices of the United States, like Marshall, Taney, and Hughes, and about

---

[9] Neal McDonald, *The Study of Political Parties* (New York: Random House, 1955), p. 152.   See also, Maurice Duverger, *Political Parties,* 2nd ed. (New York: John Wiley & Sons, 1959).

the mores and customs of the Supreme Court. Important decisions of the Supreme Court, presented as case studies, entitled *Judgement*, are prepared by the National Council for the Social Studies and by the Civic Education Service. The *Judgement* series, which are prepared with great skill and a scholarly attention to detail, should be used extensively by civics teachers across the land.

But here, too, it is important to infuse some life and interest into the study of the judicial branch of the government. Students should be allowed a glimpse into the austere proceedings of the Supreme Court. The work of the nine justices of the Supreme Court can be presented, for example, by a detailed explanation of how the Court deals with the hundreds of petitions for review that are presented each year.

A citizen may appeal from a decision rendered by a state court to the Supreme Court only if he can prove that the state court had decided a significant question of a *federal* law or that his rights under the Constitution have been infringed or violated by state authorities or by the state court. In such cases, the petitioner applies to the Supreme Court for a *writ of certiorari* or a writ of certification that the Court agrees to hear his case. A vote of four judges is needed for the issue of the *writ of certiorari* which is followed by a hearing before the Supreme Court attended only by the lawyers for both sides in the case.

The number of cases brought before the Supreme Court is large and increases each year. In 1963, 2,800 cases were brought before the Supreme Court. Of this large number, the Court considers only a small fraction. It has the authority to screen the cases and selects for argument and decision only those which in its judgment raise some important constitutional question or affect the lives and well-being of large sections of the population. Using this criterion, the Supreme Court selects for consideration only six per cent of the cases, about 150 to 170 cases each year. To make sure that even marginal cases do get consideration, the Court, which usually requires a majority of five for a decision, has limited the minimum number of justices who may decide on whether to review a case or not to review it.

The application for petition is usually brief and attached to it are copies of the opinions given in the case in the lower courts. Both the petition and the reply on behalf of the lower court decision must contain an argument discussing the "federal question" involved, namely the litigant must attempt to prove that a substantial issue concerning federal law has been involved. Each justice receives copies of these documents and makes his decision whether the petition shall be granted or denied.

In making up their minds at this initial stage, the justices do not consult with one another. Supreme Court justices must do their own work, which cannot be delegated to anyone else. Each of them has a law clerk, usually a young lawyer, but since their decisions affect the lives and fortunes of individuals or of thousands, or sometimes even millions of citizens, the justices must weigh each case personally with the greatest of care.

During the regular Court term, which begins on the first Monday in October and ends in May or early June, the nine justices usually meet on Friday of every week. These conferences begin at 10:00 in the morning and last until 6:00 with a half an hour taken out for lunch. The conferences are held in an oak-paneled chamber adjoining the office of the Chief Justice. A lone painting, a portrait of Chief Justice John Marshall, hangs on the wall. Only the justices are present at the conference. Law clerks, secretaries, and pages are excluded. The junior justice, the one last appointed to the high bench, acts as the guardian of the door to receive any messages from the outside.

Every effort is made to assure the secrecy of the proceedings so that the judges may voice their views in complete privacy, which also assures that no decisions of the Court would be disclosed prematurely. The justices are summoned to the conference by a buzzer. They enter the room and according to an old custom shake hands with one another to signify their friendship and mutual respect in spite of any differences that may arise at the meeting. The seating is strictly according to seniority of service. Each justice has before him a long list of the cases submitted for review by the Supreme Court. The Judges are called upon to select the cases in which the *writ of certiorari* will be granted or to rule on cases received from the inferior Federal Courts.

The Chief Justice begins the discussion of each case and each justice then expresses his views. They are called upon to speak in order of their seniority. However, when the voting starts the order is reversed with the junior justice voting first. The purpose of this custom is to make sure that the junior justices would not be unduly impressed by the votes of their senior and more experienced colleagues.

The discussion of the case proceeds at the regular Friday conference when a vote is taken. The Chief Justice assigns the member of the Court who is to write the opinion for the majority. The justices who voted in the minority agree among themselves who is to write the minority opinion. The writing of the opinions is a long and painstaking process which often takes weeks. Each justice who has voted either with the majority or the minority may attach his own additional opinion to the reports. The opinions of the court, those of the majority and of the minority and of the individual justices, are published. In our free society even the Supreme Court must explain to the citizens its decisions and bare its disagreements in public.

The lessons devoted to the study of the constitutional provisions concerning the House of Representatives and the Senate would benefit greatly by the addition of the procedures and mores that have evolved in the functioning of the Congress through generations and of which no trace can be found in the text of the Constitution. Neither the Constitution nor most of the textbooks give students a picture of how a congressional committee actually functions. When a hearing of a committee of Congress is occasionally televised, very few of our young people (not to mention the older generation) realize how rigidly controlled the seating arrangements of the committee members are. Even those who know something of the seniority rule do not always realize how it works. Terms like "the ranking Democratic (or Republican) member" should not be an enigma for our students.

They should know that the seating of Senators and Congressmen at the meeting of congressional committees is strictly controlled by length of service. If the majority in Congress is Democratic, then the chairman who sits in the middle of the table is a Democrat. On his right sits the "ranking Democratic member" who is next in seniority (rank) to the chairman and who would almost automatically succeed him in case of death, resignation, or defeat in the next election. The Democratic members sit on the right according to their seniority, and the seat at the far end is occupied by the Senator who has most recently been appointed to the committee. He obviously has a long climb to the chairman's chair. On the left hand of the chairman sits "the ranking Republican member." If in the next election the Republicans should gain a majority in the Senate, the ranking Republican member would (if himself re-elected) become the chairman and the former chairman would then become the ranking minority member. This system, although often widely criticized, has a great deal of merit. The chairmen of the powerful committees, who wield great power and responsibility, reach their positions after many years of service on the committee and thus gain valuable experience. The seniority rule, observed by both parties, provides in reality for alternate chairmen of important committees in Congress. Thus, continuity and orderly transfer of power is assured.

It is not enough to teach about the special powers of the Senate to ratify treaties and to confirm major presidential appointments. It is also important to provide the students with a more intimate picture of the most exclusive club in the United States. This club, which has only a hundred highly selected members, has its own rules and procedures. Much of the operation of the Senate and the way in which it exercises its enormous powers can be understood only in terms of the many sanctified traditions which are cherished by all Senators.[10]

A newcomer to the Senate or a visitor in the Senate gallery is impressed

---

[10] See Donald R. Mathews, *U.S. Senators and Their World* (Chicago: Univ. of Chicago Press, 1963). An excellent book on the Senate which contains a great deal of material easily adaptable to classroom use. Also, Lewis A. Froman, *Congressmen and Their Constituents* (Chicago: Rand McNally & Co., 1963).

by the courtesy and consideration with which Senators of both parties treat one another. This courtesy is one of the cardinal rules of the club. A birthday or an anniversary of a veteran Senator is usually celebrated by laudatory speeches by members of both parties.

In spite of the temptation of the freshmen Senators to speak to the Senate and the nation, they soon become aware of the fact that oratory is not a sign of influence in the Senate. Senator Carl Hayden of Arizona, who was elected to Congress in 1912 and has been one of the most influential men in the Senate for several decades, has seldom availed himself of the floor of that august body. He does, however, exert enormous influence as the chairman of the Senate Appropriations Committee. The freshman Senator must accept the fact that the real work of the Senate is done in the committees and in the cloakrooms and not on the floor of the Senate. He realizes that because of the complexity of legislation he must study hard and then specialize and focus his attention and energy on relatively few matters. Out of the thousands of bills that come to the Senate each year, the Senator can become familiar with only a few. On most legislation he has no choice but to accept the views of his colleagues who have other areas of specialization.

The freshman Senator, if he is to earn the respect of his colleagues, must also learn not to allow political disagreements to influence his personal relationships with all Senators. He must learn to address his colleagues as: "The distinguished (or able) Senator from ———" and he must never impugn their motives or criticize their states. He is told by his older colleagues that when he takes the floor for a speech he must expect a fellow Senator to rise and say: "Will the distinguished Senator from ——— yield for a question (or a remark)," he should answer, "I yield to the learned (or able or distinguished) Senator from ———." Courtesy and consideration are important qualifications for membership in the Senatorial club. A Senator must always remember that his enemies on one issue might be his friends on another. These rules of senatorial courtesy and parliamentary procedure may seem hypocritical but they are very important. They permit the Senate, a highly competitive and individualistic and powerful body, to function with a great measure of effectiveness.

There is an important difference in the seating arrangements in the House and in the Senate. In the House, Republicans sit on one side of the chamber and Democrats on the other. The seats of the members of both parties are divided by an aisle. There is no aisle in the Senate. Democrats and Republicans sit side by side. Freshman Senators, however, are as a rule given seats in the back of the Senate chamber. The mixed seating in the Senate contributes to the personal friendships that so frequently develop between Senators of opposing parties.

The Senator who is first elected from his state is called the "senior" Senator, and his colleague who comes to the Senate at a later date is referred to as the "junior" Senator. It is important to remember that age has nothing to do with this designation. The terms "senior" and "junior" refer only to length of service in the Senate.

The folkways of the Senate include the principle of reciprocity. A Senator who is interested in getting an appropriation for a public works project in his state can usually count on the support of his colleagues. It is, of course, understood that when the occasion arises he will reciprocate in kind. This procedure, often called "log-rolling," is much less harmful to the interests of the nation than it would seem at first glance because of the sense of responsibility of the individual Senate members. As a group they are deeply patriotic people, thoroughly dedicated to the advancement of the interests of their respective states, but conscious and proud of their title "Senator of the United States of America."

The American Creed reserves a central place for the role of the President and of the presidency. A recent study on political attitudes of children of elementary school age in New Haven, Connecticut, revealed that 80 per cent of the fourth graders questioned considered the President of the United States "the most important man in the world."[11] This attitude of young children is merely a reflection of the way most Americans view the presidency. There is something thrilling and even awesome about occasions when, impelled by an international crisis, the President appears on the television screen with the presidential seal and flag behind him. The President is introduced simply by the announcer saying, "Ladies and gentlemen, the President of the United States." There is indeed no need for a more elaborate introduction. The office is surrounded with so much tradition, honor, and respect and has so much power that Americans are always ready to give respectful attention to their Chief Executive. No wonder that the election of the President every four years is the most important event in the political life of the country. Once elected, the President is under the constant scrutiny of the press, radio and television and millions of citizens. Should he develop a running nose or be particularly jovial or irritable on a particular day, the news is reported in every paper and every broadcast, not only in America, but in many countries abroad.

Obviously the study of the presidency in civics classes cannot and should not be limited to learning the powers given to the President by the Constitution. Efforts must be made to present the Presidents, especially the outstanding ones, as interesting colorful personalities. Students ought to be encouraged by the presentation of suitable materials to form in their minds portraits of Theodore Roosevelt, Andrew Jackson, and Woodrow Wilson. They would find the zest for life of T. R., the violent temper of Jackson, and the aloofness and stubbornness of Wilson an interesting introduction to

---

11 Fred I. Greenstein, *Children and Politics* (New Haven, Conn.: Yale Univ. Press, 1965).

a more serious study of the various conceptions of the Presidency. There may be some benefit from a study of the correlation, or the lack of it, between the personality of the President and his narrow or broad interpretation of the powers of the presidency.

John Adams wrote:

> The duration of the President is . . . only few years; but his power during those four years is much greater than that of . . . the King of Poland, nay, the King of Sparta.

Andrew Jackson asserted:

> The President is the direct representative of the American people. He possesses original executive powers . . . and it is his . . . especial duty to protect the liberties and rights of the people and the integrity of the Constitution against the Senate or the House of Representatives or both together.

Theodore Roosevelt maintained:

> The President should be a very strong man who uses without hesitation every power the position yields.

But, on the other hand, a sour and disillusioned James Buchanan, who could not cope with the nation on the eve of a Civil War, asserted that:

> The business of the President occasionally great, is usually not much above routine.

William Howard Taft, jovial, phlegmatic, who really did want to be President, wrote:

> The true view of the executive function is . . . that the President can exercise no powers which cannot reasonably be traced to some specific grant of power . . . Such specific grant of power must be either in the Constitution or in an act of Congress.

Warren G. Harding, the good-looking former Senator from Ohio, who was elected in a "smoke-filled room" by the party leaders and who was unable to cope with corruption scandals which rocked his Administration, said:

> I shall not attempt to coerce the Senate of the United States. I shall make no demand upon the people. I shall not try to impose my will upon any body or anybody. I shall embark on no crusade.

Many interesting and instructive lessons can be devoted to the choosing of "great," "near great," "average," "below average," and "failures" among the Presidents. Students can be asked to make nominating speeches for any of the categories, presenting evidence in support of their nomination.

The formulation of some generalizations concerning Presidents assigned to each of the categories would lead to a better understanding of the role of the presidency in American history.

We have already indicated that many of the more important speeches of the Presidents should be presented to the students, always after the historic setting has been reconstructed. In addition, the more distinguished State of the Union Messages and Inaugural Addresses may be presented in an abbreviated form in the classroom. Several advantages can accrue from this practice. The annual presidential messages provide an excellent overview of the state of the nation in various critical periods in our history. They also provide an insight into the character and mode of operation of the President. Finally, and probably most importantly, many passages from the State of the Union and other messages form an important part of the American Creed and of the American Dream and thus can be a source of pride and inspiration to our young generation.

A few excerpts as examples should suffice. Below is part of Washington's Farewell Address of 1796.

> Solicitude for your welfare, which cannot end but with my life, and the apprehension of danger, natural to that solicitude, urge me on occasion like the present, to offer to you solemn contemplation, and to recommend to your frequent review, some sentiments; which are the result of much reflection, of no inconsiderable observation, and which appear to me all important to the permanency of your felicity as a people. These will be offered to you with the more freedom, as you can only see in them the disinterested warnings of a parting friend who can possibly have no personal motive as his counsel . . .
>
> Observe good faith and justice toward all nations; cultivate peace and harmony with all. Religion and morality enjoin this conduct, and can it be that good policy does not equally enjoin it? It will be worthy of a free, enlightened, and at no distant period, a great nation to give mankind the magnanimous and too novel example of a people always guided by an exalted justice and benevolence. Who can doubt that in the course of time and things the fruits of such a plan would richly repay any temporary advantages which might be lost by a steady adherence to it? Can it be that Providence has not connected the permanent felicity of a nation with its virtue? The experiment, at least, is recommended by every sentiment which enables human nature. Alas! is it rendered impossible by its vices?

What a pity that if and when our young people remember something of Washington's Farewell Address it is usually the oversimplified and not very accurately understood warning about "foreign entanglements." How much more important for the understanding of the greatness and the wisdom of George Washington is the passage quoted above containing undoubtedly one of the most lucid and best written formulations of United States foreign policy? How significant yet overlooked is Washington's well-expressed idea that the United States as a free and enlightened nation, pursuing a consistent foreign policy, based on justice and peace would serve as an example to the rest of mankind? Political realists and believers in power politics may ridicule such idealism, but a case can be made, and ought to be made, that the United States, with the exception of some periods of passing aberration, has heeded Washington's advice.

Thomas Jefferson, although in the long run a strong President, decided that unlike Washington, he would not deliver the State of the Union Message to Congress in person. He wished to return to "simple republican forms of government," and he felt that the ceremonious arrival of the President at the Capitol to deliver his message was too much akin to the pomp and ceremony attending the visit of the British King to open the sessions of the Parliament. Some historians have concluded that the real reason behind Jefferson's decision was his dislike of public speaking.

True to his egalitarian convictions, Jefferson began his message with the words: "Fellow-Citizens of the Senate and House of Representatives." George Washington and John Adams saluted Congress as "Gentlemen of the Senate and Gentlemen of the House of Representatives."[12]

In his first message, Jefferson gave birth to the doctrine of "states' rights" which has been supported and disputed in all the subsequent history of the country:

> When we consider that this (Federal) Government is charged with the external and mutual relations only of these states; that the States themselves have principal care of our persons, our property, and our reputation, constituting the great field of human concerns, we may well doubt whether our (Federal) organization is not too complicated, too expensive, whether offices and officers have not been multiplied unnecessarily and sometimes injuriously to the service they were meant to promote.

This passage can provide an excellent springboard for intelligent and thoughtful classroom discussions and inquiries into the growing power of the federal government and the concurrent narrowing of the scope of responsibilities and influence of the state governments.

Jefferson's First Inaugural made its own lasting contribution to the American Creed. Speaking of the bitter election campaign and the turbulent events that led to his election, the President reflected thoughtfully about the majority rule and the rights of a minority in a democratic country:

---

[12] Seymour H. Fersh, *The View from the White House* (Washington: Public Affairs Press, 1961), p. 14. See also Richard B. Morris, *Great Presidential Decisions—State Papers That Changed the Course of History* (New York: Fawcett World Library, 1966).

During the contest of opinion through which we have passed, the animation of discussion and of exertions has sometimes worn an aspect which might impose a stranger unused to think freely and to speak and to write what they think but this being now decided by the voice of the nation, announced according to the rules of the constitution, all will, of course, arrange themselves under the will of the law, and unite in common efforts for the common good. All too, will bear in mind this sacred principle, as though the will of the majority is in all cases to prevail, that will, to be rightful, must be reasonable that the minority possess their equal rights, which equal laws must protect, and to violate which would be oppression.

In 1823, President James Monroe enunciated, in a somewhat disorganized State of the Union Message, the famous Monroe Doctrine which remains to this day a guiding principle of our foreign policy.

> . . . The occasion has been judged proper for asserting, as a principle in which the rights and interests of the United States are involved, that the American continents, by the free and independent condition which they have assumed and maintained, are henceforth not to be considered as subject for future colonization by any European powers . . .

> The political system of the allied powers is essentially different in this respect from that of America. . . . We owe it, therefore, to candor . . . to declare that we should consider any attempt on their part to extend their system to any portion of this hemisphere as dangerous to our peace and safety.

Students and often even teachers tend to forget that the Monroe Doctrine, while barring any extension of European domination to the Western Hemisphere, also pledged the United States not to interfere in Europe. The passage reads:

> . . . Our policy in regard to Europe, which was adapted at an early stage of the wars which have so long agitated that quarter of the globe, nevertheless remain the same, which is, not to interfere in the internal concerns of any of its powers . . .

Andrew Jackson's message to Congress of 1834 which vetoed the bill renewing the charter of the Bank of the United States, contained a passage which reflected his bluntness, his dedicated concern for all the people and his great political acumen. Challenging the powerful Biddle and his Bank, Jackson wrote:

> It is to be regretted that the rich and powerful too often bend the acts of Government to their selfish purposes. Distinctions in society will always exist under every just Government. Equality of talents, of education, or of wealth cannot be produced by human institutions. In the full enjoyment of

the gifts of Heaven and the fruits of industry, economy, and virtue, every man is equally entitled to protection by law; but when the laws undertake to add to these natural and just advantages artificial distinctions . . . to make the rich richer and the potent more powerful, the humble members of society—the farmers, mechanics and laborers—who have neither the time nor the means of securing like favors to themselves, have a right to complain of the injustice of their Government.

This message, if taught in the context of the long, bitter and victorious encounter between Biddle and President Jackson, can be of great help in explaining to the students the essence of "Jacksonian Democracy."

What better way could a teacher have to impress upon his students the political genius of Abraham Lincoln than by bringing to their attention suitable excerpts from Lincoln's messages to Congress? Upon taking office, Lincoln suspended the writ of habeas corpus, although the Constitution does not expressly give this power to the President, even in time of armed rebellion. Thousands of suspected active Southern sympathizers were jailed without specific charges brought against them. When Congress convened on July 4, 1861, Lincoln, in his State of the Union Message, reported on the suspension of the writ, asserting that he had to take the step to save the Union, but adding that if Congress felt that it ought to pass a law authorizing the President to suspend the habeas corpus privilege he would have no objection. Then he added:

It was with deepest regret that the Executive found the duty of employing the war power in defense of the Government forced upon him. He could but perform this duty or surrender the existence of Government . . . And having thus chosen our course, without guile and with pure purpose, let us renew our trust in God and go forward without fear and with manly hearts.

Historians are unanimous that Lincoln's messages to Congress have an unexcelled persuasiveness and eloquence. Consider this passage a message on which Lincoln recommended the adoption of his plan for the gradual emancipation of slaves:

It is doubted then, that the plan which I propose, if adopted would shorten the war, and thus lessen its expenditure of money and blood? Is it doubted that it would restore the national authority and national prosperity and perpetuate both indefinitely? Is it doubted that we here—Congress and Executive—can secure its adoption? Will not the good people respond to a united and earnest appeal from us? Can we, can they, by any other means so certainly or so speedily assure these vital objects? . . . The dogmas of the quiet past are inadequate to the stormy present. The occasion is piled high with difficulty, and we must rise with the occasion. As our case is new so we must think anew and act anew. We must disenthrall ourselves, and then we shall save our country.

These examples, we hope, should suffice to make our point—that a thoughtful and careful selection of presidential messages and addresses can add a great deal of life, drama, and color to the teaching about the presidency and the American Creed.

There is indeed no reason why the study of civics cannot become an effective and even inspiring educational experience. What is needed is commitment on the part of the teacher to the basic genius of the American government and politics and a willingness to use the available materials with imagination and skill.

13

On the Teaching of Geography

It should not be considered unusual for a historian to write about the teaching of geography. The affinity and the complementary nature of these two disciplines made this task possible and advisable. The affinity and the complementary nature of these two disciplines made this task possible and advisable.

Geography, like history, is a core discipline using data, concepts, and insights from humanities, natural sciences, and the social sciences to illuminate the complex character of a particular place or a particular space relationship. Both geography and history are man-centered. The geographer studies the physical environment, but only as a reservoir or the theater of operations of man. It is the way in which man uses, shapes, lives in the physical environment that is the major concern of the geographer. To understand the interrelationship and the interraction between man and his physical environment or region, the geographer studies cultural and social factors, the many ways in which people earn a livelihood, the system of communication, the distribution of population and resources, and the forms of government. Thus, the geographer, although using different perspectives and foci, is, like the historian, interested in the total, integrated human experience. History studies and describes this experience in the framework of time relationships, while geography focuses on space relationships.

The relationships of geography and of history to the social sciences are quite similar. Both use the methods of social sciences, but are in fact not social sciences or are social sciences only in part. Geography, like history, shuns broad generalizations and geographers, like their colleagues in history, aware of the variables in man-space relationship and the complexity of the human condition, are wary of firm identification of cause and effect, of developing broad theoretical models and of formulating predictions. Furthermore, geography and history have close ties to the humanities and some geographers maintain that their discipline is "a high integrator of the natural sciences."[1] In examining a particular place on earth, the geographer sometimes uses a useful social science concept, not like a social scientist in its own independent context, but in the context of the place or area under study. The historian does the same thing when he uses, for instance, the concepts of status and social mobility to the study of the Bolshevik leadership in 1917.

Professor J. Wreford Watson of the University of Edinburgh made an exceptionally thoughtful observation on the relationships between geography and history:

> Few subjects have greater importance for the child today or the citizen of tomorrow than geography and history. These provide a world view and a view of the world's past without which it is impossible to understand either earth or man. History offers a sense of proportion, geography an idea of pattern, together they give scale and meaning to life. . . . Geography lives in the realm of physical, biological and ecological forces. It rests in nature. It is rooted in the earth. History lives in the world of ideas, reasons, emotions, motives, and drives. It springs out of man. It is the child of the spirit. Each is distinct, and distinctive. Each has its own function, point of view, and approach.[2]

History and geography are distinct and distinctive disciplines, but can be of great use to one another. Historians welcome the use of historical chronology and perspective in the study of characteristics of places or the study of configurations of social-cultural and political factors in various regions. Geographers are less happy when told by historians how useful geographic knowledge and research and tools like maps are in their work. For understandable reasons, geographers are somewhat self-conscious about their discipline. They want its integrity and usefulness preserved on its own terms. They object when it is not considered a field of study worthy of attention for its own sake, and are not happy when arguments supportive of geography are based on its usefulness to other disciplines, especially history. It should be reasonable, however, to acknowledge both the integrity of geography as an independent discipline and its great usefulness to historical research and understanding. A historian needs to know all that the geographers can tell him about the Valley of Kashmir or about Sinkiang, Outer and Inner Mongolia to write intelligently about the history of the Indian-Pakistani conflict and the story of the growing rifts between

---

[1] George B. Cressey, "Geography," in Erling Hunt, ed., *High School Social Studies Perspectives* (Boston: Houghton Mifflin Co., 1962), p. 85.

[2] Quoted in an article by Ruby M. Crowe, "Problems and Possibilities for Curriculum Change," *Focus on the Social Studies* (Washington: National Education Association, 1965), p. 47.

mainland China and the Soviet Union. An anthropologist or a political scientist who tries to understand the complexities of the tribal, religious, and political conditions in Nigeria must learn all he can about the man-land relationships, the distribution of population and resources and the distinctive characteristics of the several distinctive regions in that country.

During the writing of this chapter, newspapers reported that tension between East and West Pakistan was growing to a point which threatened to split the nation into two separate countries. This item of news is completely unintelligible without consultation of a map and a good geography textbook. Such an inquiry would produce the information that the distance between East and West Pakistan is 1,230 miles, a distance greater than that between Spain and Poland, that while West Pakistan has an area of 310,403 square miles with 47 million people, East Pakistan with an area of only 55,126 square miles has a population of 55 million. In addition, East Pakistanis who live in a largely arid area, dotted with great deserts, are wheat-eating, while West Pakistanis live in the humid, flooding Punjab and are rice-eating. While the West Pakistanis speak a number of languages, the East Pakistanis all speak Bengali and are fiercely dedicated to their language. Such information and the understandings which can be derived from it seem to be essential for any meaningful inquiry into the grave problems facing Pakistan. Similarly, knowledge of the differences in landscape, climate, special regional characteristics, and areal relationships between the North and the South as they developed in the period between 1820 and 1860 are essential in any meaningful study of the causes of the Civil War.

Knowledge of geography and its basic concepts are essential for effective teaching of the American Revolution, westward expansion, the sectional conflict, the period of imperialism, and in fact of all United States history. The struggle over "Bloody Kansas" in 1854, for instance, which came in the wake of the popular sovereignty principle included in the Kansas-Nebraska Act, cannot be understood by students without a thoughtful consideration of the potential relationship of slave labor and the economic opportunities and relationships in Kansas based on the geography of that state.

Finally, we now live in an interdependent world where places once too distant to be of concern impinge directly on our lives and have a direct bearing on the maintenance of world peace. Every day news comes from far corners of the earth which affects our economy and our security. A *coup* in Zanzibar, a famine in northeastern Brazil, a sudden shift in the foreign policy of Cambodia all have an effect on our lives. Our students must be helped to understand these and other events and geography is essential to such an understanding.

It may be said that geography has had rough sledding in high schools in recent years because geographers had a rather difficult time in agreeing what geography really was all about and because geography as taught in schools was usually dry and descriptive. Textbook geography was usually physical geography which surveyed countries by taking a dull inventory of their main rivers, mountain ranges, physical regions, capital city, and items of export. This was a boring and senseless enterprise for all concerned. A somewhat more advanced study of geography centered on the "science of man-land" relationship which often led to the simplistic deterministic assumption that man, tribes, peoples, and nations are what their geographic, physical environment willed them to be. Thus, people in the hot "torrid" zone were indolent and shiftless, while those in the cold and "temperate" and "frigid" zones were energetic and responsible. Geographers have long pointed out that in many places the temperate zone is more "torrid" than the torrid zone and that sweeping generalizations on the influence of climate on personality characteristics are inaccurate and misleading.

Professional geographers suggest that the teaching of geography as an unending stream of information items about a country or a region and the assumption that geography is basically concerned with the influence of the natural environment on man are not in keeping with what the discipline of geography has come to be in recent years. "(Geography)," Professor Gilbert F. White wrote,

> deals with our persistent curiosity as to how man affects the face of the earth and, in turn, is limited in his activities by limitations in the resources of his particular corner of the earth; it asks what have been the unique historical circumstances shaping particular landscape features of hill or farm or town; and it inevitably is forced into regional generalizations about areas large or small.[3]

Man, modern geographers insist, acting in his environment is the determining factor. How he uses the available resources, how he adapts himself to the physical environment, and how he changes his landscape by using his skills and knowledge—these are the matters studied by the geographer. Man-natural environment is a two-way not a one way relationship. To organize his knowledge, geographers seek patterns of similarity in small or large regions of the world. These patterns include the study of the physical, cultural, economic, and political characteristics which give a particular region some degree of unity. Geography, by looking and analyzing regional or areal associations and the complex functions and relationships of places, makes a unique contribution to the better understanding of the modern world.

---

[3] Gilbert F. White, "Rediscovering the Earth," *American Education* (February 1965), p. 10.

A historical geographer, Professor William D. Pattison, attempting to describe the history of geographic thought in this country, distinguished four basic traditions. The four traditions are:[4]

EARTH SCIENCE TRADITION—focuses on the study of the earth, mountains, oceans, atmosphere and the relationship between earth, sun, and the planets. Professor Pattison points out that historians and other social scientists do not share the recent tendency of professional geographers to minimize the importance of this branch of geography. On the contrary, they find the earth science of great use and value in their investigations.

MAN-LAND TRADITIONS—which for many years emphasized the environmentalism, the overpowering influence of the environment on the physical features, way of earning a livelihood, mores, political and social organization and history, has moved gradually, as we have said, to inquiry into the inter-relationship between man and his environment. Man's use of scarce resources and the culture that developed in the process are (significant) areas of interest in this tradition.

AREA STUDIES TRADITION—this tradition asserts that the earth can be divided into areas which exhibit certain patterns of similarity or distinctiveness. Teachers of geography have often favored this approach because it makes it easier to study the world. Regions can be divided by special characteristic phenomena found in them or special functions that they perform. The Tigris-Euphrates, or the Nile Valley regions are homogeneous because of special irrigation and land usage, while the Urals may be looked upon as special region because of the special configuration of its industrial complex.

SPATIAL TRADITION—this tradition stresses the importance of spatial relations and spatial analysis which centers on where places are and on the patterns of distribution and similarity or contact among them. In addition, spatial tradition includes the study of maps, geographic patterns and directions.

Professor Pattison concluded that "the four traditions though distinct in logic are joined in action. One can say of geography that it pursues concurrently all four of them. Taking the traditions in varying combinations, the geographer can explain the conventional divisions of the field."[5]

What are the uses of geography? What understanding and skills can geography teach our students?

Professor George Cressey has this to say about basic geographic understandings:

---

[4] William D. Pattison, The Four Traditions in Geography. Professional Paper No. 25, National Council for Geographic Education (May 1964).

[5] Ibid., p. 216.

The merits of geographic study are at least threefold. In the first place, it contributes to an understanding of the relations between man and his world. . . . Second, an understanding of geography involves an appreciation of the marked differences which make one place so distinct from another. . . . Finally, since these differences can be plotted on a map, geography is able to measure and appraise, and to provide the inventory base essential for all planning.[6]

Another geographer who pioneered in area and cultural geography, Professor Preston James, suggests that the main goal of geography is to teach the particular characteristics of places and areas on the surface of the earth and to explore the patterns of arrangements and associations of the discovered phenomena within the given area and among the areas. The geographer, according to James, is also interested in the connections and movements between the areas.[7]

In general, geography teaches us to observe intelligently and perceptively our surroundings, the area we live in, the town or city, the country, the region, and the world. This observation would, of course, not limit itself to physical characteristics, but would rather focus on man's occupations, designs, and activities in a particular area. The student, studying the area would try to understand the areal associations which would include the availability and the use of resources, population distribution, the hierarchy of the central places and their supporting areas, and the pattern of transportation and communication.

Geographers who have written about the problems of teaching geography in high schools stress that since it is impossible to study all the areas of the world, the emphasis in the teaching of spatial relationships and spatial dimensions in a given area should lead to the development of limited generalizations which may apply to other areas. These generalizations may also be useful in the study of new phenomena of spatial interaction or whenever a student attempting to understand a part of the world asks the questions, why is this area as it is or, how is any phenomenon spatially related to another? Professor Clyde F. Kohn, who has been closely connected with the National Geography Project, has complained that area and regional geography is not very successful or effective because the teaching concentrates on unrelated facts about the natural and cultural characteristics of a region or an area without an attempt to develop and apply gen-

---

[6] George B. Cressey in Erling Hunt, ed., *High School Social Studies Perspectives* (Boston: Houghton Mifflin Co., 1962), p. 96.
[7] Preston James, "Geography," in Gordon B. Turner, ed., *The Social Studies and the Social Sciences* (New York: Harcourt, Brace & World, 1962), p. 45.

eralizations or statements of "relationships between sets of geographical facts."[8]

It would be difficult to quarrel with Professor Kohn's injunction except that he leaves his statement as a postulated desideratum without giving some examples of the generalizations which can be drawn from the study of geographic areas and regions.   One would assume that these would have to be some lower order generalizations because geographers have long stressed the importance of the understanding of the special and unique character and the dazzling variety of the various regions of our planet.   No two places on the surface of the earth are identical, and regions have patterns of similarity only if defined for special purposes.

The basic skills that students in geography classes would acquire from effective teaching of new geography, include the following:

1. The development of a sense of space and time, distances and relationships.

2. The ability to read maps and globes.

3. The development of a skill for useful observation of natural phenomena including the analysis of obtained data.

4. The ability to take and to examine photographs in order to identify physical and cultural characteristics of a region or area under study.

5. The ability to identify patterns of interrelationships among areal, spatial phenomena leading to the formulation of valid generalizations.

6. The ability to comprehend the particular personality of a place and to appreciate its uniqueness in relation to other places.[9]

The skill of map literacy is of special importance to social studies teachers, especially since it seems to be a lost art.   History teachers who stress the cause and effect relationships realize or ought to realize the importance of the contribution of geography to the understanding of how things are located in relation to one another at the same time.   These areal relations which explain the location of things and people are best set down on maps. The narrowness of the English Channel, which for so many centuries influenced the relations between England and France, and the isolation of Tibet, which determined the cultural and religious conditions of that coun-

[8] Clyde F. Kohn, "The Geography Component," in *Focus on the Social Studies* (Washington: National Education Association, 1965), p. 24.

[9] For discussion of skills in geography, see: Thomas F. Barton, "Geography Skills and Techniques," in Wilhelmina Hill, ed., *Curriculum Guide for Geographic Education* (Normal, Ill.: National Council for Geographic Education, 1963), Chapter IV and Lorrin Kennamer, Jr., "Improvement of Instruction in Geography," *Social Education* (November 1965), pp. 452–459.

try during much of its history, are quite evident from a glance at a map. Geographers are correct in complaining of the map illiteracy of our students. It is surprising and often shocking to visit classrooms where the teacher teaches about Napoleon's retreat from Russia or about the conquest of Peru by the Spanish conquistadores without reference to a map. The use of maps by a teacher who is himself literate in map reading can be an important motivating factor for more effective teaching.

Geographers who are aware of the widespread unpopularity of geography courses in the past, are now suggesting that a "new geography," be taught on the high school level.

What do geographers mean when they talk about the new geography? What are the basic concepts of the new geography?

The "new" geographer asks three major questions. He asks about the spacial structure in social organization. In other words, a city as a social organization is defined in terms of its function of providing services, like retail stores, banking activities, and market facilities to the surrounding area. The geographer observes the regularities that underly the structure of urban activities. Using the concept of central place the geographer looks for the relation of the special pattern of settlement and the hierarchy of functions which starts with the small town and ends with cities like New York, Tokyo, London, and Paris.

The second basic question asked by the geographer pertains to the differentiation and contribution to the status of human existence in terms of individual places. These questions relate to the special character of places. The answers describe the special location of the place and interpret the consequences of that particular location as far as the people inhabiting it are concerned. Modern geography maintains that studies of many places have led to the conclusion that the dependent variable in economic and social change is the special character of the place.

The third set of questions relate to the human condition in terms of his habitat. In the study of the man-land relationship, the modern geographer stresses that while natural conditions may severely limit man's choices in earning a livelihood, means of transportation, as for instance in the Sahara Desert or a region like the Mekong River delta of Vietnam, may offer its inhabitants an almost unlimited potential, what *actually* happens is determined by man. Only man can convert "natural resources" into useful implements according to his cultural values and attitudes. A farmer in Iraq or in Pakistan may possess acres of fertile land but insist on plowing it with a wooden plow not because he does not *know* that a modern plow or tractor would not bring better crops, but because he *feels* that the methods used by his father and grandfather should not be abandoned and what was good for his ancestors ought to be good for him.

A modern geographic analysis of floods aims at the integration of our knowledge of nature in a particular region with the habits, mores, and skills of the people inhabiting it. Thus, the study of the flood conditions of the Yangtze River would include the study of man-land relationship as a unified whole. How the Chinese peasants emotionally and religiously regarded the peril of floods is as important to the geographers as the study of what they did to control the mighty river. Man is constantly changing the landscape of the earth, but how he changes it depends not only upon the part of the surface of the earth he deals with but upon his own cultural heritage.[10]

What are the basic concepts that geographers believe should be taught to high school students?

"Basically," Professor Kohn writes, "the study of geography is commonly organized around one of two major concepts: "regional differences" and "space associations.""[11]

The Regional Concept   Modern geography sees the world divided into regions which exhibit some homogeneity of natural and cultural character-istics. "Fertile Crescent," "The World Island" (Africa, Europe, and Asia, combined), "The National Core Area of U.S.A.," and "The C.B.D. or the Central Business District" are examples of such areas. The special char-acteristics of an area may consist of a variety of elements, such as special functions or the cultural and technological knowledge and skills of the people that inhabit it. "The region," Professor James writes, "is a geo-graphic generalization, an intellectual concept. . . . There is no such thing as a "true region," or one that might not be further subdivided if subdivision were desirable. *Regions are defined for specific purposes, and for each purpose a different regional system may be needed.*"[12] The gen-eral purpose of a region is to define the patterns of similarities and the differences on the surface of the earth.

The Concept of "Areal Association," "Areal Coherence," or "Space Rela-tions"   Geography today rejects the approach of traditional geography which, especially as taught in schools, emphasized the listing or inventory taking of geographic regions. Instead, the new geography seeks to estab-lish a pattern of causal interrelationships among the physical, cultural, economic, and political factors of any given geographic region. The assump-

---

[10] The author wishes to acknowledge his indebtedness to his colleague Professor Wil-liam Pattison, for ideas included in this part of the chapter.
[11] Clyde F. Kohn, "The Geography Component," *Focus on the Social Studies* (Washing-ton: National Education Association, 1965), p. 21.
[12] Preston James, "Geography," in Gordon B. Turner, ed., *The Social Studies and the Social Sciences* (New York: Harcourt, Brace & World, 1962), p. 51 (italics mine).

tion is that these phenomena do not exist in a haphazard incidental manner, but that "rather, they exist together in association, open to rational organization and comprehension."[13] The search and the inquiry for this association for the distinctive character of a geographic region should prove to be an exciting and instructive undertaking in high school classrooms. In addition, the finding and the comprehension of meaningful relationships or the general outline of a region may make much of the history of that region more comprehensible. The process of searching for the distinctive pattern of areal associations, which, as geographers remind us, is difficult and complicated because of the many variables involved, is strikingly similar to the inquiry of the historian to a complicated historical issue. He, too, puzzles over many associations of physical, cultural, political, and economic factors in order to find some plausible explanation of the fall of Rome or the course and the outcome of the English Civil War.

The Concept of Spatial Interaction Different places on the surface of the earth exist not only in association, which can be studied and comprehended, but they are also interdependent. Especially when viewed as regions, they interact with one another.

A center of a huge telephone network serving, for instance, the eastern part of the United States, supplies telephone service to hundreds of cities, towns, and rural areas which are dependent upon the proper functioning of the center's facilities. There are social sub centers and relaying stations between the control station and the serviced areas. Geographers speak of these interconnections and interdependence of places as spatial services. Whether a place is centrally located or not determines its character, and a study of its function and potential may lead to an educated prediction as to its future development.

The Concept of the Uniqueness of Places The position paper prepared by the Advisory Board of the National Geography Project for pilot teachers describes this concept.

> The student of geography should be guided toward an awareness that every place is unique, that its distinctive character is based upon complex interrelationships of many elements, and that any change or modification of any single element—either in time or in space—may produce changes in any of the others. This has been termed as the "integrity of the place."

Here, too, it is of interest to note the affinity between this geographic concept and the stress in history on the uniqueness of historical events and

---

[13] Jan O. M. Broek, *Geography, Its Scope and Spirit.* The Charles E. Merrill Social Science Seminar Series, Raymond H. Muessig and Vincent R. Rogers, editors (Columbus, O.: Charles E. Merrill Books, 1965), p. 73.

situations. Historians, like their colleagues in geography, are wary of drawing hasty conclusions from superficial comparisons of similar sets of historical "facts." They also realize that any change or modification of any single element in a complicated historical problem or situation may have a decisive effect on the entire configuration.

The Concept of the Ever Changing Face of the Earth The earth does not stand still; neither does its surface remain unchanged. In fact, it changes all the time. The landscape is constantly changed, either by the forces of nature, hurricanes, earthquakes, floods, and even more so by man. Areal and spatial associations are in a state of constant change and fluidity. "Central places" often do not remain central for very long, and places which are important suppliers of services change with great frequency. For instance, the technological advance and the introduction of modernization and industry in the developing countries changes the configurations of special interaction almost daily.

These changes, however, can and should be studied in order to detect the trends and to form useful generalizations about areal associations and especially about special interaction of various regions of the world. Thus, the geographer, like the historian, must always remain alert both to the patterns of regularity and similarity and to the constant change and fluidity which are an integral part of the human condition and of the history of man.

The Concept of Man-Land Relationship We have already discussed the concept of *Man-Land Relationship*. The new geography rejects the older notion of environmentalism which postulated that what man is and does is determined by his environment. New geography rejects this simplistic approach. It suggests that physical conditions influence man, but adds that man has a powerful influence on his natural environment. Using his skills, intelligence, and technology, he exploits natural resources, builds irrigation dams, and, when enlightened enough, embarks on a program of conservation which leads to a wise use of available natural resources.

What are the values and attitudes that geographers see as objectives of new geography?

Through the study of various regions (basically as cultural regions), the student ought to gain an understanding and respect for the variety of cultures and modes of living. Such a study, free of ethnocentric biases and prejudices, would lead him to the perception of interdependence in the world. "Modern geographers," Preston James writes,

insit on the principle that the significance to man of the physical and biotic features of the earth is a function of the attitudes, objectives, technical skills, and other aspects of culture of man himself. In other words, the physical environment has different meanings for different groups of people, or for the same group at different stages of development.[14]

The student of modern geography should gain a perspective on the variety of conditions of human existence and human interrelationships in the modern world. Such a geographic perspective, just like a historical perspective, may serve him well in appraising critically the issues and problems faced by the world today.

Professor Clyde Kohn has suggested that six thinking processes are involved in the teaching of modern geography. These include:

PERCEPTION. This process involves the ability to discriminate and differentiate the properties of objects or basic human activities and to interpret their meaning.

ASSOCIATION. This is the process of linking or relating symbols—words, signs, and the like—with things that are experienced.

CONCEPT ATTAINMENT. This includes the process of discriminating specific properties of objects and events and obstructing or generalizing common elements so that they can be classified or grouped together.

RELATIONAL THINKING. This includes the process of relating facts, understandings, and concepts to form generalizations of one kind or another.

CRITICAL THINKING. This includes the use of standards, values and purposes to evaluate the effectiveness of some action.

CREATIVE THINKING. This process involves expressing thoughts and feelings in original ways.[15]

One may properly ask why these modes of thinking are particularly related to geography and how much do we really know about teaching creative thinking. However, there is no doubt that modern geography as taught by teachers competent in geography and which stress areal associations, spatial interaction, and the new approach to man-land relations may well contribute a great deal to students' intelligent and critical understanding of our changing world.[16] Modern geographic concepts also seem to be almost indispensable to the study of history. Historians would be well advised to use the concepts of areal associations and of spatial interaction for a better understanding of such traditional terms as "spheres of influence" and "balance of power." Modern geography can do a great deal to mini-

---

[14] Preston James, "Geography," in Gordon B. Turner, ed., *The Social Studies and the Social Sciences* (New York: Harcourt, Brace & World, 1962), p. 48.

[15] Clyde F. Kohn, "Basic Concepts of Geography and Their Development in the Classroom," in Edwin Fenton, ed., *Teaching the New Social Studies* (New York: Holt, Rinehart & Winston, 1966), pp. 412–413.

[16] Excellent suggestions for the teaching of new geography are contained in the chapter Broek's *Geography, Its Scope and Spirit* (Columbus, O.: Charles E. Merrill Books, 1965), pp. 80–114.

mize the ambiguity with which these terms have been used by historians and political scientists.

In general, the traditional close bonds between history and geography will undoubtedly be strengthened by the new tendency of history to use concepts from behavioral sciences to go far beyond the political aspects of past human experience and by the tendency of new geography to look for patterns of association among physical, historical, economic, political, and biological factors in various geographic regions of the world.

14

For a Mankind Perspective in the Teaching of World History

There is general agreement that a thorough revision is needed in the teaching of world history on the high school level. The present social studies curriculum usually provides for the teaching of world history in one year, based on a very thick textbook sometimes reaching to 700 pages and "covering" the story of the mankind from about 6,000 B.C. to the most recent years. The social studies teacher is seriously enjoined by the curriculum makers and curriculum enforcers to teach a story covering eight thousand years and to find and analyze the proper associations between the events of the past and the problems of contemporary society. There are, of course, hundreds of teachers across the country using their skill, ability, and competence who do succeed in making the study of world history exciting and effective. But the same instruction in many classrooms is dull, lacking of purpose, and results in a mumbo-jumbo of unconnected information, much of it undigested and trivial.

It has to be admitted that the problem of teaching of world history in one year is indeed a tough one. The difficulty is greatly eased in those schools where world history is taught in two consecutive years. The offering of electives in world history on India, China, Russia, Africa, Latin America or the Near East alleviates the problem, at least for the more able students. However, for the great majority of schools, a rethinking of the objectives and a new rationale for the decisions on what to teach in world history is needed.

There probably is a general agreement that high school students ought to get a broad understanding of the story of the world and become acquainted with the world's main civilizations and religions. In the world of today, when the survival of Western civilization is seriously challenged, it would be unthinkable for high school graduates to be ignorant, for example, of Athens as the cradle of popular democracy, of the glory that was Rome, of important events in the history of the Catholic Church, of the dramatic story of Luther and the rise of Protestantism, of the emergence of modern nations, of the English Civil War, the French Revolution, the Bolshevik seizure of power, and of the two World Wars. But it is equally unthinkable for our students not to know something about the long history of Chinese civilization and its dynasties, about the rise of modern India, Japan, and Pakistan, and about the complicated history of Latin America. Even this very fragmentary listing of needed knowledge and understanding points to the enormity of the task facing the high school world history teacher. What is the "something" that he is to teach? How can he avoid superficial coverage of all these topics whose end result is a conglomeration of meaningless bits of information and misinformation? These difficult problems may be easier to tackle if objectives were to be, however briefly, re-examined.

World history should give students an historical perspective of the endeavors of successive generations to order their lives and achieve the goals of the "good" life as they have perceived it.

The outstanding variety of the postulated objectives of the ideal life, the baffling variety of methods used in pursuing the goals, and, even more important, the often truly astonishing and unexpected results of human strivings and conflicts ought to develop in the student a sophisticated and thoughtful approach to contemporary human affairs and social problems. A student who has studied the fascinating story of the Congress of Vienna and the visits and conferences of heads of states in Europe on the eve of World War I will view modern "summit meetings" more perceptively. "History," Edith West wisely remarked, "does provide a better guide to the future than does sheer guesswork."[1]

Shirley Engle sees the particular contribution of history in the opportunity that it presents to the student to see the story of humanity in a broad perspective. Through the study of world history, the student ought to see the broad lines of "both continuity and change in human society, the significances of uniformity and variety among human institutions, the persistent problems faced by all human societies, and the resources for improvement in human affairs."[2]

---

[1] Edith West, "Selecting and Organizing for a World History Course," in Shirley Engle, ed., *New Perspectives in World History* (Washington, 1964), p. 587.

[2] Shirley Engle, "World History in the Curriculum," *Social Education* (November 1965), p. 459.

In order to achieve these objectives, Engle suggests, some basic reforms are needed: First teachers of world history must become educators and not merely conveyers of information. A teacher should not relay information, but engage with students in a process of critical inquiry which may hopefully lead to the formulation of some pertinent generalizations and give students experience in acquiring the skill of critical thinking. Second, intelligent and effective teaching of world history cannot be based exclusively on textbooks. A good textbook may be of great help to teacher and students, but it must be supplemented by skillfully chosen and intelligently used primary sources and documents. The third and probably the most important reform has to do with a need for a radical change in the basic understanding of world history. The sorry fact is that the history taught today as world history is not really *world* history, but mostly the history of Western civilization. Thus, the story of about four-fifths of mankind is largely ignored. Some of the newer textbooks in world history include chapters on non-Western cultures and that in itself is a great improvement.

Geoffrey Barraclough might have been a bit harsh, but he was nevertheless correct when he condemned the excessive European bias in the writing and teaching of world history.

> The older historiography, with its myopic concentration on Europe and on the European powers and—where it looked further afield—its independent treatment of the history of America and the overseas territories as distinct units or spheres moving in a separate axis, has discredited history and denuded it of sense and significance.[3]

Less than fifty years ago, when the *Cambridge Modern History* first appeared, thirteen of the fourteen volumes were devoted to Europe and one volume dealt with the United States. There has, of course, been a great improvement in presenting a more balanced view of world history, but, on the whole, Europecentrism still reigns supreme. The roots of this unbalanced view of the world may well be traced to the idea of "progress." Faith in the inevitability of progress, evidence, which is to be found mostly in European civilization, caused and still causes many historians to focus their attention on the history of Europe and look on the rest of the world only as far as it is related itself or was related by force to European powers.

R. H. Tawney's idea that capitalism was indigenous to, and rooted in, the Protestant ethic and Toynbee's almost passionate faith that only a Christian revival can save Western civilization have contributed to the strengthening of Europecentrism.

Obviously, the fact that modern political and economic ideas, which have

---

[3] Geoffrey Barraclough, *History in a Changing World* (Norman, Okla.: Univ. of Oklahoma Press, 1955), p. 137.

been used and adopted all over the world by colonial peoples striving to free themselves from alien rule, and by newly independent nations, have emanated from Europe has made the emphasis on the history of European civilization quite understandable. Educated people everywhere studied and applied in one way or another the economic ideas of Adam Smith and Karl Marx and the political theories of Jean Jacques Rousseau, Immanuel Kant, Voltaire, and John Locke.

On a more practical level, the European ascendancy, power, and prosperity was attributed on all subjugated continents to the superior technology developed by European nations. In spite of the fact that the ancients had no notion of "progress" and neither did most oriental nations, European technological advancement, primarily the implements of war and industrial machinery of all varieties, was accepted by most of the overawed peoples and races of the world as a desirable mark of progress. Inhabitants of a Burmese village or the members of the Watusi tribe in Africa in the 1870's or 1890's understood that the Europeans among them were "superior" because they were capable of subduing their resistance at will and taking from them what they liked. No wonder that historians, almost all of them Europeans and a few Americans, wrote world history with the history of Europe as its core and dealt with the rest of the world only as it related to Europe. The history of the world was, and still is to a large extent, written from "an unbiased Western point of view." The Western bias, which often is unintentional, results from a limited focus and a wrong perspective. Non-Western history is often studied "from a deck of a gunboat." India became a subject of interest with the conquests of Clive, Africa from the time of Livingstone and King Albert, and Japan from the time that Europeans became interested in its trade potential.

There is no need to belabor the point that this approach has become obsolete. Europe's hegemony in the world has ended. Imperial and colonial possessions are now, with few exceptions, independent states. Nothing illustrates better the new balance of power in the world than a meeting of the General Assembly of the United Nations, which is increasingly dominated by the growing number of Afro-Asian nations.

The emergence of the nations in Asia, including an independent India, Pakistan, and China, is not only a new political reality, vitally important to the progress of the "revolution of rising expectations" and to the issue of war and peace. Equally important is our growing realization that the civilizations of China, India, and Japan are as much a part of our own historical background as is the rich heritage of the European civilization. There is an increasing measure of concern about the relations among different cultural and religious societies in the past and in the present. We want to know more, and teach our younger generation, about the cultural traditions of Asia and Africa in order to better understand the elements of unity and diversity in all of human society. We want to know and we need to know the essentials and histories of other cultures and of their points of contact and interdependence.

Nothing has been more dramatic than the emergence of many new nations in the "dark" continent of Africa. This new development has revealed how rich is the historic background and how great are the social and political changes that have taken place in Africa in a relatively short period of time. The destinies of Togo, Gabon, Nigeria, the Congo, and Tanzania are now clearly and intrinsically interwoven with the destiny of England, the United States, China, India, and the Soviet Union. We know now that in reality there is not one Africa, but many Africas, and that the ethnic, cultural, national, and economic diversity among the tribes and peoples of Africa can no longer be ignored. Nothing has probably so dramatically illustrated the changing situation in the world than the announcement, during the recent armed conflict between India and Pakistan, over Kashmir, that the President of Pakistan, Ayub Khan, had accepted the mediation offer of the President of Kenya, Jomo Kenyatta. This announcement came after a similar offer of mediation by the Canadian Prime Minister, Lester Pearson, had been ignored.

The emergence of new nations necessitates a shift in perspective in historical studies of the world. We can no longer ignore four-fifths of mankind. There is great urgency in the writing of a universal history which would be both global and unifying in outlook and pay profound attention both to the diversity and to the unifying factors of cultures and civilizations. Of course, world history cannot be an aggregate of national histories. The injunction of H. G. Wells, whose deservedly popular *Outline of History* was written from a universal point of view, must be heeded. He emphasized that universal history is at once "something more and something less than an aggregate of national histories." A useful guideline can be found in the definition of universal history by Lord Acton in his *Lectures on Modern History*, published in 1906.

> By universal history, I understand that which is distinct from the combined history of all countries, which is not a rope of sand, but a continuous development, and is not a burden on the memory, but an illumination of the soul. It moves in a succession to which the nations are a subsidiary. Their story will be told, not for their own sake, but in reference and subordination to a higher series, according to the time and the degree in which they contribute to the common fortune of mankind.

Such a world history would be concerned with points of contact and interrelationships among cultures, peoples, and nations. As such it would be much less interested in Toynbee's approach in the *Study of History*, which emphasized the growth, rise, and fall of separate civilizations and more in the approach of William H. McNeill in his *The Rise of the West,* who described the history of the human community in terms of a variety of cultures and civilizations, acting and reacting upon one another without cease.

It may well be that the writing of a truly universal history presents at this time insurmountable difficulties. The concept itself still needs a great deal of elaboration and elucidation. Furthermore, there are still important gaps in our knowledge of the history of Asia and Africa and there are still too few scholars and historians in the non-Western world competent to deal with history on a genuinely world scale. Nationalistic traditions and prejudices still becloud the vision of many historians in the West, and the world is still divided into two major ideological camps, a division which makes the prospect of an early agreement upon a unified approach to the history of the world improbable.

The experience of the UNESCO publication in 1965 of *History of Mankind: Vol II: The Ancient World, 1200* B.C. *to* A.D. *500,* by Luigi Baretti and others, dramatically illustrates the difficulties in writing a universal history. The volume was criticized by some as inaccurate and lacking perspective and interpretation. J. H. Plumb, reviewing the book in the New York *Times,* charged that the book was a poor product of scholarship-by-committee, and was not interpretative. William Spencer, a member of the publication committee, admitted in a letter to the *Times* that nationalist biases among historians have caused the publication to undergo a process of scrutiny which "removed all semblance of originality and interpretative brilliance." Nevertheless, there is great merit in the *UNESCO History of Mankind.* It is not a universal history of mankind, but it is an important first attempt to write a history of the world by pooling the contributions of historians from many countries. Louis Gottschalk, one of the editors of the UNESCO History put it this way:

> Needless to say, consensus on the course of human events is not yet at hand . . . Yet, if reason does not lose its race with disaster, consensus may still emerge from a current tendency to recognize that, while each area of the world has its own internal culture, which may be worthy of laudatory consideration in a universal history, the peoples of the world have nevertheless lived through millenia of diffusion and interchange of cultural traits.[4]

If the writing of a universal history is, as yet, impossible, what can be done, and should be done, is to make an attempt to look at selected periods in world history from a global, mankind point of view and particularly to trace the history of the concept of the unity of mankind.

---

[4] *Conference on History and Mankind—A Report,* Committee for the Study of Mankind (Chicago, 1963), p. 10.

It would seem almost superfluous to marshal arguments to prove the validity of approaching the study of history from a global view which would embrace the whole of mankind. Few people today, even those whose vision is narrowed by parochialism, isolationism, or narrow vested interests, fail to see that the major problems facing the human race today can be examined and eventually solved, not on a national, but on a mankind level. In fact, the problems of war and peace, the feeding of the hungry and the sick, the question of overpopulation, to name but a few, would clearly be insoluble if tackled within national or even regional boundaries. The revolution in the field of communication, the great advances in science and technology, the rise of the scores of independent nations in Asia and Africa, and, finally, the threat of global atomic destruction have made the earth more than ever truly "One World." Eugene Staley of Stanford University wisely wrote in the *Bulletin of the Council for the Study of Mankind:*

> The common interests which men have as members of a world community are not likely to be adequately evaluated by adding up the interests they perceive when they think as members of separate nations. As a practical matter, even the true interests of each nation can be found only by supplementing national thinking with a broader approach. For example, a major part of the national interest of the American people in assisting development outside our own boundaries is to shape the kind of world we want to live in. That kind of world can become reality only as we and other peoples think of the common interests of mankind as part of our own interests.[5]

It would, however, be a mistake to overlook the fact that the process of broadening the scope of vision and the attempt to find a universal organizational framework for all mankind has often manifested itself from the beginning of mankind's history. The reality of the existence of other lands and other peoples in the world has grown steadily from ancient times through the Age of Enlightenment to modern times.

The Macedonian Greek, Alexander the Great, deserves his title not so much because of his military conquests, but because he gave his life for the idea of a cosmopolitan world where all men would live as equals, in spite of their religious, social, and political differences.

The Romans, within a little more than a hundred years (241–133 B.C.), extended their power and influence over much of Europe, Africa, the Middle East, and Asia Minor. They were determined to unite all peoples and nations of the world under the orderly, but often tyrannical rule of Roman law and the *pax Romana.*

In the Middle Ages, the Roman Catholic Church, as its name implies,

---

[5] *Bulletin of the Council for the Study of Mankind,* mimeographed (Santa Monica, California, 1966), p. 3.

stressed the universality of its appeal and aspirations. Similarly, Muhammad, the prophet of Islam, enjoined his followers on the penalty of death not to discriminate among those who accepted the creed on the basis of race, color, or nationality. It is, in a large measure, this policy which aimed at converting all of mankind, which made it possible for Islam to gain millions of adherents among the black peoples of Africa and the millions of Indians and Chinese.

Modern imperialism, which had its cradle in Western Europe, while rapacious in its goals and means, did harbor within it the concept of a unified mankind. To be sure, it was a mankind which was to be "civilized" by Western men. But, in fact, the age of imperialism or the Age of the Enlightenment did break down barriers of separation and put the peoples of the world in contact with one another.

Philosophers and historians have made continuous attempts to find a general pattern of development or a general law governing all history. Macrohistory or metahistory has had a great fascination for many historians. These attempts at macrohistory have not usually been well received by professional historians. Lewis Namier and Pieter Geyl were particularly contemptuous of any attempts to find a rhythm or unifying pattern in the history of mankind. However, the writing of macrohistorians, including Spengler's *The Decline of the West*, Wells's *Outline of History*, Toynbee's *Study of History* and McNeill's *The Rise of the West*, was extraordinarily successful with the buying public. It may well be that these attempts to find a deeper sense in the history of man respond to a deeply felt need of the mass of the people.

It is not often remembered that Voltaire was not only a great philosopher but also a distinguished historian. Voltaire believed in the constant advancement of the human spirit. To Voltaire history was not the story of prominent men or great heroes, but the history of the human mind. In fact, he believed that details about kings and generals, about wars and diplomacy merely obscured the important and vital currents of history which truly reflect the development of the spirit of men. Voltaire, the "citizen of the world," was concerned not with the history of individuals or nations, but with the study of "humanitas"—the study of mankind. In the first paragraph of *The Age of Louis XIV* Voltaire made clear that his objective was not to give a detailed account of the life of Louis XIV, but to leave to posterity a report on the spirit of the time. Voltaire was the first to attack historians who stressed patriotism, wars, and heroes. "The progress of mankind," he wrote, "can be understood only if one takes into account the growth of religion, art, science, and philosophy." Voltaire did not write a history of the human mind, but he paved the way for a different and truly universal history of mankind which is yet to be written.

Concern for and a sense of responsibility to mankind was clearly expressed by the philosophers of the Revolution and by the Founding Fathers of the United States. Thomas Paine wrote in *Common Sense* of the duty of every American to become a "virtuous supporter of the Rights of Mankind." Thomas Jefferson, in the first sentence of the Declaration of Independence, acknowledged the existence of a world community. "A decent respect to the opinions of mankind," he wrote, obliged the leaders of the American Revolution to explain the reason and causes of the rebellion against British rule. Americans felt obligated to make sure that men everywhere understood the colonists' motives and aspirations. The explanation was based on Locke's idea of natural laws reserved for the people and the right of the oppressed to rebel against those who would deprive them of their natural right to life, liberty, and the pursuit of happiness.

George Washington, in his Farewell Address delivered on September 17, 1796, expressed his hope that the United States of America would in time "give to mankind the magnanimous and too novel example of a people always guided by an exalted justice and benevolence."

If these important efforts to find some unifying threads in world history are even partially successful we need to look at the whole of world history and try to isolate the elements of unity or the evidence of mutual concern for the totality of mankind.

History, as it has been written, largely overlooks the concern for and the constant striving toward unity and cooperation. As a rule, historians have been preoccupied with relating the course of events in fragmented parts of mankind, with the history of wars, of religious conflicts, and have largely ignored the idea and concept of mankind in history. Equally unfortunate is the fact that so much of the history of the world has been written from a Western point of view. Consequently, much of the story of non-Western civilizations has been presented, not as it was, but as it looked in the often biased or colored mirror of the Western system of values and interests.

"A decent respect to the opinions of mankind," using Jefferson's words in the Declaration of Independence, would indicate the need to examine the history of the world from the central focus, not of nations, or of races, or of regions, but from the broader concept of mankind. It is indeed imperative to examine whether the instinct for strife, domination, and the brutal struggle for the survival of the fittest has not at least been matched by an equally powerful instinct and drive toward mutual cooperation and the commitment to the welfare of the human race.

The manufacturing of atomic bombs is not the only characteristic of the Atomic Age. Equally important are the decline of imperialism and colonialism and the great strides made in modern science and technology. Within a few recent decades, the European powers willingly or sometimes unwillingly gave up most of their colonial possessions. The rising tide of nationalism brought independence to almost all of Asia and Africa. The peoples of Asia and Africa are now demanding a share in the world's wealth and a voice in world affairs, and the two major atomic powers of the world, the United States and Russia, are competing for the allegiance and support of the unaligned Afro-Asian nations.

It is becoming increasingly clear that the threat of a worldwide atomic holocaust, ever increasing international pressures and tensions, and the unification of the world by modern technology and the revolutionary advances of mass communication give new vitality and urgency to the concern for the future of mankind. Space explorations, Telstar, and the population explosion are all manifestations of this urgency. What happens in Laos, Cuba, or Angola is today of crucial importance to people in New York, New Delhi, and in Moscow. The fact that there are today about one hundred very poor countries where most of the people go to bed hungry every night must be of deep concern to us and to other "have" nations. To paraphrase Lincoln's immortal words on slavery, the world cannot long endure half rich and half poor.

Even more important is the growing realization that some of the most crucial problems faced by mankind can be solved only on a worldwide scale and only by a conscious commitment to the welfare of mankind. These problems include distribution of food, overpopulation, international trade, disease, and the armament race. As a matter of fact, it is more true today than ever before that the survival of mankind now depends upon the ability of men to deal with these problems on a universal basis. The solutions, if they are to be effective, must take into account the welfare and well-being of the entire human race. The emergence of many free nations in Asia and Africa and their struggle for higher living standards and political influence seems to necessitate a new approach to world problems.

The rapid advancement of science and technology has clearly outstripped man's capacity to order his world in a way which would make the destruction of civilization impossible. Technology has brought the human species closer together, but it has also increased the chances for a disastrous conflict. The concept and the application of the idea of a concern for mankind may be very helpful in solving the problems and conflicts which beset modern society. In the words of Professor Hans Kohn: "The concept of mankind corresponds or responds to a real and vital need and this coincides at the same time with a unique opportunity in history."[6]

The trend toward unity and universal peace and understanding has been more than matched by the forces of disunity and divisiveness. There is no need to even summarize the long, dreary, and bloody story of wars, reli-

---

[6] *Conference on History and Mankind—A Report,* Committee for the Study of Mankind (Chicago, 1963) p. 17.

gious wars, invasions, and international quarrels and conflicts. This story which, as Voltaire has pointed out, usually fills history books, does suggest that excessive nationalism was, and is, a major source of disunity and strife in the world.

On the other hand, one should not overlook the positive side of nationalism as a creative force for cultural advancement, and great economic and technological achievements, and as a catalytic force for acts of heroism and self-sacrifice. However, the history of the world does support a general indictment of excessive nationalism as the major breeder of wars and conflicts. There are in the world today several foci of infection which poison the international atmosphere, sometimes causing "small wars" and always threatening to trigger a world conflagration. These disputed territories include, among others, Berlin, Formosa, Sinkiang, Danzig (Gdansk) and East Prussia, Silesia, Tyrol, Sudentenland, the Saar, the Gaza Strip, and Cyprus. Of these potential sources of conflict, only Berlin and Formosa have some connection with the Cold War between the communist and non-communist nations. All others have been bones of contention long before the Cold War, and there is no reason to believe that they would not continue to inflame the world should the East-West conflict somehow be settled. Both Turkey and Greece are members of the North Atlantic Alliance and both are strongly anti-communist, but these countries, if left to themselves, would not hesitate to go to war over the long-standing conflict between the Greek and Turkish communities on Cyprus. No Polish government, free or communist, could remain in power if it were to renounce Polish claims to the Baltic port of Danzig. It is becoming increasingly clear that the basic quarrel between Communist China and the Soviet Union has little to do with the interpretation of Marxism-Leninism. Essentially, the conflict is a continuation of the nationalist rivalry and of the territorial and border disputes between China and Tzarist Russia. Nationalism has proved itself to be stronger than socialism or communism and an easy victor in any contest with the movements for international understanding and cooperation.

The "one world" of today makes a new approach to the writing and teaching of world history imperative. In addition to Toynbee's *The Study of History*, two other efforts should be noted. One is the UNESCO project of the publication of a new *History of the Scientific and Cultural Development of Mankind*. The scholars of many nations who are responsible for this monumental project feel that it will be an important contribution to historical knowledge. The UNESCO history is, in the words of Professor Louis Gottschalk, the author of one of the volumes, "a general effort to describe the mainstream of mankind's development and to point out the major tributaries running into that stream." However, as we have noted, no claim is made by the editors of the UNESCO history which was written by international teams of historians, including communist historians who cannot find a communality of language with their Western colleagues, that it will be a world history written from the mankind perspective.

The other effort in writing a comprehensive world history is William H. McNeill's widely acclaimed *The Rise of the West—A History of the Human Community*.[7] McNeill casts serious doubt on Toynbee's assertion that different civilizations had separate and autonomous histories. He argues that world history presents a picture not of separate civilizations rising, flourishing, and falling, but rather of a variety of cultures, acting and reacting upon one another without cease. The existence of this constant interaction of civilizations presents an intelligible pattern when limited to the influence of a particularly attractive core-area of civilization. Moreover, more often than not, other attractive centers exerted their influence simultaneously. The result was that, for instance, in the Middle East, an area particularly subject to outside invasions, penetrations and to the cross-currents of culture, there was constant merging, assimilating, and mingling of cultural patterns. At a conference on "History and Mankind" sponsored by the Council for the Study of Mankind, Professor McNeill stated:

> In my view, there has always been a process of cultural interchange; cultural flow and cultural stimulation between adjacent societies. I think the process of collision and contact, peaceful and warlike, between peoples of different cultures is the central motor of historical change; that is, the generation of new styles of life seems to be related to the intensity of contact between people having alien ways of life.[8]

McNeill is convinced that the emergence of the free nations of Africa and Asia and their throwing-off of the yoke of Western rule and tutelage need not be fatal to Western civilization. The rise of the West is still maintained, according to McNeill, because the new nations have assimilated and are using Western techniques, ideas, and attitudes. Even Spengler's spectre of Asian domination does not cause McNeill to be fearful of the future:

> At least in its initial stages, any world state will be an empire of the West. This would be the case even if non-Westerners should happen to hold the supreme controls of worldwide political-military authority, for they could only do so by utilizing such originally Western traits as industrialism, science, and the public palliation of power through advocacy of one or other of the democratic political faiths.[9]

---

[7] William H. McNeill, *The Rise of the West—A History of the Human Community* (Chicago: Univ. of Chicago Press, 1963).

[8] *Conference on History and Mankind—A Report*, Committee for the Study of Mankind (Chicago, 1963), p. 65.

[9] *Ibid.*

One wonders whether this sanguine faith in the future relations between the West and the new nations of Africa and Asia is not overlooking the national rivalries, the struggle for power within the newly independent countries, and the long accumulated distrust and hatred of the West. One has only to contemplate Indonesia's determination to destroy the Malay Federation, the border war on the frontiers of Kenya and Somali, and the fragile nature of the democratic faith of most of the new nations to conclude that perhaps McNeill's optimistic expectations may not be fully realized in the future.

At any rate, it is quite clear that we need a new and truly universal history. This new history must be global history, free of any Western or European-centered bias. It is not necessary, of course, to accept the extreme position of G. Barraclough who, in his *History in a Changing World* (1955), suggested that world history as written and learned has lost all sense. Professor Barraclough wrote that he regretted the years he has spent in studying the papal chancellery or the story of the European emperors in the Middle Ages. He thought that it would have been more useful to study the history of the Slavs and the Tartars. In his essay entitled "Farewell to Europe," Professor Barraclough dismissed Bismarck, Louis XIV, and Napoleon as "neolithic figures." The point that Barraclough was trying to make—that the Western-oriented history ignores the story of four-fifths of mankind—was well-taken. However, his depreciation of the spiritual, political, and technological heritage of the West is a distortion of history. It makes no sense to get rid of a biased Europe-centered history only to replace it with a biased Afro-Asian-centered history of the world.

The goal of Barraclough's essay was to suggest that the new universal-global history would have to be written and taught from the frame of reference of mankind as a whole. The entrance of whole continents which were, until comparatively recently, "dark continents" and the entrance during the last two decades of over fifty nations on the world scene has made thinking in mankind terms imperative. Leaders of nations and scholars, regardless of their particular disciplines, are called upon to look at the past story and the problems of the world by consciously transcending national regional boundaries and by describing and dealing with the total experience of the human race.

Obviously, the writing and teaching of world history will not be adequate and effective until and unless it ceases to be a history of the world taught from "an unbiased Western point of view." The Western bias, which often is not intentional, results from a limited focus and a wrong perspective. Someone has wisely said that most high school students usually begin the study of the non-Western world "from the deck of a gunboat." India becomes a subject of instruction with the conquests of Clive and the study of Japan begins with the entrance of Commodore Perry's flotilla into Japanese waters. Thus, the story of western civilization is considered the main-stream of world history and other cultures, nations, and civilizations are studied only in relation to the Western world. Consequently, great so-cieties in the East and in Africa have remained relatively isolated, silent, and unknown.

As we have said, just adding the study of non-Western civilizations will not make for real universal history. What is needed is a change of perspec-tive—from the horizontal groundhog point of view to the global-mankind perspective. It has often been suggested that the teaching of world history can be improved by adding the study of several non-Western countries and civilizations. The thinking on this matter follows this line: "We have taught biased and ethnocentric world history because we have left out, among others, the history of Japan, India, and Africa. Once we add these countries and continents to our course of study we will be teaching the real history of the world." The fallacy of this statement may become obvious if we compare it with this line of reasoning. "We have been teaching United States history inadequately because we have taught only the his-tory of twenty-five states; consequently, in order to teach the true history of our country we must add the teaching of the histories of the other twenty-five states." This line of thinking is obviously absurd. The history of the separate fifty states is not the history of the United States. Neither is the history of the separate countries—or even civilizations—the true his-tory of the world or of mankind. The global view of world history, as if seen from a suspended satellite in space, would not and should not ignore the achievements and the great contributions of Western civilization, but it would allow the student to see that culture in its true interrelationship with other cultures and other civilizations. Thus, the story of the Indian subcontinent would not be merely a study of the history of India, either from a Western or an Indian ethnocentric viewpoint, but a study of the interaction of three great civilizations, the Hindu, the Islamic, and the Western Christian. It is expected that history taught from the global point of reference would affect the established criteria for deciding the relative importance of personalities and events in history. It may well be that in a history taught from a global-mankind point of view, Genghis Khan would loom as a more important figure than Henry VIII, and Simon Bolivar greater and more influential than Charles V. The Mogul ruler of India Akbar may emerge as a greater figure than his contemporary, Elizabeth I in England.

Global history would not eliminate or diminish the importance of the history of individual nations, but it would temper the ethnocentric interpre-tation of history. It would also place, as much as possible, each separate national history in its proper context, not only to some of the other national histories, but also, if, and wherever feasible, to the total experience of the human race at any given period of time.

The need for the writing and teaching of a truly universal history, which would give due attention to the concept of mankind as a whole and gradually develop a concern for the welfare of mankind, is quite clearly indicated by the danger to human survival posed by thermonuclear weapons, by the unification of the world by science and technology, and by the revolutionary advance of mass communications. Africa is no longer a "dark continent," and Rangoon is no longer the remote capital of Burma, a British colonial possession. African representatives sit in the halls of the United Nations in New York a few feet from U Thant of Burma, the United Nations Secretary General. The emergence of the greater part of mankind from political subjection to political independence and influence necessitates a shift in historical perspective and a shift in the framework and perspective of world history as taught in high schools.

The task of teaching world-global history, which would include due emphasis on the concept of mankind, will not be easy. Not the least of the difficulty will be caused by lack of materials. With the possible exception of H. G. Wells's *Outline of History*, published in 1919, there are no histories written from a universal mankind point of view. While Wells' history is now largely outdated, a teacher of world history must remember the injunction of H. G. Wells that "universal history is at once something more and something less than an aggregate of national histories." We must acknowledge the truth that the writing and consequently the study of a truly universal world history is still in its beginnings. But this realization should not, however, free us from the responsibility of making a start toward better teaching of the history of mankind.

The study of world history from a global point of view, during several carefully selected historical periods, would allow for the diligent appraisal of important generalizations in the teaching of history. There is need for high school students to study the validity or the lack of validity of Hegel's great generalization that "the history of the world is none other than the progress of the consciousness of freedom." The same is true of the generalization of Voltaire that history involved the idea of progress, Marx's generalization about the role of economic determinism in history, Spengler's views on the decline of the West, and Toynbee's theory of cycles in world history.

The most promising developments in the direction of formulation of a truly world approach to world history resulted from the publication of McNeill's recent work. In many parts of the country, committees have been working on the development of new world history curricula based on McNeill's concepts of cultural diffusion, of cultural interchange among civilizations, and the concept of the ever changing ecumene or centers of culture both in the West and in the East which exerted much influence on large areas of the world. These influences were strong in times of peace and in times of war. A curriculum in world history which would consist

BIBLIOGRAPHY

ACTON, LORD. *Essays on Freedom and Power,* ed. Gertrude Himmelfarb. Boston: Beacon Press, 1948.
———. *A Lecture on the Study of History.* London and New York: The Macmillan Co., 1905.
ADAMS, HENRY. *The United States in 1800.* Ithaca, N.Y.: Cornell Univ. Press, 1957.
ANDERSON, C. ARNOLD. "A New Frame for the Social Sciences," *The School Review.* Volume 72, Number 4, Winter 1964.
ANGLE, PAUL M. (ed.). *The American Reader.* Chicago: Rand McNally & Co., 1958.
ANGLE, PAUL M. and EARL SCHENCK MIERS (eds.). *The Living Lincoln.* New Brunswick, N.J.: Rutgers Univ. Press, 1955.
AYDELOTTE, WILLIAM O. "Notes on the Problems of Historical Generalization" in *Generalization in the Writing of History,* ed. Louis Gottschalk. Chicago: Univ. of Chicago Press, 1963.
BAILEY, THOMAS A. "Revitalizing American History," *Social Education.* December 1960.
BARRACLOUGH, GEOFFREY. *History in a Changing World.* Norman, Okla.: Univ. of Oklahoma Press, 1955.
———. "Universal History" in *Approaches to History,* ed. H. P. R. Fineberg. Toronto: Univ. of Toronto Press, 1962.
BARTON, THOMAS F. "Geography Skills and Techniques" in *Curriculum Guide for Geographic Education,* ed. Wilhelmina Hill. Normal, Ill.: National Council for Geographic Education, 1963. Chapter 4.
BAXTER, MAURICE G., ROBERT H. TERRELL, and JOHN E. WILTZ. *The Teaching of American History in High Schools.* Bloomington, Ind.: Indiana Univ. Press, 1964.
BEARD, CHARLES A. *An Economic Interpretation of the Constitution of the United States.* New York: The Macmillan Co., 1935.

————. "Written History as an Act of Faith," *American Historical Review.* Volume 39, 1934.

BEARD, CHARLES A. and MARY R. *The Rise of American Civilization.* New York: The Macmillan Co., 1927.

BECKER, CARL. *Every Man His Own Historian.* New York: Appleton-Century-Crofts, 1935.

BELLACK, ARNO. "Structure in the Social Sciences and Implications for the Social Studies Program," *The Social Studies: Curriculum Proposals for the Future.* Stanford University, 1963.

BENSON, LEE. "A Tentative Classification for American Voting Behavior," *Sociology and History.* New York: Free Press of Glencoe, 1964.

BERNSTEIN, EDGAR. "Structural Perspectives: The Social Science Disciplines and the Social Studies," *Social Education.* February 1965.

BETTELHEIM, BRUNO. "Notes on the Future of Education," *The University of Chicago Magazine.* Volume XI, Number 5, February 1966.

BIERSTEDT, ROBERT. "Comment," *The American Journal of Sociology.* Volume 70, March 1965.

BLAU, PETER M. and JOAN V. MOORE. "Sociology" in *A Reader's Guide to the Social Sciences,* ed. Bert F. Hoselitz. New York: Free Press of Glencoe, 1959.

BLOOM, B. S. and D. R. KRATHWOHL. *Taxonomy of Educational Objectives: Handbook I, Cognitive Domain.* New York: David McKay Co., 1964.

BOLSTER, ARTHUR S. JR. "History, Historians, and the Secondary School Curriculum," *Harvard Educational Review.* Spring 1962.

BOWERS, CLAUDE G. *The Tragic Era.* Boston: Houghton Mifflin Co., 1929.

BRINTON, CRANE. *The Anatomy of Revolution.* New York: Random House, 1957.

BROEK, JAN O. M. *Geography, Its Scope and Spirit.* Columbus, O.: Charles E. Merrill Books, 1965.

BROOM, LEONARD and PHILIP SELZNICK. *Sociology.* 2nd ed. New York: Harper & Row, 1958.

BROUDY, HARRY S. and JOHN R. PALMER. *Exemplars of Teaching Method.* Chicago: Univ. of Chicago Press, 1965.

BROWN, RICHARD H. "History as Discovery: An Interim Report on the Amherst Project," *The New Social Studies.* Amherst, Mass.: Amherst College, 1965.

BROWN, ROBERT E. *Charles Beard and the Constitution.* Princeton, N.J.: Princeton Univ. Press, 1956.

BRUNER, JEROME S. "Education or Social Invention," *Saturday Review.* February 19, 1966.

————. *On Knowing.* Cambridge, Mass.: Harvard Univ. Press, 1962.

————. "Man: A Course of Study," *E.S.I. Quarterly Report.* Watertown, Mass., Summer 1965.

————. *The Process of Education.* Cambridge, Mass.: Harvard Univ. Press, 1960.

Bulletin of the Council for the Study of Mankind. Mimeographed. Santa Monica, California. January 1966.

BURY, JOHN B. *The Ancient Greek Historians.* London: The Macmillan Co., 1909.

————. "History as a Science," *Varieties of History.* Cleveland, O.: World Publishing Co., 1963.

————. *The Idea of Progress.* London: The Macmillan Co., 1921.

CAHNMAN, WERNER J. and ALVIN BOSKOFF (eds.). *Sociology and History—Theory and Research.* New York: Free Press of Glencoe, 1964.

CARR, EDWARD HALLETT. *What Is History?* New York: Alfred A. Knopf, 1962.

CARTER, HODDING. *The Angry Scar.* Garden City, N.Y.: Doubleday & Co., 1958.

COLEMAN, JOHN R. "When Secondary School Teacher and College Economist Meet," *The Bulletin of the National Association of Secondary-School Principals.* Number 304, November 1965.

COLLIER, MALCOLM. "A Question About Questions," *Social Education.* December 1965.

COLLINGWOOD, R. G. *The Idea of History,* ed. T. M. Knox. London: Oxford Univ. Press, 1946.

COMMAGER, HENRY STEELE (ed.). *Documents of American History.* New York: Appleton-Century-Crofts, 1949.

A Compilation of the Messages and Papers of the Presidents, James D. Richardson. Washington: Bureau of National Literature and Art, 1908. Volume 6, p. 565.

A Conceptual Framework for the Social Studies in Wisconsin Schools. Social Studies Bulletin issued by Angus B. Rothwell, State Superintendent of Public Instruction, Madison, Wisconsin. December, 1964.

COURT, W. H. D. "Economic History" in *Approaches to History,* ed. H. P. R. Fineberg. Toronto: Univ. of Toronto Press, 1962.

COX, C. BENJAMIN. "An Inquiry into Inquiries," *Social Education.* May 1965.

COX, LAWANDA and JOHN H. *Politics, Principle, and Prejudice, 1865–1866.* New York: Free Press of Glencoe, 1963.

CRAVEN, AVERY. *The Coming of the Civil War.* 2nd ed. Chicago: Univ. of Chicago Press, 1957.

CRESSEY, GEORGE B. "Geography" in *High School Social Studies Perspectives,* ed. Erling Hunt. Boston: Houghton Mifflin Co., 1962.

CROCE, BENEDETTO. *Theory and History of Historiography.* London: G. G. Harrap, 1921.

CROWE, RUBY M. "Problems and Possibilities for Curriculum Change," *Focus on the Social Studies.* Washington: National Education Association, 1965.

DAVIS, JEFFERSON. *The Rise and Fall of the Confederate Government.* New York: Crowell-Collier & Macmillan, 1961.

DEFOREST, J. W. "The Man and Brother," *Atlantic Monthly.* 1868.

DETOCQUEVILLE, ALEXIS. *Democracy in America.* New York: Random House, 1945.

DEWEY, JOHN. "Experience and Nature," *The Paul Carus Lectures*. LaSalle, Ill.: Open Court, 1929.

———. *Lectures in the Philosophy of Education: 1899*, ed. Reginald D. Archambault. New York: Random House, 1966.

———. "Social Science and Social Control," *New Republic*. 1931.

DONALD, DAVID. *Charles Sumner and the Coming of the Civil War*. New York: Alfred A. Knopf, 1960.

DUBERMAN, MARTIN. "The Limitations of History," *The Antioch Review*. Summer 1965.

DuBOIS, W. E. B. *Black Reconstruction in America*. New York: Russell & Russell, 1953.

DUVERGER, MAURICE. *Political Parties*. 2nd ed. New York: John Wiley & Sons, 1959.

EASTON, DAVID and ROBERT D. HESS. "The Child's Political World," *Midwest Journal of Political Science*. Volume 6, Number 3, August 1963.

———. "The Role of the Elementary School in Political Socialization," *School Review*. Winter 1962.

ENGLE, SHIRLEY H. "Decision-Making—The Heart of Social Studies Instruction," *Social Education*. November 1960.

——— (ed.). *New Perspectives in World History*. Thirty-fourth Yearbook of the National Council for the Social Studies. (Washington) 1964.

———. "Objectives of the Social Studies" in *New Challenges in the Social Studies*, eds. B. G. Massialas and F. J. Smith. Belmont, Calif.: Wadsworth Publishing Co., 1965.

———. "World History in the Curriculum," *Social Education*. November 1965.

ETZIONI, AMITAI. "Social Analysis as a Sociological Vocation," *The American Journal of Sociology*. Volume 70, March 1965.

EYRE, EDWARD. *European Civilization*. New York: Oxford Univ. Press, 1934–1939.

FARLAND, MAX. *The Framing of the Constitution of the U.S.* New Haven, Conn.: Yale Univ. Press, 1962.

FENTON, EDWIN. *Teaching the New Social Studies*. New York: Holt, Rinehart & Winston, 1966.

FERSH, SEYMOUR H. *The View from the White House*. Washington: Public Affairs Press, 1961.

FISHER, H. A. L. *A History of Europe*. Boston: Houghton Mifflin Co., 1935.

The Four Traditions of Geography. William D. Pattison. Professional Paper Number 25, National Council for Geographic Education, May 1964.

FRANKLIN, JOHN HOPE. *Reconstruction After the Civil War*. Chicago: Univ. of Chicago Press, 1961.

FRASER, DOROTHY. "Status and Expectations of Current Research and Development Projects," *Social Education*. November 1965.

FROMAN, LEWIS A. *Congressmen and Their Constituents*. Chicago: Rand McNally & Co., 1963.

GEYL, PIETER. *Debates with Historians.* Cleveland, O.: World Publishing Co., 1958.

GIBBON, EDWARD. *Autobiography.* Cleveland, O.: World Publishing Co., 1961.

GOTTSCHALK, LOUIS (ed.). *Generalization in the Writing of History.* Chicago: Univ. of Chicago Press, 1963.

———. *Understanding History.* New York: Alfred A. Knopf, 1950.

GROSS, RICHARD and FRED I. GREENSTEIN. *Children and Politics.* New Haven, Conn.: Yale Univ. Press, 1965.

HARRIS, SEYMOUR E. "Economics" in *High School Social Studies Perspectives,* ed. Erling Hunt. Boston: Houghton Mifflin Co., 1962.

HEGEL, GEORG WILHELM FRIEDRICH. *Lectures on the Philosophy of History.* London: K. Paul, Trench, Trübner and Co., 1896.

HESSELTINE, WILLIAM B. *Lincoln's Plan of Reconstruction.* Tuscaloosa, Ala.: Confederate Publishing Co., 1960.

HIGHAM, JOHN, LEONARD KRIEGER, and FELIX GILBERT. *History.* Englewood Cliffs, N.J.: Prentice-Hall, 1965.

HOEBEL, E. ADAMSON. "The Nature of Culture" in *Man, Culture and Society,* ed. Harry L. Shapiro. New York: Oxford Univ. Press, 1956.

HOFSTADTER, RICHARD. *The Age of Reform: From Bryan to F.D.R.* New York: Alfred A. Knopf, 1955.

———. "History and the Social Sciences" in *Varieties of History,* ed. Fritz Stern. Cleveland, O.: World Publishing Co., 1963.

HUGHES, H. STUART. *History as Art and as Science.* New York: Harper & Row, 1964.

HUTCHINGS, A. W. S. *The Teaching of History.* Cambridge, England: Oxford Univ. Press, 1950.

JAMES, PRESTON. "Geography" in *The Social Studies and the Social Sciences,* ed. Gordon B. Turner. New York: Harcourt, Brace & World, 1962.

JOHNSON, HARRY M. *Sociology—A Systematic Introduction.* New York: Harcourt, Brace & World, 1960.

JOHNSON, HENRY. *Teaching of History.* New York: The Macmillan Co., 1940.

KELLER, WERNER. *The Bible as History.* New York: William Morrow & Co., 1956.

KENNAMER, LORRIN JR. "Improvement of Instruction in Geography," *Social Education.* November 1965.

KIRKPATRICK, EVRON M. and JEANE J. "Political Science" in *High School Social Studies Perspectives,* ed. Erling Hunt. Boston: Houghton Mifflin Co., 1962.

KLEMENT, FRANK L. "Clement L. Vallandighan's Exile in the Confederacy," *Journal of Southern History.* May 1965.

———. *The Copperheads in the Middle West.* Chicago: Univ. of Chicago Press, 1960.

KOHN, CLYDE F. "Basic Concepts of Geography and Their Development in the Classroom" in *Teaching the New Social Studies,* ed. Edwin Fenton. New York: Holt, Rinehart & Winston, 1966.

————. "The Geography Component," *Focus on the Social Studies.* Washington: National Education Association, 1965.

KRATHWOHL, D. R., B. S. BLOOM, and BERTRAM B. MASIA. *Taxonomy of Educational Objectives: Handbook II, the Affective Domain.* New York: David McKay Co., 1964.

KRUG, MARK M. *Lyman Trumbull—Conservative Radical.* New York: A. S. Barnes & Co., 1965.

LASSWELL, HAROLD. *Politics, What, When, How?* Cleveland, O.: World Publishing Co., 1963.

LEVINE, LAWRENCE W. *Defender of the Faith: William Jennings Bryan—1915–1925.* New York: Oxford Univ. Press, 1965.

LEWIN, KURT. *Field Theory in Social Science,* ed. Dorwin Cartright. New York: Harper & Row, 1951.

LEWIS, BEN W. "Economics" in *The Social Studies and the Social Sciences,* ed. Gordon B. Turner. New York: Harcourt, Brace & World, 1962.

LI, DUN J. *The Ageless Chinese—A History.* New York: Charles Scribner's Sons, 1965.

LINTON, RALPH. *The Tree of Culture.* New York: Alfred A. Knopf, 1959.

LONG, NORTON E. "Political Science" in *The Social Studies and the Social Sciences,* ed. Gordon B. Turner. New York: Harcourt, Brace & World, 1962.

LYND, ROBERT S. *Knowledge for What?* Princeton, N.J.: Princeton Univ. Press, 1939.

MacRAE, DONALD G. "Some Sociological Prospects," *Proceedings of the Third World Congress of Sociology.* (London) 1956.

MADJE, JOHN. *The Tools of Social Science.* Garden City, N.Y.: Doubleday & Co., 1965.

MALINOWSKI, BRONISLAW. *Argonauts of the Western Pacific.* New York: E. P. Dutton & Co., 1922.

MARTINEAU, HARRIET. *Society in America* (abr. ed.). Garden City, N.Y.: Doubleday & Co., 1962.

MASSIALAS, BYRON G. "Teaching History as Inquiry" in *New Perspectives in World History,* ed. Shirley H. Engle. Thirty-fourth Yearbook of the National Council for the Social Studies. (Washington) 1964.

MASSIALAS, BYRON G. and ANDREAS M. KAZAMIAS. *Crucial Issues in the Teaching of Social Studies.* Englewood Cliffs, N.J.: Prentice-Hall, 1964.

MATHEWS, DONALD R. *U.S. Senators and Their World.* Chicago: Univ. of Chicago Press, 1963.

McDONALD, FORREST. *We the People.* Chicago: Univ. of Chicago Press, 1963.

McDONALD, NEAL. *The Study of Political Parties.* New York: Random House, 1955.

McKEACHIE, W. J. "Psychology" in *The Social Studies and the Social Sciences,* ed. Gordon B. Turner. New York: Harcourt, Brace & World, 1962.

McKITRICK, ERIC. *Andrew Johnson and Reconstruction.* Chicago: Univ. of Chicago Press, 1960.

McNEILL, WILLIAM H. *The Rise of the West—A History of the Human Community.* Chicago: Univ. of Chicago Press, 1963.

McWHINEY, GRADY. *Reconstruction and the Freedmen.* Chicago: Univ. of Chicago Press, 1963.

MEAD, MARGARET. "Anthropology," *American History and the Social Sciences.* New York: Free Press of Glencoe, 1964.

MENDENHALL, THOMAS C. "Social Studies, History, and the Secondary School," *Social Education.* April 1963.

METCALF, LAWRENCE E. "Research on Teaching the Social Studies" in *Handbook of Research on Teaching,* ed. N. L. Gage. Chicago: Rand McNally & Co., 1963.

———. "Some Guidelines for Changing Social Studies Instruction," *Social Education.* April 1963.

METCALF, L. E. and M. P. HUNT. *Teaching High School Social Studies.* New York: Harper & Row, 1943.

MOORE, BARRINGTON JR. *Political Power and Social Theory.* Cambridge, Mass.: Harvard Univ. Press, 1958.

MORGAN, EDMUND A. *The Birth of the Republic.* Chicago: Univ. of Chicago Press, 1956.

MORGENTHAU, HANS J. *Scientific Man Versus Power Politics.* Chicago: Univ. of Chicago Press, 1965.

MORISON, SAMUEL ELIOT. *The Oxford History of the American People.* New York: Oxford Univ. Press, 1964.

———. *Vistas of History.* New York: Alfred A. Knopf, 1964.

MORSE, GEORGE L., RONDO E. CAMERON, HENRY BERTRAM HILL, and MICHAEL B. PETROVICH. *Europe in Review.* Chicago: Univ. of Chicago Press, 1957.

MURDOCK, GEORGE PETER. "How Culture Changes" in *Man, Culture, and Society,* ed. Harry L. Shapiro. New York: Oxford Univ. Press, 1956.

NAMIER, SIR LEWIS. "History" in *Varieties of History,* ed. Fritz Stern. Cleveland, O.: World Publishing Co., 1963.

NEVINS, ALLAN. *The Gateway to History.* Garden City, N.Y.: Doubleday & Co., 1962.

———. "What's the Matter with History?" *Saturday Review.* February 4, 1939.

NEWMAN, FRED M. "The Analysis of Public Controversy, New Focus on the Social Studies," *The School Review.* Vol. III, Winter 1965.

NICHOLS, ROY F. "Postwar Reorientation of Historical Thinking," *American Historical Review.* Volume 54, 1948.

NIMHOFF, MEYER. "Anthropology, Sociology, and Social Psychology" in *High School Social Science Perspectives,* ed. Erling Hunt. Boston: Houghton Mifflin Co., 1962.

ODEGARD, PETER. "The Social Sciences in the Twentieth Century," *The Social Studies: Curriculum Proposals for the Future.* Chicago: Univ. of Chicago Press, 1963.

OLDFIELD, R. C. *The Psychology of the Interview.* London: Methuen and Co., 1941.

OLIVER, DONALD W. "The Selection of Content in Social Studies," *Harvard Educational Review.* Winter 1957.

OLIVER, DONALD W. and JAMES P. SHAVER. *Teaching Public Issues in the High School.* Boston: Houghton Mifflin Co., 1966.

Organizing Summer Institutes for Teachers: Some Reflections. Edwin Fenton and Richard B. Ford. Mimeographed and distributed in January, 1966, by the U.S. Office of Education.

PADOVER, SAUL K. *The Living U.S. Constitution.* New York: New American Library of World Literature, 1954.

PARKMAN, FRANCIS. *The Jesuits in North America.* Boston: Little, Brown and Co., 1963.

PERRUCCI, ROBERT. "Sociology and the School Curriculum," *Social Science Education Consortium Newsletter.* Volume 1, Number 2, July 1965.

PHILLIPS, U. B. *The Course of the South to Secession,* ed. Merton Coulter. New York: Hill & Wang, 1939, 1964.

PIERSON, GEORGE W. *Tocqueville and Beaumont in America.* New York: Oxford Univ. Press, 1938.

POLANYI, MICHAEL. "On the Modern Mind," *Encounter.* May 1965.

POTTER, DAVID. *People of Plenty.* Chicago: Univ. of Chicago Press, 1964.

QUILLEN, JAMES. *Interpreting and Teaching World History.* Thirty-first Yearbook of the National Council for the Social Studies. (Washington) 1961.

RANDALL, JAMES G. "The Blundering Generation," *Mississippi Valley Historical Review.* 1940.

RANDALL, JAMES G. and DAVID DONALD. *The Civil War and Reconstruction.* Boston: D. C. Heath & Co., 1961.

RAYMOND, HENRY J. *The Life and Public Services of Abraham Lincoln, Together with His State Papers.* New York: Derby and Miller, 1864.

RENIER, GUSTAF J. *History, Its Purpose and Method.* Boston: Beacon Press, 1950.

Report of the Commission on the Social Studies. American Historical Association. New York: Charles Scribner's Sons, 1932.

A Report of the Committee on Historiography: The Social Sciences in Historical Study. (New York) Social Science Research Council. Bulletin 64, 1954.

A Report of the Committee on Historiography: Theory and Practice in Historical Study. (New York) Social Science Research Council. 1946.

Report of the High School Social Studies Committee. Naperville Public Schools, Naperville, Illinois. Mimeographed.

Report of the Study Committee, "History in the Schools," Organization of American Historians. Signed by Richard M. Brown, Robert D. Cross, Angus Johnston, and Charles Sellers, Chairman. December, 1965. Mimeographed.

RHODES, JAMES FORD. *Lectures on the American Civil War.* New York: The Macmillan Co., 1913.

ROSSITER, CLINTON. *1787: The Grand Convention.* New York: The Macmillan Co., 1966.

Rostow, W. W. *British Economy in the Nineteenth Century: Essays.* Oxford: Clarendon Press, 1948.

———. "Economics," *American History and the Social Sciences.* New York: Free Press of Glencoe, 1964.

Rowse, A. L. *The Use of History.* New York: The Macmillan Co., 1948.

Rundell, Walter Jr. "History Teaching: A Legitimate Concern," *Social Education.* December 1965.

Saveth, Edward N. *American History and the Social Sciences.* New York: Free Press of Glencoe, 1964.

Schlesinger, Arthur M. Jr. "The Causes of the American Civil War: A Note on Historical Sentimentalism," *Partisan Review.* Volume 16, 1949.

———. *A Thousand Days: John F. Kennedy in the White House.* Boston: Houghton Mifflin Co., 1965.

Scott, John A. *Living Documents in American History.* New York: Washington Square Press, 1964.

Shapiro, Harry L. (ed.). "Human Beginnings" in *Man, Culture, and Society.* New York: Oxford Univ. Press, 1956.

Singletary, Otis A. *Negro Militia and Reconstruction.* Austin, Tex.: Univ. of Texas Press, 1957.

Smith, Page. *The Historian and History.* New York: Alfred A. Knopf, 1964.

Sorenson, Theodore. *Kennedy.* New York: Harper & Row, 1965.

A Soviet View of the American Past. Prepared by the State Historical Society of Wisconsin. Chicago: Univ. of Chicago Press, 1960. P. 24.

Sparks, Edwin Earle. *The Lincoln–Douglas Debates of 1858.* Springfield, Ill.: Illinois State Library, 1908.

Spengler, Oswald. *The Decline of the West* (2 vols.). New York: Alfred A. Knopf, 1945.

Stampp, Kenneth M. *And the War Came.* Baton Rouge, La.: Louisiana State Univ. Press, 1950.

———. *The Causes of the Civil War.* Englewood Cliffs, N.J.: Prentice-Hall, 1959.

Stendler, Celia. *Children of Brasstown.* Urbana, Ill.: Univ. of Illinois Press, 1946.

Sykes, Gresham M. "Sociology" in *The Social Studies and the Social Sciences,* ed. Gordon B. Turner. New York: Harcourt, Brace & World, 1962.

Toynbee, Arnold J. *Reconsiderations.* London: Oxford Univ. Press, 1959.

———. *A Study of History* (6 vols.). London: Oxford Univ. Press, 1934–1939. Vol. 5.

Trevelyan, George M. *Clio, a Muse and Other Essays.* London: Longmans, Green, 1914.

———. *English Social History.* London: Longmans, Green, 1942.

———. *History and the Reader.* London: National Book League, 1945.

Turner, Frederick Jackson. *The Frontier in American History.* New York: Holt, Rinehart & Winston, 1920.

————. *The Significance of Sections in American History.* New York: Holt, Rinehart & Winston, 1932.

WEDGEWOOD, C. V. *Truth and Opinion, Historical Essays.* New York: The Macmillan Co., 1960.

WEISBERGER, BERNARD. "The Dark and Bloody Ground of Reconstruction Historiography," *Journal of Southern History.* 1959.

WELLMAN, PAUL I. *The House Divides.* Garden City, N.Y.: Doubleday & Co., 1966.

WESLEY, EDGAR B. and STANLEY P. WRONSKI. *Teaching Social Studies in High Schools.* Boston: D. C. Heath & Co., 1958.

WEST, EDITH. "Selecting and Organizing for a World History Course" in *New Perspectives in World History,* ed. Shirley H. Engle. Thirty-fourth Yearbook of the National Council for the Social Studies. (Washington) 1964.

WHITE, THEODORE H. *The Making of the President, 1960.* New York: Atheneum Publishers, 1961.

WILKINS, BURLEIGH TAYLOR. *Carl Becker.* Cambridge, Mass.: The MIT Press, 1961.

WILSON, EDMUND. *Patriotic Gore—Case Studies in the Literature of the American Civil War.* New York: Oxford Univ. Press, 1962.

WOODWARD, C. VANN. "The Low Ebb," *American Heritage.* April 1957.

WORCHEL, PHILIP and DONN BYRNE (eds.). *Personality Change.* New York: John Wiley & Sons, 1964.

INDEX

Acton, Lord, on history, 11
Adams, Henry
  definition of history, 3
  on scientific history, 37
Adams, John, on Presidency, 242
Altgeld, John P., controversy with Cleveland, 218–20
American Creed, 206, 216, 243
American Dream
  formulated, 210–14
  national purpose, 215, 243
Anderson, Arnold C., on social studies, 79
Anthropology
  concepts, 84
  history, 67–69
Area studies tradition, 252
Atomic age, 269–70
Aydelotte, William O., on generalizations, 27

Bailey, Thomas, approaches to history, 197
Barraclough, Geoffrey, 263
  approach, 276
  on universal history, 273
Beard, Charles
  charter, 77
  on Civil War, 142, 194
  on history, 39
  making of Constitution, 228
  on social sciences, 40

Becker, Carl
  on democratic faith, 216
  on facts, 50
  on history, 18, 39
Bellock, Arno, on methods, 118
Benson, Lee, on classification system, 64
Bettelheim, Bruno, on schools, 131
"Bloody Kansas," 153
Blum, John, 161
Boorstin, Daniel, 127
Bowers, Claude G., on Reconstruction, 158
Brinton, Crane, generalizations, 66
Broudy, Harry S., on teaching, 95, 96
Brown, Richard, 137
  on new history, 184
Bruner, Jerome S.
  on history, 130–32
  on inquiry, 19
  objectives, 127–28
  on social studies, 115–22
  on structure, 76–77, 114–15
Bryan, William Jennings, speech, 190–93
Bury, J. B., scientific history, 38

Calhoun, John, 152, 179
Cambridge Modern History, 263
Carr, Edward H.
  objectives of history, 42–43
  on predictions, 27

Celebreze, Anthony, 235
Civics
    closed areas, 201–202
    nature of, 198–99
    teaching of, 198–247
    textbooks, 203–205
Civil War, historiography of, 139–55
Clay Compromise, 126, 149
Cleveland, Grover
    and cancer operation, 180–81
    controversy with Altgeld, 218–20
"Closed Areas," discussion of, 234
Cochran, Thomas, 241
Collier, Malcolm, on inquiry, 194
Collingwood, R. G., on history, 3, 5, 21
Commager, Henry Steele, on national
    purpose, 214
Comte, August, rules, 105
Concepts
    anthropological, 84
    basic, 175
    in geography, 256–59
    Hofstadter on, 62–63
    organizing, 115
    political science, 87
    in social studies, 73–78
    sociological, 83
    in world history, 275
Congress, teaching of, 239–41
Constitution
    making of, 222–26
    teaching of, 226–28
Controversial issues, 202
Cox, Benjamin C., on modes of in-
    quiry, 93–94
Craven, Avery, on causes of civil war,
    143–44, 194
Crevecouer, J. Hector St. John de, his
    letters, 207–208
Croce, Benedetto
    contemporary history, 20–21
    on history, 3
Cromwell, Oliver, 17
    letter, 9
Cross, Robert D., 137
Curti, Merle, 40

Davis, Jefferson, on Civil War, 140–41
Dewey, John
    on education, 22
    inquiry steps, 196
    on problem-solving, 95
    on social science, 108
    on teaching of history, 130
Dewey, Thomas E., 232
Discussion method, analysis of, 195
Douglas, Stephen A., 142, 143, 153
Duberman, Martin, on limitations of
    history, 65, 104
Du Bois, W. E. B., on Reconstruction,
    158

Earth-Science tradition, 252
Easton, David, on values, 133
Edwards, Jonathan, sermons, 188–89
Eisenhower, Dwight D., 11
Engle, Shirley H.
    on decision-making, 132
    objectives of social studies, 95–96
    on world history, 262–63
E.S.I., 114
    generalizations, 119
    new materials, 122
    social studies curriculum, 118
Ethnic Groups, teaching of, 235–36
Etzioni, Amitai, new sociology, 54
External criticism, 101

Fenton, Edwin
    evaluation, 136–37
    inductive approach, 110–12, 129
Franklin, Benjamin, speech, 224–25
Franklin, John Hope, on Reconstruc-
    tion myths, 170

Generalizations
    E.S.I. generalizations, 119
    Potter on, 27
    reports on, 40–41
    structure approach, 115
    Toynbee on, 32–33
    in world history, 275
Geography, on teaching of, 248–60

Geyl, Pieter, on Toynbee, 34, 268
Gibbon, Edward
  on Constantine, 46
  on his work, 12
Goldberg, Arthur, 235
Goodlad, John I., foreword, *vii*
Gottschalk, Louis
  on generalizations, 40–41
  on his historical method, 101
  UNESCO history, 266
Grant, Ulysses S., on South, 159
Griffin, Alan, on social studies disci-
  pline, 78
Gronouski, John, 235

Halstead, Murat, convention, 10
Hamilton, Alexander, at Constitutional
  Convention, 225–27
Hanna, Paul, 95
Harding, Warren G., on Presidency,
  242
Herbart, Friedrich, on inquiry, 95
Herodotus, definition of history, 4–5
Hess, Robert, on values, 133
Historical Review, 178
Historiography
  of Civil War, 139–55
  teaching of, 194
History
  and anthropology, 67
  economic, 14
  Henry Johnson on, 183
  historians on place of, 137
  historical method, 64–66
  new approaches, 175–97
  political, 13
  and psychology, 63
  questions on, 195
  social, 16
  and the social sciences, 37–72
  and the social studies teacher, 69
  teaching of, 134–36
  uses of, 20–36
  uses of historiography, 194
  what it is, 3–16

History textbooks, nature of, 17
Hofstadter, Richard, on social science
  concepts, 62–63
Hughes, Stuart H.
  on psychoanalysis, 63
  on social sciences, 42

Imperialism, in history, 268
Inductive method
  evaluated, 136
  Fenton's approach, 110–12
Internal criticism, 101

Jackson, Andrew
  message, 245–46
  and Nullification crisis, 179–80
  on Presidency, 241–42
James, Preston, on geography, 253
Jefferson, Thomas
  on mankind, 269
  message, 244
  on slavery, 149
Johnson, Andrew
  comparison with Lincoln, 166–69
  and Reconstruction, 157
Johnson, Angus, 137
Johnson, Earl, on social studies, 95
Johnson, Lyndon, 11
Journal of American History, 178

Kansas-Nebraska Act, 126
Kant, Immanuel, on progress, 28, 264
Kennedy, John F., 11, 14
  on Cuba, 100
Kirkpatrick, Evron M. and Jeane J.
  on civics, 200
  concepts, 74
  on political science, 80
  on uses of political science, 87
Kohn, Clyde F., geography teaching,
  254, 259
Krug, Mark M.
  foreword, *vii*
  Trumbull, 64

Lectures, in social studies, 195–96
Lincoln, Abraham
   comparison with Johnson, 166–69
   compromise with South, 153
   on emancipation, 104
   Farewell Address, 185–86
   message, 246
   plan of Reconstruction, 162–66
   on slavery, 145–47
   on Tennessee, 163
Locke, John, 264
Long, Norton E., objectives of civics,
   205

Madison, James, the Constitution, 227–
   28
Mankind, discussion of, 270
Man-Land tradition, 252
Marshall, S. L. A., on Cuba, 100
Martineau, Harriet
   on destiny of America, 209
   on slavery, 141
Marx, Karl
   on history, 30–31
   on slavery, 143, 264
Massialas, Byron, on social studies ob-
   jectives, 134
McDonald, Neal, 236
McDuffie, George, 149–50
McKinley, William H., on war with
   Spain, 187–88
McKitrick, Eric, on the North, 160
McNeill, William H.
   concepts, 275
   on inquiry, 103
   The Rise of the West, 211, 268
   on world history, 272
Mead, Margaret, history and anthro-
   pology, 68–69
Metcalf, Lawrence E.
   on closed areas, 201–202
   on social studies, 76
   on values, 134
Missouri Compromise, 126, 149
Modes of inquiry, 92
   historical, 96–105
   inductive, 110

observation, 106
polling and sampling, 107
Monroe, James, message, 245
Morgenthau, Hans J.
   on predictability of social sciences,
      105
   on scientism, 69–70
   traditional political science, 107
Morison, Samuel Eliot
   on causes of Civil War, 155, 178
   on history, 3
   on writing history, 46
Morrison, Samuel Clinton, on inquiry,
   95
Muller, Herbert J., on Hegel, 29

Namier, Lewis Sr., on history, 4
National conventions, discussion of,
   231–33
Nationalism, discussion of, 271
Negroes
   conditions, 161
   franchise, 164
   Lincoln and Johnson and, 166–67
   and Reconstruction, 157–58
   in the South, 160
Nevins, Allan
   on pedantic history, 44
   on social sciences, 47, 178
Newman, Fred M.
   on public controversy, 122–23, 135
   on structure, 116–17
Nichols, Roy, 40
Nullification, 179

Oliver, Donald W.
   jurisprudential approach, 217
   public controversy approach, 122–27,
      129

Paine, Thomas, on mankind, 269
Palmer, John, on teaching, 95–96
Parkman, Francis, as historian, 17, 45
Pattison, William, geography traditions,
   252
Petrarch, letter, 8

Political Science, 74
   and civics, 200
   uses of, 87
Politics, teaching of, 229–35
Potter, David
   on generalizations, 27
   People of Plenty, 88–90
Presidency
   libraries, 11
   teaching of, 241–43
   views on, 241–42
Primary sources, 98, 99
Public-controversy approach, 122–27,
      217
Pullman Strike, 218–20

Randall, James G., on blundering gen-
      eration, 143
Ranke, Leopold Von, on history, 3
Reconstruction
   governments, 170
   Negro rights, 171
   period discussed, 156–71
Renier, G. J., on history, 3
Rhodes, James Ford, on Civil War, 142,
      194
Roosevelt, Franklin Delano, 11, 233
Roosevelt, Theodore
   and assassination attempt, 181–82
   on Presidency, 242
Rousseau, Jean Jacques, 264
Rowse, A. L.
   on biography, 183
   on uses of history, 23–24
Rundell, Walter Jr., on inductive
      method, 136

Saturday Review, 130
Saveth, Edward N., on history and so-
      ciology, 83
Schlesinger, Arthur Jr.
   on Civil War historiography, 148
   on historical judgments, 103
   on social sciences, 59
Schurz, Carl, on South, 160
Secondary sources, 98–99
Seeley, John Sr., on history, 3

Sellers, Charles, 137
Senate, mores of, 239–40
Shapiro, H. L., on anthropology, 51
Shaver, James P., on public controversy
      approach, 122–23, 135
Slavery
   compromises, 149–54
   Craven on, 144
   emancipation, 159
   Jefferson Davis on, 141
   Lincoln and, 145–47
Smith, Adam, 264
Social Studies
   Bruner on, 115
   concepts in, 73–75, 83–87
   Fenton on, 110–12
   historians and, 137
   independent discipline, 95
   new curricula, 175–76
   objectives, 134
   simplifiers and synthesizers, 75–76
Sociology
   concepts, 83
   and history, 62–63
South Carolina Controversy, 126, 149–
      50, 179–80
Spatial tradition, 252
Spengler, Oswald, on history, 31–32
Staley, Eugene, on world community,
      267
Stevens, Thaddeus, on South, 104
   radical, 157, 163
Stowe, Harriet, Beecher, 152
Structuralists, 118
Structure, definition, 115
Sumner, Charles
   and Reconstruction, 157, 163
   speech, 189–90
Supreme Court, teaching of, 236–39

Taft, William Howard, on Presidency,
      183, 242
Teaching
   effectiveness, 205
   inquiry steps, 196
   objectives, 22

Thelen, Herbert, on effective teaching, 205
Thucydides
    historical method, 100
    histories, 21
    on history writing, 97
Tocqueville, Alexis de
    on slavery, 211–12
    uniqueness of America, 210
Toynbee, Arnold
    faith, 263
    on history, 3
    study of history, 265, 271
    on world history, 32–33
Trevelyan, George M.
    on appeal of history, 11, 13
    on social history, 16
    on uses of history, 26
Truman, Harry, 11, 107
Tyler, Ralph, curriculum, 205

UNESCO, world history, 266, 271
Universal history, 263–65

Valery, Paul, on history, 3
Values
    and Civil War, 139–55
    Metcalf on, 134
    teaching of, 133

Voltaire
    book of, 21, 264
    on history, 4
    on nationalism, 271
    on world history, 268

Washington, George
    address, 243
    Constitutional Convention, 224
    mankind, 269
Washington Peace Conference, 126
Webster, Daniel, 159
Welles, Gideon, diary, 99
Wells, H. G.
    on universal history, 265, 268, 275
    world community, 267
West, Edith, 262
White, Gilbert F.
    on geography, 251
    objectives of, 262–63
    proposal, 275–76
    world history, teaching of, 261–76
White, Theodore, books of, 230, 235
Wilmot Proviso, 126
Wilson, Edmund, on slavery conflict, 144–45
Wilson, Henry, on Civil War, 139
Wilson, Woodrow, 183
Woodward, C. Vann, on Reconstruction, 171
World History
    progress in, 28
    Toynbee on, 32–33

B C D E F G H I J   5 4 3 2 1 7 0 6 9 8